THE SOVIET STATE
AND ITS INCEPTION

The Soviet State

AND ITS INCEPTION

by

HARRY BEST

PHILOSOPHICAL LIBRARY

NEW YORK

1950

Printed in the United States of America

FOREWORD

ON general principles the situation as regards the Soviet Union would be worthy of and would demand the fullest and most profound attention and examination on the part of the American people. The basic and the ultimate issue, however, that is before us is the present world clash of what is known as communism, something that has been smouldering underground in more than one country of the world, has burst into violent flame in Russia, has moved to certain other countries more or less under Russian domination, and unless checked bids fair to spread to a greater or less portion of the earth. Already in not a few countries there is an admitted movement to the left—whether or not any considerable number will go to extremes here. The question of the disposition of the wealth created by the hand of man, out of which the whole issue springs, is today no longer to be confined to quiet discussions in ivory towers, but is one that is now found raging on "cold" battlefields of the world—highest Heaven forbid that it be more!

Attitudes and actions of the Soviet Union, whether or not or how far we may be in agreement with them or can give them our approval, are deserving of respectful consideration, for the good alike of that country, of ours, and of the world as a whole. They are not to be dismissed out of hand, as hardly meriting our regard, without a hearing or without notice of what they are about, what they mean, and upon what they are based. Nor are they to be held lightly, or even sneered at or made fun of—laughed out of court—they are taken in Russia and elsewhere quite too seriously for any such treatment as that on our part. Nor yet again are they simply to be deemed a menace to our security and well-being, and to that of a democratic world, with respect to which we must be on our powerful guard. Even if we in anxiety and dread, and in planned measures of self-defense, look upon the Soviet Union with its pronounced economic and political doctrines as an actual or potential danger to the peace and safety of the world, its policies and practices are all the more entitled to, have a claim upon, our deepest and most earnest consideration. America has much to learn from the achievements of the Soviet Union—what it has done to its credit and what it has done that is not so, especially in the contrast of the one with the other—much to learn to the advantage of America—by way of challenge, of spur, or of warning.

The present work has been prepared, not so much with the intent of presenting new particulars with regard to what has transpired in the Union of Socialist Soviet Republics, but rather as a general sociological appraisal of what has taken place there, or as a study of the social philosophy underlying the movement as a whole. It is based upon three sources: rather extensive reading upon the subject; opinions of persons holding different points of view who have been to the Soviet country; and personal observations made when the writer had the privilege of visiting that country at one time.

CONTENTS

PART I
Before the Revolution

PART II
After the Revolution

PART I

Before the Revolut'on

CHAPTER I

Russia and Its Geography

WHAT was once known as Russia, but in consequence of the Revolution there now a part of the Union of Socialist Soviet Republics, has for long been a land of uncertainty. It was here that there took place what in the range of its operations has hardly been surpassed among the startling events of history. For in the process there was a change in that spacious country from one of the most autocratic and least democratic lands of all time to a land under an absolutism no less real, but with a dictatorship presumed to be in the hands of the workers and peasants. Under it there transpired a vast experiment, involving not only the accustomed economic principles and bases for the production and distribution of wealth, but the adoption of a new social philosophy, a new manner of life, a new civilization, all different from what the world hitherto had accepted. Some of the things that had been made use of by man in the past, some of them venerated, had been overturned or thrust aside or crushed under foot, to make way for another order.

In the former Russian empire, or in the new Union of Socailist Soviet Republics, is embraced a far-reaching area—in fact, one-sixth of the land area of the entire earth. It is a territory in recent times exceeded in extent only by that of the globe-encircling elements of the British Empire. It takes in almost all of the eastern half of Europe and northern and much of central Asia. Its domain goes almost half-way around the earth—or over one hundred and sixty degrees of longitude.

As night is falling on its western bounds, day is dawning on its eastern.

The vastness of the Russian territory is not easy to comprehend. It stretches from polar regions to sub-tropical regions. It extends from mid-Europe all the way across the immense continent of Asia. So far flung is the dominion to the east that its eastern extremity faces the American possession of Alaska less than two-score miles away across Bering strait. In the Bering Sea only three or four miles separate Big Diomed Island of Russia from Little Diomed Island belonging to the United States. In fact, Russia at one time extended its realm into North America, owning not only Alaska but carrying settlements far down the Pacific coast into what is now California.

The Russian domain lies between the old and cultured countries of central and northwestern Europe and the even more ancient and storied countries far to the east, on the eastern edge of the Asiatic Continent—between an arm of the Atlantic Ocean known as the Baltic Sea and the actual blue waters of the Pacific. On the south it is separated by one or two smaller countries from the Mediterranean Sea and the Arabian Sea. On the north there is nothing but the bleak expanse of Arctic waters—beyond which lies the north pole, and beyond that the Continent of North America.

Wide as is the range of territory under Soviet banners, no less is the range of its climate. With a breadth that embraces one huge continent and half a smaller one, it has extremes of latitude that could be approached by no other country. It extends from ice-packed seas and everduring frozen tundras where the thermometer may descend far below zero, to hot, sweltering regions with a temperature that only torrid regions know. To the north are biting frigid winds, chilling and benumbing and freezing; to the south are parched, burning deserts, where the scorching rays of the sun might have alleviation in an oasis with a cluster of waving palms.

Not only this, but in certain parts of Russia there are in them-

selves extremes of temperature, in a particular region the thermometer possibly covering a range of one hundred degrees in
the course of the year—say from twenty or thirty degrees below zero to ninety or more above. Not many countries have
such variations in temperature. Winters in most of the land
except far to the south are long and cold, with a temperature a
considerable part of the year well below freezing, or even below zero, and with summers that are short and hot.

Russia is in great part a very cold country. The larger portion
lies north of a line extended from the southern border of
Canada. Parts are within the Arctic circle. The city of Leningrad (St. Petersburg) is of the same latitude as the middle of
Hudson Bay. Much of the northern area is swept by Arctic
winds, with little to break them.

Over a great portion of the country rainfall is scarce, often
erratic; and there may be long-continued droughts, bringing
famine in their wake. In good seasons, with the warmth of the
summer sun, even short-lived, but perhaps a period of verdant
grass and brilliant flowerings, the grain sown in the earth is
caused to grow rapidly—the growing or vegetation season may
be only three or four months or less—with intense efforts at
that to complete the harvesting. In some regions the productive
time is quite too brief for really profitable agriculture. A considerable portion of Russia is highly fertile, especially the "black
earth" region in the south. Much of the country, especially in
the north, is covered with forests. To the east are the arid
steppes of Asia, where no little part of the land, especially in
the southwest, is a semi-desert, perhaps subject to heated winds
and dust storms. A large portion of Russia has been said to be
too cold, too dry, too wet, too barren, too rough, too inaccessible
for successful cultivation.

Russia provides a succession of landscapes—bare, forbidding
tundras perpetually frozen solid a few feet under the surface;
forests no less expansive but less forbidding, mostly conifers
stretching far to the east and to the west; all but impassable

5

swamps, marshes, and thickets; treeless steppes and endless plains spreading into wastes and deserts; fair, level regions where smiling nature offers land ready to yield its abundance.

There are but inconsiderable elevations, the country being in general flat, except in the Ural Mountains, which are supposed to separate Europe from Asia, and these not high. Most of the great central plain is not over one thousand feet above sea level, with hardly more than low rolling hills. The Valdai hills in the northwest are of slight altitude, as are certain areas of the Crimea. Some of the peaks in the Caucasian region, however, are lofty ones, certain of them towering higher than the Alps. Lakes dot much of the Russian land, and noble rivers cross it.

Russia has been an ever-enlarging empire. From relatively confined regions, it has moved to the east, to the west, to the south—there was no north to which it could move. It began its march to the east not long after Moscow had become the principal city of a definite Russian territory in the sixteenth century, and after the overthrow of the Khanates remaining from the Tartar invasion had opened the way to Siberia, and later to the Pacific. Expansion to the west, which was to reach the Baltic Sea, came mainly in the seventeenth and eighteenth centuries. First what is known as Little Russia was wrested from Poland, and later portions of the Baltic states from Sweden. In the latter part of the eighteenth century on the dismemberment of Poland Russia received a large slice. Early in the nineteenth century Finland was received from Sweden.

Conquests to the south, especially in the Crimean region and near the Black Sea, and in the Caucasian regions proceeded in general a little after the expansion to the west was under way, though there were also earlier movements in this direction. In the latter part of the eighteenth century Turkish sovereignty over the Tartars here was overthrown, and the Russians established themselves in the regions occupied by them. In the nineteenth century Bessarabia (Rumania) was added, as well as the

Asiatic side of the Caucasus Mountains and parts of Armenia. This century also saw Siberia extended; the latter part of it saw Turkestan in southwestern Asia and Central Asia absorbed by the relentless Russian drive. Russia always added adjacent territory—there was never imperial expansion overseas, except as to what proved inconsequential Alaska. Territorial expansion might be said to have been rather fortuitous—it was not so much on the whole the result of deliberate design.

There was only one check to the mighty expansion of Russia —that by Japan in the early years of the twentieth century. Before this Russia was generally believed in the United States and elsewhere as unstoppable; and was feared accordingly.

Russia has had contacts with nations widely separated from each other. In early days it had contacts with Scandinavian countries (together with Finland) to the northwest; with the Baltic states, and Poland and Germany to the west (and later directly with the Baltic Sea); with the Byzantine Empire (Constantinople), and later with Turkey, to the south; with the varied races of southwest Asia, and also in time with Persia, Afghanistan, India, and China on its eastern and southeastern borders. It touched Christian Europe on one side, and Moslem Asia on the other.

The Russian people were in a way a semi-Asiatic people, standing on the edge of Europe, and during a large part of their history with their faces turned to the east rather than to the west. They had been slow finding their destinies with the people of Europe. They had looked upon the people there somewhat as strangers. In the days of Peter the Great and Catherine the Great certain attempts were made to westernize Russia, culminating in the founding of St. Petersburg (later Leningrad), which could then have a longed-for window upon Europe. Here were put on, at least in court circles, the airs of western Europe. But westernization was only a veneer for the upper classes. The masses of the population were little affected; the Russian people would have none of it. St. Petersburg re-

7

mained an upstart city, away from the life of the people. In their hearts it was little Mother Moscow that had their affection. Western Europe to them remained far off.

And Russia knew the peoples of the east, even when they had come as foes. Standing on the hills overlooking Moscow from the southwest (as did Napoleon on a notable occasion), one could easily look beyond the gleaming, white-walled city, with its glistening, golden towers and pinnacles—a very dream of beauty and romance, not greatly impaired by more modern structures—and without too great effort of the imagination glimpse the illimitable plains sweeping ever and ever on into the vast east, till they are finally lapped by the waters of the Pacific. One could still behold the hosts of Mongolians and of Tartars on horseback, sweeping west from that boundless east, hungry for the treasures of the Muscovites.

Much of the Russian landscape is bare and bleak—a vast unrelieved, inhospitable plain, though in part with growing crops and tended livestock it is potentially a land of fairly happy homesteads. Certain areas have been regions of gloom and blackness—and of a kind to make humans uneasy and fearful, to make them shudder and turn away, and wish to hie to regions where nature extended a more beckoning smile.

But the Russian spectacle has other regions, regions not only inviting, but of enchantment. In the southern areas what a storied country! What country contains so much of seductive interest to mortals—in its scenes of intriguing ancient mythology around the Black Sea and in its glamorous cities of central and southwestern Asia!

Far to the south in Crimea, in the Caucasus regions, and bordering the Black Sea, we are carried back to times beyond history, to fabled lands, to the stories of classical literature, to mythological days, to the deeds of ancient peoples, particularly to the achievements of the Greeks of those earlier days. Ruins of ancient civilizations bestrew this land.

On the east coast of the Black Sea (the Euxine of old), in

what is now known as Georgia, was Colchis, which had a part in two celebrated episodes of Greek legends. On what was called Mount Caucasus, now identified as Kazbek (some think it was Elbrus a little to the west), an extinct volcano, higher than Mt. Blanc, but far more difficult to climb, halfway between the Black and the Caspian Seas, was bound Prometheus to the cliffs, with birds of prey ever pecking at his breast, in part because he had snatched the prized boon of fire from the abode of the gods on Mount Olympus, and had given it for the use of mortal man.

Here, too, the peerless Jason had come with his daring Argonauts in quest of the Golden Fleece. This fleece had been taken from a ram that had been sacrificed to the gods after transporting a human burden, and had been hung on a tree in a sacred grove, where it was guarded by a never sleeping dragon. After accomplishing the task imposed upon him of subduing fire-breathing bulls to plow the field for sowing dragon's teeth, whose fruit was armed men bent upon his life—whom he had turned upon each other till all were dead—and after having put the sentinel dragon to sleep, all with the aid of the sorceress Medusa, his affianced, Jason seized the fleece and bore it triumphantly away. Jason was accompanied in his quest by Hercules, Theseus, Castor and Pollux, and other worthies of Grecian mythology.

In the Crimea, called Tauris by the ancients, was the sanctuary of the goddess Artemis, where she hunted deer, and to which Iphigenia came as a priestess. The latter was the daughter of Agamemnon, "king of men," and leader of the Greek army in its war against Troy, who, in punishment for his having offended the goddess, had his fleet becalmed, and who could have it moved only by the sacrifice of his daughter. Just as the sacrifice was about to be consummated Iphigenia was snatched away and borne to Tauris. "Iphigenia at Tauris" is one of the great dramas of Euripides. (In later times Racine and Goethe had tragedies laid here.) This region was said by

9

some to have been touched by the wily Ulysses in his long journeyings after the fall of Troy. Here came Io as a heifer in her wanderings under the displeasure of the goddess Juno. Here came Hercules in one of his twelve labors, involving his encounter with the queen of the Amazons. North of the Black Sea in Homeric times lived the Hippomolgi (drinkers of mares' milk). Even in Grecian and Roman thought the regions to the north were cold, outer darkness.

In the days of history as such we find here regions visited by Herodotus, called the father of history, a man who was indefatigable in his journeys and was insatiable in his curiosity —and who had the high gift of graphic writing, and the power of making some remarkably good observations; his Hyperboreans were possibly those inhabiting the vast north— what is now Russia. It was of the region just south of the Black Sea that another Greek historian has written. This was Xenophon who with his immortal Ten Thousand hued his way through the Persians to the Euxine, which evoked their happy shout "the sea, the sea!" and which could carry them to their beloved Hellas. South of the Caspian Sea was the ancient Kingdom of the Medes, now in Persia.

In the Crimean region by the sea of Azov was the land of Pontus, kingdom of Mithradates who did so much to cause trouble to the Roman legions before his betrayal. The "hill of Mithradates" is still pointed out. Farther east in the region of the Caspian Sea was the land of the Parthians who also, in their shooting backward as they seemed to retreat, were a thorn in the flesh of the Romans. Near where Russia, Turkey, and Persia meet is Mount Ararat, where the ark of Noah is believed to have come to rest after the flood.

In the storied Crimea and adjacent lands have dwelt a succession of peoples that go far back into ancient times, and that also came down to more modern days. Tauri, Cimmerians, and Scythians were known of old. According to Herodotus, the Scythians had a scorched earth policy of their own when their land was invaded by the Persians. In later times Greeks made settlements here. Byzantines of the east and Romans of the west were acquainted with the region. Goths and Huns extended their invasions to it. After the Crusades peoples from Italy came to it, to establish colonies and trading centers—to found some sort of empire—Genoese, Venetians, Florentines, Pisans. These had in time to give way to Tartar and Moslem hosts sweeping in from the east—Kurds, Khazars, Turks. It was in the Crimea that Florence Nightingale made for herself an everlasting name in nursing wounded soldiers. It was here that Tennyson had the scene of "The Charge of the Light Brigade," "the noble six hundred," "when all the world wondered."

In later days and in enlarged Russia we have its glamorous cities of southwest Asia, in the land of the fabled Asiatic conquerors. This is chiefly what is known as Turkestan, bounded on the north by Siberia, on the east by China, on the south by Iran (Persia) and Afghanistan, and on the west by the Caspian Sea. This region contains the Aral Sea, into which flowed the "yellow Oxus" by whose banks Sohrab died after his strange encounter with his father Rustum, as told by Matthew Arnold in his poem which has the unforgettable ending:

> But the majestic river floated on,
> Out of the mist and hum of that low land,
> Into the frosty starlight, and there moved,
> Rejoicing, through the hushed Chorasmian waste,
> Under the solitary moon—he flowed
> Right for the polar star, past Orgunje,
> Brimming, and bright, and large; then sands began
> To hem his watery march, and dam his streams,
> And split his currents; that for many a league
> The shorn and parcelled Oxus strains along
> Through beds of sand and matted rushy isles—
> Oxus, forgetting the bright speed he had
> In his high mountain-cradle in Pamere,
> A foiled circuitous wanderer—till at last
> The longed-for dash of waves is heard, and wide
> His luminous home of waters opens, bright

And tranquil, from whose floor the new-bathed stars
Emerge, and shine upon the Aral Sea.

The region was the early seat of human civilization. It is
mentioned by ancient writers. It has to do with the Book of
Wonders of Zoroaster. It is better known, however, for the exploits of mighty conquerors who hurled themselves upon it, or
who made it the center of their far-flung empires.

An early conqueror was Alexander the Great, who fell upon
it in his sweep of the known earth several centuries before
Christ, and who wept because he had no more worlds to conquer. It was pounced upon by Saracens, the fierce followers of
Mohammed, in the seventh century in their resistless upsurge
to the south and east of the Mediterranean. It was overrun by
the mighty Ghengis Khan from China whose hordes had burst
upon Russia and overpowered it in the thirteenth century, his
generals advancing to the Volga on the west, and to the Persian Gulf on the south, extending his sway from the Hellespont
to the Ganges, and making him lord of Persia, Mesopotamia,
and India—plundering and destroying cities and snuffing out
human lives by the wholesale as he went. A century and a half
later came another unbelievably cruel conqueror, who delighted
in pyramids of human skulls—Timurlane (the Lame), who
combined central and western Asia into one powerful kingdom.

The city of Samarkand (the Golden) has had a distinguished
part in the conquests that swept over the territory in which it
was located. It was here that Alexander the Great, besides
sacking and burning the city, killed at a drunken banquet his
favorite general Clitus who had once saved his life. Ghengis
Khan made the city his capital and seat of empire. Timurlane
followed the example of his illustrious predecessor, and fixed
upon it as his capital, conducting here a brilliant court. All
the conquerors of Asia in fact stopped at Samarkand—it had
a succession of conquerors, and of royal courts. More than
a hundred thousand foreign architects and artists, it is said,
were brought in for its beautification. This city, located in a

fertile and well-watered area and once the meeting place of the art and architecture of Persia, China, and other Oriental lands, contains what is left of the mausoleum of Timurlane surmounted by a brilliant blue dome, in the crypt of which was his tomb — the body having been wrapped in linen, anointed with musk and rose water, laid in an ebony coffin, and placed in a sarcophagus of jasper—with a record of his exploits and his genealogy high above in golden Arab characters; and all transplendently decorated. On his tomb are inscribed the words: "And were I alive today, the world would tremble." In Christopher Marlowe's "Tamburlaine the Great" the city is thus addressed by the mighty conqueror:

> Then shall my native city Samarcana
> . . . Be famous through the furthest continents,
> For there my palace royal shall be placed,
> Whose shining turrets shall dim the heavens,
> And cast the fame of Ilion's towers to hell;
> Through the streets with troops of conquered kings
> I'll ride in golden armor like the sun.

By the American poet Edgar Allen Poe in his "Tamerlaine" the city is mentioned in the following words:

> Look around thee now on Samarcand!
> Is she not queen of Earth? Her pride
> Above all cities? In her hand
> Their destinies? In all beside
> Of glory which the world hath known
> Stands she not nobly and alone?

This heartless but fastidious monarch built other mausoleums as well. He erected a special mosque for his favorite wife. It was Ghengis Khan who had ninety elephants carry stone from India to construct a mosque here. Samarkand has had many beautiful, gaily-colored tile buildings, together with numerous imposing slender minarets. It was once called the "Athens of Asia."

Possibly a more important and more renowned city was Bokhara, once razed by Ghengis Khan, and once a capital city

13

before the removal of its court by Timurlane to Samarkand—
once the citadel of Arab-Persian culture, and a focus of Moslem
pilgrimages. It was surrounded by walls, the gates of which
were closed from sunset to sunrise. It was built of low, flat-
roofed, windowless houses, facing courts within. It was famed
as a center of learning; it had at one time over three hundred
mosques, besides a number of theological seminaries. It contained a high tower from which criminals were hurled to their
death (somewhat like the Tarpeian rock in ancient Rome).
Its celebrated bazaar received visitors from far-off regions—
Tartars, Afghans, Turkemans, Uzbeks, Tajiks, Armenians, Hin-
doos, Kirghizes, Persians. Here were brought carpets, fine silks,
copper and other metal work, lambskins, and further prized
articles.

Another city of repute in the region east of the Caspian Sea
was Merv, one of the oldest cities in the world. It was mentioned in the early Holy Books of the Persians. Located in an
oasis in the desert, it was regarded as one of the wonders of the
earth. It rivaled even Baghdad of the Arabian Nights stories,
the home of the illustrious Haroun Al Raschid, and in time to
be the core of the Arabian empire. Though in the east, it was
still with Hellenistic influence. In the sixth century of the
Christian era it was visited by Nestorians. It, too, fell before the
Asiatic conquerors. It was given to the sword by the son of
Ghengis Khan, it was said, because of the death of a grandson
before its walls. It is reported that one million human beings
were put to death on this occasion.

There are any number of interesting, fascinating cities scattered over Russia proper. After the modern but storied capital
of Moscow comes the late capital called in reverse order Leningrad, Petrograd, and St. Petersburg—perpetuating the name of
Peter the Great, in its western European garb, then in its Russian raiment, and finally in its distinctively Soviet habiliment,
the former national hero giving way to the Revolutionary hero
Lenin—a confused, once glamorous, and ever alluring city

14

where met the old Russia and the sprightly countries to the west. Then there is the still more ancient capital city, the glittering Kiev, which calls itself the mother of the cities of Russia. In some ways this is the most romantic place in Russia, and certainly the place of the deepest religious significance. It was here, as we are to see,[1] that Christianity was introduced into Russia. It has always been to the Russians a holy city, containing within its peculiar soil the preserved bodies of Russian saints, and formerly visited yearly by countless pilgrims.

In the cities to the west of Moscow there are reminders of Napoleon's invasion and his inglorious retreat. One can still hear the pealing of the triumphant bells from the churches of Moscow and other cities in Tschaikowsky's "1812." Not far from Kiev is Poltava where Charles XII of Sweden, the "madman of the north" whose career might "point a moral or adorn a tale," in the poem of Dr. Samuel Johnson, came in his bold campaigns far into the heart of Russia, and far from his own home, to meet defeat at the hands of Peter the Great. It was here that the victorious monarch presented a sword to an officer of his defeated enemy for conspicuous valor on the field of battle. There still is shown the chapel where the Russian emperor prayed before the issue of arms was determined. A foe of Peter in this battle was Mazeppa the Cossack who, according to the story told in verse by Byron, had once been tied to a wild horse set loose over the country.

Not far from Moscow to the south is a place sacred alike to Russia, to literature, and to humanity—Yasnaya Polyana, where Count Leo Tolstoi lived, and where he lies buried. Close by is the historic battlefield of Kulikovo where the Mongol invaders in the latter part of the fourteenth century met decisive defeat. North of Moscow is Kostroma, where Mikhail Feodorovitch Romanov was prevailed upon by the boyars to accept the Russian crown—the first of the Romanov line. Also to the north, where the Oka river flows into the Volga, is Gorki, before the

[1] See *post*, p. 45.

Revolution known as Nizhni-Novgorod, at whose great fairs the east literally joined the west, where eastern Asia and western Europe exchanged wares. This city is not to be confused with the older Novgorod called the Great, the early redoubtable republic that had wide commerce, even with Baltic and North Sea cities. A city that appeals to English-speaking people in particular is Kherson, not far from Odessa, where lie the remains of John Howard, the great prison reformer, on whose tomb is the deserved eulogy: *"Vixit propter alios; alios salvos fecit."*

There are not a few other cities and towns in Russia, each with its own story to tell—Odessa, the Black Sea seaport, with its immense wide stairway leading down to the sea; Yaroslavl, one of the country's earliest cities and perched high above the Volga; Stalingrad once with the Czaristic name of Tzaritzuin, now a name memorable forever as the place where the Germans were stopped; Kazan, a reminder of the days when it was the capital of a Tartar kingdom; Ulyanovsk, once Simbirsk, which perpetuates the family name of Lenin; Yalta (and its sister cities) beside the sparkling waters of the Black Sea, once the Riviera of royalty and nobility; Rostov (on the Don), for long a type of a brisk commercial city of Russia; Astrakhan, where the waters of the Volga break into their delta before entering the Caspian Sea, and where so much of the esteemed caviar is obtained; Kharkov, the center of the iron and coal industry of south Russia, the Russian Pittsburgh; Tiflis in the historic Caucasus, the "city of seventy languages"; Baku on the Caspian Sea, with whose surrounding easily lighted oil wells there may have had some association by Zoroaster and his Persian fire worshippers.

The Union of Socialist Soviet Republics is a territory of great wealth so far as natural resources are concerned—in not a few respects being second to no other country on the globe, and being for the most part self-sufficient. In some portions the soil is quite rich. The "black earth" region of the Ukraine and

16

certain regions toward the Volga River are notable for their fertility. In different parts, with fair rainfall and good cultivation, a bountiful harvest is to be expected. Russia in fact constitutes one of the granaries of the earth. It produces about three-fifths of the rye of the world, and one-fifth of the wheat, barley, and oats; it is first in all these cereals. Other agricultural products range from potatoes and tea and sugar and tobacco to cotton and flax and hemp and silk. The country is preëminent in sugar beet possibilities. It possesses vineyards and rice fields. A great future is possible for such farm industries as the production of live stock, fruit, eggs.

Natural resources other than the soil are abundant and varied, with nearly all the elements known to man. The country has the principal raw materials for a first-rate industrial nation. In timber it comes first, having nearly three-tenths of the world's present reserves. It contains the richest deposits of manganese in the world. It is foremost in stores of potassium and platinum. The country has almost measureless sources of potential wealth such as oil and coal and iron. Its oil fields in the Caucasus and Caspian regions are vast indeed. It is among the leading countries in coal, having great deposits in the regions in the south and in Siberia. It is not easily surpassed in the possession of iron ore, which in general is rather near the coal areas. Such substances as bauxite, phosphates, and peat abound. Such metals as lead, zinc, and copper are to a certain extent to be found. Gold alone offers a source of great wealth, notably in Siberia, there being here some of the richest mines of the world. There are other mineral deposits of wide variety and in no small quantities. All kinds of stones, including precious stones, are possessed. There are materials for making plastics and artificial rubber.

Further forms of wealth does the Soviet Union have. Of the development of the fur industry only a beginning has been made. The same is true of the fishing industry. The extent of water power cannot easily be computed.

17

It is to be added, however, that there cannot be certainty how far some of the foregoing substances are inexhaustible in the land. Certain materials as nickel, copper, tin, sulphur, tungsten, antimony, and natural rubber would, it seems for the present, have largely to be imported. There is not certainty whether the country can supply itself with sufficient all-important steel for wide general use. Such may be also the case with oil. Some regions in Asia appear to be slowly drying up.

What country has such rivers? The Volga, over 2,300 miles in length and at some places several miles in width, is the largest river in Europe. The Don and Dnieper are two of her other great rivers. Russia has been sadly lacking in seaports, especially warm water seaports. The Caspian Sea has no outlet. The potentially finest harbors are upon the frozen Arctic. The most useful ones have been on the Baltic and on the Black sea. Unfortunately, egress from the latter is subject to the dominance of other nations. Russia has always coveted strategically located Constantinople. Certain rivers flow in part through marshy soil.

Strangely enough, some of Russia's most important rivers have their rise not far from Moscow, thus through a system of canals affording her a water outlet—the Volga flowing to the Caspian Sea, the Dnieper flowing to the Black Sea, and the Dwina flowing to the Baltic Sea. The Neva coming from Lake Ladoga connects Leningrad with the Gulf of Finland.

Russia is no longer official name of a country, and will not be as long as the country is in the hands of its present rulers. What was once known as Russia is embraced in the Union of Socialist Soviet Republics (U.S.S.R.). This may have annexed to it and united with it any region in the world subscribing to its political and economic formula; the name of the whole remains unchanged.

The U.S.S.R. is a congeries of almost two hundred different races and nationalities, with more than eight-score languages and dialects. Embraced within its wide bounds is a descending scale—with diminishing political and economic power—of areas, territories, or groups—union republics, autonomous republics, autonomous regions, national areas, besides undesignated districts—the lower forms being mostly in tribal condition or in sparsely populated or nomadic territory. As any unit becomes politically fit, it could rise to a higher order. All domain is in general under the control or supervision of a full republic.

Not all of old Russia, nor "all of the Russias" (as the former Czars used to call it), came under the Soviet government. All the nationalities to the west were sloughed off for a time, taking advantage of troubled conditions when the Czar's government suffered collapse—Poland, Lithuania, Latvia, Estonia, Finland. Towards the east, in Asia, however, the U.S.R.R. had hold of practically all of the farthest reaches of the former Empire, including some doubtful or disputed territory.

It is those who are known and will continue to be known as Russians—Russian Slavs—who constitute much of the larger proportion—not far from nine-tenths of the population of the Union. It is to be remembered that the Russians are themselves divided into three distinct groups: the Great Russians, who center about Moscow (the Muscovites), constituting a little over one-half of the entire population; the Little Russians, who inhabit southern Russia and front upon the Black Sea (the Ukrainians), numbering a little over one-fifth; and the White Russians, who live in southwest Russia and are nearest to western Europe, amounting to about three per cent. There has been another Slavic group in Soviet Russia, though not identified with the Russians proper—a considerable group of Poles who once had become separated from their fellow countrymen in what was Poland.

Smaller proportions are of various nationalities. The largest proportions of non-Slavic elements, with something like two or three per cent for each, are Uzbeks, Tartars, Kajaks, and Jews (the last mostly in White Russia). Other smaller groups (together less than one-tenth of the total), usually concentrated in some section, are Germans, Finns (eastern and western), Turks, Caucasians, Georgians, Azerbaijans, Armenians, Greeks, Persians, etc. Spreading across Asia is a heterogeneous mass.

Projecting farthest into Europe are the Slavs, together with less extensive clusters of other whites (including those who inhabit the Caucasus regions). Lying in eastern Europe and western Asia are peoples who are largely Turco-Tartar, finally shading off into Mongolians in farthest Asia. Some groups in the latter Continent are hardly more than nomadic tribes.

The vast Soviet land in its complete stretch is as yet quite underpopulated, though already with not far from two hundred million people, and, resources permitting, potentially capable of containing several teeming billions. There was a pre-Soviet population of some one hundred and seventy millions, perhaps increased by over twenty million with the addition of new territories, and with a net natural increase of several million (with allowance made for the considerable numbers lost through war, famine, and disease).[1] In some areas the population is quite scant, though in most of these it is increasing in greater or less measure. Well over three-fourths of the population has lived in the western fourth of the land.

[1] See *post*, pp. 288, 358.

CHAPTER II

Russia and Its History

THE early Russia of a thousand or more years ago, of which history records so little, consisted of tribes more or less scattered over the land. (In the seventh century a group known as Bulgars on the Volga River are said to have been driven out by the Khazars.) People lived in clearings here and there in the forests, or in some relatively favored place on the steppes, or by the riverside, engaged in hunting wild animals or in such agricultural operations as were then possible, and subsisting upon what could be obtained from these activities.

In the course of time, as wares or commodities began to be exchanged between different communities, trading posts were established, especially on the great rivers. These rivers became, in fact, arteries of trade. In general the peoples of the north were desirous to exchange what they had in the way of furs and other articles for food from the south. What cities were established were naturally fortified centers. Barbarous tribes were also engaged for a time in chasing each other over the land; in time those that survived settled down in more or less fixed habitations, but with boundaries vague and shifting.

As mighty chiefs or princes, emerging from the forests and steppes, arose among the people and gained or assumed power, they had jurisdiction over a more or less wide and ill-defined territory, dividing up the country into principalities, some of considerable size. As they took possession of the towns or cities —such as had been created—they sometimes, if not already stockaded cities, set up kremlins or small fortresses in the cen-

21

ter or on a bluff overlooking a river, for their own protection —against rival chiefs from another principality, or against a possible uprising of their own people within the city.

Powerful chieftains had their own bodies of retainers, and there were frequent if not constant wars and feuds among them. But in general, as trade increased, there was less marauding and depredations, the princes gradually striking root in their own principalities. Now and then traders were asked or invited or encouraged by the princes to set up trading centers or cities. Trade was now becoming a leading occupation.

In time the country might have been called a loose spreading association, a vague conglomeration, hardly a confederation, of almost independent principalities and certain town states or more or less free cities, varying in size and importance, and with no central government. This was the situation in the main till after the expulsion of the Tartars and the ascendancy of Moscow among the principalities, as we are soon to find.

In those early days Russia could little be expected to be subject to aggression from foreign countries lying to the west. The barren wastes of what was known as Russia could have small appeal to them, their own problems and growth and wars being enough themselves to keep their eyes away. To the south, people called Cossacks proved stalwart defenders from any possible incursions of Turks or others inhabiting that region. It was from the limitless tracts to the east that could first be expected anything to disturb on a large scale the secluded ways of Russia.

In more or less historical times Russia may be said to have centered about two cities—Novgorod to the north and Kiev to the south—both somewhat to the west. The former was once a flourishing free city, a sort of burgher republic, located on the upper Volga River, and having trade with the Baltic and Scandinavian countries. It was in fact in touch with the cities of northern Europe which were members of the famed Hanseatic League. It was believed to have been founded by non-Russian

22

people, Varags or Varangians. According to legend, possibly based upon some true incident and recorded in early chronicles, in the latter years of the ninth century one Rus or Rurik, a Scandinavian, was called in to be its head—he being told: "Our land is great and fruitful, but there is no order in it. Come and reign and rule over us." By some it is believed that Rurik was at the time on his way, largely by water-routes, to far-off Constantinople in the south. At any rate, he seems to have yielded with no great reluctance to the overtures made to him, bringing with him many of his hardy brethren. He made Novgorod the capital of a large region to the north. He or his followers also conquered other regions, and extended his sway till he found himself in possession of the fair city of Kiev on the Dnieper—much to the south. Their raids and exactions of tribute had extended far.

Kiev had a noble history of its own. It was an old city—it called itself the "mother of all the Russian cities." It was the capital city of southern Russia. The Grand Princes of Kiev had no little territory for their domain. By means of the Dnieper River and the Black Sea Kiev had contacts with the Byzantine land; it was from that land that Russia was to receive its religion and no small part of its institutions, including some of the alphabet. It was, relatively speaking, a city of light when much of Europe was in the shadows. The city was under considerable Greek influence. Under its ruler Vladmir, in the later years of the tenth century, it accepted Christianity. It had the first Russian code of laws. Kiev has ever been proud of its culture, and of the less rude and more gentle manners in it than prevailed in other Russian centers. There were in time, however, quarrels and dissensions in the city, especially as to who should rule it. There arose prolonged internal wars, and the city was weakened. In the end dynastic feuds plus the Tartar invasion proved too much for it.

Besides the contacts with Constantinople, Kiev had other notable contacts. It even had a sort of international alliance through intermarriages not only with the family of the emperor at Byzantine, but with those of Poland, Hungary, Norway, France, and England.

Russia was in general to have intercourse with other regions largely by means of its great rivers. Not only was this possible by the Dnieper and the Black Sea to once mighty Byzantine, but through her great Volga she was to reach regions far to the east—the bazaars of Baghdad and trading centers of Persia, India, and Indo-China.

It was her rivers at the same time that were to have much to do with cutting Russia off from western Europe. It was their course that set her off from any considerable notice by these countries. Flowing from north to south as they largely did, and not from east to west, they kept vital trade from passing to the west. This circumstance was to have great influence on the life of Russia. Russia did not understand the west; it did not understand her. When ties were at last riven, it was perhaps too late for effective entry into European concert. Russia was to miss alike the Renaissance, the Reformation, the French Revolution.

Trade between different parts of Russia, as well as to an extent with the outside world, had now begun, and was to grow with the course of the years. It was given an impetus through the movements of the daring and sturdy Varangians, some no doubt hardly more than freebooters or buccaneers, who traded their wares for those of the south. The Russians took with them such things as furs, grain, honey, and even human slaves; they brought back fruit, wines, textiles, tools, weapons, and sundry other manufactured articles. Trading towns in general now increased in number and in size.

However slowly Russia was developing and in whatever degree it was settling down to peace and order, it was bound in time to feel the impact of foreign foes. It was in the early and middle parts of the thirteenth century that it had to deal with the vigorous and pressing order of the Teutonic Knights on

24

its western border, and also with Swedes. The former antagonists suffered defeat on ice-covered Lake Peipus at the hands
of the nation's hero and saint Alexander Nevsky.

It was, however, in these times that Russia had to have business with a far more powerful foe, and to suffer a far more
deadly blow from outside in another direction. This was nothing less than the Tartar invasion from the east. (That part of
the Mongolians that affected Rusisa were generally known as
Tartars.)

During the thirteenth and fourteenth centuries, Tartar and
Mongolian hosts sweeping across almost the entire continent of
Asia fell upon doomed Russia—not once, but time and time
again. Russia, which had never been a united country, so far,
was dazed and stunned; it reeled and staggered under the fierce
blows of the strange and mighty intruders who poured upon
it. In the quaint words of an old chronicle: "For our sins unknown peoples have appeared. No one knows who they are, or
whence they have come, or to what race and faith they belong
... who they really are is known to God, and perhaps to wise
men deeply read in the books."

In wave after wave the Asiatic hosts descended upon the
land. Their first victory was a great battle near the sea of Azov
in the earlier part of the thirteenth century, when the Russians
in what numbers and with what preparation they could gather,
met decisive defeat. By the middle of the century all Russia
had been overrun—opposition no longer showing its head. In
the earlier days the leader of the invasion horde was the dreaded
Ghengis Khan, who had already put the conqueror's foot on
much of Asia, even reaching the outskirts of India in the south
of that continent. In fact, no man hitherto had ruled over so
vast a territory (somewhat on the order of the later Czarist
empire or of the Soviet Union). This renowned but merciless
Mongolian warrior had defeated all rivals. He is said to have
declared: "As there is but one God in heaven, so there should
be but one ruler on earth." Ghengis Khan sacked and de-

stroyed; he ravaged towns and villages, spreading devastation wherever he set his foot, slaughtering in his mad onrushes untold numbers of human beings, men, women, and children. It is well that when he turned his eyes on Russia, the days of his drama of life were nearing their close, and Russia was spared much of the woe he had brought to other lands.

After the passing of Ghengis Khan there was a succession of Grand Khans, though none of them with hardly his cruel power. There followed a perceptible weakening of their hold on Russia, though a grandson overran Russia and even invaded Poland and Hungary. A Mohammedan Khanate of Tartars included a group under the picturesque name of the Golden Horde. It was a branch of this group that settled on the Volga, and was the last to be overthrown; in fact a remnant remained in and about the city of Kazan.

The other great Asiatic conqueror, Timurlane (the Lame) also visited Russia later in the fourteenth century; but though his lieutenants were able to occupy Moscow for a brief time, the movements in Russia on the whole amounted to little.

The Tartars were to hold Russia in thrall in greater or less measure for the better part of three centuries. In Russia under its Tartar rule, though whole cities were razed and untold damage done, there was not the wild slaughter that had attended the Tartar conquests in Asia. To Russia were brought tents and flocks and herds; the Asiatics settled down as if permanently to occupy the land, especially the eastern part. The Russians were treated with a certain tolerance and even consideration. There was little attempt to interfere with the Russian language or religion—largely Moslems though the Tartars were in their religion. They were content mainly with submission to them and the payment of tribute from the conquered people. They even introduced a postal system in the land.

Effective efforts to remove the Tartar yoke in Russia first showed themselves in Moscow. It was this city that, though repeatedly sacked by Tartars or other Mongols, was to be the rallying point for their expulsion.

During the period of the Tartar conquest certain principalities, especially that of Moscow, began to dicker with their Asiatic guests in the matter of money and other tribute they had to pay. (In Moscow is still pointed out the maidens' field, where they were gathered before being passed on to the conquerors.) The Muscovites displayed a particular subtlety and cunning in their bargaining. They somehow contrived to get on the good side of the Tartar visitors, and to secure favor. They acted as intermediaries in collecting tribute from other Russian cities. They ingratiated themselves by ostensibly helping to suppress disturbances and uprisings elsewhere in the land. They played off one Khanate against another. They were not above the use of bribery in advancing their ends.

Through all these means the Tartar hold on the country was steadily weakened. In time, Moscow was ready to resort to stronger measures. In the latter part of the fourteenth century the Moscow princes, with the assistance and support of princes of other regions, administered a severe defeat to the Tartars, including the renowned Golden Horde, which loosened their hold on the land. Moscow now proceeded to relieve one city after another from Tartar control. As the Russians grew stronger, the Tartars grew feebler. The Khanates became divided against each other. Finally, toward the end of the fifteenth century the Grand Princes of Moscow, aided by numerous other Russian cohorts, were powerful enough to shake off the long-imposed Tartar yoke—to put an end to Tartar domination for good. The Tartar invasion had done one good thing—it had made the Russians feel the need of each other's help; it had developed something of a spirit of national unity.

With the expulsion of the Tartars from Russia, and with the liberation of the land, the star of Moscow was riding high in the skies, in later years to rise even higher. As the princes of Moscow had taken the lead in this epochal event, as they had asserted primacy in times of war, they saw little reason for declining it in times of peace; they were not averse to its continued retention. Moscow had in general progressed more rapidly than other regions; and, with its central location—early a trading center[1]—it felt itself entitled to priority in the new Russia that was coming into being. With its own government amplified and strengthened, it was now ready to reach out and absorb other areas; it was now of itself to assume authority and to extend it; it was to spread in all directions. It was edging out other cities, which had had considerable dominion, and had been more or less rivals to it. Different principalities turned and looked to it, some not disinclined to yield it obeisance. Those that were not disposed to bow before the Muscovite banners had due force applied to make them do so.

Moscow was also becoming the new center of religious Russia—something of itself of no small significance. In its eyes it was holy Moscow; at the time it was thinking of itself as the third Rome. By the middle of the seventeenth century Moscow was definitely recognized as the head city of Russia; on no side was its position of overlordship longer in question. The Grand Princes of Moscow had emerged supreme in the land.

Russia had now begun the process of unification—under Moscow's direction and under its hegemony. This was perhaps largely a unification of the principalities, but it represented a step towards that end for the country as a whole none the less. Moscow was in fact the symbol of unity. Not only did one after another the principalities come to join in the creation of the rising empire, but certain elements in the population of the country were also to see the pointing of the way. The owners of large estates in particular were realizing the importance if not the necessity of a strong national government; they were willing not only to witness the ascendency of Moscow, but to attach themselves to it.

---

[1] On Red Square in Moscow at one time were "piled up rare furs from Siberia, silks from Paris and Turkey, cotton goods from Khiva and Bokhara, English cloth, and Venetian glass." *U.S.S.R. Information Bulletin*, April 16, 1947.

As the unification of Russia had commenced, so had its expansion. As we have just seen, the vast later empire of Russia
(and of the Soviet Union as well) had its origin and seat in the
city by the Moscow River. This principality, already started on
the way, gradually added to itself other principalities, in time
reaching the Volga on the east, and then extending itself in
other directions. Areas that did not voluntarily adhere to it
were overpowered and their allegiance forcibly secured. In the
course of the years there was a wide expansion of Muscovite
Russia to the east, to the south, to the west.

Along with the growth in power of the princes of Moscow,
there developed a sort of gentry class; with the increase in
strength of the city, there sprang up a territorial peerage. Those
who had won princely favors could expect sooner or later to
become landed proprietors. Particularly for military service, or
in return for contributions on the field of battle, there were
awarded certain manorial rights; seignorial privileges in land
could become in time those of practically absolute owners or of
those in practically full possession. There was thus created a
body of grandees on their estates, which crystallized into a
landed nobility, and which in time came to have much power.
The name given them was generally boyars. It was this class
who were later to choose the last reigning house of Russia.

We have now entered the period of Russian history where
we can identify its rulers, and can point to particular reigns.
We may begin with the monarch Ivan III, known as Ivan the
Great, Grand Prince of Moscow, who sat on the throne from
the latter part of the fifteenth century to the early part of the
sixteenth, and who in many ways may be regarded as the real
founder of the Russian empire. It was he who took over the
remaining neighboring principalities; he extended Russian territory in general.

Already the Mongolian enemies to the east had been disposed
of; but there were new foes to be faced, this time from the opposite side, or from the west, in part induced by the troubles

coming from the Asiatic regions. Russia was called upon to do battle with the Lithuanians who sought to extend their kingdom to the Black Sea, cutting across part of Russia for that purpose. With Poland there was almost continuous war, that country more than once taking advantage of her Tartar predicament, and seizing some of her territory. For a time Poland and Lithuania were in combination against her. Sweden was another nation to enter the lists. White Russia on the western border and Little Russia somewhat to the south became regions under the feet of contending armies. The country was now definitely in touch with the west, and with western enemies. Russia was approaching the Baltic Sea.

From the south, too, there were important events transpiring. It was during Ivan's reign that great Constantinople fell; and this could hardly escape the serious concern of Russia. It had for long years been exposed to Byzantine and Greek influences, though not of warlike kind. Numbers of educated Greeks now found a new home here. In certain public buildings, and notably in churches, Greek architecture was in evidence. Ivan was so much in touch with non-Russian Europe that he felt he could bring in Italian architects to try their hand in beautifying the city of Moscow, the center of his empire.

After Ivan the Great there came, though not immediately, another Ivan, with the justly earned blood-curdling name of Ivan the Terrible, whose long reign extended through half the sixteenth century. When he was crowned by the Metropolitan at Moscow, it was not longer as Grand Prince but as Czar of all the Russias. He proceeded to extend his empire to the east, and was grasping at the great wastes in Asia reaching to the Pacific and known as Siberia. His attention was also to be directed to his not too well disposed neighbors on the west. Under this Czar Europe in general began to take notice of Russia. It was during his reign that certain commercial negotiations were begun with England.

The sobriquet bestowed by history upon Ivan proved to be

30

one well won. Before his reign was half over, this bloodthirsty monarch had begun a campaign long to be remembered for its terror and unmitigated cruelty. His quarrels started with his nobles, whom he put down with a heavy hand; they spread to other groups, finally reaching virtually all classes. Any signs of opposition or rebellion or even incurring his displeasure were met with horrible punishment from his Janissaries. Individual executions were unending; there was no less wholesale slaughtering. Before he was through, it seemed that he was killing for the sheer joy of it. It was he who did so much to make the ruler of Russia an absolute autocrat. It was he who created for Russia a system of secret police, something that was to play so great a part in the later history of the country.

Ivan the Terrible had a weak son to succeed him to the crown; but there was a quite energetic and ambitious brother-in-law, the renowned Boris Godunov (Feodorovitch), whose strange story is told in Moussorgsky's opera. Just as the sixteenth century was coming to a close, having slain the last of the true line of descent of the last Czar, he had himself elected Czar; but his reign was disturbed by confusing reports of a pretender to the throne, the false Dmitri, the late Czar's younger brother, who was declared to be alive, and who received recognition and support for a time from a part of the people and from Polish or Swedish armies. At one time Moscow was in the hands of the Poles.

Boris proved to be a harsh, despotic ruler. He was popular with neither nobles nor people; discontent and opposition were general; there were repeated uprisings. There were also heavy sufferings from famines in the land.

At this point in the life of the Russian people, known as the "time of trouble," a wave of nationalistic feeling seemed to take possession of them. There asserted itself a measure of patriotism largely unknown hitherto. There was now less patience with and less toleration of those regarded in the land as foreigners, and not genuine Russians. Under this new spirit,

31

shared in by nobles and peasants alike, a real Russian country was believed to be called for. There was a demand that Russia be made strong and secure, with a ruler capable of appealing to the people and wisely guiding them.

A few years after the passing of the unhappy Boris, early in the seventeenth century, the nobles or boyars took matters into their own hands; in a sort of national assembly they chose from themselves a new Czar—Mikhail Feodorovitch Romanov, the founder of the last dynasty that was to rule Russia. His reign was marked by the extension of territory, especially to the west —Russia and Poland were contending for the Ukraine—and by increased contacts with western lands. Not long afterwards Little Russia was wrested from Poland, and part of the Baltic area from Sweden.

The ablest and the most celebrated of the Romanov line was Peter the Great, whose reign embraced the last score of years of the seventeenth century and the first quarter of the eighteenth. This progressive and truly remarkable monarch, who did much during his reign for his country, turned his eyes to western Europe; it was with it, he believed, that Russia's brighter destiny lay. It was the countries of that region that he wished as associates for himself and his people. For himself he put in a period of study in the west, the better to acquaint himself with western thought and culture and customs and ways. He returned to Russia brimming over with plans of modernization and industrialization.

Later he felt that his remote land would be better off "with a window toward Europe," as he put it; so on the marshes and swamps of the Neva River he built himself a new capital called St. Petersburg. Realizing that if his country was to prosper and be worthy of its western neighbors, it must have a far greater industrial life, he encouraged manufacturing in his domain, using both peasant and prison labor as operatives for the purpose. He instituted various internal reforms, more or less violently, in administration, finance, etc. He simplified the alphabet. He created an Academy of Sciences. Peter's reforms, however, were not looked upon altogether with favor by his people, even if they were to gain somewhat through them. He had trouble with the boyar class in particular; by ruthless means he brought them under. All internal disaffection he summarily suppressed.

With the situation within his empire under some measure of control, Peter was ready to devote his attention to his external foes, for he had some powerful ones to deal with. Conspicuous was the Swedish Charles XII, an extraordinary monarch and general, who though coming from a smaller country was able to conquer no little of Europe, and to penetrate deep into Russia. It was at Poltava near the Azov Sea where he finally met defeat at the hands of Peter. Peter then proceeded to strengthen his hold on the Baltic, especially in Latvia and Estonia. He renewed his attentions to the south where he had to engage the Turks, though he was never able to gain their Constantinople. Russian territory was extended to the Caspian Sea.

It was the energetic, redoubtable Peter who enjoined upon Bering the Danish navigator to find out whether the new world or the western hemisphere was separated from Siberia by water. It was this that led, for the obtaining of furs and fisheries, to the taking of Alaska and to claims to the Pacific region far down into what is now the United States. Not long after Peter's death part of Finland was taken by Russia.

Russia was now entering upon involvements with the west, which were to continue and to increase. Concern in the European political scene was in the offing; alliances with western monarchs were to follow.

Twoscore years after Peter's reign another great sovereign appeared—Catherine the Great, of German origin, and made a ruler of Russia through intermarriage. This able ruler brought to her adopted country not only German blood but no little German influence. She was engaged in various wars, and had part in the dismemberment of Poland. Lithuania was absorbed into her territory. With her renowned general Potemkin she won areas on the Black Sea, including the Crimea, from the Turks. She even dreamed of a fresh Byzantine empire over which she was to be sovereign.

Like her predecessor on the throne, Peter the Great, Catherine was much concerned in internal reforms in her land. Though not in the fullest sympathy with her serf population, and really strengthening the system, she thought of their eventual emancipation; their problem had already come to be regarded as a serious one, and one inviting imperial attention. She even thought of a national parliament. She in part secularized church estates. She proposed a wide legal system for her realm. She established secondary schools in the chief towns. She sought to build up cities and to bring industries to them. She gave no small attention to matters of culture, which was to be on the order of that of western Europe. She encouraged dramatic production. She permitted a degree of religious liberty. She invited philosophers and reformers to her land, especially from France; in her court there was a decided French atmosphere. She was not afraid to offend the existing nobility; she wanted a strong nobility, largely of her own creation, and resembling as far as possible that of France. She was known for her court favorites.

We are now approaching more modern days and more modern history in the life of Russia. At the beginning of the nineteenth century there ascended the throne Alexander I, who lived a dozen years after the end of the Napoleonic wars, and who had a word to say in shaping the face of Europe thereafter, seeing his nation become a full-fledged member among the nations of Europe. He started out with some liberal and progressive ideas, and was interested in some definite reforms. He is even said to have desired a constitution for his country. He sought to do something if not much for the poor of his land. He contemplated the emancipation of the serfs. He built some hospitals. He encouraged education and schools to a certain degree. He sought to systematize the laws of the country. He improved its financial order. He showed a toleration towards dissenters in religion.

With the planting of the seeds of unrest and dissatisfaction, including the formation of more or less revolutionary secret societies, now making an appearance in Russia (to be considered later)[1], Alexander experienced a change of heart, becoming more reactionary in his later years. During his reign there was taken Bessarabia from Turkey and Finland from Sweden.

The successor of Alexander was Nicholas I, a less enlightened and more despotic monarch. He established a pale for his Jewish subjects; he sent political offenders into exile in Siberia; he created an army of spies, and reinforced his secret police, for those who might be entertaining revolutionary or too radical ideas; he established a rigid censorship over speech and press; he persecuted both religious and political dissenters; he ruled in general with a rod of iron. He had the state laws codified. He witnessed some industrial developments in his realm, including the planning of railways. He carried the imperial eagles into the southwest; but in the Crimea as a result of contentions with Turkey, he fought a disastrous war with England and France.

There now comes upon the scene, shortly after the middle of the nineteenth century, one of the country's most intelligent and far-sighted sovereigns, one whose earlier years promised much for his country, but one whose reign was to have tragic termination. This was Alexander II. The bright jewel in his crown was the emancipation of the serfs, which occurred shortly after his coronoation. He instituted various internal improvements, including the erection of hospitals, the building of roads, the bringing of waste land into cultivation, and the development of natural resources. He instituted financial reforms. In some measure he extended and advanced popular education; he promoted the establishment of universities. He

[1] See *post*, p. 105.

gave certain strength to local self-government units. He encouraged cultural organizations. He remodelled the legal system with improved judicial practice, and with the extension of trial by jury. He conquered the Caucasus region, and extended his dominion into central Asia, even to the frontiers of China.

Though a secret police was maintained, the censorship of the press was relaxed; it was given some liberty. The Czar came near granting his people a constitution, even agreeing to a call for the purpose.

Under Alexander II a feeling of liberalism was spreading over the land; great things were hoped for and looked for. The impression found lodgment with not a few of his people that Russia could be placed on the same order if not put on the same plane in social welfare matters and in political objectives as the countries of western Europe, which had hitherto been so far in advance of it; at least some steps in this direction could be counted on.

But all did not turn out well. Perhaps too much had been expected. Possibly because Alexander did not feel that there was sufficient appreciation and support of his reforms, or because he regarded himself as in greater or less degree frustrated by the hidden or open activities of the radical elements or revolutionary parties in his country, he became increasingly reactionary with the passing of the years. The eager hopes that had been built up began to fade; in their place gradually came disappointment and depression. The expectant feelings that had been aroused changed to somber forebodings. Fears arose that the reign of the present monarch was not after all destined for notable advancement in the land. Over the country there was a growing realization that proposed or hoped-for internal reforms were not to materialize, or at least on any considerable scale.

The press now felt something of the displeasure of the Czar; in greater or less measure it was curbed. He began to bear down with increasing vigor and wrath upon different elements of the population. To the Poles was handed severe punishment for attempts at insurrection. Even the great work of emancipation was to have some untoward results, though with blame not falling wholly on the Czar. There were rumors among the peasantry that he proposed to give the land outright to them, instead of allowing a period for payment (as was the case), but that he was thwarted by the lords of the estates. In this matter there arose much misunderstanding and trouble.[1] With the growth of revolutionary political parties, there were a series of disturbances and disorders in the larger cities. There were secret associations vowed to overturn the government; with the radical elements there was deadly opposition, at times openly displayed, and causing wholesale arrests on the part of the police, often attended with imprisonment or banishment or execution. By way of revenge police or government officers had to meet assassination. Increasingly tense grew the atmosphere. (These matters are considered more fully later.)[2]

The more radical or more desperate fraction of the population was now maddened and was blinded. It did not know that, or did not care whether, the Czar, who at least at one time had proved himself of good and progressive intentions, might have been willing to come to some sort of terms, to mend unhappy matters in greater or less measure, to listen to reasonable proposals brought to his attention. It would yield or compromise not at all. It would be satisfied with nothing less than carrying out its more or less revolutionary program. The Czar and his officials for their part, no longer believing that effective reconciliation was possible, came to the feeling that there was nothing for them to do but to fight fire with fire.

One day in the year 1881 when Alexander was returning to his Winter Palace from a military parade not far away, a half dozen men approached his carriage and threw in bombs, blowing his body to pieces. The last attempt on the life of this harried monarch had met with success. Those of the assailants

---

[1] See post, p. 60.
[2] See post, p. 118.

who survived, after a formal trial, were marched in carts through the city, for all the people to see, who stood in a sullen silence broken only by the solemn rolling of the drums, to the scaffold, where in the presence of thousands of spectators they were hanged.

Over the place where Alexander received his death wound, there was erected the magnificent Church of the Resurrection (sometimes called the Church of the Expiation), built of granite, marble, and colored brick, with nine domes, the main one overlaid with mosaic, and the others with brilliant enamel. The exact spot of the assassination was enclosed with rare silver, and was marked by a canopy borne by four columns of polished jasper. Each of the doors to the altar contained over one-half a ton of silver. In the structure there was four times as much mosaic as in St. Mark's at Venice. On the walls were heavy pictures set in gold, and studded with gems; ikons flashed with precious stones. Paintings were of scenes from the life of Christ. On the piers of the central dome were apostles, prophets, martyrs, and church fathers.

If the Nihilist or other revolutionaries felt that Alexander II was reactionary, they were not to find an improvement in the Czar who followed him to the throne, Alexander III. Here was a monarch who could prove from the start himself highly disposed to the old order of oppression—perhaps made all the more so in consequence of the fate that had befallen his father.

Very soon began a bitter persecution of the Jews—something largely responsible for the great tide that set in among them toward the United States. Heavier restrictions were placed about the Jewish people—about the occupations in which they could be engaged, about their education, and about other matters affecting them. The Poles, too, were made to feel the wrath of the new sovereign. Upon all his subjects strenuous efforts were made to impose the Russian language, in all too many cases against their will. In the Baltic states in particular attempts to "Russianize" only seemed to crystallize nationalistic sentiments. Lithuanian mothers cooed their babies to sleep in their own language so that these babies when they grew up would have it. There was keen discrimination against foreigners in the land. There were inequalities in the dispensing of justice. Strong restrictions were placed upon all attempting to practice any but the Orthodox religion. Education was frowned upon, in the belief that it made the people restless. Local self-government was abridged. Upon the press and upon the universities was laid a stern oppressive hand.

On the other hand, there were some constructive measures during the reign of this Czar. The trans-Siberian railroad was begun. The debts which the peasants had been required to pay for the purchase of their land were in part cancelled. Loans in some measure were granted to some of the poor. Attempts were made to check usurious practices. There were efforts to curb the drinking of alcoholic vodka. Conquests were extended even further into central Asia and towards India.

After Alexander III there was but one other Czar to reign over the Russians. This was the ill-fated Nicholas II, the last of the Romanovs, as well as the last of the Czars. He was a good man, but weak, and quite unfitted to occupy the throne of the troubled and heated days ahead. Despite a harshness towards Finland, continued attempts to "Russianize" minority groups, and intolerant attitudes towards certain religions, Nicholas was considerably less tyrannous and oppressive than some of his predecessors. He possibly aspired to leadership and a sort of protectorate over the Slavs in southeastern Europe. He completed the Siberian railway to the Pacific. In that region, however, in a war with Japan he lost Manchuria, the first and only Russian territory to pass into the hands of another nation. It was Nicholas II who granted to the Russian people a duma or parliament and a constitution, as we are to see,[1] but who in the "Revolution" to follow was to lose his life.

[1] See post, p. 127.

CHAPTER III

Russia and Its Government

R USSIA from its earliest days to the Revolution was largely under autocratic rule—in the person of the Czar after the country became a nation. This autocratic rule was for the most part of an extreme order, little tempered with any expression of popular opinion; the reign of the Russian monarch was as a general thing an absolute one. So far as there might be counsel in his ears, this came mostly from those appointed by him, ministers of his own creation, who always remained subject to his imperial will; at best they constituted little more than an advisory council; as officials they could do only his bidding. The Czar was much on the order of an Asiatic monarch. The early influence of Constantinople, the Tartar invasion, the arbitrary rule obtaining in the former principalities, the blessing of the Church upon the ruler, together with the flow of the rivers north and south, all had a part in turning the face of Russia from the more democratic nations to the west.

In the early days of a city like Novgorod there was a government not a little on the order of a republic. For a long period in various communities there was a resemblance to a town meeting, with a certain approach to democracy. For one or more epochs in the more general history of the land there was something on the order of a limited national assembly. This was particularly true of the early days of Moscow, even before the Tartar invasion. A form known as the Sobor, to a great extent of religious bearing, was active in the first half of the sixteenth century, but more fully developed in the seven-

40

teenth. It was a loose sort of assembly, but in a way stood for the collective vote of most sections of the population except the peasants in general. It represented largely the nobility, the clergy, the merchant class, and a limited segment of the peasantry. It met irregularly, most likely at times of national trouble. It might be called by the ruler on some particular occasion to render assistance. It might have a real participation in the affairs of government, notably in the election of a Czar. (Godunov and the first Romanov were thus chosen.) In later days when the Russian Czars felt themselves possessed of so great power that they had no need for the continuance of such a body, it fell into desuetude. From time to time in the past there were formal assemblies of the nobility.

On the whole, however, before the arrival of the duma in the early years of the twentieth century, and in fact not greatly modified by it, power in Russia rested in the throne of the Czar—and with his small body of official advisers who were immediately responsible to him. Administration was formally left in great part to this Council of Ministers (Council of Empire), there being in addition what was called the Ruling Senate, a sort of Supreme Court, and also having the function of promulgating the laws of the land; there was, moreover, the Holy Synod, lying somewhere between the state and the church and participating in authority in both.

The country was divided into some three-score government divisions or provinces, each with its own governor, who was appointed from St. Petersburg. This governor might be assisted by or receive advice from deliberations of the local bodies which we are shortly to examine, but final power was in his hands.

Until almost the time of the Revolution there was no legislative body, apart from the restricted local assemblies, to have a part in legislation in the land. After the creation of the duma, it had certain powers along with an imperial council, as we are later to see.[1]

[1] See *post*, p. 128.

41

Of the local institutions the best known was the mir. This was a peculiar institution in Russia, an institution seemingly of immemorial character, in existence both before and after the emancipation of the serfs. It was in a way, as we have just seen, a sort of town meeting. Each village constituted a more or less permanent assembly. As a community activity, it had its origin in an ancient communal system—a group system coming up from the past, and based upon a collective status and with certain rather definite responsibilities. It had a limited autonomy or self-government. It had no inconsiderable civic and public powers, though not as to the most important political matters. It had some police, judicial, and similar functions. It could see to the construction of bridges and roads, recruiting for the army and providing of quarters for soldiers. It had some word as to the restricted education facilities that could be offered. It was responsible for the collection of taxes for the government. It was answerable for the repayment of loans made to its members. It could allocate land and decide as to the character of the work to be done on it. It could prevent the leaving of any of its members for other regions.[1]

The mir was of no little value in teaching some measure of self-government and in developing a community sense. It had, however, its human weaknesses; such a thing as "politics" was distinctly possible in its operations. Like all institutions of its character, it was at times in the hands of a local "boss." It was not always beyond corruption or graft. It was not always known for the efficient handling of its affairs. A good part of the leaders as well as of ordinary members were, however, honest and straightforward, acting to the best of their ability.

Above the mir was the volost, a sort of union of mirs, a peasant assembly to which a given number of mirs elected representatives. It had some control of such matters as education and health, and especially over certain civil relations and criminal acts. Both the mir and volost were subject to the gov-

[1] See *post*, p. 61.

ernor of the area concerned, the latter to a greater extent. Above the volost was a state district called the uyezd.

Another local body vested with certain public functions was the zemstvo, a much later creation than the mir, and of somewhat different order and basis. Though in part of elective character, it was set up from above and had its source of authority largely in the government at St. Petersburg; it was in some respects a branch of the Czaristic government. It was of two gradations: the lower one was the district body, which could elect delegates to the higher or provincial body. It was composed of two groups. On one side were the nobles and landed proprietors, and on the other side a group composed largely of peasants. Of the two groups the former was much the more powerful. To the relatively affluent classes was thus entrusted major authority in the zemstvo. It dealt with taxation, local credit, education, health, roads, methods of farming, and other more or less local concerns, sometimes conjointly with the mirs, having in part the same fields as they. Its acts, like those of all the other bodies, were subject to the approval of local representatives of the imperial government; this had power of veto over its enactments. Occasionally there were national assemblies of the zemstvos. Some members were of progressive character, with rather liberal sentiments.

As the years passed, greater restrictions were imposed by the central government upon the local assemblies; the powers of the governor, who was the direct representative of the central government, in general became more rigid. In the earlier years of the twentieth century the zemstvo, to appease popular feelings, was permitted to regain some of its former powers. On the whole, these several local bodies may be said to have promoted rather than impeded liberal sentiments as well as self-government in general.

To some of the larger cities special powers were granted by the central government, certain ones having fairly broad charters, but none outside the Czar's general direction and oversight.

An additional source of authority over the land with no responsibility to any local bodies was the Czar's police, including the secret police; it received its orders directly from its St. Petersburg headquarters.

Practically speaking, Russia was in the hands of a gigantic, strongly organized, highly centralized, all-powerful bureaucracy acting in the name of government and at the nod of the Czar. It did not pretend to have popular backing. The system was overdeveloped; it was characterized by lengths of red tape. It was not distinguished for its efficiency; it was in fact to a large extent glaringly inefficient. Its actions could be slow and dilatory. Not only this, but they might be arrogant and imperious. Russian autocracy was for the most part one of incompetence or one of harshness, at times of both together. Its movements could be governed by arbitrary caprice or by brute force. The government was not without corruption in different parts, which could grow in high places and in low. Bribery of public officials was far from an unknown practice. Officials were not often punished for their dishonesty or other misdeeds. It is not to be thought, however, that there were no straightforward, competent public officials in Russia—for of such there were a number.

The people of Russia were hardly acquainted with full civil rights, or with really notable rights of any kind. The freedoms that Anglo-Saxon peoples have enjoyed were quite beyond their ken. Even freedom of movement was in practice pretty much denied—not only because one did not have the wherewithal to travel, and often no place to which to go, but because one's local community might have power to interdict any attempted action in this direction on his part; he could also not escape the local taxes laid on him, and which had to be settled before he could take his departure. The government at Moscow could, furthermore, keep a watchful eye on the movements of its subjects over the land, with possibly a sort of internal passports.

CHAPTER IV

Russia and Its Religion

THE Russian Church had its origin in, or was originally part of, the Eastern Orthodox Church, which had its seat in the city of Constantinople (Byzantium)—the Church of the countries of eastern Europe in general. The story goes that it was deliberately chosen for Russia, after a hearing given to different religious systems of the period. Emissaries from Russia who visited Constantinople were said to have been deeply impressed with the magnificence of St. Sophia, declared to have been the costliest religious structure at that time ever erected. They were dazzled with the splendor of this mighty temple, "the throne of the glory of God," and all the more with its treasures within. They gazed with awe and wonder upon its vast vault, its soaring dome suspended overhead; its walls gleaming with light and color, its hundreds of gorgeous windows, its scores of marble columns, its immense galleries and bold arches, its exquisite altars, its variety of beautiful pictures, its magnificent mosaics, its multitude of jewelled sacred vessels, its appurtenances of gold, silver, and precious stones.

After the view of the edifice and of the ceremonies taking place in it, it was declared that "not upon earth is there such a sight or beauty." With its profound emotional appeal such a Church was not unlikely to secure a hold upon a people like the Russians.

When this religion came to Russia, in the later years of the tenth century, it was by way of Kiev, the holy city of Kiev, beside the Dnieper River, in whose waters so many of the peo-

45

ple were baptized. Though spreading slowly at the beginning, the new religion in time seemed to receive the veneration and homage of practically all the people of the land. It was Bishop Cyril who in his missionary activities gave to Russia the peculiar alphabet which was so long used in the land, called after his name, partly Roman and partly Greek. So much power and influence did the Church attain in the next few hundred years that this period has been called the "Golden Age of the Church in Russia."

From the introduction of Christianity into Russia to the days of the Tartar conquest, a period of about two hundred and fifty years, the Church was naturally a part of the patriarchate of Constantinople. With the overthrow of the Tartars in the fifteenth century the Russian Church assumed a degree of independence, largely throwing off the Byzantine connection, and ceasing to recognize its supremacy. The Russian Church now established an authority of its own—though still at least nationally under the general ecclesiastical jurisdiction of the Eastern Church, and having a metropolitan who received his appointment from that Church. With the fall of Constantinople towards the end of the fifteenth century, the Russian Church owed allegiance to no outside ecclesiastical body.

The Russian Church, however, always greatly valued and esteemed its former connection with the headship of the hallowed city on the Bosporus. It was quite proud of its claims upon that city on religious grounds; it even dared to hope that in time it might have physical claims in consequence of possible advances toward the eastern Mediterranean—claims that long remained fixed within the Russian mind. In early times a claim to the Byzantine throne was offered through intermarriage between a Byzantine princess and a Russian sovereign. Russia considered itself not a vassal to Constantinople but an inheritor to it.

In the days when Moscow was attaining an ascendency

46

among the Russian principalities, and when there was no longer a tie to Constantinople, a patriarchiate was created in that city; in fact, "holy mother Moscow" came to be looked upon as the rightful heir of the Byzantine city. The power of the Moscow official, ecclesiastical and political, likewise increased in strength; by the middle of the seventeenth century the leadership of Moscow was recognized for the ruling of the country in the Church as well as elsewhere. By it great power came to be possessed, both temporal and spiritual.

Early in the eighteenth century, however, under Peter the Great, the patriarchate was abolished, no new patriarch being appointed on the death of the old one. It was feared by Peter, who wished to be all powerful in his realm, that the patriarch might not prove sufficiently amenable to his plans of progress and reform, and perhaps not always easily managed. From this time on the Church came to lean upon the Czar largely as the head not only of the Russian nation but of itself. He became the defender of the faith and the father of the faithful, as well as in some part the administrator of Church affairs. The first Romanov Czar was the son of the Moscow patriarch, and succeeding Czars were to a greater or less extent in a position of primacy in the direction of the Church system.

Under Peter the Great, somewhat as a substitute for the patriarch, there was created the Holy Synod, which was to be the paramount organization of the Church, and its supreme judicial court. It consisted of high church dignitaries, a collegiate body of practically government officials. The Czar was personally represented by a procurator, a layman who must approve all proceedings; it was he who introduced the subjects to be discussed, and who had to give consent to all resolutions adopted. The Russian Czar thus obtained a powerful hold upon the Church, and could in large measure wield it as he might wish.

Church and state in Russia were now intimately united. The powers of the Church and of the Czars were nominally or to an extent co-equal; but with the Czar in the superior position, the Church lost much of its temporal power. In time in a sense the Church became a department or arm of the state.

In later days the Czar continued to have a definite and conspicuous part in the life and functioning of the Church. He had a prominent place in solemn, imposing religious processions and ceremonies, including the quaint but impressive blessing of the waters of the Neva at St. Petersburg. In coronation of the Czar the Church had a paramount and spectacular part.

The Church retained control over such matters as marriage and divorce. It could officiate at baptisms and burials. The Holy Synod had some concern with education; under its jurisdiction were a considerable portion of the schools of the land. The Church engaged to a greater or less extent in charitable activities. But it was in general less given to works and deeds, these things being left, so far as they were to be performed, to the state.

The Church was now in position to turn its attention to its own internal affairs and to its ecclesiastical organization—and to its more spiritual matters and concerns. In this aspect it became wrapped in formal worship, elaborate ceremonies, and monastic contemplations.

The Church body was divided into a little over three-score dioceses under archbishops and bishops. The metropolitans were its ecclesiastical officials of the highest rank, there being three of these, located at Kiev, Moscow, and St. Petersburg. Discipline in the Church was strict, dissidents or disturbers receiving short shrift or befitting punishment.

The clergy in Russia were in general of two orders. One was the so-called black clergy largely attached to the monasteries, who held the highest church offices, and who had general charge of the work of the church. They were best off in this world's goods and rather looked down on the white clergy. The other group known as the white clergy were the real pastors and ministers over the land, in direct touch with the people. These depended for livelihood in large measure upon fees for weddings, baptisms, and burials.

In many places throughout Russia the church buildings were a conspicuous feature in the landscape. Nearly all the larger cities had cathedrals, some imposing. Who that has beheld the Russian churches can forget them? Outside you might see them gilded or silvered, or otherwise brightly colored, and with strange onion-shaped domes, usually five in number, with the highest in the middle, all perhaps highly and richly decorated—one to represent Christ, and the other four the Gospels—with triple crosses to indicate the three Persons of the Godhead. Within you might find bare space sans seats, but that is the only thing lacking. All else is a bright and moving array. There are resplendent and impressive appointments. There are ikons and sacred pictures which can be carried in majestic procession. There are perpetually burning lamps. There is incense pleasing to the senses. There are the rich and imposing vestments of the clergy.

As there is much to greet the eye, so there is much to greet the ear. There may be no organ or other instrument to peal forth music, but what is to be likened to the rich sonorous voices of the male choirs? And who can fail to remember the stately solemn ritual and liturgy? And what of the holy days? In particular what is to be said of the gorgeous presentations at Easter? Symbolism was carried far in Russian churches.

The monasteries, of which there were some eight-score dotting the land, were also peculiar to Russia's religion. They were really collections of churches, each a small village of its own, sometimes within the walls of a kremlin. Most were quaint according to our notions; there were some exquisite and beautiful; there were some that were prison-like structures. There were four lavras or chief monasteries, each with a charm of its own.

Names applied to religious places were of deep significance, calling up vividly Christian beliefs and practices. At the Kremlin in Moscow there was the Gate of the Redeemer, the Convent of the Assumption, and the Church of the Archangel Michael.

The Church in Russia amassed great wealth. It had costly vestments for its priests, and vessels and ornaments of silver and gold, perhaps bedecked with jewels, and sometimes of priceless value. The Church had in fact accumulated wealth from the beginning, or from far in the past, commencing with the presentation of land and other gifts to it by rich converts and by princes and nobles. This practice had long continued.

In the Church superstition had secured a foothold; Russian religion became heavy with it. In times of drought in the country, processions moved into the fields with banners and ceremonies, to pray for rain. Ikons were carried to the homes of the sick to effect their cure. There was abundant kissing of relics. In not a few places were there nails of the true Cross to be seen. There was worship of the bodies of saints. The shrine of the Iberian Virgin at Moscow, the wonder-working image at Kazan Cathedral at St. Petersburg, various objects of devotion at holy Kiev—all attested the overtrustful faith of the people.

Religions other than the Eastern Orthodox Church had for the most part a difficult time in getting a hearing in the land. To both the church and the state they were little short of anathema. The people were to be carefully guarded against them. Not only could the formal religion of the land to an extent pass into superstition, but it could become an intolerant one.

At the same time the Church claimed some of the ablest and best educated and noblest in the land to its bosom. Many priests were gentle, mild, simple, devoted to their work—some showing an apostolic faith on their countenances. In the days following the Revolution, who that had seen them could forget these patient, sad-faced men as they quietly and unobtrusively made their way in the city or in the country?

On the other hand, there were some priests of whom not such good things could be said—priests more concerned with performing the functions of their offices than with the cure of souls. A considerable number were with but meagre education. Some were chiefly interested in what their labors could bring them of a material nature. Some knew how to extort money from the poor peasantry for their services or for their lack of services—some having no other sources of income. Not a few earned little respect from the people with whom they dwelt— the portion of certain ones was open derision.

For too long there was a belief shared by many that the Church was in the hands of the rich and powerful of the land. It was looked upon as a sturdy vested interest. More particularly it was regarded as a sort of tool of the state—in social, economic, and political matters. The closeness of the Church to the Czaristic power led it to reactionary attitudes; it was too much for maintaining the status quo. At times the very priest was thought of in a way as a policeman for the Czar. Even the confessional, it was charged, could become a vehicle for espionage; through it could be discovered or brought to light alleged political delinquencies or misdeeds or plottings.

The Church, it was further charged, was not only an ally and representative of the Czar: it was under his close and immediate care. In turn it threw its ardent protection around him, and around his family, and also around his nobility in general. Pictures in the church or in the home could show that all these were under the special guardianship of Christ and His holy angels.

A deep-rooted mysticism penetrated the religion of the Russians as befitted their nature. The forms and rites of religion meant much to them. They could stand on their feet for long hours during a religious service; they could devoutly prostrate themselves to the earth. Hardly a week passed without one or more religious festivals. But with all their high liturgies and ceremonies and ikons and crossing of selves, which were only of the outward appearance, the Russians were a profoundly religious people. Religion entered the lives of a great portion of the population; it truly gripped their hearts. In the Easter greeting—"Christ is risen; He is risen indeed"—there was a tone of genuine warmth, of an unmistakable sincerity. In cemeteries could be seen framed pictures of loved ones who had gone before. Religion with the Russians was to be thought of as considerably more than a sense of mystic contemplation, as a display of imposing ceremonies. It had an intimate effect upon the lives of the people. It was a real deterrent from evil ways. It brought to its followers noble conceptions of peace, of charity, of justice among men. It inculcated in them piety, humility, brotherly love. It taught them to endure—shall one say too much?—and to suffer. Some entered the monastery, not necessarily for the performance of good works, but for the humiliation of the flesh. Religion made noble souls of some, some worthy of the martyr's crown. Russia would have been much worse off without its religion, such as it was.

With all its shortcomings and weaknesses, the Church had a powerful hold on the mass of the people of the land—especially the country peasantry. Their faith in it was a resolute, indomitable one; with many it was so strong that they could see nothing but the virtues of the Church. They yielded to it not only their utmost faith, but their unquestioning obedience; not only their hearts, but their minds and souls. With some, however, particularly among the intellectual classes and among the city workers who had listened more or less to socialistic or revolutionary ideas, the Church was no longer a compelling or inviting force or institution. Upon them it had lost its hold; if not directly hostile to it, they were quite indifferent.

The Eastern Orthodox Church, the "Russian Church," was the state church of the land; it was the outstanding, the prevailing church. But it was not the only one. Besides it there were other religious bodies. Closest were the "Old Believers," who in the latter part of the seventeenth century had broken off from the regular church because of their objection to certain ritual changes (perhaps on the whole not great), and had created a schism. They were at times bitterly persecuted.

The Roman Catholic Church cannot be called indigeneous to the Russian soil. It was the Eastern branch of the early church, with its seat at Constantinople, that secured so strong a foothold in the land. Russia was little moved by the religious convictions and practices of western Europe. Its face was turned to the city on the Bosporus rather than to the city on the Tiber. Curiously enough, it had no part in the Crusades, though they passed close to its southern bounds. As the country went its way removed from the Roman Catholic Church, it was likewise untouched by the Protestant Reformation. There were Roman Catholics, however, in various cities of the land into which they had infiltrated. In the Polish and Lithuanian regions in the west the Roman Catholic was the prevailing religion.

Among Protestant bodies the Lutherans were in evidence in the Baltic states, and in divers places over the land to which Germans or Scandinavians had come. Protestant bodies such as the Baptists and others were also to be found, in spots having a considerable following.

There were also strange, mystic sects whose origin cannot always be easily explained. Some were of highly abstemious habits, perhaps flagellants or engaged in some severe, self-imposed hardship or infliction which they bore. Some were of an order not far removed from dervish dancers. Persecution was often the portion of these irregular sects.

Jews were, especially in later years, confined mainly to a "pale," in general in White Russia. In the south, in trans-Caucasian lands, and in central and southwestern Asiatic lands there were adherents of Mohammed—in some areas in great numbers. In Asia there were represented more than one Asiatic religion, especially ones from India.

CHAPTER V

Russia and Its Peasant Farmers

IN the relatively early history of Russia, or up to the thirteenth century, there was no great amount of agriculture in the land, the inhabitants living largely on whatever of wild life they could find, with perhaps a small clearing here and there for the growing of some crop. During the next two or three centuries there was a considerable increase in agriculture, it now becoming the predominant industry of the land. At this time those whom we call peasants were in general relatively free, carrying on their farming operations as best they could on the land they occupied. During this period, approximately from the fifteenth to the early seventeenth century, a large part of the peasants were having ever increasing difficulty in eking out an existence on their holdings in this rough country. As had been the case in other countries under similar circumstances, they gradually found themselves squeezed out of their own possessions and drawn into the big landed estates of the nobility, to a great extent represented by the boyar class, who were so largely in ownership of the territory of Russia. At times, especially after the Tartar invasion, wandering peasants could find security and protection only in this condition. Many also overburdened with debt if not with taxation could obtain relief only here. All this meant that the peasants were reaching a stage where they were to be tied down to the estates, were losing part of their ancient liberties, and were entering a condition of serfdom.

As the years passed, this situation hardened. The peasants

became more rigidly and more tightly held to the land. Before long they could even be sold with the land upon which they dwelt. By the close of the sixteenth century they had been reduced to a practically complete state of serfdom. To maintain and strengthen the system, attempt was made to keep the peasants from moving from one place to another over the country; in later years, or after the middle of the seventeenth century, they were definitely denied the right of free migration. After the time of Peter the Great they were generally considered as attached to the land. They were now largely a helpless class.

As the Russian empire expanded, so did serfdom. It was strongest around Moscow and the older parts of the country in general. It became a vast, wide-spread, accepted institution, though with time a relatively decreasing one.

At the middle of the eighteenth century probably well over one-half the population was in this condition; at the time of the emancipation (a little after the middle of the nineteenth century), not less than one-third. At that time the number was somewhat over twenty million (besides almost as many "state" serfs). There were more than two hundred thousand serf owners, some owning many, some only a few.

There were two forms of serfdom—one that of private landlords, and the other that of the crown and imperial family (royal demesne). Between these two the serfs were divided about evenly. The state or crown serfs were in general the better off. For one thing, they were less subject to personal service; though they had taxes and dues to pay, there was for the most part little interference with their daily lives. The serfs on the private estates made payments either in money or in labor, or in both. In the event that they should happen to be able to substitute cash (or some valuable commodity), their work on the lord's estate was reduced accordingly. In great part they paid with their labor or physical exertion. They usually gave the major portion, or not less than half, of their time to the lord's service—as a rule not less than three days a week. There was not infrequent violation of this allotment of time. The balance of the time the serf could put on the little home with its garden and a few sickly acres which had been allowed to him. He could also have a horse, a cow or two, and some poultry, besides his rude agricultural implements.

When the serf was required to devote a large amount of time to the lord's estate, he must labor at very early and very late hours of the day on his own plot if he were to extract something from it. The serf was also expected to bring his own agricultural implements and work horse when he came to the lord's estate to do his work. A small portion of the serfs were retained by the lord as his domestic servitors; some of the lords had a considerable retinue of such household attendants, sometimes more than there was work for. On the other hand, when a serf had a grown son, he could often send this son to the lord's estate to work in his stead, thus allowing him more time for his own domestic affairs. At times serfs attached to one lord, and not immediately needed, could be hired out to another lord, with the division of the amount involved between the serf and his own lord.

No serf could have such land as he had, entirely as his own individual property. The land which was allotted to the serfs and which they could cultivate for their own uses, was largely under the direction of the mir, an ancient institution in Russian life (already described).[1] The serfs themselves generally lived in village communities from which they went out to do their work.

The landlords sought to get all the labor possible out of their vassals. They could lay a heavy hand upon the serfs under them. There was almost complete control over the peasants' bodies; there could be exercised powers of discipline and punishment, perhaps including flogging (though in later years forbidden). The landlord might have a good deal to say with

[1] See *ante*, p. 42.

respect to the marriage of the peasants or of members of their families. The peasant had in general no legal means of protection or defense from the lord except in the event of extreme cruelty or abuse, in which case conviction was difficult. If the landlord bore down too hard, there was little avenue of escape on the part of the peasant to the town or city, as was often possible in western Europe. Besides, in Russia large towns were not numerous, or were some distance away. A runaway might find himself sooner or later in the arms of the police; in addition, he might have his family at home to worry about. If his escape had been made good to a city or to the sanctuary of a monastery, he could depend only on temporary alms for his subsistence. All persons without definite employment otherwise were supposed to be attached to a land somewhere and had to make explanation if not.

Some landlords proved themselves exacting, harsh, cruel taskmasters; some were, indeed, close to being barbarous. Some of them were extravagant, perhaps often themselves in debt—perhaps now and then taking it out on their helpless underlings. Conditions were the worst under the stewards or overseers of absent landlords, or under those who had bought land largely for speculative purposes, perhaps only for a short period, and who were mainly concerned with getting the quickest returns possible. In this case there was little helpful interest either in the peasant or in the land, both usually suffering considerably in consequence. The peasant, furthermore, had upon his shoulders an undue proportion of the taxes of the country.

Yet the lot of the serf was not an altogether baneful one so far as his physical well-being was concerned. As with slave labor elsewhere, the individual master might have a kind heart within his breast and a warm, humane disposition. There might also be certain mitigating features to the general evils of serfdom. Even though the serf might not be a free citizen on the land, yet he might be absolved from personal cares and worries. He had to pay no great amount, perhaps very little, for his food, his clothing, his fuel, and other necessaries of life. If he was ill or destitute, he might be taken care of. Now and then a generous landlord would extend pecuniary aid in time of special need. While the serf could be sold with the land, there could be no separate individual sale on the auction block, at least in the later years.

Serf labor, however, like any other kind of unfree labor, was bad all around—for all the parties concerned, including the nation. Apart from the building up of a caste system and an autocracy, and apart from its holding back education and general progress, it was a poor means of producing wealth, agricultural or other. It was characterized by industrial inefficiency. It offered little incentive to the worker. It was clumsy and wasteful. It stood directly in the way of social and economic advancement.

Effects upon the landlord class itself were anything but desirable, as is always the case with anything resembling a slave-holding class. To the nation, as to all nations that have practiced any sort of slavery, it was nothing less than a curse; and so it was to Russia. In that land, furthermore, as was to be expected, serf labor for the most part became reluctant, apathetic, careless, shirking labor, as far as was possible or expedient. Even in the breasts of the patient, long-suffering Russians there arose in time discontent, vexation, resentment, animosity. Among many immediate relief was found in excessive drinking.

Though there had been been consideration of the possible emancipation of the serfs of Russia at one time or another before the actual event, not a few in the land being aware of the evils and weaknesses and disadvantages of the system (certain of which had been slightly mitigated a few years before), it was not till the early 1860's that the great edict went forth (under Czar Alexander II), having been precipitated, it may be said, by the Russian reverses in the Crimean War.

Emancipation was to apply to both the landlord serfs and the state serfs. For those on land belonging to the government there

58

was no indemnification called for with respect to any one; they simply received the land on which they had dwelt, whether or not the matter would eventually turn out well for them. With the serfs on the estates of the landlords the situation was quite different. In that portion known as house serfs, who were really little more than domestic servants around the lord's house, and who cultivated no land, there were no land allotments—there was freedom alone; in their case it usually meant loss of maintenance and their drift into the ranks of wanderers seeking employment.

For the general body of the serfs who were in the hands of the landlords emancipation was not simply a legal removal of the bonds of serfdom lying upon them. The land with which the peasants were now to be endowed belonged to the landlords. It had to be paid for; the previous owners must be compensated for their loss.

To this end the government agreed to advance the necessary funds. It was to pay for the land, at three-fourths or four-fifths of its value. Of the sum to be yielded to the landlords, it was to provide four-fifths, the peasant being theoretically expected to furnish the remaining one-fifth—though as a matter of fact the peasant in the end paid little here. For its advance the government was to have repayment or redemption from the peasants over a period of forty-nine years, with interest at six per cent; after that they could own the land as in freehold. The ex-serf had thus to do his part; he had to assume the obligation of paying back his portion to the government. Any claims of the landlords were to be duly satisfied; obligations to them could be settled in money or in labor.

If emancipation was to mean very much, the serf had to be supplied betimes with land taken from the landlord, and in an adequate quantity. Orderly taking over of this land, however, proved a slow and by no means easy process; there were various obstacles in the way. Part of the land was still to remain in the ownership of the lords—and it was they in general who got the better land. The rest of the land was largely collective property in the hands of the local mir, or turned over to it. If any portion had been under individual proprietorship, it remained so. Approximately half of the land went to the peasant; the other half remained with the landlord, crown, or church.

There was, unfortunately, not a little misunderstanding in the whole undertaking, particularly as to the nature of the transaction involved. The peasants assumed, or somehow got the impression, that the Czar was seeking to give the land free to them, but was being held back by the wicked landlords and others. When one discovered that he had to pay interest, and taxes also, he experienced no little resentment; he felt that the land on which he and his ancestors had so long lived was now rightfully his, with no obligations anywhere. The peasants also found or believed that they had been cheated or over-charged in the purchase of the land from its former owners; they were convinced that they had to pay too high a price for the land they were now using. This attitude of the peasants was more than once reflected in actions of violence on their part.

In the emancipation of the serfs the landlords did not appear to be great gainers either. They had to witness the shrinkage of their lordly estates; they saw themselves possessed of a smaller share of the country's wealth. Some found themselves deprived of a class of cheap labor, and unable to hire other kind, though others discovered a pool of such labor eventually to await them. Certain ones, especially those whose estates were under German managers, could continue to make out fairly well; they could get along somehow. Others experienced great difficulty in adjusting themselves to the new situation. Those that had always carried on in quite unbusinesslike fashion were hit the hardest. Some faced bankruptcy. Among the landlords in general there were few that recognized any considerable responsibility or lent a friendly hand toward their newly emancipated neighbors.

All was thus not going well with the new economic and social set-up. The peasant, thrown on his own resources, early
discovered that his emancipation was more formal than real.
As long as he had to advance money for payment for the land
he was using, he felt himself not actually to be freed. Though
his serfdom was nominally at an end, he was held under the
tight bonds of the communal system of land control. His movements were restricted; he could go when and where he pleased
no more than he could before; he was confined to his local territory. He still had financial obligations and liabilities to the
mir to which he belonged. Through it the land he was to cultivate was allocated. To or through it he had to pay his share
of dues and taxes. Without its consent he could escape none of
his responsibilities here. Until he had fulfilled all his obligations to the mir, including any possible indebtedness, he must
remain with it.

The peasant found himself in further troubles in the new
order. The land allotted him was not always in the most desirable or most accessible location. He had lost the right of
pasturage for his cows and pigs, and the right of cutting wood
for the big stove in his home and for various other purposes.
He now had to pay something if he was to have these things.
He had to buy the necessaries of life with hard cash—there was
now little that was really free. As under the new dispensation
there might be less home or communal work that could be
carried on, he might have to pay more for his clothing, his
house furnishings, and the like.

Under the new system of land cultivation, furthermore, the
peasant found that, with the reversion of some of the land to
the landlords, he eventually had actually less land to till than
was the case before. As, too, the population continued to increase, his share of the land was bound to decrease. The proportion of the land which was his to cultivate shrunk with
time. (It was the chief householder, not the family, that was
as a rule entitled to inherited land.) The land allotment quite

61

too often, as had long been the case under the serf system, proved insufficient for the support of a family. What he had was seldom more than a scant score of acres, often less, perhaps much less. The awkward and cramping strip system, which was not easily to be done away with (described later), was in addition to his difficulties.[1] With the small acreage of land available to him, the peasant was at times compelled to secure supplemental land. This was possible only through the leasing of such land, which could be done only on high, perhaps exorbitant terms demanded from the landlord or from the government or from one of the few fellow peasants that were better off.[2]

Under all these circumstances the peasant, but lately removed from serfdom, had little difficulty in falling into debt. This debt proved not an easy one to pay off, and was likely to have constant additions; in time arrears could grow into quite sizeable proportions. Interest on his indebtedness was anything but low; it readily passed into genuine usury. Extortionate interest charges in fact led to further unhappy borrowings. A class of usurers arose to take advantage of the situation, and to profit greatly from the extremity of their wretched neighbors. Some had been peasants themselves; it was largely through the necessities of fellow peasants that they had been enabled to enrich themslves. Constituting from three to ten per cent of the rural population, they became a generally hated group in the land. The name given them was "kulaks"—an evil name which the Soviets were later to exploit so vigorously. By way of settling an indebtedness, creditors might get control of the labor of the borrowers, which labor they proceeded to drive for their further profit. In certain business transactions besides, the peasant was often an easy mark for the swindler or other spoiler who knew how to exploit or take advantage of him in some dealing or other.

[1] See *post,* p. 79.
[2] On other possible sources of income, see *post,* pp. 67, 81.

The taxes which the peasant had to pay were heavy and grievous ones—often more than he could bear—possibly consuming half or more of his slender earnings, at times even exceeding these earnings. Taxes were not infrequently on the basis of twice the value of the land used or its nominal rental value. Defaulting in taxes was a widespread practice. (There had been a poll tax, which was abolished after the third quarter of the nineteenth century.) In his general efforts for the redemption of his land, the peasant might have to pay from 50 to 100 per cent more than it was actually worth; much of the land bought from the landlords was overvalued at too high a price. Bending under all these burdens, the peasant could not always be expected to keep going — too often he must be crushed under.

No wonder that there grew up in the land a mass of dissatisfied, restless, embittered peasants. Many who could escape left for other parts, especially for the city, in search of work. The proportion that thus set forth to better their fortune was said in some regions to be from one-fifth to one-half.[1] Numbers who could not get away simply reverted to agricultural laborers on the landed estates from which they thought they had so recently been freed.

As the years went by, the Czaristic government became increasingly concerned over the land situation. It felt that something had to be done. There were sincere, well-intentioned efforts to alleviate the lot of the peasant. At the same time the government for its own sake was asserted not to be averse to building up a strong, contented, conservative-minded class of small landowners.

The twentieth century was not far advanced when a series of agrarian reforms was instituted, the essence of which were assistance to the peasant in acquiring land of his own and freedom of his movements. Remitted were all arrears in dues to the landlords. Redemption payments were cut in half, and

[1] See *post*, p. 81.

finally given up; all unpaid balances against the peasants were wiped out. Cancelled or reduced were debts to the mir.

The control, moreover, of the mir or local communal organization over the land was broken, the peasants being given the right to separate themselves from it and to keep their shares of land as their individual property. They could thus become full owners of the soil on which they toiled, with strips furthermore merged into single compact holdings. The consent of the mir was now no longer necessary to sell one's land. The peasant, in addition, could live where he wanted; he could leave his old locality and move to another if he so desired. The compulsory power of the mir was thus greatly modified and restricted. Not only was the individual ownership of land encouraged and provided for, and peasant proprietorship promoted, but the peasant was to have a greatly enlarged freedom in general. He might now enter college or the state service of his own free will. He appeared well on the way toward a full citizenship status.

Great and almost revolutionary as were the reforms initiated for the benefit of the Russian peasants, these were as a whole slow to appreciate and act upon what the government was doing for them. They were to a considerable extent in the dark as to what was involved in it all; they were distrustful, fearful, uncertain. The larger number failed to take advantage of the benevolent, fairly generous governmental gesture extended to them. Despite their previous hardships, despite their grievances and complaints, they were far from rendering an eager or warm response. They seemed loath to take hold of the new order. It is to be said that there still remained certain restrictions upon the ownership of land; in particular it was not to be sold except under strict conditions, and there was a limit upon the amount an owner could acquire.

With the passing of the years, more and more land came into the hands of individual proprietors. But the movement was with leaden feet. The distribution of the communal land, even in the years just before the First World War, never proceeded rapidly; the collective or communal ownership of the land was still the prevailing type. Some of the peasants who had obtained land individually were unable to carry on under the new arrangements and sold it back to the mir. Others no more successful could only become agricultural laborers or betake themselves to the city. The more clever and astute among them simply increased their holdings.

At the time of the First World War a little over one-third of the agricultural land of Russia was in the hands of the landlords or other vested interests, about one-fourth in the hands of the mir or of individuals, mostly known as kulaks, who had amassed more or less of wealth, and the remainder, about two-fifths, in the hands of the peasants themselves. Private landlords numbered somewhat over one hundred thousand. Most of the land belonging to the state or crown was forest land, and embraced little of what could be used by the peasants for farming. Land in the possession of the church, including monasteries, was not at this time considerable. Those of the kulak class, or those who had profited in the procedure, constituted about one-tenth or one-eighth of the peasant population in general. More than half of the peasants were hardly other than landless tenants or farm hands. Somewhere between one-third and one-fifth appeared able to make a living from the farms. Though the peasants were one hundred times as numerous as the landlords, the land of the former amounted to only four times that of the latter. From one-tenth to one-sixth of the housholds seem to have received consolidated holdings of an individual freehold nature.

Yet without doubt what had been attempted by the government in Russia was distinctly and importantly a step forward toward general individual peasant ownership of the land. Individual holdings were now recognized; it had become much less difficult to acquire this form of holding. Peasant movements were freer, at least theoretically. Agricultural conditions, however faulty and imperfect they remained, were steadily improving up to the time of the First World War. Quite possibly, if not probably, the governmental policy might in time have attained a fair or even considerable measure of success. Could the movement toward peasant proprietorship have continued unabated a score of years longer, it is just possible that the Revolution might have been averted. There was too little time or opportunity to prove the value of the new policy or to demonstrate its advantages. Agricultural reform in Russia came too late; already revolution was in the air.

CHAPTER VI

Russia and Its Industries

THOUGH in the earlier years of the nineteenth century there were in Russia few of what could be called "factories," it is not to be thought that there was at that time no manufacturing of any kind in the land, and no production of articles other than general agricultural products. There must have been some means of creating such things as even primitive man had to have. This manufacturing was done mainly in the homes of the people—such home industry having played no small part in Russian life for long years. Aside from the necessity for the creation of certain articles, it was no less needful that many, particularly among the peasants, be engaged in some occupation besides their farming, to help them eke out a bare existence, income from their farming operations quite too often being insufficient. Not a little could be done on cold winter nights after the day's work was done, and frequently in the cold hours of the day as well, in this form of subsidiary toil. Various articles could be produced in the period when the modern factory had not put in an appearance—especially various articles of clothing and household furnishings.

There were what were known as village or "kustar" industries, depending largely on the character of the raw materials at hand or within reach. Handicrafts might be engaged in by a collective body or coöperative group, perhaps including the members of a family. The principal articles made, apart from household and family requirements, were wooden work, woven work, embroidery, leather work, metal work (especially in iron and copper), work with linen or wool or silk, work with bone, work with furs, pottery, cutlery, rug making, making of toys or folk jewelry, silver ornamentation, making of samovars, basket making, and other like work, besides lacquer work, ivory carving, and painting of various articles, including religious ikons.

Not a little skill was often displayed here—some persons became quite proficient. Some villages were fairly well known for the particular industries in which they were concerned. Some articles had a considerable sale, largely local, though certain ones were sold at distant places, some even outside Russia. Some craft associations bore a resemblance to the old craft guilds known in western Europe. Some of the articles thus made were exchanged or bartered for other articles. Sometimes there was an entrepreneur who distributed the raw material and collected the finished product. The work was, however, as a rule not a highly paying one. It usually involved long hours and small profits. It was at times exploited by middlemen. At the beginning of the twentieth century, or shortly before the Revolution, there was an appreciable percentage of the population definitely engaged in "kustar" industries.

A particular cause of the industrial retardation of general Russian factories lay in the circumstance that there was little capital available in the land, with little credit attainable. Another factor was that there were poor means of transportation, especially in the paucity of railroads, with the necessary fuel also in part unavailable. It was likewise true that the home market was small; the populace was with little purchasing power. Though the population as a whole was large, it was for the most part thinly distributed over the land.

There were several events to cause Russians to realize the great need of industrial development, some in part the result of wars. First were the Napoleonic wars; later, the Crimean war; and, finally, the war with Japan. Long before these particular events, however, the progressive and indefatigable Peter the Great was aware of the situation. He set about creating what factories he could, though these were mostly small, with the labor force mostly poor and inefficient, and with goods mostly for home consumption. He copied from other countries and brought in artisans from them. There were also certain manorial factories attempted on a limited scale, none of them of importance—besides an occasional small state one.

In time it was realized that free labor in the land was on the whole considerably to be preferred to serf or controlled labor. This circumstance had an important bearing upon the action of Alexander II in emancipating the serfs. It was realized also that Russia must engage in far greater export trade if it was to attain to any degree of prosperity—must sell its goods outside for the money to be brought in.

With the entry of foreign capital, especially from western Europe, into the country, there could be marked development of the nation's industries and resources. This was to be furthered with the importation of machinery, especially from Great Britain and Germany. A high protective tariff which was eventually adopted helped to encourage national manufacturing and production.

It was after the middle of the nineteenth century that Russia began to engage in manufacturing to any appreciable extent, and after the third quarter of the century to any considerable extent. In the closing years of this century and in the beginning years of the next century, industry was in general advancing steadily even if not always rapidly. Here and there in the land factories of large size were springing up. When the First World War occurred, industry was on a decidedly upward swing. By some it was believed that the nation was on its way to become in no small measure an industrial one, with a fairly bright future.

Some of the industries making advance in this period were those having to do with the manufacture of sugar, hats, paper, glassware, leather goods, chemicals, steel, textiles, wooden ware, etc. Coal and iron production in particular greatly increased.

Textile and metal production were finding a place in central Russia, and iron and coal production and sugar production in the south, while in the north, especially in the St. Petersburg region, there was production of machinery and chemicals, as well as some textile and metal production.

Railroad building, though never on a wide scale (Russia having a special narrow gauge of its own) was by no means negligible, the trans-Siberian railway being a very important phase. Transportation facilities were, however, for a country the size of Russia entirely inadequate. It was to this factor that was largely attributable the loss of three great wars—the Crimean, the Japanese, and the First World War.

Factory employees were becoming a sizeable part of the population, and in fact in some of the larger cities so numerous as to constitute a conspicuous element. In large measure, especially in the years following the emancipation of the serfs, they had come from peasant farms where they had had such difficulties in extracting a living. In the case of a portion it was still possible to return to the country if city work did not turn out well. Some had come for only a part of the year, but later decided to make the city their home and stay on for good.

Under the Czars, foreign capital was the main source for the establishment and promotion of industries—factories, railways, banks, etc. It had to come from outside because in Russia there were relatively few who were in position to advance it. There was no little of selling concessions to foreigners, where the chief concern was dividends accorded to foreign stockholders. Most of the stockholders resided in western Europe, notably in France, and also in Belgium, Germany, and Great Britain.

Not only were the entrepreneurs and managers of Russian industries to a great extent foreigners, but the external commerce was largely in their hands as well. The Germans had a great deal to do with industrial affairs in Russia. They allowed wide credit on goods purchased. They had branch banks over the land. There were German manufacturers, merchants, artisans, custodians of estates, etc., as well as German physicians and German churches in the larger cities. In the seventeenth century in particular, certain soldiers of fortune, who had come into the land from Germany and also from other countries, settled down as merchants or artisans.

The foreign trade of Russia was considerable, but never as large as could have been expected with respect to a country of such vast natural resources and of so large a population. The chief exports were timber, cereals, petroleum (besides certain other minerals), sugar, flax, eggs, and butter. From one-third to one-fourth of exports were to Germany, with a proportion slightly less to Great Britain. Of imports about one-half came from Germany, and about one-sixth from Great Britain.

Trade in pre-Revolution Russia was of a quite primitive character. There was relatively little formal buying. Except in the larger cities where regular stores might be found, and except for an occasional store in smaller areas, most of the purchasing of goods was through peddlers who moved about the country, through bazaars which were fairly numerous, or through fairs in different cities which were held from time to time, and which were attended by the people in considerable numbers. Even in the larger cities wares were also commonly sold on the streets. The interior of Russia was served mostly by the village market, the peddlers' pack, and now and then a small country store. There was no established merchant class in the land outside the large cities.

In the days before the Revolution, the Russian people were not unacquainted with some form of a coöperative movement, especially that form known as the "artel," which went back for several centuries, having at the beginning to do with such matters as joint hunting, fishing, and lumbering enterprises. There were organizations that had relation to production and consumption alike, and also to a considerable extent to credit; they were to be found in both farm and factory. The consumers' organizations were very extensive, having come into being at about the time of the emancipation of the serfs, and developing in later years. Just before the First World War there were said to be something like eleven thousand such associations in the land, with not less than one-third of the population affected. The organizations were much on the order of the Rochdale pioneers of England. Producers' associations had their principal illustration in home or village industries.

Coöperative movements were something that seemed well fitted into Russian life, already so largely on a communal foundation. They would have been much farther extended but for the ignorance or lack of education existing among the Russian people, for the great distances separating them, and for the want of acquaintance with the principles of trading. Such organizations as were brought into existence were not marked by the fullest efficiency; in not a few ways they could have been improved or made of a higher order. Some had only a short life.

Labor legislation in Russia for the protection of the workers was slow in advancing. Factory conditions were for long of a deplorable character, with low pay, long hours, unhealthful and unsanitary surroundings.

As far back as the 1860's there was certain limited social insurance provided for state mining operations, later extended to private. In the early 1880's further labor laws were enacted, dealing mainly with factory inspection and with child labor. Children under twelve years of age were forbidden to work, and those from twelve to fifteen had their hours limited to eight per day. Limitations, though not severe ones, were also placed upon the unconscionably long hours of adults. In later years labor laws were somewhat improved. Further provision was made for factory inspection, which was not often of a high order. Workingmen's compensation laws were introduced to a limited extent, in some part in 1912. Larger industrial establishments were required to set up hospitals for injured employees. Early in the twentieth century trade unions were nominally legalized.

CHAPTER VII

Russia and Its Economic and Social Life

R USSIA was a country very loosely held together. Only the large cities were connected by railways; and train service in Russia was never noted for its efficiency. Most of the country had to do without it. Highways or public roads were for the most part in a quite unimproved state; they were few in quantity, and such as they were, poor in quality. They were usually more or less streaks of dust or mud, according to the season, across the country. Riding in sleighs over snow-covered earth in the long winters was often the readiest and easiest mode of travel. River transportation was of some help, but rivers were usually frozen in winter, and not infrequently shallow in summer. Poor and limited facilities for transportation seriously interfered with the even distribution of food and other articles over the country.

There were relatively few large cities in the land. The Russian people were mostly collected in villages—real farms or country homes seldom being found—from which they generally went out to the country to do their work. A village was a drab affair, perhaps containing not over a dozen dwellings; if it approached the size of an actual town, there might be one or two hundred. The village for the most part ran along a straggling, grass-grown street, in the larger places perhaps of cobblestones, with the houses of the inhabitants on either side. In addition to the rows of dwelling houses, there was usually to be found the village church, its curious shaped dome often the dominating feature of the place, and with an architecture that belonged only to Russia. There were also perhaps the village school building or a communal meeting place; in the larger places there might be a store of some kind, and very often a place for a vapor bath. Villages were frequently subject to fires; when once started, they were not easily to be put out.

The homes or dwellings in which the Russian people passed their lives were in general uninviting; they were such as could be occupied only by a poverty-stricken people. In those regions where there were few trees the houses were made of mud or clay, perhaps whitewashed. Where timber was available, they were usually of logs plastered with clay, or with interstices filled in with earth, moss, or other substance. In the towns houses of some of the well-to-do were of stone, and were perhaps painted; such houses were more likely to have a second story. The coverings of dwellings were often thatched roofs. Floors consisted of rough boards or plain earth. Where windows existed, they were frequently broken—and boarded-up in cold weather. A considerable part of the houses were without chimneys, at least in the earlier years. Not many houses had more than two rooms—not a few only one. In some of the houses there might be lodging also for domestic animals, they sharing the quarters with the humans. Here and there, especially in southern Russia, homes lost something of their dismal and cheerless appearance by having flower pots in the windows.

Furnishings in the dwelling did not go far. The furniture consisted of a bed or couch, a chair or two, a table, a bench or shelf—and always a stove, possibly of brick, and usually a good-sized one, which was necessary for so rigorous a climate. In a way the stove was the chief article in the house, occupying a large share of its limited space. It had various uses. Besides supplying heat to warm the occupants, to cook their food, to dry their clothing, and to afford a steam bath on occasion, its top when not heated could well serve for sleeping purposes. A vapor bath with steam arising from water poured on heated coals was a frequent Saturday night luxury or necessity, largely serving the purpose of soap in cleansing pores of the skin.

The principal bed covering was a sheepskin coat, which could in fact do double service, being worn during daylight hours by different members of the family. This sheepskin coat was an important article of clothing from the fact also that in general there was insufficient clothing to withstand the winter weather and the frequent bitter cold of the country. Trousers, smock, and boots were the main other articles of clothing worn by men. There was usually little underclothing for the members of the family. Such clothing as was worn was changed too infrequently for the health or cleanliness of the person.

The fare of the Russians, what they had to eat on their tables in their dreary homes, was flat and simple; they could discover little variety in their daily menu. Their meals for the most part consisted of black bread made of rye or barley, cabbages or cabbage soup, boiled potatoes, onions, one or two other vegetables, possibly a porridge, sometimes a melon (especially cucumber), and from time to time some milk. In season there were added fruit or berries, and at times acorns. Eggs in less favored areas could be regarded as something of a luxury, as was tea, most often a weak variety. Butter was from time to time, but not too often, on the table. Here and there honey had a place. Meat for a part of the population was to be had a few times in the year, though some fat was more frequent. Those living near the water could add fish to their diet. In some parts of the land at times so much grain was exported that there was not enough left for the people.

The Russians had a peculiar drink made sometimes from rye, sometimes from barley, often from potatoes—vodka—a drink of terrific and deadly power, made the worse by its being frequently taken to excess. In addition, there was some mild beer brewed from barley or rye known as kvass. In certain parts of Asiatic Russia there was a drink from fermented mares' milk.

The pleasures of the people were plain and homely, perhaps

in part a bit rough. They could enjoy some kind of rude, turbulent, primitive sport. Religious festivals generally had wide celebration. A wedding was an event of which much was made. A thing like hunting was rather for serious purposes. With some elements falconry was engaged in. The hardness of the life of the people was occasionally relieved by something on the order of a circus or an acrobatic or juggling exhibition. Folk dancing, some including movements of high skill, were always popular. The Russians delighted in holidays, revels, and such merry-making as they were capable of.

The people of Russia were themselves of a kind to win men's affections. They were simple, honest, generous, warm-hearted, patient, long-suffering, passive, non-resistant, of high imaginative powers—at times perhaps passionate, perhaps quick in headstrong action or in despair; they could pass from melancholy or low spirits to bursts of excitement or of gayety. Despite their privations they had cherished a love of art and other of the finer things of life. The vast distances of the land, with its limitless stretches, told upon the people; this was written in their character and in their vision.

Though essentially an agricultural country, Russia made poor and limited use of what agricultural resources she had. Just before the First World War less than half the total land area was under tillage, the remainder being in forest or barren steppes. Russian agriculture such as it was long remained in a very backward state. It was in general at a low ebb, with progressive farming but little understood or practiced.

After the emancipation of the serfs the land was not turned over directly to the individual peasant for his own use or as his personal possession; there was nothing like what we know as ownership in fee simple. It was the mir (which has already been described)[1] that assumed charge of the situation. Communal distribution and control of land was something that had long been known in Russia. The mir had power not only

[1] See ante, p. 42.

to allocate the land that was to be tilled, but to determine in general the character of the agricultural operations to be pursued, just as it had power over many details of the life of the village community. In many cases, however, the peasant might have a little ground of his own, for the production of his own crops or livestock, separate from his communal allotment—a small tract of arable land and an orchard and garden, besides the house in which he lived.

There existed over a large part of Russia a curious arrangement for the tilling of the soil. No one could claim a permanent holding. Land was redistributed from time to time, allotments being periodically granted, say, every twelve, fifteen, or twenty years, to different persons.

Communal land was in general of several kinds—the land on which the village was built, the arable land which was used for the growing of crops, the pasture land, and the meadow land (besides the forest land). The arable land was itself divided into three parts or strips, each a rather narrow one, averaging half a score, some only a few yards in width, and averaging about six score in length. A peasant might be allowed from ten to fifty or more strips, not necessarily contiguous to each other, but more likely some distance apart; he usually found them widely scattered around his village. His farm was thus composed of fragments, of separate plots—with incidentally no little time to be consumed in going from one to another. The boundaries between different individual holdings were marked by still thinner strips, perhaps overgrown with weeds. The strip system had a long and established usage in Russia (as well as in other countries of Europe). It was something not easily to be done away with; even the fairly broad land reforms in the early twentieth century did not abolish it altogether.

Cultivation of the soil was based upon rotation of crops. One of the strips was to lie fallow each year, one was planted perhaps to a winter grain, and the third to a spring grain. At times a crop like potatoes or legumes might be substituted or added. Smaller areas might be given to vegetables, flax, or other growth. Meadow land could be allocated annually or mown in common. Pasture and forest land by the village was usually held in common. Sometimes a given area might be devoted to the same cereal for several years, and then when exhausted permitted to lie fallow for several years.

The mir, as we have seen, had general charge of the matter, not only allocating the land to be cultivated by each peasant, but deciding what to plant or sow. Nothing was to be attempted without its consent. For his allotment the peasant had to pay by rent or labor. The peasant lived in the village, and went out each day to work on the plot of ground which had been assigned him, which was possibly some little distance away.

The strip system was a highly wasteful one; there was also considerable waste in the boundaries between strips. In part by reason of this system the land was steadily impoverished. By the allotment plan, furthermore, no one could claim permanent holding of a tract of land. In consequence of the form of land tenure, and also because of the redistribution of land from time to time, there was little incentive to improve the soil or to employ scientific procedure in dealing with it, on the part of the immediate user. Few could be expected to take a deep or abiding interest in land which was in one's possession and for one's use only for a season. Few could be concerned in, or could care to undertake, the lasting improvement of the soil.

Under the land system of Russia the peasant's farm, his share of the communal land, was quite too small for satisfactory or successful cultivation. For any approach to efficient farming operations from twenty-five to fifty acres at the least would have been necessary for profitable operations on the part of a peasant. As it was, his allotment was often hardly more than a few acres, perhaps half a dozen, perhaps a dozen, perhaps even a score or more. The situation grew worse with the years.

78

At the time of the emancipation average holdings were of one or two dozen acres; at the beginning of the twentieth century, half as many. As the population increased, the average size of the holdings became less. There was not land enough for all.[1] Holdings were never adequate for a population like that of Russia, and the only possible result was steady deterioration of land and peasant alike.

Even though the land was equally distributed, the results might not be the same for all the families concerned. One family might have a greater number of individual members to work on it than another family; or there might be a greater number of mouths to be fed from one allotment than from another. If additional land was necessary in a given case, it would have to be rented—something to come high. But where was the land to be found? Where was the rent money to come from?

Agricultural methods were for the most part primitive and antiquated. Under the strip system mechanized farming was largely both physically and financially out of the question; modern farm machinery could only sparingly exist. Farm implements used in plowing did not permit of a deep turnover of the earth; the rude plow in use barely scratched the surface and left only shallow furrows—most plows were without metal parts. The harrows that were used were crude affairs. In the harvesting it was the scythe, sickle, and flail that were largely employed. There was poor seed to be sowed in the soil, and poor fertilizer to be applied to it. (Some valuable fertilizer material was burned as fuel in the home.)

The animals made use of on the farm were in general small and of low grade. Good or scientific breeding was largely unknown. Pasturage was usually poor; in some areas it was quite inadequate. In fact, there was no great amount of livestock raising in the land; what there was, was on the decline. One-third or one-fourth of the farm households owned no horses;

[1] See *ante*, p. 61.

a like proportion owned only one—perhaps a horse had to be hired to do the farm work. The poorer peasants did not even own a cow. There was some raising of hogs, and limited raising of sheep. The smaller number of peasants possessed farm implements of their own; such implements as were used had often to be rented. Capital was in general wanting for needed improvements on the land.

Familiar to the harried peasant were bad harvests and crop failures, followed by famines in the land; from these things the people were never far removed. It was under threat of them that was maintained their constant struggle for their scanty harvests.

Another drawback to happy farm life lay in the general cold climate of the country, with its long torpid winters, allowing only a short but hot planting and harvesting season. This limited the practice of agricultural operations and put a tax on the powers of endurance of those carrying them on.

Finally, the Russian peasant had meagre resources or outlet for disposing of whatever of his products he might wish or be able to sell. Distances to centers of population were great; means of transportation were poor and scant. To make matters worse yet, the peasant might have to sell his produce at harvest time, when prices were lowest.

As though the woes of the peasants were not crushing enough, there were imposed upon their shoulders usurious interest charges for the money which they were compelled to borrow from time to time, and a ponderous government tax from which they could not escape. No wonder the Russian farmer often looked upon himself as doomed, as destined to remain a hopeless creature with slender possibilities of ever rising. Truly the plight of the Russian peasant could become one of despair.

The Russian government was not unaware of the situation on the farm of the peasant. It took a certain interest in it, and tried to some extent to deal with it. It sought in some measure to teach better agricultural methods, conducting a number of agricultural institutes over the land. Its accomplishments in this direction, however, did not go far, or at any rate not far enough.

To supplement the earnings that were possible from his agricultural endeavors to eke out a living, it was a fairly frequent practice of the Russian peasant to engage to a greater or less extent, especially in the long winter evenings, in other occupations, including village industries or home fabrication of certain articles, to be used by the family or to be sold outside. (This matter has already been considered.)[1] The whole family often engaged in the process. Children, following the footsteps of their parents, might take up their toilsome tasks in their tender years; for them there might not be much of childhood.

Owing to the dwindling size of the farm of the Russian peasant, with an ever growing population, and owing to the inconsequential income to be extracted from it even by diligent and ceaseless toil, he sometimes had no other recourse but to betake himself from his rural home to the crowded ways of the city, to try to find work as a factory hand in the not too numerous industrial establishments existing there, or as a domestic servant in such homes as could pay even the small wage to be had in that occupation. With some the visits to the city were only temporary or for a season, especially in the winter, with return to the farm for the rest of the year when farm operations could be engaged in. (Even though one left his land for a time, he could retain his former connection with it and rights to it.) As the years passed, residence in the city secured an ever stronger hold, and the ties to it became of more permanent character. As we have seen,[2] many who came to the city decided to remain there for good, forsaking all their country allegiance.

The income of the hard-pressed, poverty-ridden family in

[1] See *ante*, p. 67.
[2] See *ante*, p. 63.

Russia seldom exceeded two or three hundred dollars a year; often it was considerably less. Per capita earnings for the general population were seldom as high as fifty dollars, not infrequently forty or even thirty. If one hired himself out in the country, he could not often expect over thirty or thirty-five cents a day. The maximum wage of factory employees in the city was somewhat higher than that of the worker in the field, but never really large. It might be something like eighty-five cents a day, but frequently less than half that sum. Competition for such jobs as existed had a part in keeping earnings low. Collateral or incidental or subsidiary work might constitute from one-eighth to one-half of a family's total income.

If the Russian peasant on his farm was often called indolent or shiftless or inept or in a state of inertia, if he was said to have little of a spirit of enterprise or progressiveness—and perhaps inclined at times to too large a sip of his vodka—the fault was hardly to be placed at his door; it lay in no innate traits in his character. It was rather the result of conditions over which he had but limited control. It lay in the rigors of the climate in which he had to live, in the tiny acreage of land he was allowed to cultivate from which little more than a pittance was to be extracted, in the general nature of the system of land tenure in which was involved no permanent possession or use of the soil that was cultivated, in the backwardness of the agricultural processes which he had to employ, in the ignorance or lack of modern scientific knowledge which could be applied to his farm, in the puny but heavily taxed income which he was able to wring from his tedious and arduous endeavors, in the ever increasing number of mouths which had to be fed on an ever decreasing allotment of land, in the generally hopeless estate in which he found himself from the rising of the sun each day to its setting.

In view of the unhappy conditions under which the Russian peasant had to live, was it so great a matter of wonder that he was driven to seek relief in his fiery vodka? And from such excitable potions were there not to be expected from time to time altercations and brawls with his family or with his neighbors? Was it not little more than the letting off of steam? Was not the peasant's heart in the right place after all, but his living under such conditions as to make him beside himself at times?

Illiteracy spread over Russia like the plague. The land was steeped in it. What education there was did not reach far. A great portion of the people were without it. At the end of the third quarter of the nineteenth century over two-thirds of the people were not able to read or write. At the end of the century the proportion was about one-half; at the time of the First World War it was about one-fourth. In urban sections the proportion was much lower than in rural. The richer families could employ private tutors for their children, or occasionally send them to a private school.

Schools were relatively few in number; they were seldom housed in inviting quarters; they were not distinguished for the quality of their work. Schoolbooks were often hardly worthy of the name. Those who did the teaching were not infrequently themselves not far advanced in education, and had in general little training. Compulsory education had hardly any effective beginning until the years of the twentieth century. Per capita costs of education were unbelievably low.

Many villages were without what might be called high schools, or schools beyond the elementary grade, though these were slowly increasing. Universities were to be found in a number of the cities of considerable size. The first was created as early as the early part of the seventeenth century; and the movement was slowly making its way over the land. There were also a limited number of professional and technical schools. In the universities was about the only light shining in the nation, a light with a flame largely borrowed from western Europe, and a light already somewhat colored with more or less radical doctrines.[1]

[1] See *post*, p. 113.

Even though low educational levels prevailed widely in Russia, it was not in general so much the people's fault. Means or avenues to education were mostly closed or denied to them. When they were given the chance they were quite willing, if not avid, to drink from the fountain of knowledge. Many of those who were in position to attend a university at one of the principal cities did so. Students were in considerable part in quite poor circumstances, but they were as a rule ardent and much in earnest in their quest for knowledge.

It was charged that the Czaristic government did not do more to advance and promote education for the reason that it feared the thing and what it might do for the people. There is little doubt that if education had received its due in Russia, the land would have escaped a great part of its later difficulties and unhappy experiences. It is to be stated at the same time that before the First World War conditions as to education were in most respects undergoing improvement, and that there was a definite upward trend, even though one far from rapid. Illiteracy was steadily, if slowly, declining in the land. The government was putting forth sincere and measurable, even though belated and inadequate, efforts to deal with its great problem.

In a number of cities there were maintained museums, some of which were quite worthwhile, for the spreading of knowledge. Collections of works of art, some well-known, were to be found in the chief cities. In St. Petersburg (Leningrad) was an unequalled collection of rare manuscripts. The Imperial Library there was one of the great libraries of the world.

Newspapers were to a great extent unknown outside the larger cities, and there only to a limited extent .They were without notable influence—the influence of a newspaper generally corresponding to the extent of the reading ability of the people. It was among the intellectual radicals that the printed sheet had the widest sway.

Russian literature none the less was hardly other than a mighty thing. It held on its roll of honor great names, some of world-wide recognition. The golden age of literature in the land is regarded as that during the reign of the last three or four of the Czars. What country would not cherish a poet like Pushkin, or a painter in words like Chekhov? And had not Russia excelled in the novel, with its Tolstoi, Turgeniev, Gorki, Dostoievsky, Gogol, and not a few others? The country had men of letters of note in various other fields. The natural sciences were always cultivated in Russia. There was particular activity with respect to biology, physiology, and other such sciences. There were medical men of renown.[1] Who has not known of Pavlov with his conditioned reflex? There were names high in music, too—Tschaikowsky, Glinka, Moussorgsky, Rimsky-Korsakov, and all the rest. The people had their many folk songs. Who does not know the "Song of the Volga Boatmen"? In painting did not Russia have a name such as Vereshchagin? Russian writers and artists depicted and dwelt upon the sorrows of their land. Not a few took the side of their oppressed countrymen.

The birth rate and the death rate in Russia were the highest in Europe—the two things usually going hand in hand. The former was often around 45 or 47 per 1000 of population in a year's time (not far from the 50 which is regarded as the maximum for the human race). The death rate was correspondingly high, often close to 30, a very high figure indeed for the white race, and one of the highest for the entire world. Both the birth rate and the death rate were not far from three times as great as the rate for the countries of western Europe.

There were a number of reasons for the high death rate in Russia—inability to read and write, and consequently inability to receive proper health instruction; inadequate or unnourishing daily diet; general unhygienic living conditions; verminous conditions in the crowded peasant hut; little control of spread of infectious diseases; general absence of isolation and other hospitals in rural areas; keeping of animals in rural

[1] The Institute of Experimental Medicine was opened at Leningrad in 1890.

homes; paucity of physicians, especially in rural areas; general absence of trained nursing; overcrowded and unsanitary conditions in the home or work place of the city dweller. In addition, it is to be stated that in isolated lonely sections of the countryside killing of human beings by wolves or bears was not unknown.

The infant mortality rate (deaths during the first year of life) was often one-third, varying in different areas from one-fourth to one-half—an abnormal rate even among people of low culture. This astounding rate was in part due to the circumstance both that Russian mothers lacked knowledge of infant care, and that they had to engage so heavily in physical labor.

Disease in general was not easy to check. Pestilence or plague could count its victims by the tens or hundreds of thousands. The larger portion of the population was said to be suffering from disorders of some kind or in need of medical attention in some degree. Outstanding infections were tuberculosis, venereal disease, and eye complaints. There were few physicians in the land, in some areas but one to every score thousand of population, while some of those practicing medicine were far from being properly qualified. There were few dentists. There was considerable of medical fakers, soothsayers, and witch doctors in some parts of the land. Hospitals were hardly to be found beyond the large cities, and even here were mostly inadequate. Trained nurses were almost totally lacking. Only a certain physical robustness and stamina kept the people from having illness to a greater extent, considering their general untoward living conditions.

With poverty so widespread over the land, and with so large a part of the population in dire want, there was in Russia a vast field for deeds of benevolence and social service. The situation could be met only in small measure. The Russians were warm-hearted and generous to a degree, and a people given to charity, but few were in a favored position to come greatly to the succor of their brethren in distress.

Such charity as was provided in the land came from those individual citizens who were concerned and who had some financial means. There was, however, no little unassuming generous giving on the part of the poor out of their slender means to their neighbors in time of need. Bestowals of charity among the more affluent classes were too often for the good of the soul of the giver, with less consideration for the general effects upon the recipient. Begging was a nation-wide practice; beggars seemed to be everywhere. Around church doors in particular were their beseeching hands.

There was little of what we call organized charity. Russia was too big and too unwieldy and backward for such movement to have gone far. A semblance of private charitable or relief societies existed in a few of the larger cities, but their operations were limited. What hospitals and orphan institutions were to be found were often a direct gift of the Czar or of his family or of one of the nobility. In St. Petersburg and Moscow there were large foundling hospitals. The church did some charitable work, though seldom on any considerable scale. A general system of public relief was all but unknown; there was little of a compulsory relief system—though in some local communities there might be restricted attempts in this direction. What we regard as social welfare measures in general were circumscribed; such as they were affected only small numbers of the population.

While in controversies and contentions between peasant and peasant rude justice was in general to be expected in the local courts, such was not so likely to be the case when there were differences between the lowly peasant and one of the proud upper classes. Here too often the former found the scales of justice not evenly balanced—balanced against him. The other side could not infrequently look for favoritism, partiality, protection at the bar of the law.

Punishment in Russia for crimes, or for misdeeds, or for the incurring of the displeasure of the Czar or his ministers, or perhaps of some of the nobility, was hard, harsh, very often cruel, and at times barbarous. Punishment could be for relatively trifling offenses, if the government was concerned. It was the political offender who quite often had to suffer the most. In punishment torture was by no means unknown. The use of the knout, generally made of dried thongs of raw hide interwoven with wires, was once a favorite and peculiar instrument of the land for beating a victim on his knees. Long imprisonment under horrible conditions might be ended only by merciful death. The fortress of Sts. Peter and Paul at St. Petersburg had many an anguished story of durance vile to tell, as did similar prisons over the land. Endless lines of exiles marching to the cold and desolate regions of Siberia aroused the interest and excited the compassion of the world.[1] The scaffold or the firing line was seldom long without use.

Apart from the regular police, and apart from the Czar's secret police, there was a body of executioners of the Czar's orders and of protectors of his throne and its privileges, a mounted body composed of Cossacks, who made that term a dreaded one in the land. Woe to those they ever rode down!

A great source of weakness to Russia was the lack of a strong, intelligent middle class. In the days before the First World War and the Russian Revolution, not less than three-fourths of the population were peasants. Something like one-eighth were industrial workers. Small traders, professional classes, government employees, and other similar groups constituted a somewhat smaller proportion. In regular military service was one or two per cent. The remainder was to be placed within the ranks of the nobility, of an even slighter figure. Russia, it thus appears, had very little of a real middle class. On top were the monarch and the aristocracy; at the bottom were a vast landless peasantry and a mass of low paid industrial workers; wedged

[1] During the nineteenth century not less than one million persons are said to have been ordered to Siberia, and during a single year in the early twentieth century several score thousand.

in between was a thin layer of small shopkeepers and professional groups.

Apart from the nobility and monarchy only a very small part of the Russian people really owned land. Natural resources, to the extent that they were developed, became the property of the monarchy or nobility—so far as they did not pass into foreign grasp. The government had in general the power and was in a position to create or add to the nobility as it pleased. It had a ready means of reward for valued service to it or for pleasing activities in its behalf.

Among the nobility there was a considerable measure of German influence, there being not a few German managers or custodians of the landed estates, some of whom were hardly more than exploiters, and some perhaps even on the order of spies.

The upper classes were largely known for their luxurious, extravagant, and spendthrift living—and for their excessive gambling. Monte Carlo and all the casinos of Europe had their acquaintance. Among them was probably the grandest set of gamblers on the Continent. They liked to live in the city, retaining their country manors. Apart from gambling and garish palace parties, the chief diversion or pursuit of the nobility was hunting wild game.

The opulence of the Russian nobility, however, was largely superficial; not a considerable portion could be called decidedly well-off; upon no small portion rested a ponderable burden of debt; there were very few of the mansions not mortgaged. Despite its trappings and garnishings, despite its elaborate and ornate country and town houses, it was really to a great extent impecunious. For the most part, it was chronically short of funds and in need of ready cash—something that in considerable measure explains its thirst for gambling. It was also now and then this need of money that accounted for no small part of the bribery that could infest government circles.

The nobility aped the gay and expensive ways and doings of

89

envied western Europe. They acquired a western veneer which was quite foreign to the masses of the people. Some of them were rather upstarts and sophisticates, quite out of keeping with the simple ways of the Russian people in general. Their Russia was not to be outdone by what was exotic to its nature and character. An exquisite Peterhof near St. Petersburg was to be on the order of Versailles—in fact a second Versailles. There grew up a conflict between the dainty, elegant court life of St. Petersburg and the plain manners of Moscow, the ancient heart of the country of the Slavic people.

With certain glowing and noble exceptions, the nobility, often dissolute and dissipated, was a heavy burden and trial to the Russian people. To no small extent it was an irresponsible lot. Of a portion much better things could be said.

It is only fair to add that it is believed by some that in the years shortly before its Revolution progress in Russia both educationally and industrially was clearly in evidence, with the probability that this movement would with the years be at an accelerated rate; that the country was in fact on the eve of notable advance along economic, social, and political lines; that there was genuine promise of its onward march as an enlightened, forward-facing nation, under a constitution, on an ever enlarging democratic basis, and with ever widening democratic conceptions—but that all this happy outlook was staved off, was thwarted, was nullified by the radical tendencies of the times, culminating in the Revolution. It will forever be a question how far there is truth here. There can be no doubt that Russia was progressing in greater or less degree. But whether this progress was rapid enough, or was sufficient or adequate to forestall violent changes in the nation's make-up is a matter upon which there may be debate that is endless.

CHAPTER VIII

Russia and Its Ingestion of Revolutionary Doctrines

IN the change of Russia from its Czaristic days to those of the Soviet power, there were two forces or movements converging upon each other, and preordained to meet in the fullness of time. One was the radical or revolutionary movement, creeping over a greater and greater part of Europe, and not entirely slighting Russia— a movement having existed underground in Europe for over a century, and now taking organized shape as communism. The other movement was that of the vast Czaristic empire slowly tottering to its dissolution.

In a fashion the revolution in Russia can trace descent from the French revolution of the latter days of the eighteenth century, or at least in some measure from the thoughts loosened by that revolution—furthered by the rapid developments consequent upon the industrial revolution, especially in its use of steam power and in the concentration of men in factories for the making of things to supply human wants.

The causes of the French Revolution need not be entered into here. The long smoldering discontent with injustice and oppression along with wretchedness of living among many in the land of France, and with the domination of the land by the selfish "aristocrats," had finally burst into flame in the struggles under the name of that Revolution. This great upheaval in the affairs of men was, however, not so much concerned with the ownership of property as such, but rather with the abuses of ownership, and with the "rights" of man. Socialism as we now understand it had little genuine connection with

91

the French Revolution; nor was it a direct growth from it.

It is to be remembered that man's condition in society had about this time been drawing attention from several directions. In France in particular, actually before the great Revolution, questions as to man as a social being had been receiving pronounced consideration (as in the writings of Rousseau and others). Conceptions as to human liberty were likewise becoming the subject of men's thoughts—something that for not a few years had engaged speculation in England. In France, to take up the subject in pre-Revolution days, and in a way to herald the Revolution, were men like Diderot, d'Alembert, Voltaire, and other of the so-called Encyclopedists, with their somewhat radical political and economic doctrines, conceived, as they claimed, in the light of reason, with the extolling of science, and with particular hostility toward privilege and other obnoxious features of the old order. The general welfare of the people had a place in all these considerations.

After the days of the Revolution and after the days of their successors, the imperial sway of Napoleon Bonaparte, there was a great advance in agriculture, industry, and trade over western Europe, especially in France, England, and the Low Countries. After what was known as the Industrial Revolution, which had barely preceded the French Revolution, the factory system was steadily establishing itself, displacing now out-moded means for the production of goods. Home production, which had hitherto prevailed, had little chance compared with factory production, while what had been known as journeymen workers were now little called for. One who in the old economy was able to rise to the position of master in a given trade found himself in a quite different situation: he could as a general thing under the factory system expect only to be converted into one of the thousands of men who become little more than cogs in a gigantic power-driven machine. But whatever the shift in the position of the industrial worker under the new system, there was under it a vast, towering increase of wealth among men.

This wealth, however, was little shared by the workers in the factories. All the tremendous advantages and gains that had come through the factory process of production left them hardly better off economically than they had been before; there was no great benefit to them in the new procedure. Their general earnings were little increased, whatever might be the size of the earnings accruing to the owners of the factory or of the machine. The whole business was avowedly driven for the profit of these owners—the stock-holding capitalists. The workers were simply "hands"—a necessary part of a machine that was hardly human. Their actual directive participation in the operations of the factory in which they worked could not be great or go far—though it was these operations that affected practically their whole being. Not only this, but there was often little regard for their working conditions—they might have less consideration than sturdy working animals. Their health and safety were in themselves of secondary import. It was not even pretended that the welfare of the workers was the uppermost or a prime consideration in the operation of these factories. Wages could be low, perhaps a pittance; hours could be long, unbearably so; conditions of work could be anything but conducive to soundness of body or mind or to human vitality, but quite antagonistic thereto—they could at times be described as not less than horrible or shocking. Child labor could be employed, even the labor of children in their tender years, unfitting them for their future years, causing them to compete with adult labor, and taking the bread away from the heads of families. And all this was for the financial gain of the factory owners; put forward was no other motive.

Government interference or even regulation in the matter, so far as it was thought of, could amount to little. There were few in a position or concerned or willing to take proper or adequate action. The doctrine of *laissez-faire* was supreme; it rode roughshod over all other considerations. Whatever of public reform was to be injected into the situation would have to wait.

In time, however, the matter and its significance were to receive notice from two groups—thinkers or the intellectual classes, or the so-called intelligentsia, on the one hand, and the workers themselves who had directly and practically to experience it, on the other.

Following the French Revolution and the changed conditions of labor now becoming general, there were various proposals for a new and different order in the production and distribution of wealth. In France in particular, the home of the French Revolution, there was a whole line of projects offered, some of highly fantastic nature, by St. Simon, Cabet, Babeuf, Fourier, Proudhon, Blanc. All more or less or in some measure favored the abolition of the capitalistic system, together with the leisure class in society, and the competitive wage system.

These proposals, some perhaps more or less in the direction of socialism, had little really to do with the actual introduction and growth of that system. Possibly a more scientific foundation for socialism came from certain of the political economists of other lands, especially England, who had been examining the matter, and who were advancing their theories on the subject. There was also influence from certain of the philosophers of these and earlier days, especially in Germany.

The workers in the factories, who seemingly were not regarded by the owners as capable of full intellectual processes, were also doing some thinking. They were becoming alive to the conditions in which they were finding themselves.

In the factories these workers were thrown together; they were in position to discuss common interests as they learned or became aware of them. Gathered in the same work places, they could ask questions of each other during and outside working hours. They wanted to know whither they were proceeding. An important query in their minds was why they had to work so hard, and under such disadvantageous conditions, while others who worked but little could so largely enjoy the fruit of their toil. They made inquiry as to the sources of wealth—and its disposition—its production and its distribution. They turned their attention to the whole capitalistic system, whereby accumulated capital was used for the production of further wealth for the benefit of those who owned the capital; they wondered if all this was the best thing for them.

And so in the later years of the first half of the nineteenth century there was arising the conception of a system that would be antithetical to existing capitalism—on a different basis, and with a different purpose—that is, socialism. It was in large part against the injustice and inequities piling up during these and preceding years that there arose the conceptions of this great new economic and social system.

In the earlier periods in most of the countries of Europe the proposals under the new light were not so much of a theoretical order; they were rather conservative or of a practical character; they were primarily concerned with measures of social reform, which were to proceed bit by bit; for the most part they were not of a particularly radical cast. Immediate aims or those for the time being were chiefly: greater participation in government by the working classes, extension of the franchise to male adults generally (especially without property qualifications), sounder bases of parliamentary representation (especially equal voting areas), voting by ballot, annual parliaments, payment for members of a parliament, wider education, more equitable schemes of taxation, improved labor conditions, more humane criminal codes, and similar measures of social and economic betterment. The Chartist movement in England was something of an illustration of these attitudes.

There was, however, one outstanding telling document that appeared about the middle of the nineteenth century (1848)—what was known as the Communist Manifesto, a blast prepared by an international group. This document was pretty radical, of all but volcanic character; it was harsh, materialistic, somewhat unfair—but withal a thought-provoking thing. It was a fiery indictment of a capitalistic society, and included its stirring appeal to the working classes of the world to unite, who had "nothing to lose but their chains," and "a world to gain." It declared that the issue in capitalism was the nature of ownership in the production of goods, with the desire for world markets. Under its contemplation was the "violent overthrow of the whole contemporary social order." In its opening sentence it characterized itself as the "specter haunting Europe" (as it indeed was). The workers were told that it was their historic mission to bring in the new order.

The Communist Manifesto was of two parts—one dealing with socialist principles, and the other with proposed measures of early social reform. In the latter category or program were in the main: abolition of property in land, heavy and progressive income tax, abolition of inheritance of property, transfer of ownership of estates to the state, cultivation of waste land and soil improvement, universal free education for the people, including industrial education and technical training, equal liability of all to labor, no child labor, extension of state factories and other instruments of production, state ownership of means of communication and transportation, centralization of credit in a state monopolistic bank, equitable distribution of population, and gradual abolition of distinctions between town and country.

The adoption of any measures of reform during the period in question faced a stone wall. Though a certain part of what was then demanded (apart from much of the Communist Manifesto) now receives general assent, the proposals at the time incurred deep opposition from the ruling powers, and in more than one country there was an abortive revolution (notably in France)—a repercussion of which was the migration of some excellent citizens from a country like Germany to a more liberal America.

The time was now ripe for the entry upon the scene of one of the great figures of all history, a man comparable to Mohammed for his success in building up a following of uncountable numbers who accepted with little question his deliverances—a man who still holds dominion over the thought of a large part of the world. This was Karl Marx, the scholarly German socialist. It was he who had a large part in the writing of the Communist Manifesto.

It is to be said, however, that certain of his co-laborers at this time, especially Engel, Rodbertus, and La Salle, had much to do with the movement now set on foot. Certain German philosophers like Kant, Fichte, and Hegel are to be credited with having furnished some of the basic conceptions. The gentle Kant had set forth the notions of the good of the state, of its organization and discipline, of one's duties to it, and of a world order. Fichte had made no small impression upon Marx by his emphasis upon the place of the state in human affairs, which tended toward state supremacy, state absolutism. Hegel had made a powerful appeal with his conceptions of social growth or the evolutionary processes in human institutions, and of the conflicts of opposites, and of the authority of the state. English political economists like Ricardo with his labor theory of value, or subsistence or wage fund, passing into the iron law of wages—wages being largely determined by the amount of food and other necessaries of life available for the supply of workers concerned—also had an important part in the formulation of the new doctrine. Darwin's recently announced postulate of the survival of the fittest in the evolution of man was also not without influence. In the system were combined both economic and political principles. The summation of Marx's views was in his great work *Das Kapital* (1867).

Marx aimed at quite summary procedure—a direct appeal to the working classes of the countries of Europe, and indeed of all the world. He sought to show them how they had been exploited, and would continue to be exploited, till they themselves took possession of the machinery of capitalism. His great philosophy of life—for it is nothing less—centers about and is built upon the material forces (in particular food, raiment, and shelter) upon which man has to count for his living. These became the only forces to be reckoned within man's social life, or indeed in his civilization. It is the "economic interpretation of history" which is Marx's starting point. Man's struggle for tools (besides land) for the production of things for the satisfaction of his needs is the primary and underlying struggle of human existence. The class struggle is the struggle between the owners of these tools (the capitalist class) and those who are not owners but are compelled to work for the owners (the proletarian class). The bourgeois class, composed mostly of small traders and groups themselves owning little capital—sometimes regarded as part of the capitalist class itself—are really allies and beneficiaries of it. Wealth more and more is concentrated into the hands of the few, especially in the combination of producing interests, with economic power quite likely to rest with the shrewd and grasping among the capitalist class. This class is ever seeking wider world markets for the goods it produces, and with ever wider world power. In capitalistic rivalries lie largely the roots of war. The middle class tends to disappear between the upper and nether millstones of economic conditions. The working class, beaten so far in the conflict, have to accept wages from the capitalist class for the labor they perform, their physical toil being all they have to give in return for their means of living, and constituting what is looked upon as a reserve of labor. They have thus the status of wage slaves.

The wealth created beyond what is returned to the workers as wages is surplus value, which is entirely unearned on the part of the capitalist class. The profit, interest, and rent now accruing and which are received in society are unfair, and come really from the despoiling of the workers. Under these circumstances, perhaps attended with a series of industrial crises, each more serious than its predecessor, the condition of the working class goes from worse to worse, their misery increases, till finally, losing more and more control of the tools of their labor, goaded beyond all endurance, and seeing the futility of individual action and the necessity of action by the workers in concert, they rise up and seize for themselves the tools of the capitalist class—unless, indeed, capitalism, intrinsically unsound at the core, and carrying within itself the seeds of its own destruction, sooner or later falls to pieces of its own weight, spelling its doom of itself.

As the capitalist class knows no country, but extends its operations everywhere, so the working class will do likewise; theirs will become an international movement. A powerful class consciousness will grip the workers of all nations; together they will march to victory.

In extreme Marxian thought, finally, when socialism is in complete mastery of the field, there will be no need of force or of the agencies of government in the affairs of men, but only voluntary coöperative activities among the citizenry. By that time the people will have adapted themselves to the new order, and will know how to get along together; they will have become accustomed to elementary conditions of social existence, without subjection to outside compulsion. There will be an abundance of goods for man's consumption, and none need be in want. Sources of friction or competition, conditions breeding contention, will disappear. There will now be a classless society, and the state will "wither away."

Not only this, but the "morality," the "civilization" of capitalist countries is based upon capitalistic principles, and reflects capitalistic attitudes. Accepted standards in what have been afforded in religion, arts, literature, law, philosophy are thus likely to be wrong from top to bottom. No individual is to blame—socialism never becomes personal—but the system is altogether bad; and it is the system that must be destroyed.

It was this doctrine of Marx which swept over great areas in Europe, and has held so vast a sway. It is classical, orthodox, Marxism socialism.

Though at the time of the adoption of the Communist Manifesto there were revolutionary uprisings over a large part of Europe, those regions which were supposed to be concerned with radical economic reform, especially central and northern Europe, in later years followed Marx at a greater or less distance, but with an increasing measure of conservatism. There grew in general little faith in violent revolution, as this was believed to be a real detriment to the cause; activities were more and more confined to an appeal to the suffrage. With the extension of the ballot, there could be reform through evolutionary process. Even the theories of Marx underwent a process of toning down. Under Bernstein in Germany in particular, with his "revisionist" policy, the Marxian philosophy was considerably moderated, becoming less dogmatic and more opportunist. Some of the leading postulates of that philosophy came to be regarded in no little degree as fallacies, more or less at variance with the unfolding facts of human experience. For one thing, the theory of increasing misery of the working class under the capitalistic system could not be accepted; on the contrary, the condition of this class was for the most part seen to be improving. Nor were there clear signs of the breaking down of the capitalistic system. The middle class was not disappearing, but possibly increasing. Whether the class struggle was becoming more intense was a question. Some industries were continuing to operate on a small scale; not all were being absorbed into large combines. Not a few of the workers were themselves found to be owners of securities in one corporation or another. Nor was to be overlooked the part of technology and scientific knowledge in the increased production of goods. The general wealth-producing powers of the capitalistic system were being more and more clearly discerned.

There were now springing up certain so-called socialistic parties of Europe, often known by some such name as social democratic, which could be denominated as only partly socialistic. They were generally "right wing" groups. Their programs were not very "red" after all; hardly enough indeed to cause dismay among fairly conservative people. They were as a matter of fact engaged in a mighty battle against "left wing" elements, which were decidedly radical and revolutionary. The combat between these two groups in time raged vehemently; it was often more bitter than any combat between them and other groups.

For the really revolutionary groups of Europe the orderly processes of socialism would not do. They were not thorough enough. The kingdom was to be taken by violence. Developments here resulted in the more extreme variety of modern communism in Europe. The newer system may be said to have had its formal beginning in 1863 in London.[1] (It was in England that such movements could be started without police interference.) There was formed what was called the International Workingmen's Association, or the first "International," with sections in different lands. It lasted till 1876. Other "Internationals" were to follow, as we are later to see.[2] In 1871 there was in Paris, France, just after the Franco-German war, a brief but sanguinary experiment under what has been known as the Paris Commune.

It was to some extent from the first International that organized radical communism may be said to have had its origin— for it emphasized the international aspects of the movement even more than did the more sober brand of socialism. It may be said to have arisen largely under Bakunin (once an officer in the Russian army, who like other Russian revolutionaries had escaped from prison), and was for a time called the "International Social Democratic Union." Though at the beginning of rather confused character, without an altogether practicable or coherent program, and in some respects verging toward anarchism, it was able to secure a certain following in some

[1] Curiously enough, one of the principal purposes of the gathering here was to protest against Russia's oppressive treatment of Poland.

[2] See *post*, p. 332.

countries, especially in southern Europe, and to a limited extent in Russia, there showing itself largely in what was called "Nihilism" (to be considered later).[1] This movement was of openly destructive character, the torch or the bomb being a recognized instrument of its procedure. Much of its virulence was directed towards the crowned heads and ministers of state.

The movement did not confine its operations to the economic readjustment of society, though its operations were declared to spring from this motive. It set forth particular opposition to the inheritance of property. It demanded the abolition of class and social inequalities among individuals. It declared for the **common ownership** of the machinery and instruments of production and for the absolute distribution of the wealth produced, declaiming against private ownership of property. It affirmed science to be all in all. It was not only prepared to attack capitalism, but it may be said to have demanded a wider emancipation: from the tyranny of the state, and of religion, and perhaps to some extent from that of strict marriage ties— virtually the overthrow of established authority everywhere. (Toward some of the things included here Marxian socialism is supposed to have very liberal views; but in general under it certain of these matters are taken as purely personal ones, and not within its prerogatives.) Under the more violent communism, as then proclaimed, all these things were believed to interfere with the freedom of the individual, and at least to some extent to buttress hated capitalism.

So far as there had emerged a difference between communism and socialism, the one was much more intolerant than the other, and asserted itself in much more dogmatic terms. Communism was the more likely to look upon force as a rightful, appropriate, and necessary weapon for the attainment of its ends. It could more easily pass into despotism, or into a species of totalitarianism. Socialism could rather regard itself as based upon and tending toward liberal principles. According

[1] See *post*, p. 108.

to strict dialectics, socialism emphasized one's endeavors in respect to the receiving of consumption goods; communism emphasized one's needs.

Whether looked upon in connection with the movement in Russia or not, communism stood forth as one of the great, overshadowing problems with which modern society had to deal. Apart from totalitarianism in other forms, it had, in its momentousness, been second in the minds of men to only one other thing—war. In more than one country of Europe it had been the overmastering, the fundamental problem. Extra police vigilance and preparation for certain days of the year or trepidation over mysterious watch fires on some mountain top had been sufficient attestations of the gravity of the situation.

Communism appealed with particular force to the most ignorant, the most discouraged, the most wretched, the most desperate, and those with the least to lose among the masses of men—those with the least of tradition to govern them and with the least of restraint upon their movements. It had its source, its springheads in human misery, in unrelieved human wants, perhaps in a counsel of despair. It could well be compared to cancer in the physical body. Neither was well understood, and adequate measures for dealing with neither had yet arrived; but greater progress was doubtless being made with respect to physical cancer than with respect to communism in the state. Communism was indicative of unrest and threatened revolt—that all was not well in the nether regions of society. Humankind, with all its learning and skill and ingenuity, had seemed quite unable to find a complete cure. Its continued presence constituted an indictment against man's civilization.

It was the way of communists, with their radical political, economic, and social program, to bide the time when they could proceed to put their program into practice. They might have used peaceable means to obtain their objectives; if such were not at hand, resort might be had to violence, to the use of physical force. Communism might be said to have been constantly lying in wait for such deep-seated dissatisfaction or disturbance, especially of an industrial nature, as would sweep them into their desired power. They stood ready to play upon industrial disputes, to seize upon and exploit troubled industrial situations. They exaggerated evil living or working conditions—bad as they might already be. They fanned whatever flames of industrial discontent they could discover, adding fuel to the spreading flames. They sowed seeds of discord and dissension in the industrial life of a people. They encouraged, fomented, and provoked clashes with the police or with those charged with the keeping of order and the peace, berating and denouncing officers of the law, and seeking to awaken hostility towards existing government. If necessary, they were prepared to take a more decided, more active stand. All the while they declared themselves the one retreat and refuge of the underpaid and overworked in human society, of the oppressed and dispossessed; they pointed to the happy haven to be reached when power was entrusted to them. The various tactics employed by them were to redound to their benefit and advantage. To the communists the world was a mission field.

Communism (or radical socialism), as was to be expected, had hardly started upon its way when it began to clash with government, in particular with the officials of government. Its leaders, at times men of force and education, were hunted from place to place, much as outlaws, and had to spend most of their time in hiding. But the fires of the movement, smoldering though they were, were kept alive, and were ready to burst forth into flame at the opportune moment.

In Russian history earlier years were not without instances at one time or another of upheavals or outbreaks on the part of the downtrodden serfs. Even before the nineteenth century these things had occurred among the peasantry, elemental stark revolts of oppressed poverty-stricken people. Such movements, however, did not go far, and accomplished little.

A decade before the end of the eighteenth century there

were in Russia certain echoes of the French Revolution—not loud, and for the most part passing unnoticed. Virtually as far back as the beginning years of the nineteenth century there were what may be called revolutionary stirrings, though largely of exotic origin, and winging their way into the country from the west. Within the first few decades of that century there had here and there come into existence secret revolutionary societies.

Not long after the end of the Napoleonic wars there occurred disturbances or uprisings on a small scale on the part of groups known as Decembrists, composed mainly of young Russian officers who had seen service in western Europe. They had received some insight into what was engaging men's minds there, and were made conscious of the industrial and cultural backwardness and generally low living levels of their own country. On their return to Russia they were bold enough to think of a more democratic order in it, with even a constitution. Their activities, however, which were serious enough to call for the military, were quickly brought under, with short shrift to the leaders, some meeting execution and others exile.

Notwithstanding this abortive undertaking, there was now the sowing of the seed of more or less revolutionary doctrines, and the inspiring of certain revolutionary dreams in the minds of some of the Russian people. There had been the beginning of a sort of liberal education that was showing, if not openly, at least by underground operations, what was brewing. A force had sprung up in the land, composed rather of the upper or the intellectual classes, and without support from or contact with the masses of the people, that could dare raise its head against imperial autocratic authority.

The effects of acquaintance with western Europe were by no means ended. Later were to be borne further and fuller fruits. Much lay in the travels and studies of those Russian citizens who could reside for a greater or less length of time in that region, mainly youths who had taken up residence at some college or university there, especially Switzerland. As the years passed, and as such persons pursued their visits to the west, they were increasingly imbued with the desire to start something in their own land—quite often of more or less revolutionary character. Some on their return to their native heath instigated and fostered radical underground tactics. Certain ones went so far as to disguise themselves as workers or peasants, or even as physicians, to get closer in the confidence of the people in the rural areas. As they passed over the land, they were ever seeking to inculcate their doctrines to whatever extent they could. This procedure was in some fashion off and on continued over a considerable period.

In some measure these labors were in vain. The peasants may or may not have been interested—perhaps in their general ignorance they could not well understand what it was all about. Some of the peasants proved actually hostile to the new teachings. In more than one instance they betrayed their disguised revolutionary visitors to the Czar's secret police.

City workers who had never left their native soil also tried their hand from time to time with their peasant compatriots. They invaded rural regions in efforts to bring the peasants over to a more revolutionary way of thinking. They, too, made no great apparent headway. In fact, agitators coming directly from the city had become considerably discouraged over the apathy they found, perhaps more or less embittered toward the poor peasants in consequence. Some felt called upon to declare that the emancipation of the peasants had simply created a new class of capitalists, with whom it was next to impossible to join hands.

Yet though as a general thing little seemed to have been immediately accomplished through these several missionary undertakings, and though it was very hard to arouse or stir up the country peasant in comparison with the city dweller, there is no question that seed had been sown over the countryside. In some places there was effected the organization of a club or society, even though not often of far-reaching character. Secret bodies of some sort were growing over the land.

A particular influence of moment in the spread of revolutionary ideas came not long after the middle of the nineteenth century with the appearance of the arch-revolutionist Bakunin, to whom reference has already been made.[1] His views were so extreme that he was often set down as an anarchist more than anything else; but he had a certain following over the country —which following may be said to have been in great part the kernel of the later successful revolutionary movements. Many of his adherents were at the same time to be found in countries outside Russia.

After the middle of the nineteenth century revolutionary leaders who had emerged here and there—with whatever following they may have had—asserted themselves in ever growing boldness and strength, their numbers steadily increasing with the passing of the decades. Most of these leaders were themselves of Russian origin or extraction, there being only an occasional apostle from some country to the west who dared or found it desirable to bring in his doctrine from outside.

There was, however, to be some definite contact with the movement that had been set on foot in western Europe known as the International Workingmen's Association (the first International), which had shown itself in limited strength in England, France, Germany, and a few other countries of Europe. The most notable effects were to be seen in the larger cities, even though here they were not widespread for some time.

The general movements in western Europe, relatively conservative in character as they were, were on the whole passing Russia by. The very fact that Russia was off to itself made it the possible prey eventually of fiery revolution when the day of vengeance should arrive. In the event of a political upheaval in Russia it was the extreme or left wing element of the radical

[1] See *ante*, p. 101. See also *post*, p. 109.

107

movement that would mount the saddle, and would have no more regard for moderate socialism than for downright capitalism. In it would be embraced in greater or less measure the revolutionary conceptions as to the state and as to capitalism, and also as to religion and as to the family. It would attempt to set up a new social order, a new civilization, based upon a philosophy different from anything the world had tried before.

It was in Russia only that such a curious force as "Nihilism" —empty, incoherent, shapeless thing that it was—could come into life. It was a bed-fellow of anarchism, and represented something of the blackness and terror and despair that had brooded over the land and was finally enveloping it. The so-called Nihilist movement sprang up not long after the time of the emancipation of the serfs in the early.1860's, in no small part under the influence of the doctrines of Bakunin. It bore a decidedly radical cast—so much so that it was regarded as passing into a species of anarchism. The name or nickname given it, "Nihilism" ("nothingness"), indicated somewhat its character—or rather the attitudes and motivations of its proponents—a negation of the established standards and principles of society in government, religion, family. It had, however, some quite positive presentations. It declared itself only for the worship, following, and guidance of science, in particular the natural or physical sciences, which were to have exclusive domination in society—a sort of scientific materialism. It was, though of acknowledged violent tendencies, in part an outgrowth of a certain philosophy that had arisen in Europe of distinctly peaceable character. This was in particular what was known as "positivism," which asserted that as man had passed the religious and metaphysical stages in his onward progress, he was now only to depend upon and live in the pure light of the natural sciences. The system was in considerable part based upon the doctrines of Comte, and in lesser part upon those of such men as Buckle and John Stuart Mill with their several social, economic, and political views.

As expected, the new cult in Russia announced itself as having little use for such institutions as religion or the family, private property, and centralized government; in fact, it showed a particular aggressive hostility towards religion—not altogether different from what was later to be in evidence under the Soviet system. There was confessed hatred for authority (whence really the term "Nihilism"), including that of state and of religion alike. Even though Nihilism was not widespread over Russia at this time, it had a very considerable influence in shaping future thought. It evoked opposition and alienation, not so much because of its innate doctrines, but because of its open espousal of the use of terrorism—of dynamite, of firebrands. Many of its followers were imprisoned or exiled or executed. Its answer was assassination or attempted assassination—more terrorism. In fact, Nihilism had passed into terrorism.

After this period revolutionary agitation in Russia never ceased; propaganda on more or less radical lines was constant; there was unabating turmoil which from time to time was to boil over into serious disturbances.

In the years following the middle of the nineteenth century there were formed one after another more or less revolutionary circles over the country. By the end of the third quarter of this century local societies of this nature, whether calling themselves "Nihilists" or not, were fairly numerous—more or less on the order of the later Soviet organizations. Radical literature, with a decidedly communistic cast, especially in the form of pamphlets, began to stream from secret presses and to make their way over the land. Covert meetings of like character sought to escape police attention. Preachments passed into practices, with possible application of physical measures. Terrorist bands were about, which balked but little at the destruction of their enemies. Some became skilled in the use of the bomb.

What was now entering Russia was a violent brand of communism—such as had its roots largely in the teachings of

Bakunin and his disciples rather than in the milder and more peaceable doctrines of Marxian socialism. The latter had come into Russia in the early 1880's with the translation a few years before of *Das Kapital* into the Russian language. By many students and by many of the intelligentsia of the country, as well as by some of the city workers, its teachings were speedily accepted. By others nothing of so moderate and temperate a bearing could answer—could meet their demands. The socialist movement in Russia was coming to a point where it was being divided into two parties—relatively conservative socialists and radical revolutionary communists. It was the latter that in the end were to gain the ascendency.

The second great event responsible for what was to happen in Russia was the approaching dissolution of the Russian Czaristic empire, an institution sooner or later doomed through its inherent weakness to perish under the conditions of modern civilization and social progress. There was no other hope for it unless there could develop with or without the Czar and his ministers some sort of democratic constitutional government—something of which, as we have found, we could not be altogether sure. When men come to think of it, they may well wonder that such an autocracy as that in control of this vast land could have been projected into Europe and could have remained so long side by side with western civilization.

Russia, while ostensibly a European nation, and actively in alliance with some of the advanced peoples of Europe, was in part somewhat on the order of an Oriental despotism, in some respects with only a thin veneer of European culture and efficiency. Not many of its rulers had been strong or commanding personalities, or really capable of leading a great people. Most of the Russian Czars had lived peculiarly sad lives; their golden crowns had too often carried tragedies with them. Ever since the imperial diadem was placed on the brow of the first of the Romanovs some dread disaster seems for the most part to have pursued the imperial family. Life for them had been insecure and uncertain, and apart from the world round about them, despite legions of troops for the protection of the Little Father. Probably there had been few really happy days spent by most of the Czars of Russia.

The Czar's ministers, those he gathered about him in his councils, were too often a set of men facing backwards, rather than facing forwards, though there were at times among them genuine statesmen. The nobility of the land, those to whom the people could look for light and leading, was in little better case. It was all too often a prodigal, self-indulgent lot, as a general thing with little sense of responsibility; in large part it was without feeling of obligation to help better the life of the common people lying below it.

For the great mass of people life was hard and mean. A large part of the population was living in wretchdness and hopelessness. Conditions were unquestionably more or less or in some respects improving; but the improvement was too slow to count for much in the material and spiritual well-being of the people. The vast peasant class seemed to constitute a solid plodding army of the fortuneless, while the estate of a large segment of their city brethren was not greatly different. Indigence, penury, destitution like a black cloud hovered over the land. Possession of any considerable portion of the good things of life was the lot of relatively few. Many of the peasants were on the verge of starvation much of the year. Serfdom had been abolished, but despite its formal end policies and regulations as to land tenure still bore hard and were oppressive; the actual liberation of those who tilled the soil had not proceeded far. The limited industrial undertakings in the larger cities were in considerable part in a backward state. Largely barren alike were rural and urban life.

Disease crept over the land only under partial check; the death rate long remained the highest in the world. For offenders against the law, not a few of whom were political offenders, punishment could be brutal and heartless; the world knew the story of the long lines wending their heavy way to Siberia. Cultural opportunities, especially in the way of education, were meagre and poor; to a considerable part of the population they were practically denied. National and linguistic groups were ruthlessly ground under foot. Social welfare measures for the great body of the population existed only to a slight extent. Legislation in the interests of the working classes had gone only a little way. The essence of religion was to no small extent wrapped up with stately ceremonialism. Spiritually and culturally, as well as economically, Russia was to the world a byword for backwardness. The people were living in the sixteenth century. With them religion had soon passed into something not far removed from superstition; regard for a ruler, into a lively worship of the Little Father. From oppression and crushing misrule, from the denial of the rights that should be accorded to any people, from the want of education and what it could give, the people had suffered for long, long years; in their faces were written these long, long years of suffering. Russia was a land largely filled with unhappy, miserable human beings. It was an American poet who in his "The Man with the Hoe" asked if the Russian peasant were not "brother to the ox."

Nor did matters better themselves greatly with time. Those who ruled Russia in general could not or would not see. If there appeared a glimmer of relief or surcease from oppression, it was likely to be followed by reaction and renewed severities. If promises were secured from the government, they turned out to be in great part untrustworthy, perhaps meaningless. Whatever redress was obtained was by no means sufficient. Reform did not go far.

Down to the time of the Revolution the Czar's government, with occasional bursts of light, pursued its despotic, cruel way, for the most part refusing to hear the cries going up from its subjects or to offer any wide or substantial program for the amelioration of their condition. Reasonable demands of the people were too often rejected; those that were granted were yielded with reluctance. Leaders who were moderate in their proposals and who were as much opposed to revolution as were the Czar's counsellors usually met only rebuff or worse for their pains. The Czar and his ministers knew how to deal with mild elements of his subjects seeking mere redress no better than they knew how to cope with violent parties bent upon his overthrow.

Russia suffered much for lack of a great middle class— something between a small body of enlightened citizens and an illiterate, unknowing mass hardly as yet fitted for self-government or for the construction of an orderly, progressive commonwealth. In the large cities where opportunity was full-est for discussion of public questions, and where liberal but not necessarily radical doctrines could have had a hearing, already revolutionary propaganda was afoot and at work, with notable effects upon the proletariat. In rural areas most of the people simply endured, even if sullenly, with little understanding of the significance of events or uncertain as to what might be done about them. The nobility, hardly better understanding, was in no position for leadership.

Apart from various scattered public-spirited citizens over the land, virtually the only class of persons who could appreciate the situation and give it intelligent consideration were the pro-fessors and students in the country's universities—and these largely as a result of contacts with western Europe. Students were mostly from the upper classes—from the families of the gentry, well-placed clergy, well-to-do merchants and manufac-turers, and high government officials. Such did not altogether constitute a large group, relatively speaking, but it was a select one. They were carefully making note of the conditions and happenings of the day, and were deeply impressed with what they observed. Reports of arrests, of imprisonments, of con-demnation to Siberian exile, of tortures inflicted, of executions for political offenses, all these provoked and stirred them. As they were the most sensitive among the Czar's subjects, so they were the most audacious. They could demand certain liberties and the mending of certain abuses. Many were qualified or undisguised socialists, or even of more radical hue. Not a few came to feel that the only way to reform the government was through revolution; that anything less was a waste of time and of energy. In Russia there was an exceedingly high proportion of the intellectual and educated classes in the revolutionary party. In this land revolutionary conceptions had their birth principally, not in the minds of the masses, but in the minds of the upper classes, especially those with an academic background and an academic stimulus.

In the eyes of the government ministers and police, the universities were in large measure hot beds of discontent and of revolt, a view by no means without foundation. What went on there was watched, spied upon, probed. Into the hands of the Czar's officers came no little evidence of subversive tendencies and activities, some of it false and some of it true. On the universities the government bore down. Their work was interfered with, was halted. Professors were disciplined, perhaps dismissed. Ring leaders among students were seized and severely dealt with, their movements curbed, their assemblies banned.

Nor did the activities of the out-and-out radical and revolutionary elements of the country in general, and of the cities in particular, whether in orderly discussions or in more forceful practices, pass without the notice and concern of the Czaristic government. It hardly comprehended, and hardly knew how to proceed. It set itself in general to a policy of blind repression. Prisons were filled to overflowing, and long lines started toward exile in Siberia. For conspicuous offenders against the government there was the scaffold or the firing squad. But what it did here did little for the mending of matters; it mostly made them worse. Efforts to muzzle or stamp out anti-governmental doings only invited deadly reprisals.

When there was increased censorship of the press or more

cracking down on public assemblies, revolutionary movements could go underground, there to flourish with unabated vigor. When the pursuit of some leaders became too hot, these leaders could betake themselves to foreign countries, where with no less effectiveness, and with greater safety to themselves, they could keep in touch with the situation at home and manipulate the strings of revolutionary activity there. Refugees and exiles alike found happy employment for their time in egging on malcontents on the home front. Galling personal experiences and relentless persecution of the leaders in general only aroused them to intensified bitterness, and fired them to more profound hatreds. They could strike out in retaliation and revenge, and with possibly a more definite goal in view. There had grown up a body of professional revolutionists.

In the cities generally where crowds could be readily collected to discuss their grievances and to think up more or less radical remedies to deal with them, the situation had become a seething one, if as yet not boiling over. But disquiet was entering the country districts as well; here the situation could be called at least a simmering one.

With time changes were evident in the attitude of the rural dwellers, who had for the most part held themselves aloof from movements bordering on the revolutionary. Slowly enough doubtless, but steadily the newer doctrines were infiltrating into the country. Apart from the general flow countryward of these doctrines, there was a special means for their introduction, especially in later days. This was through the city workers who went back to the country from year to year to assist in farm operations, carrying with them more or less revolutionary ideas and setting them forth there, perhaps succeeding in arousing at least a little interest in them. But the peasants came themselves to realize what crying evils of their own they had; they were not in great need of outside incitation or exhortation to move them; they found they had sufficient cause to do some hard thinking of their own initiative and accord. With backs stooping low, a state that had become their wont, they could not but feel their crushing burdens, and ask how these burdens came there, and whether any relief was ever in store for them. In time the country no less than the city was to fill itself with bitterness and discontent. Was not an upheaval here to be anything but a break in their otherwise unending patience and resignation? Was it not to be expected that in due season the peasant, too, would rise up against what he deemed his oppressor?

While the peasants had as a general thing been passive and quiescent, and seldom unruly with regard to social and economic ills in the land—so far as participation in revolutionary movements was concerned—it is not to be thought that they had been altogether calm or complacent. There were occasions in one place or another where they had flared up, and had, so to speak, shown their fangs. Among them from time to time there were outbreaks with deeds savoring of the insurrectionary, though never on a country-wide scale. With a certain but small number there was unmistakable revolutionary doctrine at work. In different areas there was now and then something like actual rebellion, with some peasants engaging in passive resistance to the demands of the state or of the landlord, and with others displaying more active opposition. There might be attempted boycotting of appointees to local government posts. There were instances where peasants burned or otherwise destroyed property belonging to the landlords or to the government. There were instances where estates were sacked or put to the flames. There were instances, especially of later years, of the seizure or the attempted seizure of an estate. Occasionally the peasants came to blows in pitched battle with a landlord or government official. There might be a sort of limited guerrilla warfare initiated. There were hundreds of peasant uprisings requiring military intervention.

To offenders or insurrectionists could be meted out severe physical punishment, perhaps deportation or worse. The landlord, in case action was to be on his part, could strike back with fury and with brute force. The least that might be done in curbing or subduing recalcitrant peasants was the raising of rents or the reducing of wages. Another mild recourse was the levying of heavier taxes, direct or indirect. Action more harsh was possible.

During this period there was more than one appeal or demand from rural assemblies for national reform of a general nature or in some particular or other—even for a constitution or parliament.

It is not to be thought that the Czar and his government were not alive to or not genuinely concerned over the condition of the people, even though they were slow to see, and their seeing was with half-blinded eyes. On their part was at times a sincere and realistic effort to deal with the peasant problem, and with the land situation in particular. But whatever forward measures the government promised and whatever the steps taken to that end, they did not go far enough. The people remained anything but satisfied—there were increased clamors for thorough-going reform—or for more drastic action. The situation grew ever more tense.

It is also to be remembered at the same time that the extreme radical or revolutionary elements, especially in the cities, wanted no such thing as reform. They were too far committed to revolution—a violent upset or overthrow of the government, or its complete destruction. They had gone to such lengths that they could be content with nothing less. They were prepared and determined to reject, to rebuff any peace overtures from the government, even though these might have been of considerable account.

Loose now in the land was wild terrorism, ready to strike, and to strike hard, whether blindly or not, against anything in its revolutionary path. Rough, brutal handling by the government and its police only intensified a desire for revenge. If repression became too heavy, revolutionary thought and planning were driven underground, or were transferred to foreign lands, for their continued operations.

The best the government could do to meet a situation becoming ever more acute was to strike back savagely—and about as blindly—something that could only promote renewed attempts at reigns of terror, in which the assassination of public officials was bound to have a part. There was open, acknowledged war between government and revolution.

Upon different gradations of political dissidents descended the heavy hand of the autocratic state. Included were some of the ablest and most exemplary citizens. There were those whose ways were only the ways of peace, who were only liberal-minded, and who were concerned only in some moderate reform, as improved education or agricultural conditions or a parliamentary assembly or a national constitution. There were those to whom was imputed guilt by association, having perhaps members of one's family or friends or companions who were charged with complicity in some anti-governmental activity or with other more or less serious offense. There were those who, out of patience with attempts at reform, or exasperated over government cruelty or injustice or lawlessness (as penalization without trial) or harsh treatment of themselves or of their comrades, despaired of remedy by slow process, and entered the ranks of the revolutionaries. There were those whose bitterness of spirit had so passed all bounds that their role had become that of terrorists.

Absolutism was bearing down hard, but to no avail, with anything but success. The Czar had a powerful and diligent police system throughout his dominions. He also had a relentless, untiring, unsleeping secret police, which to an extent was known for its efficiency. In a sense its greatest efficiency was in making enemies for the government it served. Public gatherings, so far as they were not restricted, were under intimidation; people could take part or even attend at their peril. Labor organizations known as homes for radical doctrines felt the iron fist; nothing less than their destruction was sought. Police spies were everywhere. The haunts of radical leaders were ferreted out. Secret police wormed their way into the confidence of persons who could tip them off or inform them as to the movements of, or could expose, disguised revolutionaries. Rebels and revolutionary or radical leaders were hunted down like wild animals. State prisons were gorged with political offenders; the long lines wending their way to Siberia continued with ranks unbroken. Some who escaped—and there were always some who did—possessed in their flaming eyes only the wild desire for revenge, and with a sole mission in life—to bring on the revolution. It was now called *the* revolution, which was regarded as inevitable.

As if nothing else was needed to stir up feelings and create bitterness of sentiment in the land, there were revivals from time to time of anti-nationalistic activities, to make alien nations under the Czar's yoke ferment and to glower at their oppressor.

During all this period of increasing bitterness and dissension, there were fingers pointed, particularly by the radical forces, at the excesses and indulgences of the rich and powerful of the land, in contrast with the general wretchedness of the masses. At hand, right before the eyes of the people for them to see, was ready material—material for scornful gibes and biting taunts—palaces, costumes, lackeys, frivolous pastimes, prodigal ostentation and display. Angry feelings were not relieved by the knowledge and by the tales that reached the ears of the people—of the ornate and pretentious mansions of the princes and the nobles and the wealthy, of the smart and costly raiment that clothed their bodies, of the sumptuous viands that were heaped upon their tables, of the extravagant, far-fetched diversions and dissipations with which they tried to fill their empty hours of leisure.

Attempts of some grand duke or other of the nobility here and there to open a sympathetic heart to the people, to take

119

their side, to try to improve their condition were mostly lost sight of in the prevailing unseeing attitudes of this class. What stood out, what was held in mind, was the crass indifference of the upper classes in general to the crushing and suffering of the masses of the population beneath. Nothing that was before the eyes—and sometimes before the imaginations—of these masses was lost on them. All was stored away in the hearts of the people: they were doing for their remembrances much as Madame Defarge was found doing with her knitting in the days before the French Revolution, as told in Dickens' "Tale of Two Cities."

Among all classes was growing unrest and discontent and rancor. As the days wore on, protests and uprisings became more numerous and more open. These were in the main of local or isolated character, but some were not without sanguinary accompaniments. The severe punishments meted out only added to the gloom in the land. Russia in time became a land that in wide areas was filled with men and women awaiting a day of national vengeance.

CHAPTER IX

Russia and Its Revolution

IN the last decade or two of the nineteenth century the situation in Russia was becoming loaded with explosives; it could not much longer be contained. Not only were the smoldering embers of revolution being fanned into flames, but they were spreading farther and farther over the land. The situation was made worse by nationalistic waves, which had been provoked by anti-nationalistic campaigns in respect to certain non-Russian groups living under the Czar, including attempts at the repression of their language. Poland was dragged down to deeper depths. Upon hapless Finland were imposed further limitations and additional hardships. As the nineteenth century was nearing an end, a crushing hand was laid upon that country, which, practically a separate nation under the Czar, had been a self-governing duchy for almost a hundred years. The Finnish constitution was abrogated; the Finnish army was incorporated with the Russian. The whole country gasped at this outrage.

Upon Jews were renewed visitations of sufferings. There were particular persecutions levelled at this wretched people, at times in the form of bloody pogroms. Prime rights and privileges were taken from them. They had heavier burdens piled upon them. They were compelled to live in a restricted territory known as the pale. One result was that great numbers of Jews fled the country to find refuge in the promised land of America.

Russia was now rocking through its length and breadth.

121

Over the country from end to end there were ever more marked disturbances, and with corresponding acts of repression. Towards the close of the century there were great strikes flaring up in some of the larger cities, notably St. Petersburg, the country's capital. Everywhere unrest deepened.

As the new twentieth century dawned over the ill-omened empire, matters only worsened. As the working classes learned more of happier conditions in western Europe, and realized more their own low estate, and with the never-ending incitement emanating from the universities, there was intensified resentment over the lot of the Russian people, and a yet more powerful urge toward rebellion. Strikes became more frequent and more widespread, not merely in demand of higher wages or shorter hours, but as an instrument to express disapproval of conditions in the land; they became chronic. There was also greater inclination to resort to sabotage as a weapon. In rural areas there were increasing outbursts of violence.

The tenor of the times was further in evidence from the vehement demands and determined struggles for liberty and political rights arising over the land, particularly among the factory workers in the large cities. Petitions to the same effect presented by other bodies of citizens were a gentler but no less emphatic procedure. Cries for genuine political liberty—including now the grant of a constitution and of a parliament—were coming forth from every hand, and in ever louder tones. From the presses poured newspapers and pamphlets, some with one mandate at their mastheads—a better day for the land, by force if necessary.

As the unhappy years dragged themselves along, disquiet, restlessness, ferment, agitation, confusion, turbulence, turmoil, disorder, outbursts, all raged through the land. A greater or less part of the population was being lashed into a fury. In hardly any place was there not at least an undercurrent of discontent. The larger cities were seething; strikes multiplied; streets were reddened from encounters between police and revolutionaries.

Dissents were ripening into armed clashes.

More numerous, more vigorous, more determined waxed the protests against the actions of government, even against government itself. There were taking place important meetings and conferences outside Russia; there were central or controlling committees being located away from it. The people were refusing any longer to take seriously the declaration of vital reform or of promises of substantial improvements on the part of the government. (A few years before the First World War the great Tolstoi died, and the people knew they had lost a friend and champion.) Dissatisfaction was spreading over the land—even into the rural regions. In the cities it had passed into something more—into not merely revolutionary conceptions but revolutionary plannings. Everywhere revolutionary protests were growing in volume and in violence.

Almost the order of the day became the conflicts between the government and the industrial classes, general strikes with the paralysis of industry, inflamed mass meetings, audacious, provocative processions. May day demonstrations could grow to vast proportions. At times so far had opposition to government proceeded that police and soldiers were affected, taking the side of the people, and refusing to fire or move against them.

In 1905 there occurred a peculiarly unfortunate, but entirely avoidable, incident which left a deep mark in the minds of the people. This was in St. Petersburg on what has since been called "Black Sunday" or "Red Sunday" or "Bloody Sunday." Toward the Czar's Winter Palace there marched a crowd with religious banners and singing hymns, which carried a petition to the Czar, calling attention to harsh working conditions in the city and praying for various reforms, including an eight-hour working day, amnesty to political and religious offenders, freedom of speech and press, separation of church and state, compulsory education, transfer of land to the peasants, freedom of labor organizations, call for a constitutional assembly, a national parliament, and other matters. It had been warned not to assemble. Though led by a more or less radical group—declared by their enemies to be trouble-seekers, fishing in troubled waters—the demonstration was not of a violent or riotous nature, but of quite peaceable character. Instead of gaining a hearing, however, to say nothing of possible redress, the protestants were surrounded by the Czar's soldiers, fire was opened upon them and they were mowed down like sheep—several hundred being killed outright and several thousand wounded. This action was followed by a flood of disturbances, especially in the form of strikes in different cities—here and there with sharp clashes with the police or military—together with the burning of the homes of some of the nobles. In turn there were renewed governmental reprisals—closing of universities, suppression of newspapers, exiles, and other of the government's favorite means of hitting back.

The time was proving most propitious for the activities of the radical and revolutionary groups, some of which were busying themselves in setting up or strengthening or revolutionizing what they called soviets or councils of workers in the larger cities—of which we are soon to hear more.

During this period of excitement and disturbance over the land, certain political parties had come into being, were now in the field, and in the event that a parliament was set up would have a greater or less part to play in its actions and deliberations. The main ones were as follows:

1. The Octobrists or Constitutionist Monarchists who were the most conservative of all the parties, forming what might be called the extreme right—composed to a large extent of feudal landlords and great capitalists. They generally favored the status quo, though there were some who would have preferred a constitution. A slightly more liberal wing were known as the Nationalists.

2. The Constitutional Democrats, sometimes called Cadets —midway between the rightists and the leftists—fairly liberal, hardly to be called a conservative, and certainly not a reaction-

ary, group, composed for the most part of public-spirited professional persons, small business men, merchants, university professors and some of the more enlightened capitalists, and various broad-minded thinkers and intellectual groups. They were not a large body, but represented a solid section of the country much concerned with its well-being and progress. Their principal aims were a national constitution, a parliament, ministerial responsibility, generally increased democratic powers, and various social reforms.

3. The Social Revolutionaries, composed largely of peasants and rural dwellers in general, including some small peasant capitalists. They were rather liberal in their general principles, but for the most part hardly to be called radical, except with regard to some particulars of land reform. They were in general much concerned with such reform, especially with the limitation or doing away with of the great estates, or with the reduction of feudalism—and perhaps the transfer of land to the peasants—the land to be "the property of the whole people." They were in part successors to a "Populist" party which had embraced, on the one hand, some more or less radical elements, even some regarded as terrorists, and, on the other hand, some with rather mild tendencies—both these wings continuing with the party.

4. The Social Democratic Party, which was created to a great extent on the principles of Karl Marx and the Communist Manifesto. Hardly had it been started, however, when it split into two branches:

a. The Mensheviki, who were much on the order of the German Social Democrats, believing in an evolutionary process toward the socialist state, and desiring immediately a constituent assembly. They sought various reforms, both economic and political, including land reform or the better division of the land of the nation. They were not opposed to the temporary use of capitalism.

b. The Bolsheviki (literally "majority" party), the extreme

left, who were decidedly radical and openly revolutionary—admittedly communistic. They declared uncompromisingly for the "dictatorship of the proletariat," and favored the expropriation of private holdings so far as should be necessary in the accomplishment of their purposes. They encouraged and were prepared to promote violent action to gain their ends. These aims were quite definite, and for their achievement strict discipline was enjoined upon the party's followers. Though made up chiefly of workers in city factories, they were willing to have coöperation with the peasants of the country, but on the basis of radical socialism.[1]

There were several other parties, with only a small following, and not of great consequence. These different parties had in general crystallized into their present forms in the late years of the nineteenth or early years of the twentieth century.

As had already been indicated, however, it is not to be thought that during all this time, especially as the early years of the twentieth century crept along, there was no effort on the part of the imperial government to quiet or placate in some measure the disturbed atmosphere, to conciliate so far as possible opposing elements, or to institute important or necessary reforms. There were certain more or less liberalizing movements set on foot. We have already considered efforts of the government to increase peasant holdings.[2]

At times fairly generous breezes seemed to sweep into the royal palaces. There seemed to be evidence of the coming of political and social improvements or reforms. Even if such happy prospects turned out to be mostly delusions, and if substantial gains proved slight or even negligible, the very fact that betterment of conditions in the land was receiving attention from the Czar and his ministers was an indication that the government was not asleep altogether, or was devoid of con-

[1] Both wings of the Social Democratic party often had their formal meetings outside Russia.

[2] See *ante*, p. 63.

science, or was capable of turning a completely deaf ear to public outcries. But what it seemed to promise for the most part failed to materialize. What it actually did was quite too little, or was too late. Even for its good intentions it was likely to receive not approval and thanks, but some measure of condemnation. Against the Czar and his government fate was plainly working.

During all this period of increasing agitation and disturbance over the land, what had become of the ever widening and more insistent pleas, calls, urgings, demands for the granting of a constitution and the setting up of a parliament? The coming of these things would denote a definite political advance and material social reform, with a recognition of the limits to be fixed for absolutism and the general powers of the Czaristic government.

The demand for a constitution and a parliament, though for a considerable time contemplated and strongly desired in the hearts of a part of the population, became more articulate and more pronounced in the early years of the twentieth century. Not only were the liberal elements and the so-called intelligentsia insisting upon these things, but a large portion of the working classes in the cities and a certain but smaller portion of the peasantry, especially in the rural assemblies, were agitating to the same end. In time this agitation became unceasing, and all but universal.

In 1905 when the situation in imperial Russia was so acute, just after the chastening defeat by Japan, there was hope in the hearts of many that the time had arrived for the remedying of the most intolerable of the abuses in the land. It was in these circumstances that the Czar, at least as some measure of appeasement, was prevailed upon to promise, or saw the necessity of action with regard to, the eagerly sought constitution for his country. Through an imperial manifesto or edict it was duly promulgated to the people. In it were to be recognized certain rights of the citizens; in it was granted a quantum of individual liberty, of conscience, and of opinion, including to an extent freedom of press and of assembly.

Though this constitution failed to allow full or adequate representation of the people in government and was thus without full popular support, and though the "rights" and "liberties" set forth were considerably restricted ones, the instrument was a distinct and really important step forward. All things considered, it was a tremendous event in the life of the Russian people—all the more if it should work fairly well in practice. A constitution, such as it was, was in being; and it authorized a duma or parliamentary assembly to an extent to take the place of the old bureaucratic régime. Even if the duma was not to be fully representative, and even if the roots did not go down deep, it was none the less a momentous advance movement in the land.

In particular the constitution provided for the election and operation of an imperial parliament or duma which was to be based ostensibly upon national representation. In urban regions there was to be direct voting; in rural regions election was to be through delegates from lower bodies to higher. There were to be something over four hundred members elected for a term of five years.

The duma, however, was not a fully representative body; it failed to speak for the masses of the people. It rather stood for the most part for the propertied classes of the country—the landed gentry, the commercial classes, and in general the well-to-do and the comparatively well-off, with inadequate representation of both peasants and industrial workers. It was thus a body with control vested mainly in the weighted upper classes, and without the backing of the people as a whole. The suffrage authorized for the country was thus but a limited one.

Popular legislative power was even further restricted by the fact that the duma was but one of the two chambers in which the law-making power was to be vested. The first chamber or upper house was composed of a Council of Ministers, an Imperial Supreme Council (Council of Empire), a sort of hang-over from its Czaristic predecessor, of approximately one hundred members nominated by the Czar, and a like number elected (for nine years) through local assemblies, but composed chiefly of representatives of the nobility, land owners, and other propertied groups. The upper house, moreover, had more than coördinate power with the lower body; it was in possession of certain fundamental powers, particularly as respected foreign affairs.

Much control of legislation thus remained with the Czar—delegated by him in the Supreme Council. There was also, as we have seen, a body known as the Ruling Senate, which was largely to attend to the formulation and promulgation of the laws. There was, finally, the Holy Synod, which was to govern in the affairs of the Church.

The powers, furthermore, of the duma itself were definitely circumscribed. Drafts of laws were to be determined by the Council of Ministers, who were responsible to the Czar, and not to the duma. The duma had no power over the army and navy. It had little control over the budget or over judicial appointments. All acts of the duma were subject to the Czar's approval.

Sessions of the duma—their frequency and their length—were to remain to a great extent in the hands of the Czar. If it was his will, he might dismiss a session; it could be dissolved if it became too fractious or too unruly. The Czar had power to convene, adjourn, prorogue, and dissolve a session; he could veto what it did. The Czar even had power in supposed emergencies to declare a state of siege and to suspend the laws which had been duly enacted. When the duma was not in session, the Czar might issue temporary decrees, which had the force and effect of statutes; during its recess the Czar could assume wide powers. The duma's existence was in considerable degree to be but a formal one.

With all these restrictions and impediments upon anything

resembling popular law making in Russia, there was notwithstanding definite and manifest gain. There was, as has been said, a really momentous step forward—there was progress in the direction of liberalism. The duma could debate upon various matters and put them under the light of public discussion —and this truly meant something. Even though it was largely a deliberative and consultative body, with highly restricted actual powers of legislation, it represented a certain introduction of the people into the affairs of government. An undisguised absolutist régime was at an end, or at least had brakes placed upon it; there had to be recognition, even though to a small extent, of the existence of a law-making element not directly of the Czar's creation. The duma did have a degree of responsibility, and did afford a certain check to Czaristic activities. In any event there was provided a training ground in parliamentary principles and in parliamentary tactics for a considerable part of the population, limited though that part was, which had hitherto been denied participation in government. And there had come into being a forum for the consideration of public affairs, through which public opinion could have some vent. The creation of the Russian duma was after all a milestone in human progress, at least in Russia.

On the announcement of the constitution, and with a parliament assured for the country, there were high expectations, and even a measure of enthusiasm, on the part of much of the population. This was true in general of the liberal elements, and of the educated classes. By these it was believed that there was about to be inaugurated a new and better era in the land, and that Russia was now to be numbered with the enlightened nations of the world. There were other groups in the country, however, who did not share so fully in these warm hopes. One was a considerable portion of the peasantry who were in general in too great a degree of ignorance to understand what was going on, or the significance of the new developments. Another was the radical communistic or revolutionary party who would have little sympathy with any such moderate program as was now on the way; with them there was just one demand —revolution.

In 1906, the same year that Russia received its constitution creating a parliament, there was, after due election of its members, convoked the first Russian duma.

In the majority were the Constitutional Democrats and their allies. The more radical elements, particularly that faction of the Social Democrats known as Bolsheviki, had limited representation, in part because of their having largely boycotted the election, and in part because of their fear that it might not be well for them or their cause if they appeared in considerable numbers.

The duma at the outset took a quite advanced stand—one not by any means expected by those who had called it. It proved in fact to be much more of a radical body than had been looked for from any side—though attempting or projecting little that was beyond a really democratic legislative body. In a bold declaration at the start it asserted that no law of the land was to be valid without its approval. It sought to extract from the Czar much more than he had contemplated granting. It made no attempt to placate him or his ministers. It set out in definite opposition to some of the Czar's favorite policies. Before long it was proving a decidedly recalcitrant or even hostile organization. It made no pretense to patience with the existing order. It showed little of a conciliatory spirit. It was carried away with the conceptions of democracy and of its mission in that direction. It would be content with no gradual attainment of that thing; it wanted it there and then. Whether for good or ill, Russia seemed a country which could expect an evolutionary government from neither its conservative, its liberal, nor its radical parties.

The new duma sought at once to take matters into its own hands, to assume the real reins of government. It demanded various reforms, including parliamentary government, with ministerial responsibility—the ministers of government being made answerable to it and not to the Czar; the guarantee of certain civil rights; the suppression or doing away with its haughty and too powerful rival, the Imperial Council; the abolition of capital punishment; the improvement of labor laws; better and free educational facilities for the people; wider popular representation in local government; the greater or less expropriation of the landed estates (with due compensation to the owners) and distribution of the land among the peasants; an equitable taxation system; the abolition of class, social, and other distinctions. It wanted a more direct and broader appeal to the people through universal suffrage (even though the people could not then prove altogether qualified or responsive). It wanted amnesty for the great number of political offenders wasting away in prison or in Siberian mines. It demanded the ending of martial law over the country, leaving the civil law to prevail.

Though what the duma asked for was only in keeping with enlightened democratic principles, Russia was hardly prepared for any such program at this juncture in its political life—desirable and beneficial as it might have in general been. Probably the members of the duma were surprised at their own temerity; probably they did not expect any full realization at the moment of what they had set forth. But they had the satisfaction of knowing that they had thrown the gauntlet down to absolutist Czaristic government.

The Czar and his adherents were little short of stunned at what had taken place—at the character and boldness of the demands that had been enunciated by the duma. The Czar's party hotly resented the suggested infringements upon what had so long and without questions been his sole prerogatives. They had no thought of giving them up or even of modifying them in any marked degree. The Czar and his ministers, it is true, wanted a measure of reform; and they were willing to give the duma a chance to coöperate to this end. They really and sincerely were desirous of benefiting their common country. When the government made some attempt at conciliation with the people by the offer of certain mild reforms, it expected its action to win due appreciation and gratitude; the government had done its part—let the people now express their dutiful thanks. What the government now saw was a duma hard to deal with and to get along with, little disposed to be satisfied with what had been offered, much less to indulge in a paean of thanksgiving. The government was not only shocked; it was highly angry.

The Czar and his ministers looked upon the situation with indignant and hateful eyes; their only response to what the duma had asked for was an order for its dispersion. They would have no such duma—no such defiant body at the very sanctum of government. They had also become alarmed over this manifestation of popular feeling, and wanted out of the way any such body giving vent to it.

Not only the Czaristic government itself, but some of the middle class and even of the peasant class had seen the behavior of the first duma not without certain misgivings; they had become a little uneasy, a little fearful over what they regarded as its extravagant and extreme demands. They would have liked to see a more conservative and a safer body convened at St. Petersburg.

The duma, or at least a considerable part of it, doubtless having realized what the Czaristic response was likely to be, was ready to stand its ground. A section of it, jealous of its position, highly conscious of its new responsibilities, and feeling itself called upon to defend any new powers conferred upon it, or any powers it felt it ought to assume, resisted the imperial command—a couple of hundred hied themselves to Finland to try to continue their legislative deliberations. But they were too weak for a power like that of the Czar's; his forces countered by fitting arrests and new forced deportations to Siberia.

After the dissolution of the first duma, the government

wished to take no more chances with an antagonistic, stubborn, and unruly assembly; it would see to it that a more tractable and submissive body filled the legislative halls. This was to be accomplished by changing the electoral system and adopting a more restrictive franchise, which would keep trouble makers out. Suffrage qualifications would give greater representation to the land-owning and other propertied classes, and less to liberal and nationalistic groups.

The result was that the second duma elected in 1907 turned out to be a considerably more docile and pliant body than the previous one. There were not many on hand who could be called dangerously liberal or radical; some of this group had proved ineligible, and others had been prevented from being elected because their followers refused to have anything to do with the election. Over the second duma as it assembled the Czar's ministers and police kept a watchful eye. Some who were believed to be moving or plotting against the government or antagonistic to it, were placed under arrest forthwith; some were exiled. Attempts at any drastic measures could now not go far—could hardly get under way. Besides, there were clashes between different groups in the duma itself, something that further served to check any liberal activities.

Despite the purging of the duma, and though on the whole there was little liberal advance, there was some constructive and beneficial legislation now enacted. Social insurance laws were broadened. There was liberalization of laws relating to religion. Land reforms included, as we have seen,[1] the abolition of the communal ownership of land, and some release from financial burdens, and greater freedom of movement to the peasants. Some of these laws the conservative elements in the duma helped in securing.

With succeeding dumas (the third and fourth)[2] up to the First World War, so far as was concerned the manifestation of

[1] See *ante*, p. 64.
[2] The first duma was in 1906, the second in 1907, the third from 1907 to 1912, and the fourth from 1912 to 1917.

liberal principles, the story was much the same. There were always some who were true to their convictions in this respect, and who were never willing to give up, asserting at times a considerable measure of independence, but not having power enough to override the strong governmental interests. In the main the dumas were docile and submissive, and to an extent even reactionary. The Czar emerged with little actually diminished strength or prestige. It was made plain that it was he who ruled the Russian empire. Preponderance in the suffrage remained with the propertied, ultra-conservative classes; the government also retained its free hand in managing elections pretty much as it wished. There continued to be some useful legislation enacted, but of a kind not to weaken the Czaristic government. Liberal or advanced legislation was kept under; there was little to warm the hearts of those who desired to see a progressive Russia. The "rights" supposed to have been granted in the constitution proved of little avail in the practical political life of the land; they turned out to be mostly a vain hope, a dead letter.

So far as real parliamentary government and the creation of a liberal commonwealth were concerned, the Czar's forces seemed hardly more than trifling with the people. All these circumstances played powerfully into the hands of the radical or revolutionary elements in the land. They were observing closely, and were storing up strength against the day when this strength would be put to most profitable account.

When the First World War broke out, the duma—still holding some liberal elements—was quite patriotic. It was altogether willing to lend what support it possessed to the Czar's government. Though not forgetting some pressing internal reforms that it would have liked to advocate, it urged the vigorous prosecution of the war, readily recognizing that Germany was fundamentally the enemy of anything having to do with liberalism. While not favorably impressed with the government's war efforts, it abstained at first from destructive criticism, in the hope of making these efforts more effective.

The government on its part became even less concerned with the approval or disapproval of the duma. It grew more reactionary, and less inclined to seek to coöperate with the duma or to placate it, or to ask its advice. The war had gone on less than two years when the Czar was dismissing the liberal elements in his government, and was opening the doors to his old-time tyranny and absolutism.

The duma in its turn, and for all its apparent acquiescence, was now both disturbed and affrighted. It showed more and more increasing distrust of the existing government. It demanded more and more vigorously a responsible ministry to conduct the affairs of state. It viewed with great alarm what was going on. It declared its belief that "dark forces" were in control. There were even charges that the Czar was surrounded by a pro-German element—for there was no question that there had been German influence at court before. By this time the duma was losing all patience with Czaristic actions; it had about gotten out of control. It was becoming more and more disposed to take the reins of government in its own hands. It was feeling that it was the only organization in the state capable of carrying on in these desperate hours.

The Czaristic party at this juncture began to display signs of weakness, which became plainer and more in evidence with every passing day. It could no longer show marks of vigor or strength. It was becoming paralyzed. Evil shadows were falling upon the Czar. His throne appeared to be tottering, and its fall could not be far away. Faith in it was passing.

When the war started, radicalism was not at the fore in Russia, no matter to what extent it was smoldering beneath the surface. So patriotic were the Russian people that they were quite ready to forget their own ills. They were also eager to befriend and protect their fellow Slavs in Europe, who were endangered by the aggressions of the enemy power. As the war proceeded, internal conditions in Russia grew steadily worse.

From one end of the country to the other the situation was getting out of hand. Old peacetime difficulties and dangers were multiplied and accelerated in wartime; they were now bursting loose.

More and more peasant farmers, as well as other persons, were being called into army service; and there were few left on the farms to produce food alike for the people and for the fighting forces. There developed a food shortage over the land, and one that was rapidly growing worse. Many horses, furthermore, had been taken from the farms for war service, a large part of which had been killed; there was now an insufficient number of horses to be used on the farms.

On the already highly restricted industrial resources of the country war necessities were putting a heavy strain, a strain beyond their powers of endurance. Nor was there enough labor in general to carry on the work of the nation. On every hand there was a shortage of manpower; there was difficulty in its replacement alike on the farm and in the factory. The currency of the land, too, became a source of great trouble. It became of less and less value; more and more of it was required in exchange for an article to be purchased. Even when there was food to be sold peasant farmers were unwilling to accept the depreciated currency. Trade was almost at a standstill. To make matters worse yet, railway service was breaking down. It was harder and harder to get trains across the country or to the war front to carry either soldiers or supplies. Movements of trains with soldiers or any one else or anything else were everywhere held up. Insufficiently and inefficiently manned and equipped trains could not be expected to run otherwise than in most lamentable fashion. There was close to a collapse in transportation.

The country, moreover, was unsuited for carrying on war. Russia, for all its array of soldiers, was in war clumsy and slow-moving; it was quite unprepared for military operations, especially those on an extensive scale. The far-reaching bureaucracy of the land was at its worst in time of war. Because of unfit weapons, inadequate supplies, poor transportation facilities, lack of proper war organization, general incompetence in providing material for the conduct of war, and not infrequent incompetence in military operations at the front—to say nothing of possible graft and corruption behind the lines—the country presented a sorry spectacle in time of war. One result among others was an extremely high proportion of battle casualties. The whole military system of Russia along with its government was on the verge of prostration.

There was no spot in the land where great hardship and discontent were not in evidence. In many places revolt could hardly be restrained from showing its head; it could not be kept under much longer. The surging tide was to make its way to one place where its ravages would likely prove fatal. This was the Russian army, which had hitherto been the mainstay of the Czar. It could not and did not escape.

The revolutionary party, now better known as the Bolsheviki (and later as the Soviets), were quick to see what strength would come to them if they had the army with them, and on their side. Hence they proceeded to bore in—though their actual secret operations in this direction had been going on for long before. Workers from the city who were in the army could be approached without difficulty, and with welcome. They had already been infected with revolutionary doctrines; they could quite readily be entrusted with the banners of revolt. A large part were already ripe for the "revolution." Peasants from the country who were in the army were a raw, undisciplined, and largely ignorant mass; they had hitherto been largely immune to Bolshevik dogma. They might in the past have been slow to listen; but now with their experience in the army they were not likely to turn a deaf ear; they, too, could become quite fertile soil for the sowing of the Bolshevik seed. They could in the present straits become easy prey to revolutionary appeals.

At the front the Russian soldier was brave, and gave his life without complaint. The munitions and supplies that came to him were scant in quantity and poor in quality. Perhaps he had inferior weapons or no weapons; even with weapons he could not count upon the quality of his ammunition supply if indeed he had any. He had at times to fight with a club or with his bare hands—perhaps he had to wait till a comrade by his side had fallen, and then seize the released weapon and fight on. And in addition there was lack of hospital equipment and all else that goes with war to rob it of some of its horrors. A great many who had suffered in battle had received little or no medical or nursing attention, and had died of gangrene. The Russian soldier had been poorly supplied alike with weapons for combat and with facilities for mending the wounds taken in combat. He had little protection from the cold; a limb froze, or perhaps his entire body. There was a persistent enemy always at his side—hunger. The food he had to eat was often hardly fit for the human stomach; but even so, there was seldom enough of it. He was called upon to do battle, famished and quite ill-equipped as he was, with a strong, highly trained, and efficient foe in the German uniform. Because of general Russian inability for carrying on war, losses in battle were frightful. Disillusionment and disorganization could not be far away from the soldier at the front.

The Russian soldier, weary and hungry, not understanding why he was still fighting, was now ready to listen to any program that would promise him surcease from his woes. It was the revolutionary party, always active in subterranean channels, and long biding its time, that came with soft whisperings in his ear. It alone, it told him, opposed continuation of the execrable war. It was through the use of four magic words that his adherence could be won—peace, food, liberty, land. He might comprehend little of the high-sounding and intricate phrases of communism, but he did know what these magic words meant. He knew what peace meant, because he had gone through months of bitter war, with untold suffering, and amid heaps of dead men's bodies. He knew what food meant, for during most of that period he was not far from starvation. He knew what liberty meant, for all his life he had seen only the heavy yoke of oppression. He knew what land meant, for this he had craved from his earliest days.

The army proved a mighty recruiting ground for communistic indoctrination. The Bolsheviks showed themselves past masters in the art of this indoctrination. They eagerly and joyfully took advantage of the situation placed before them. What they could do here they did with telling effect. When revolutionary doctrines had infiltrated into the army, their eventual victory was assured. When the revolutionary party had won over the soldiers, their *coup d'état* was all but complete.

The fateful year 1917 had hardly begun when it appeared on every side that the Czaristic government could not hold up much longer; it was now unmistakably tottering to its fall. People over the land had about entirely lost faith and confidence in it. There were renewed reports, not always unfounded, that the German element, which for long had had no little influence in court circles, was stirring up what trouble it could. Palace scandals as they came to light could only cause disgust and aversion. Business and industry in the land were fast becoming paralyzed. Strikes were becoming a common occurrence in one city and another. On streets were bread lines— and barricades and riots. In city and country alike was growing an ugly temper. Arising and spreading were disorders, revolts.

Troops called upon to suppress outbreaks or to fire upon insurgents or revolters refused to put their guns to their shoulders; they at times even fraternized with those they had been ordered to shoot. Soldiers in large part declined to fight longer. They would not obey orders. They threw off all authority. They disowned and insulted their officers. Discipline in the army melted away; it was on its way out. Soldiers left their ranks; in great numbers they deserted. They took free rides on the trains. Some on their departure simply went home; others went wherever their fancy or their need took them. Some went back home to take the land as their own. Walking the streets in the cities or wandering over the countryside were heaps of demoralized ex-soldiers.

There was none now who did not see that the Czaristic government could no longer remain on its feet, that its downfall was at hand. An imperial order came to the duma for its dissolution; it refused. Certain of its leaders, especially from the Constitutional Democratic party, and in part from the Social Revolutionaries, and notably two men named Kerensky and Miliukov, took upon themselves to set up a provisional government to last till a permanent one could be secured, thrusting to one side the Czar and his ministers, and depriving them of any further real participation in the government. A program of reform was offered for the country's well-being and advancement, embracing no small part, or much on the order, of the proposals of the first duma, with the power once vested in the Czar now hardly more than nominal, if even that. There would be granted such things as a liberal parliamentary government, civil liberty, universal suffrage, political amnesty, abolition of caste, freedom of speech, freedom of religion, freedom from arbitrary arrest, generous treatment of non-Russian nationalities, right of labor to organize, and other principles and rights dear to the democratic heart, together with an enlightened social welfare program in general, including partial breaking up of landed estates. Above all, it was directed that a constituent assembly be held, which was scheduled to take place a few months hence, to ascertain views of the people, and to fabricate the future political structure of the land.

An executive committee took into its hand the reins of government. Kerensky was put at the head of the new order. Very soon, so hurried and so dark were the troubles descending upon the land, it was seen that it would not do to have the Czar any longer on the scene. He was asked to abdicate, which he did.

The duma was now the only body in the land with any semblance of authority.

But things did not go well with the provisional government. All about was confusion and uncertainty. Its task, and especially that of Kerensky, was a hopeless one, as was soon to appear. His committee was mostly a series of unstable, quarreling, short-lived, inter-party combinations, forever at cross purposes; they were compromises somewhere between the relatively conservative elements of the duma at one extreme and the radical and ever unsatisfied local Petrograd Bolshevik soviet[1] at the other, the former constantly but vainly seeking to compose or at least to quiet its differences with the latter. Before long many of the more conservative element had been driven out; those of moderate tendencies grew less and less. Whatever exercise of governmental power was attempted by the provisional government was hampered and thwarted on one hand or another; its work was largely fruitless and came to an early end. Most of what it set out to do it was too weak to accomplish. It found itself with little backing anywhere.

The position of Kerensky himself was fast becoming desperate. He stood all but alone. His pathway was strewn with woes. Whatever hopes or aims he may have had were speedily to be dashed. Whatever course he embarked upon was now of little avail. It was furthermore too late. He never had a real chance.

At the outset Kerensky sought, for the sake of his country, and to keep faith with its Allies, to go on with the war with Germany; he was keenly conscious of his international obligations. He promised the Allies that he would be with them "to the victorious end," though he asked them to be a little more specific in stating their war aims. To do his part in the war, he endeavored by all possible means to get his demoralized army back on its feet, to make it an effective fighting force, and to put it into the field against the Germans. In deal-

[1] The "soviet" or council coming into use with the disturbances of 1905, and at first rather a sort of strike committee, was the term applied to the fundamental unit in the new movement. In time it became the general term.

ing with it he tried to be stern and strict. But he was to reckon largely without his host. Army and people alike had become utterly war weary; there were few who wanted more of it. The very suggestion of it was enough to cause immediate revulsion. Besides, by the radical elements Kerensky was charged with being in the hands of the international capitalists, with being but their tool.

As if his cup was not overflowing with adversity, Kerensky had to have quarrels and encounters with some of his generals who were supposed to be at the front doing what they could against the still powerful German armies, but who did not always see eye to eye with him. One of his generals had in his efforts to secure discipline in his command, and believing that he had the support of Kerensky, gone far, practically announcing himself as dictator; on his armed advance on the Russian capital he was placed under arrest by Kerensky's orders, and was deposed.

Occupied as Kerensky and his new government were with the battle line, they had to face something more formidable at their rear. A more dread, more determined, more subtle, and more bitter enemy lying in wait were the irreconcilable Bolsheviki whom they had tried to no purpose to appease and win over. These were most eager spectators of what was going on; they were watching with unconcealed glee the tragic course of events. They were shortly to become the supreme actors in the national drama.

In the general turmoil, confusion, and disorder of the day only one thing was needed to galvanize the Bolshevik party into effective and successful action. This was the arrival upon the scene of an iron-willed man who was in his life to be the arch leader of the Soviet state and after his death its patron saint. His name was Nicolai Lenin.[1]

[1] A youth in a Volga town, Lenin had seen his brother hanged for his alleged part in a plot against the life of a Czar, and had thenceforth vowed himself an unswerving, uncompromising revolutionist, living most of his years outside his coun-

The Bolsheviki knew almost instinctively when the time would be ripe for them to take over. For a brief while they acted circumspectly—something they well knew how to do—and could bide their time and play safe, assured that patience was all that was now required of them. At one time when they felt that they were under suspicion of being in collusion with the Germans, their leaders went into hiding.

At this stage there were two parties in Russia that could have done much to decide the issue of the future rulership of the land, according to whichever side they elected to throw their massed weight. Whatever action they saw fit to take could move the scales, and would spell the fate of the provisional government as against the Bolshevik elements. They could, if acting as a whole, support it and give it strength to weather the storm; or they could by withholding their support bring about its downfall. One of these parties was the Social Revolutionaries (agrarians); the other was the Mensheviki (conservative socialists). Both together had a considerable following.

If at this time Kerensky had adopted, or had been able to adopt, firm and vigorous measures in dealing with the matters before him—the Czaristic régime, the army, the insubordination of the generals, the continuation of the war, the disposal of the land question, the dissatisfaction of the industrial workers, and the Bolshevik threat—he might have had all but the full strength of both of these parties with him; as a general thing they were considerably more sympathetic with his views than with the views of his Bolshevik antagonists.[1]

Kerensky seemed, however, not to be particularly popular with either party, or in fact with the masses of the people in general. The roots of his power never sank deep into their

try, and using to advantage the libraries of Zurich, Munich, and London, who had been a fugitive of recent years, and who had been sent back to Russia by the Germans in a sealed car in the well-founded belief that his instigations would disrupt the Russian military efforts against them.

[1] In the local Petrograd soviet the Bolsheviki were for a time outnumbered, the other groups declining to take part in their revolutionary program. At the same time in both of these groups there were more or less radical elements.

hearts. He was hardly in greater favor with them than he was with the Czaristic faction. He had little actual following from any source. Many had become estranged in consequence of certain recent happenings: some were turned from him because of his quarrels with his generals, others because of his insistence upon keeping the nation's obligations with its allies, which seemed perhaps meaningless, and upon the continuation of war, which seemed hardly less than wicked. Not a few were driven away by divided counsels in the new provisional government, not knowing whom to back. Besides, it was not fully realized how little the threatening Bolsheviki could be governed by principles of majority rule.

With the peasants there was another factor—to them an exceedingly pressing one, and the one by far the most important of all. This was the land question in which they were so profoundly and so vitally concerned. Kerensky appeared too high-minded to take advantage of the peasants in any way; he wanted to do the fair—and above all the constitutional—thing. He sought to satisfy the claims of the peasants by telling them that the land allotments would have to wait till after the constituent assembly, which was only a short time off. The Bolsheviki were held back by no such scruples; they announced forthwith that the land which the peasants had so eagerly desired these past years had already been given back to them; it was now theirs to keep. The Bolsheviki, also realizing that the people in general were exhausted and weary with the war operations, and having little regard for such an abstraction as international obligations, played up their opposition to any continuance of the war with Germany.

It was all these things that kept the allegiance of the major portion of such groups as the Social Revolutionaries and Mensheviki from the Kerensky cause—or at least led to their unwillingness to take effective action in its behalf. If Kerensky had acted more promptly and less punctiliously, and perhaps more realistically, he might have won to his side these bodies, together with the general mass of the people, and might have turned the struggle in his favor.

Events were now playing cumulatively into the hands of the Bolsheviki—internal dissensions among their opponents, general weariness with the war, demand for land expropriation, wide-spread dissatisfaction and feelings of revolt among peasants and city workers alike (aside from the overthrow of the Czar with which the Bolsheviki had had nothing to do, but of which they took full credit and full advantage). They were prepared to capitalize upon the situation that had been created, to reap its fruits. It was the Bolsheviki lurking in the shadows to whom the finger of destiny was now pointing.

The Bolsheviki had never taken kindly to the efforts of those who desired constitutional government in Russia. A constitution would not do for them—only revolution. The idea of a constitution may of itself be said to have set a wedge between the two groups. To the Bolsheviki the provisional government had never appeared imposing or formidable. They had never had much respect or use for it. In the present crisis they were not slow in showing their scorn and disdain. They were happy in the realization of the great part they were to have in its approaching downfall. The Kerensky party had tried hard to appease, to soothe, to mollify, in order to win their coöperation if not their support, but to no purpose. The Bolsheviki had been invited into the counsels of the provisional government, an invitation which was accepted, but not in good faith. Here they took part only to such extent and in such fashion as would embarrass their opponents and advance their own ends. The weapons of war that were placed in their hands to fight off what were regarded as common enemies in the quarrels with the generals were only to be carefully preserved and in due time turned against their givers. Kerensky had helped tie his own hands by listening to Bolshevik suggestions as to restrictions upon troop movements. In his policy of amnesty in releasing political offenders he had opened prison doors to a swarm of Bolshevik foes. This party did not hold double-dealing in reprobation when its ends were involved. It had no desire to temporize or have aught to do with anything that savored of orderly processes in setting up constitutional government; it was all out for the revolution—and now seemed its golden opportunity.

Power was amassing in the hands of the Bolsheviki. What were called "soviets" or councils, if not already in existence, were springing up in various parts of the land, especially in the large cities or industrial centers; in them were to be discerned more and more radical tendencies. Infiltration had proceeded far into trade unions and other organizations of workingmen; these were already largely captured. Factory committees were formed in one place and another, and were instructed both in sabotage and in factory management. In more than one gathering armed drilling went on. A large part of the country peasants, even though not comprehending altogether, were at least in a restive mood; they were at any rate ready to envision something quite different from the old order. The winning over of the army by the Bolsheviki had proceeded apace.

The hour was now fast approaching, was indeed at hand, for the revolutionary Bolsheviki to take possession of the scene—the hour for which they had longed, and for which they had so diligently prepared themselves—for which they had bided their time, and which indeed they had expedited—and which had played into their waiting hands, or rather into their alert and energetic hands. Their activities with the army in particular had given them the scepter to wield, had sealed the situation in their favor; as they well knew, mastery had now fallen to them. They were about to mount the saddle.

The Bolsheviki were to receive the reward for their faithful and unstinted labors, which labors they had carried on with great determination and with great efficiency. The adroitness and resourcefulness and resolution which they possessed—the sure knowledge of their goal and of the necessary steps to reach it—and shall we add their general unscrupulousness?—were in strong contrast with the inertia, the halting, uncertain, temporizing, even if punctilious, tactics of their opponents. They knew just what they wanted, and how to go about getting it. They had one thing no other party had—a definite, planned program. They had a very carefully prepared line of action, with all its philosophy and all its theory; they needed only the opportunity for its practical application—this they were now to have.

The organizational procedure of the Bolsheviki was not far from perfection. They were masters of the art of intrigue and of propaganda. Some of their leaders were idealists; some were astute practical politicians—all were opportunists whose day had arrived. There were some among them of genuine ability and highly skilled—some with no little education. Some were little short of geniuses at organization. Not a few were schooled through hard Czaristic experiences. The number of actual machinators, or of those in the inner circle, was relatively small— only a sprinkling of theorizers and of practical city workers, representing all in all a very thin section of the Russian population. But whatever its size or numerical inferiority, it was quite equal to the occasion. Perhaps never in history has there been at a time of national political crisis a group or party so cool, organized in so high degree, so primed, so entirely prepared to seize upon the mastery of a situation.

With the situation now within their grasp, the Bolsheviki moved rapidly. They proceeded forthwith to take over the functions of the duma. It was they who were now to give orders.[1]

Army units one after another had gone over to them—what remaining opposition might exist was too weak to count. There was now little left of the provisional government or of the

[1] The famous order no. 1 of the Bolsheviki was to the effect that theirs was now the body to be looked to for authority, with military units creating their own committees.

Kerensky party—only a handful of gallant and devoted followers. When the powerful Cossacks of the south, long the dependable standby of Russian government, threw their allegiance with the revolutionaries, the result was no longer in doubt. The issue came to a head on the streets of St. Petersburg (Leningrad), where it was fought out—where there had seemed a sort of spontaneous revolutionary movement. Here there was joining up with the local garrison—which was of itself practically sufficient to decide the affair. The Bolsheviki took possession of strategic centers in the city—telephone exchanges, bridges, railway stations, electric light or power plants, banks, etc. Street battles followed one another, the Bolsheviki always coming out on top. Defense was finally concentrated at the Czar's former Winter Palace at the head of the Nevsky Prospekt and by the water front. When Bolshevist sailors brought up their man-of-war *Aurora* to the rear of the Palace and proceeded to shell it, its doom was sealed. When it fell, all was lost; the Bolsheviki had won. The city was now in their hands and under their control. An All-Russian Soviet Congress of Workers' and Soldiers' Deputies in St. Petersburg at the time was presented with a *fait accompli*.[1]

Bolshevik forces with little delay went on to the rest of the country. In time, sooner or later, the battle was carried to other cities, always eventually with like results .The fall of the Kremlin in Moscow was the death knell to all opposition. Except in this and a few other cities, the revolution was accomplished without great bloodshed in actual battle, though not a few of those felt to be hostile to the Bolshevik cause or undesirable on general communistic principles were unceremoniously done away with. The task of overcoming resistance was less difficult in those places where soviet councils had been set up for a longer or shorter time. To ensure their victory or their security, the Bolsheviki had no hesitation or compunction in demand-

---

[1] With so little disarrangement and interference did the general activities of the city of Petrograd continue on this historic night that dramatic production proceeded largely as usual.

ing hostages. Everywhere they were known to be deadly in earnest. When dissenting White Russians came in from outside to contest the issue, and in the end lost, the issue was settled for good—there was to be witnessed the coronation of the Bolsheviki cause. It was the banner of the hammer and sickle that was in triumph to wave over the land.

When the Bolsheviki had taken possession of St. Petersburg (Leningrad), their first act was to abolish the duma, whose functions they already usurped. This body had been the sponsor of the provisional government succeeding the Czaristic régime, and which had been nominally in charge of the affairs of the nation. It had lasted hardly half a year. On the dissolution of the duma the revolution was proclaimed. Russia was declared to be in the hands of its soldiers, workers, and peasants. All power was to the Soviets. This was in November of 1917—the famous November (October by the Soviet reckoning) that has had so important a place in the calendar of the Soviets.[1]

The Bolsheviki now proceeded to take over the Kerensky army—or what was left of it—which was facing the Germans on the war front. Russian battle lines appeared in chaos; the Germans were advancing. The Russian army ostensibly opposing it was already in large part steeped in Bolshevikism and was in no condition or mood to oppose the Germans. A truce was established, which was to lead to a treaty between Russia and Germany, and the withdrawal of Russia from the war.

Competent as was the Soviet party to take over power, it was no less competent at wielding power when once in its hands; and with power it was ready to exercise a ruthless dictatorship, giving no other party or group any chance of contesting its rule.

In early Soviet days, or shortly after the revolt—in fact only two months after it—there met, to determine the form and nature of the future government of the land, a constituent assembly, or All-Russian Congress, which had already been for-

---

[1] The term "soviet" was now gradually to take the place of "Bolsheviki."

ınally called by the short-lived provisional government, and had, all things considered, been elected on a fairly equitable democratic basis. It came nearer to representing the masses of ıhe population than any body yet brought into being in the land. It was to a large extent composed of the agrarian Social Revolutionary party—that is, peasants from the country— though there was also appreciable representation from what was left of such groups as the Mensheviki and the Constitutional Democrats. The Bolsheviki were greatly outnumbered, having not over one-fourth of the total votes. If the election had taken place a little later, or after the success of the revolution had been more fully demonstrated, their vote would probably have been materially larger. On the other hand, but for intimidation the vote of their opponents might have been larger.

The majority of the delegates were not in favor of Bolshevik rule, and were prepared to vote it down. The Soviet party when thus failing to get the upper hand should by rights and by all the proprieties have yielded up its power. But it did no such thing; by sheer force it held on. When it was found that the action of this body would not be to its liking, it was promptly dissolved. The delegates, abashed, overawed, intimidated, and more or less confused, were physically prevented from continuing their deliberations; by armed troopers they were ousted from the convention hall—they were dispersed to their homes. It was claimed by the Soviets that in the meantime, or since the promulgation of plans for a constituent assembly, the political and social theories of the people had undergone change, and that accordingly the assembly no longer properly represented them. To a great extent it was all a victory for the city workers, perhaps a bit more clever and a bit more adept in organization or in mass movements than the crude and stolid peasantry from the country. The discipline and authority thus inaugurated by the Soviet party was to be maintained in later days.

151

Under the unselfish and benign solicitation of the Germans, and desirous no longer of having part in a "capitalistic" war, the Bolshevik power now definitely deserted the cause of the Allies and withdrew. It entered into a treaty with Germany (at Brest-Litovsk), which involved the ignominious surrender of much Russian territory—the Baltic states on the west—and a considerable part of the Ukraine to the south. Russia gave up one-third of its best agricultural land, one-half of its manufacturing industries, and three-fourths of its coal and iron.

Shortly after the Bolsheviki entered into power, they opened the state archives to see what they could find there, seeking especially something of an incriminating nature against the old Czaristic government and its Allies with which it had been fighting. Here they discovered the secret treaties which had been made; these they at once and with great gusto published to the world. This was no small coup on the part of the Bolsheviki; it strengthened no little their hold in the seat of power. The war-weary Russian people were much impressed; they believed the Allies to be simply imperialistic, and were all the more ready to sever connections with them, whatever of dishonor might attach to that action. The Allies were asked to restate their aims, in the expectation that whatever might be said would be to their embarrassment and discomfiture. The Bolshevik plan was announced as a "peace without annexations and indemnities."

It was during this period of confusion and unsettling, when the Bolshevik power was all engaged with its internal difficulties, that the Baltic states, taking advantage of the situation, detached themselves from Russia and set themselves up as independent states. These were Finland, Estonia, Latvia, and Lithuania. Poland also emerged as a separate nation, with some former Russian territory. In addition, at the end of the war Rumania took over the province of Bessarabia.

The internal power of the Soviet forces was solidified by certain happenings at this time, for which they were not altogether responsible, but which served to put them in high feather. But for those occurrences it is just possible that the government might have been wrested from their hands. After the Soviet party had taken over control of the old Russian Empire, attempts were made by incensed enemies who were called "White Russians"[1] to drive it out and to repossess the land. In these movements there was some aid or instigation from the Allies who had fought the World War, and who now regarded Russia as having defected from them, and no longer on their side.

Through this action was brought about an old situation in the history of nations—when a nation is invaded by armies from outside, it turns instinctively to any defenders it may have from within, no matter what its feelings may have previously been towards them. There was repeated in Russia what had happened in France just after its revolution when soldiers in the uniforms of foreign sovereigns moved upon the land. What the Allies, together with the "White Russians," did, played directly into the hands of the Soviet power. This intervention, whether wrongly conceived or not, only served to give it strength and prestige.

From one direction and another the White armies—with superiority in trained officers, money, supplies—in everything except popular support—advanced upon the country, and at times succeeded in penetrating far within. But they were too much consumed with rage and with desire for vengeance; and upon helpless and innocent inhabitants of the countryside and the towns occupied by them fell maddened onslaughts. Not always with discrimination in the matter of possible aid and comfort to the Bolshevist forces, men and women were tortured and executed and their possessions seized. There was a "White terror" no less than a "Red terror." The White armies were no less willing to shoot down or hang any not believed to be in sympathy with them, and by wholesale. The White

---

[1] "White Russians" as opposed to "Red Russians" (or Bolsheviki) are to be distinguished from those persons who inhabit White Russia, a region in the southwestern part of Russia.

armies pillaged as did the Red; each left a trail of desolation in its wake.

But the people were more embittered toward the White armies. If they were inclined to rise up against the Reds, they were even more inclined to rise up against the Whites. The old order, it was believed by many Russians, was under the Whites largely to be restored. The people feared a new Czaristic government, and there were many old autocrats among the Whites of whom the people were particularly afraid. As between the Red and White armies some Russians might in large part have remained neutral; but the former made it appear that the latter were operating in behalf of foreign capitalists who were trying to conquer the country, and this was enough to win their allegiance. The several White armies, moreover, quarreled among themselves. Their leaders were often rivals, each trying to get to Moscow first. Besides, there were too many officers, and too few soldiers under them. The Red armies, furthermore, got some help from the Germans. In addition, they had the advantage of operating from interior lines.

The actions of the White Russians proved fatal to them; there were evoked toward them resentment and antagonism. The population of the territory invaded was made to turn as to friends to those who had tried to protect them and their country, and to regard them as their real brothers in arms. These were none other than the Bolsheviki. Nor were the Bolsheviki slow to take advantage of the situation and to turn it to good account. It was this stroke of fortune that gave them a grip upon the country as a whole that otherwise they could scarcely have had.

Whether or not they had taken actual part in the anti-Bolshevik war—and many had not—there were killed off or driven out a large section of the well-to-do of the land and no small part of the dissenting educated classes. A very severe loss resulted to Russia in the expatriation of a great number of her best and worthiest citizens. All over Europe and in other parts of the world were exiled men and women who loved and cherished their native land despite its revolution and its new governing party. Many experienced keen suffering through what transpired; many lost their all. A large part could not return to Russia; or, if so, only with the loss of their self-respect. As with other countries in the world's history, persecution at home drove into the arms of other lands some of the choicest of the population.

At the same time there were some former Russians out of the country that Russia, or any other nation was better off without. There were persons who had a blind hatred towards those who differed with them—certainly as great a hatred as had the Bolsheviki. If they could once have secured control of the government, they would have had little beyond a spirit of vindictiveness, which very likely would have vented itself upon quiet, inoffensive citizens as well as upon active enemies. In addition, not a few of them would have been imbued mainly with a desire for the exploitation of the land for their private benefit. Such emigrés were of the kind who learn nothing and forgive nothing.

Though power fell to the hands of the Bolshevist party like ripened fruit, there was yet before it the task of making sure its hold. It had to rid itself of all enemies, actual and potential, if its tenure was to be permanently secure. The Soviet forces, not inclined to gentleness by nature, did not refrain from the sternest, even most brutal, measures, in putting down all opposition. They had been used to receiving violence at the hands of those who oppressed them; now that the seat of power was with them, they were prepared to deal out violence. Those enemies of the new order who remained in the land must be brought low and rendered harmless to it. It must be seen that the new government was neither overthrown nor undermined.

In dealing with enemies or obstructionists of any kind, the Bolshevists' power proceeded without knowledge of compassion. To those who stood in its way there was little shown of pity or mercy. Its work was attended with outbursts of savagery. Individual or wholesale massacres became the order of the day; there were single shootings and there were mass shootings. In making its place secure in the earlier days, the new régime leaped forward with the spirit of the tiger. If it did not take over its power in a sea of blood, it sealed that power in such a sea. There was a "Red" terror that no man might forget. But however bitter the conflict, it was the new authority that carried the day, that emerged with the upper hand.

It is not to be thought that there was a real revolution in Russia, in the sense that there occurred a heavy clash of armed forces, with resulting assumption of power by the victorious side. The matter was not so simple as that, or perhaps was simpler. The Bolsheviki did not seize power. Such action was not necessary. It was ripe to their hands, or to the hands of any organized group with any following who could pick it up. Though once recognized as one of the mightiest empires of the world, and protected by myriads of soldiery, the Czaristic government was builded upon the frailest of foundations; beneath it was no enlightened democracy or popular will, or even popular understanding. When the storm broke upon it, as in time it was bound to do, there was nothing to stay its collapse.

There might have been set up in Russia a liberal, progressive, constitutional government thoroughly opposed to the old darkened autocratic absolutionist régime; but those who stood between it and the new communistic order were not given a chance to show what they could do; they were literally squeezed out. In the conception of the new victors, a bourgeois revolution would not do—but only a full-blown one of the proletariat.

As the transient government glimmered out, and as order faded away, the Bolsheviki marched in and took possession. Into the vacuum that had been created they had merely to step. It may be questioned if there was a real state of anarchy at the time. The revolutionary party proceeded directly, methodically, and in keeping with its carefully made plans. As power grew in their hands, even though there were still enemies to be subdued, they simply took over. No movement ever appeared at so propitious a time for itself as did communism at the time of the collapse of the Russian empire.

There was never anything quite like it in human history. Within less than a period of a year a minority party, perhaps not exactly insignificant, but at any rate numerically a distinctly minority party, with a following that represented only a slight portion of the Russian people, had leaped into the saddle and was riding the land, making itself a force that swept all before it.

But the full story had not been told. A mighty movement that had for long been operating underground was now showing its head above the surface. For the first time the world was confronted with a new philosophy which believed itself destined to rule the earth—if necessary by ruthless force.

PART II

After the Revolution

CHAPTER X

The Soviet State and Its Getting on Its Feet

A new régime could not have started off less auspiciously, matters could not have been worse for a new political organization arriving upon the scene or taking over the reins of government, than was the case when the Soviets[1] came to power in Russia. It had difficulties and obstacles exceptional and of huge dimensions placed before it. It was face to face with all but overpowering troubles. It was confronted with a situation rarely before met by a government.

The country was truly exhausted after its part in the First World War, though it had deserted its allies, and had secured a patched-up peace with its former foes, which left it shorn of a very large part of its industrial resources. At the conclusion of this war it had had to stand up to a counter revolution undertaken by the enemies of the new order. When both these war clouds had been dissipated, not only had a vast amount of the wealth of the country been destroyed, but great numbers of its agricultural and industrial workers had been killed, maimed, or otherwise lost.

There were distress and privation on every hand. There was a shortage of food, and also of fuel and factory materials. The productiveness of the country, never at a high ebb, was brought very low. Agriculture, which had never been of an efficient order, was hardly in position to meet the present fresh demands upon it. Peasants in the country were none too friendly, and were disposed to look upon the new government with suspicious eyes. Industry had come practically to a standstill, and

[1] On this term, see *ante*, p. 142.

the manufacture of goods of any kind was to be attained with endless difficulties. Many of the ablest business and industrial engineers had fled the country. The transportation system had almost completely broken down. A suitable currency was lacking. There was inherited the general inefficiency of so many years of Czaristic rule. The country and its socialistic inclinations were regarded with little favor, and had little of a helping hand, on the part of foreign nations. A blockade was thrown about the land, which bore hard upon it.

When the Soviet party had established its rule, and felt itself actually in the seats of power, it proceeded to certain definite measures. The introduction of some sort of a socialistic program for the new state would naturally be the initial proceedings with which it would try its wings. In whatever degree any such proceedings were now feasible, what had to come first was grappling with the immediate situation before it.

Apart from a prompt "Declaration of the Rights of the People," setting forth various matters and calling for the abolition of classes and civil ranks among the people, the early socialistic program to be called for and to be put into effect to a greater or less extent might include such considerations as the following: the general nationalization of the means of the production and distribution of wealth; the transfer (by confiscation so far as was necessary) of the landed estates for the peasantry; the complete appropriation of the national resources of the nation, such as forests, mines, etc.; the taking over by the state of banks, railways, etc.; the direct seizure of factories and other industrial establishments (especially the larger ones); the confiscation or abolishing of private property when it was needed by the state and without compensation to the owners, or a certain dispossessing of the propertied classes; the providing by any means possible of food and other necessaries of life to those lacking these things; the conscription of labor to secure workers for the state; the seeing that profits arising from any process accrued to no individual, but to the state alone; and the exclusion from a voice in government of all but the proletariat.

The prime responsibility which the new Soviet government felt to be laid upon its shoulders was the creation of an army to protect and safeguard it in these trying hours, from both internal and external enemies, actual and potential. The old Czaristic army may be said to have passed out, to have fallen to pieces. It had become demoralized and undisciplined, as well as poorly equipped and accoutered. Besides, so far as it had active soldiers ready to fight, these had largely passed over to the Soviet side. This army, taken over in the Revolution, had to be transformed into a new effective fighting machine. Such an army the Soviet power set out at once to obtain. It was to be composed to a great extent of material of the old army, but under the spell of the new revolutionary spirit and equipped with the best that could be gotten for it under existing conditions, or as soon as it could be made ready. With a powerful, disciplined army in their control, the Soviet authorities could stand prepared to defend and make secure the power that had come to them.

To ensure the survival of the Soviet state, and to prevent the collapse of the "Revolution," its leaders had the further and hardly less immediate task of making available to the people food and other necessaries of life. Indeed, this action was fundamental; it was imperative before anything else. Food in particular had somehow to be gotten to the people if they were to be spared starvation, and if the new state was to endure.

Food supplies at the beginning could by no means suffice for the population, decimated though it was. In many areas food was not to be had, or was to be had with the greatest difficulty. Crop failures in the early days made the situation worse and augmented the country's woes. At times the country was all but stripped of food. Starvation stalked the land, and many fell its victims. Whole cities were on the brink. Suffering was widespread and acute.

163

At the outset all the available food was requisitioned by the Soviet authorities; it was to feed the army, and as far as possible the rest of the population that was in dire need. Rationing of food in the cities was introduced. (Ration cards were more sparingly issued to old Czaristic elements.) Communal kitchens to provide food were established. Agricultural surpluses or what the peasants did not need for their own consumption were wrung from them and turned over to the state. Grain, livestock, and other foodstuffs were taken from them, possibly with promise of payment, but really confiscated, to be distributed among those in want. This treatment was resented by the peasants, who proceeded to cut down production to avoid handing over the fruit of their toil without recompense. Part of their land they refused to cultivate; part of their products they hid or destroyed. Many withheld requisitions. Some declined altogether to sell their products. There were even peasant uprisings.

A particular source of grievance with the peasants was the taking of much of their food for the benefit of the city dwellers, who, the peasants always believed, were benefited at their expense, and constituted a favored class in the Soviet economy. They felt that the burden of support of the new nation was falling unduly upon their shoulders, with other workers producing much less. For a long time the peasants, if not hostile to the Soviet régime, were critical of it. As food was essential to the life of the state, its seizure by those in power was readily justified; there were few scruples. By the Soviet authorities the whole procedure was called war or military communism, and was declared to be only temporary, only for a season.

Nor was food alone wrested from those who had it. With so many homeless and shelterless, besides being foodless, it was decreed in early days that dwellings, whether occupied or not, especially those of any size or with multiple apartments, should be thrown open to those in need. Some of the mansions of the nobility or of the wealthy were converted into hospitals, day nurseries, and the like. Persons who had other possessions which the state desired or believed necessary for the sustenance of the people, including more or less of concealed valuables, suffered similar divestment. Those having a surplus of an article or commodity that could be employed for the benefit or advantage of others might have to turn it over to their less fortunate brethren. Supplies of different goods in private possession might have to be shared or distributed according to common needs. To the necessitous in general, and to some setting themselves forth as such, much was given gratuitously, including free rides on railway trains and free telephone service to an extent.

Without delay and without remorse the Soviet power proceeded to seize and take over whatever of private substance or possessions was left in the land and was required for the subsistence of the people. Supplies were now in some measure to be had which were so desperately in demand, and which otherwise seemed impossible to obtain. When there was objection on the part of the owners, bald confiscation was a speedy resort. All these operations could hardly be expected to be carried out without the exercise of more or less physical compulsion; and more or less of violence and bloodshed was not an unknown occurrence in consequence.

The production of different kinds of manufactured goods was a pressing necessity. Something like industrial chaos reigned in the land. Factory production had fallen to a low ebb. From some factories goods only trickled out if they came forth at all. Factories were often badly damaged or run down, and often hardly capable of operation, what with their war experiences and other misfortunes. Even with an adequate and qualified staff of workers the goods that could be turned out were far below what was required. The actual workers into whose hands was to be committed the operation of the industrial establishments were hardly fitted for so intricate and complex a task.

Directors and managers were in little better case. Not many

had had any industrial or engineering ability or experiences. Though the Soviet government made what use it could of those who had been so engaged in the old Czaristic days, these could hardly look for the full confidence and trust of the new socialist rulers, and could expect watchful, even suspicious eyes upon them. With them, furthermore, there was repeated interference in operations on the part of self-appointed critics among the workers or in the new government, usually to the detriment of successful operations. Sabotage by enemies of the new order was a possibility, and at times a fact. There was in general much of inefficiency and no little waste. Matters were decidedly worsened by the bitter civil war that had overtaken the land, as well as by the blockade imposed by former allies and which kept needed goods from reaching the country.

Nor was it easy for the factories and shops to get, under a system of transportation that had all but broken down—many railway bridges, for one thing, had been destroyed—the materials and natural resources, as well as fuel, they so greatly demanded. After whatever processing or manufacturing was possible, it was no less difficult to get the wares or goods to the waiting consumer. At best there was greater or less delay. To make matters worse still, money was in limited use; and it was difficult to pay employees. With many there was no pay at all for a time, but only the meting out of such things as were requisite to sustain life. Without money workers were not able to buy food or other necessaries—much having to be taken from the peasants by force, as we have seen.

Industry was slowed down, and in some cases almost ceased to produce. With the great shrinkage in industrial production workers were disposed to go into the country where they felt they could be surer of getting a living; and some factories lost part of their employees in consequence. It is almost a matter of wonder that industrial production did not come to a standstill; in fact more than once it appeared about to do so.

To remedy industrial conditions, to get manufacturing going, the Soviet government was prepared to take, and did take, drastic measures. It moved with vigor and determination. All productive property was taken over without ado. Owners of factories who could be made to continue production were compelled to do their part, even though their response was halting and faltering. Often factories were turned over directly to their workers, perhaps into the hands of such unions as had been organized. The larger or more important industrial establishments, especially those having over a certain number of employees (as five or ten) or operating by power machinery, were confiscated at once or a little later taken over by the state. All were to be duly "nationalized."

Conscription of labor was enjoined. The whole population was made into an industrial army. Workers had to go where they were needed most. There were severe penalties for shirkers and dodgers—for there were some of this kind. Hours were lengthened so far as seemed feasible under the circumstances. Premiums or bonuses or extra pay were offered to encourage the fullest response. Strikes were forbidden. Membership in trade unions was for a time made compulsory. Coöperative societies were encouraged, especially among consumers; for a time consumers were to a considerable extent required to join such societies.

For the greater or less amount of technical skill and experience which were required in the industrial operations, those in the old régime in possession thereof continued largely to be pressed into service. As rapidly as others could be prepared or trained, they were enlisted.

There was a strong psychological appeal made in the whole proceeding. Responsibility for production was placed upon the workers. They were told that industry now belonged to them; that it was committed to their hands; that it was theirs to decide what was to be done about it. They were urged to put forth their utmost endeavors to make a success of the country's industrial efforts. Workers at the same time were firmly re-

167

minded of their obligations as citizens in the new socialistic state. Quite positively the people were told: "If a man will not work, neither shall he eat."

During all these efforts to get food and other necessaries of life for the people, proceedings continued for the "nationalization" of such private property as the government felt essential for its purposes. In general such property was to pass over into state control or was to be taken over by the state except certain personal or household articles of relatively small value or articles such as could not be used for the creation of further wealth for the individual. Means for the production and distribution of wealth were to be in the hands of the state alone.

It was the relatively wealthy land owners and affluent industrial classes that were to feel most heavily the immediate dispossessing arm of the government. To some extent the business of ordinary private citizens was not proscribed at once in wholesale fashion; state expropriation here was more gradual. Limited individual buying and selling, often not far removed from barter, might in some measure continue under state regulations.

As with all revolutionary movements, the one in Russia was accompanied with its contingent of criminal elements, including bandits and other evil-doers; but their allegiance was rarely sought. Especially in the earlier days, there was a certain amount of plunder and pillage, particularly of the property of the well-to-do classes, on the part of the needy, covetous, or rapacious. But this practice was without the endorsement of the Soviet authorities; it was never encouraged in any way. In fact, these authorities took special measures to thwart and check any such actions; for those found guilty of it appropriate punishment was provided. If there was to be any taking over of private property, it must be by the hand of the state, and for the interest of the state alone.

No little attention had to be given to the peasants and their problems. Involved were other matters besides the providing of sustenance for the nation. Hardly had the old Czaristic government fallen when the peasants with little delay or ado set about taking over the estates of the landed proprietors. This parcelling out of peasant holdings was an announced policy as well of the Soviet government, which at the outset wanted to have the credit for its initiation. The government was to bide its time when the collectivation of farms could be effectively imposed in the socialist manner. It had formally bestowed the land upon the peasants, and with its blessings. It seems to have been intended at first that only the larger estates should be expropriated, but it soon appeared not easy to draw a line, and landed proprietors in general stood to be dispossessed. The peasants, as they had had no hesitation, so they had no qualms or scruples in what they did. They thought that they were to become individual owners of the land—socialism at the start having little place in their mental processes. It was this attitude in general that was later to prove so great a source of embarrassment and harassment to the Soviet authorities.

Another sore plague to the new government lay in its money troubles. There was want of a generally accepted currency in the land. A paper money issued in the early days had before long become almost worthless, with large quantities necessary to have any purchasing power. There had been a period of inflation—something that had been inherited more or less from the old Czaristic régime. When this paper money was not made use of, the country had for a time to get along without money. This lack of a satisfactory medium of exchange or currency system was a particular source of trouble with the peasants, something that intensified the unhappy relations with them. Already anything but eager to do business with the Soviet agents, they were loath to accept a paper money next to worthless that was offered them for their products. With no proper money available they demanded high prices for what they were willing to dispose of. In lieu of money in the factories, furthermore, workers had to a considerable extent to be paid in "tickets" which entitled them at certain stores to food and other necessary articles. Those possessed of surplus wealth in the form of jewelry and the like were glad to exchange it for such a requirement as food.

There was in fact little buying or selling in the land—barter having largely to serve as a means of exchange. At some stages there was no inconsiderable amount of barter—goods or services being swapped for other goods or services, without the intermediation of specie. This was the particular means for the exchange of agricultural products for industrial products. There remained, however, peculiar difficulties in effecting proper exchange between these two kinds of goods—between the actual costs of production and the arbitrary prices set for articles—something that was the basis of what was later called the "scissors" problem.

Nor was there any but the slightest banking business done in the first Soviet days. The country was thus further handicapped in promoting commercial transactions or traffic. The Soviet government did not, however, let the matter of a circulation medium remain long a hindrance to its operations. As we are to find later, it proceeded to establish a sound and effective monetary system, together with an appropriate banking system.[1]

Foreign and domestic indebtedness in the Soviet state was for the most part cancelled or repudiated at the beginning; debtors no longer had to think of their creditors, at least so far as these debtors were of the proletariat.

In its beginning days, purportedly as a war emergency measure, and continuing for a time, there was set up for the administration of the affairs of the new state, a central national governing authority, called by some such name as the supreme council of national economy. In its hands were placed productive units in general, business enterprises, means of transportation, large-scale trade and exchange facilities, and all other things needful that pertained to the going of the Soviet state.

[1] See *post*, p. 191.

There was also a governing body under the name of council of people's commissars. After a little time there was a definitely and formally organized government established, which was by authorization and direction of the constitution adopted for the land.

In theory the organization of the Soviet government now set up was far from being a bad one. To students of political science the plan of government of the Union of Socialist Soviet Republics, the official title of the country, novel though it was to the ears of other nations, had some quite commendable features; there were few who would condemn it altogether.[1]

Beginning with the lowest or smallest political unit in the state, which in industrial areas was made up of occupational groups, and in rural areas of territorial groups (not altogether different from the arrangements of the old Czaristic duma), delegates were elected to a higher and larger one, and so on, till the supreme government at Moscow was constituted. The system was thus a pyramided one, rising tier above tier. In its composition recognition was given to one's standing alike as a citizen and as a producer. In later days the relation of the individual to the government was made of somewhat closer character, and with less differences between rural and urban workers.

The general government was set forth as a federated one, rather than a centralized one, as under the old Czar. To the several political bodies or national units making up the general union there was left a considerable measure of self-government or of cultural autonomy. Matters of a strictly domestic nature were to be passed upon by the different republics or other political units concerned. A republic was given the formal right to withdraw from the Union. (During the Second World War each of the republics was given power to conduct independent international relations with foreign countries.)

[1] On the activities of the Communist party, see *post*, p. 315.

The general government finally emerging for the nation as a whole consisted of a union congress or parliament, known as the supreme soviet or supreme council, meeting twice during the year. It was made up of two bodies of equal power, one a union council based upon and representing the entire land; and the other a council of nationalities, with delegates duly apportioned among the several political divisions, higher divisions having more and lower less. By the supreme soviet was elected a central executive standing (or steering) committee, known as the presidium, and consisting of a president, a number of vice-presidents (one for each republic) and a like number of other members. This body had wide powers. It could act between sessions of the supreme soviet, its acts being subject to the approval and ratification of that body. It could interpret the laws, and formulate broad principles of legislation. It could carry on the general administration of government. It had charge of international matters, appointing ambassadors and ministers to foreign countries. There were chosen also a somewhat larger number of commissars (Council of People's Commissars, later called Ministers), a sort of cabinet of department heads, which were vested with immediate administrative powers. By it was chosen a premier. Though both the presidium and the council of commissars were supposedly in large measure administrative or executive bodies and accountable to the supreme soviet, their decrees or edicts had much the force of the regular laws of that body (somewhat on the order of the procedure with the former Czaristic duma).

There were also state agencies for planning projects, for the banking system, and for cultural activities. In addition, there was a graduated judiciary, including a supreme court appointed by the presidium. There was a procurator, or attorney-general, with subordinate officials over the land. Smaller political divisions had an analogous or corresponding set-up to that of the general union, but without a council of nationalities, and in general of narrower scope. Recall of officials was possible in the Soviet Union. The supreme soviet had power to amend the constitution.

The general union or central government had broad powers —over foreign affairs or international relations (including military matters, defense, foreign trade, etc.), admission of new areas, boundaries, qualifications of citizenship, and also such matters as heavy industry, general judiciary, trade, banking, currency, natural resources, railways and other means of communication, and basic nation-wide interests in health, education, labor, etc. Smaller units had charge of their general internal affairs, to an extent paralleling the work of the central government, including additional functions if necessary, but always subordinate to its broader authority. At the bottom of the scale were "soviets" on the order of a city council or other local governing body, possibly in cities together with district or ward soviets each with its own several committees. All local autonomy was subject to review at the Kremlin.

In the hands of local Soviet authorities could be placed in large meaure various matters, mainly of local concern, as land distribution, schools, health measures, welfare activities, and general local improvements. Political subdivisions or local communities, perhaps through village authorities or coöperative bodies, were encouraged to attend to their own economic wants which were of a small scale and relatively simple nature, thus avoiding too great congestion of business with the central government, and in some measure reducing possible cityward migration and crowding of traffic ways, but with the central government prepared to extend oversight, advice, or other assistance. Larger industrial enterprises were left to the general government.

The leaders of the Soviet Union, especially those that had taken part in the Revolution, were not to be set down, outside their particular all-consuming body of convictions, as a lot of malevolent or unprincipled men. No small part were of the devoted, high-minded sort, within accepted communistic boundaries, and with uncircumscribed energies. Not a few were so convinced of the desirability, the efficacy—the utter necessity—of the cause of communism, that they were willing and quite prepared to meet danger, to experience hardship or suffering, to face death itself, for its advancement or realization. They were zealots with a fanatical zeal, burning with nothing less than a consuming fire. Seldom has the world beheld a torch carried in so consecrated hands as a firebrand.

Some of the leaders were men of talent and rare ability. A considerable portion were widely read, acquainted with the social sciences and versed in the doings of the world and of men. A notable portion were of the intelligentsia; not a few were university trained and highly educated—some the intellectual pick of the Russian universities who had continued their studies through life. These may have been terrorists to a greater or less extent, but they were men of education none the less. Only a relatively small proportion of the leaders had been actual manual laborers or members of the so-called working class. Not often in history has a powerful political movement or a political revolution been so definitely in the hands of the educated élite of a country. In the case of the Russian revolution the proletariat must have had abundant faith and trust in such leaders—leaders who had previously been mainly masters of theory, a sort of lordship of economic transcendalists.

Whatever the character of the leaders in the Russian revolution, whatever their merits or virtues, their points of excellence, in nearly all there was a narrowness or obtuseness of vision, a dogmatic intolerance of attitude, a bitterness of spirit, towards those in their own land or in the rest of the world whose political or economic opinions did not coincide with theirs or who dared to differ with them in such matters.

What made the Soviet movement of such grave concern and of such potential danger, not only within its borders, but to the whole world, whether more or less pronounced in later than in earlier days, was this flaming impatience with respect to all who did not share its point of view and its principles—or with respect to all who did not see eye to eye politically with those who happened to be in the Soviet seats of power. To the Soviet people, especially in the first days, there was preached an everlasting, truceless war against the foes of communism; into the hearts of the people was burned a class hatred, bitter, implacable, ready to stop at nothing with respect to any who stood in their way. Upon the Soviet people was enjoined the utter destruction, the extermination of the "enemies of the revolution"; they were charged to be relentless and pitiless towards these enemies.[1] Nothing of good was to be seen or allowed in the adversary; there was no other course but to strike him down, to put an end to him for good. There was a devouring passion, a heart-made pledge to overthrow, completely to demolish capitalism and all its works, and if necessary any who might be found standing in its defense. It was close to a savage attitude that was adopted here.

It was this attitude that rendered the Soviet power a thing of ferocity within its land, and a thing possibly boding heavy ill for the world outside. In respect to such a frame of mind it might be asked if the Soviet power was not being built upon the point of bayonets; and if a state of war was not being entered upon, a war from which there could be no surcease, the combatants merely changing positions with the course of succeeding conflicts.

The most portentous characteristic in this Soviet ideology was not so much any peculiar doctrines as to the political status of the land or as to the national economy which was to be espoused, but its being grounded upon naked intolerance and making force its supreme instrument and weapon. The world would have been much more willing—despite any possible lack of sympathy for Soviet political and economic tenets—to

---

[1] In the "Declaration of the Rights of the Toilers and Exploited People," prepared by Lenin, and the basis of the first constitution of the Soviet Union, the aim was "mercilessly to crush resistance."

have thought well of it, and to have held out to it the open hand of friendship, but for its all-consuming intolerance, coupled with its readiness to employ violence to gain its ends or against any and all dissenters—to use ruthless force where it appeared desirable or necessary in Soviet interests. Terrorism in greater or less degree, inherited from Czaristic days, was not to be left behind—it was to be continued, and in far wider areas. Never before had partisanship on so large a scale, so blindly narrow and of so bloody-minded a cast, taken over the reins of government in a great nation.

CHAPTER XI

The Soviet State and Its Economic Set-Up

THE Soviet state, now definitely launched as a sovereign state among the nations of the world, was committed to the socialist system, and that system was forthwith to set in. Fairly rapidly the socialist tide closed in upon the land. The three great desiderata of formal socialism—no interest,[1] no rent, no profit—were to be put in the way of achievement, together with state production and distribution of wealth to a greater or less extent. In the inauguration of the new program some matters might move along lines relatively simple, some along lines more difficult and complex. In the whole undertaking, if it was to proceed in its economic aspects according to strict Marxian gospel, it would have to be constantly recognized that the country was largely an agricultural one, and one that was not adaptable offhand to a socialist régime.

At the outset attempt would have to be made to "nationalize" all the hitherto private property of the land that was to come under state control, a procedure that with whatever interruption or intermission was to continue till the goal was entirely or substantially achieved. In keeping with this principle means of production and distribution of wealth were in general to be vested exclusively in the state. There could as a rule be no private business in the land, and no income from such. Nothing could be owned by the individual that was to be used for the

---

[1] Interest was possible through savings banks and government bonds. but all through the hands of the state. See *post*, p. 193.

production of further wealth. There could be no wealth to the individual unless immediately earned by its possessor.

Before, however, the Soviet state could proceed far with its full economic or Marxian program, it found itself face to face with certain practical considerations which had to be attended to. These must have due and full regard ere its program could be definitely and finally put into effect.

In the first few years of the new Soviet state when it was getting on its feet, and struggling forward, there was general demoralization and confusion in the land, with the production of goods at so low an ebb, and with a considerable part of the population so disaffected, as to spell danger and disruption to it, to threaten its very existence. In consequence of the troubled, well-nigh chaotic conditions prevailing, to meet the critical economic situation, and to relieve the pressing imperative needs of the times, it was felt that something must be done of drastic character, if the life of the new order was to be preserved and kept going. This could be nothing less than the slowing up of the process of making the state a socialistic one, a process which evidently had been at too rapid a pace, if not attended with too great violence, and a return in a certain measure to the procedures in vogue in countries of a more capitalistic color. In short, there had to be allowed a measure of private activities. Certain concessions had to be made first of all to the recalcitrant peasants, and also to certain other producers as well as to certain kinds of traders, for the securing of necessary consumer goods and for the making of these goods available to the people at large.

The government had already decided, after a few years, to abolish the levies upon the produce of the peasants; instead a tax was imposed. To avoid any further giving of offense to this class, as well as for other reasons, private trade which had at first been forbidden in the land, was permitted to them in some degree; their surplus products might be sold in private markets, or through the hands of private dealers, to be disposed of on the best terms possible. Persons engaged in agriculture were also allowed under restrictions to rent land and to hire labor. This new concession was to be ascribed in large part to what had been called "the peasants' strike" of earlier days.

Idle factories of inconsiderable capacity, especially those not power-driven and those having only a handful of employees—several times as many as had previously been allowed in the smaller factories—might operate in private hands, and perhaps be leased for the purpose. Other business undertakings of petty or limited character might for the time being revert to private control. Retail trade was now possible to an extent without the direct management of the state. Money was brought back into more general circulation, and became the more usual basis and means of exchange, to take the place of primitive barter. Employees could now be paid in cash. There was a step-up in the tempo of business transactions. In considerable measure private buying and selling prevailed. There was thus sanctioned in the land a modicum of capitalistic procedure.

It was the fairly well-to-do peasant, the middleman, the retailer, and the small industrialist who most took advantage of the new line of action, and of the new liberty thus accorded. Some profited a little; some profited considerably; a few profited greatly. Not many, however, fared so very well on the whole. Whatever prosperity the private producers and traders might enjoy, they had at a certain cost: they did not win general favor or popularity. From part of the population they had rather denunciation and upbraiding for their non-communistic behavior. They were under a greater or less amount of suspicion; they did not escape the vigilant eyes of the state. They also suffered civil disabilities or were subject in greater or less measure to the loss of civil rights. They had difficulty in securing supplies and in obtaining credit; they could operate in general only on a restricted scale. They were also subject to special taxation; any particular evidence of affluence on their part could be countered by extra imposts.

In its new plans, the better to meet its present difficulties, and to secure improved economic conditions among the people, the Soviet government also turned to the encouraging and promoting of coöperative organizations—agricultural coöperative bodies and consumers' coöperative bodies, together with marketing coöperative bodies, especially with respect to the necessaries of life—though such bodies were by no means new in Russian history.

Because of the lack of sufficient engineering talent, furthermore, the Soviet government for a time farmed out or allowed as concessions to outside or foreign capitalists the inauguration or operation of certain enterprises, especially those for the development of some natural resources or for the large-scale production of necessary articles or for the promotion of some important form of trade. The government kept a firm hand on all the proceedings; as a rule when it had paid back the costs of the investment, the physical equipment was left on Russian soil, and the country was that much better off. Commercial intercourse with foreign countries was at the same time promoted in some measure. For the most part the procedure worked well. At times, however, the Soviet government was taken advantage of. At times, on the other hand, there were complaints of one kind or another from the outside interests, especially as to annoying interference or unjust or unfair regulations.

There was thus in the early days of the Soviet undertaking a certain departure from strict socialistic doctrines. The exigencies of the situation did not permit complete adherence to them. There had to be greater or less loosening of their rigid precepts for the time being, and some sort of adjustment to the conditions actually being faced. The Soviet authorities recognized the issues before them, and with little ado were ready to waive any theoretical socialistic predilections. They were capable of displaying common sense and courage alike.

The "new economic policy," as it was called, though relatively brief (lasting less than a decade) and intended only as a transitory measure, seemed like a return to capitalism, and by many was so hailed.[1] It was, however, to be looked upon as a respite in the Soviet overhasty procedure; more than that, it could afford opportunity for needed educating in socialist principles of the people of the land, especially the peasants, who had found the movements a little too rapid, and who had never become completely reconciled to the new order.

Without doubt the indulgence on the part of the Soviet state that had been granted to certain groups in the population gave it a breathing spell, and tided it over these critical days. During this period it was enabled to make a study of general conditions and needs in the country, to consolidate its internal positions, and to effect some measure of economic reconstruction. In such wise to an extent or in some respects the Soviet Union in its economic launchings followed the teachings and pattern of the capitalistic state. But while such procedure may have been contrary to the doctrines of orthodox socialism, it need not have been taken as subversive thereof, or as the entering wedge for the revival of capitalism. Modifications of or compromises with socialistic principles were only temporary expedients; they did not prove fatal.

With the end of the new economic policy, all private enterprises which had been allowed existence under it were duly barred. The way was now open for the introduction of the real socialistic state so long before the eyes of its creators. The Soviet state could proceed to the desired socialization of the country. It set about its vast undertaking systematically, and according to its principles quite logically.

Wealth that smacked of private capital, whether the owner

[1] Following the Second World War there was for a time something on the order of the "new economic policy" in certain local urban and rural areas seriously devastated in consequence of the war.

181

lived in the Soviet Union or had moved away, could be expropriated readily enough by the state. For the small capitalist who resided within, there was always at hand a convenient means of liquidation—the inescapable vehicle of taxation—if there were not evoked more direct or more drastic measures. Natural resources, whether or not they had been in the hands of foreign concessionaires for a greater or less length of time, were now to be exploited exclusively by the state. They were in general to be in the hands of what were called state trusts. Such was the disposition also of the larger industries, as we are to see.

Means of production and transportation of goods could to a considerable extent pass into the hands of the state fairly smoothly, without too great violence or upheaval, and with less of disturbance in the transition period to the general national economy. Their taking over could be regarded as the most natural or most logical movement in the whole process. State ownership, as we have seen, had already applied in Russia as well as in other continental countries to common carriers and public utilities. Manufacturing establishments, controlled by capitalists, foreign or domestic, could be physically expropriated without too much distress to the Soviet conscience. Their "nationalization" presented industrial rather than political difficulties. "Nationalization" of the farms was a quite different and a far more serious matter, as we are later to see. All income was now to be at the disposal of the state, for the asserted benefit of the people.

For the carrying on and managing of the state industry after the ending of the new economic policy there were called into being the state trusts, which now took the field. These were to be followed by state planning systems by which within a given or fixed period production was to be placed under specific bounds and according to predetermined standards. (This matter is later to be considered.)[1]

[1] See *post*, p. 216.

Trusts somewhat like corporations in capitalistic countries, but with power in the hands of the state and with state monopoly alone possible, were largely organizations for the production of goods; into them were grouped industrial plants of different categories. For the purpose of supplying raw materials, conducting trade, marketing output, and securing credit, there could be created what were known as syndicates, perhaps involving unification or coördination between certain trusts; they could act as intermediaries between the trust and the market. Syndicates might pass into combines of larger scope, or overall organizations (to an extent on the order of holding companies in America), concerned in production, selling, and other matters, including the providing of supplies for a producer, besides securing government subventions and serving in a general advisory capacity. (In Czaristic Russia there were organizations on the order of trusts and syndicates, though not of socialistic character.)

These organizations might have comprehensive programs, and could adopt wide policies as to production and distribution of goods. In some cases they were set up rather along geographical lines. Trusts were to be conducted according to strict business principles. They were as far as possible to be self-sustaining. Those that were not might require state subsidization for a greater or less length of time. If requests for state aid were too insistent or too frequent, there was need for investigation. A considerable part of profits were to go to the government, while small proportions were set aside for a reserve fund, for improvements or technical developments, and for welfare work or cultural activities in behalf of the employees. The managers and directors were to be largely concerned with cheapening and improving their products and their processes of production. Prices for different commodities were to be determined in relation to several considerations: costs of production (including transportation charges), state and consumer needs, character of article in relation to other articles, and planned profit, together with the "turnover" tax (later to be considered).[1]

Though the manufacture of goods as a form of the production of wealth, no less than their sale, was essentially in the Soviet country a state affair, there were slight exceptions—but exceptions not greatly affecting the situation as a whole. In general one could manufacture for sale what was his own work alone, without the employment of another. Practically speaking, handicraft trades were in earlier days about the only ones in the land of which this was true.

For a long time in different parts of Russia there had been, as we have seen, home or village manufacturing of simple articles of one kind and another, to be disposed of as one could.[2] Under the Soviet régime home craftsmen were permitted in some measure to continue to ply their trade, and a certain amount of small-scale manufacturing was thus possible—if tacked into the general state industrial organization. Sales of articles made by this process were in large part, as we have already found, without a very definite business organization. No small portion were peddled from house to house over the land. Production of this nature, however, proceeded at a diminishing rate under Soviet auspices. It did not appeal very strongly to the state authorities, and for a time was not encouraged. Later certain advantages were seen in it; and there was even to some extent promotion of handicrafts on farms and in small shops in the towns, particularly through coöperative bodies. With the building up of factory labor forces there was less place for home workers.

Trade (apart from that involved in the operations of trusts), which was to involve the distribution in general of the wealth of the land, was on the whole a little more gradual in passing from private hands, or in suffering "liquidation." Foreign trade was of course a government monopoly from the beginning (always in the currency of the foreign nation). Private

[1] See *post,* p. 194.
[2] See *ante,* p. 67.

trade was in a small way, as we have seen, permitted for a time with the "new economic policy."

During the continuance of that policy one was allowed to sell or market one's own products: there was limited capitalism on the farm or in a modest industry. But all this was only a temporary makeshift. With the end of the new economic policy, private trade, practically speaking, stopped except in some minor or local situation. Even when private shops might legally remain in operation, they still had their way strewn with difficulties. It was far from easy, as we have seen, for a private local dealer to get stock or supplies from the proper state agency; they could not be obtained from a state emporium unless under special circumstances. Goods could not be imported. They were mostly to be had from peasant farmers, or from occasional small producers of other kinds. For what they purchased they were charged higher prices. Nor was it any easier to get credit when this was necessary to carry on one's business. There might also be severe restrictions upon such matters as the hours when private places could be kept open—in general less favorable hours than those of the state establishments. Virtually always, furthermore, whatever small and restricted business and commercial undertakings were privately owned had to face state competition, and the ever present possibility of state expropriation—to say nothing of the constant likelihood of more or less heavy taxation befalling them. It was thus next to impossible to carry on one's private business with any considerable expectation of success; it was doomed from the start. For none did the outlook appear bright, and it was usually not long before their fate overtook them.

Somewhat more indulgent was the attitude toward farm products direct from the farm. A greater or less amount of the products of collective farmers as well as of homestead farmers (so far as the latter existed) could be sold to private purchasers, though always under careful state oversight.[1] As we have seen,

[1] See *post,* pp. 212, 213.

one could as a general thing sell what he had made himself, when without the employment of another person. Nowhere was there place for the middleman.

A special form or phase of private selling which was countenanced to an extent by the state was the peasant market, something to which Russian peasants had long been accustomed. Booths and storage facilities for the purpose might be provided by the state. Here under due restrictions certain products could be brought and sold, with the economic law of supply and demand thus more or less in operation. Farmers in general appreciated this privilege, as they preferred to do their buying and selling in this way as far as they could, taking less kindly to the state's shops or stores. They had, however, to compete more or less with these shops or stores, which could always set the price—prices of agricultural products sold privately being more or less affected by the prices established by the state. Prices in peasant markets were relatively high to outsiders—something that was true in general of free markets. Sales here were largely of food products, though articles of other kinds could be included, even certain used articles.

In some areas a place, though a diminishing one, might be made for open street sales, or bazaars, long a part of the old Russia. Barter in general had a footing in the exchange of goods. It had by no means disappeared in the Soviet country.

Rural fairs were another institution that had long been known in Russia. They were retained for a time in the Soviet state. Restrictions upon them, however, caused them for the most part to be gradually given up. The old-time fairs of certain large cities might continue for a period within set bounds.

Another class who could carry on private sales in greater or less degree were, as we have seen, persons who fabricated articles in their homes or as craftsmen in some selling organization —something also long recognized in Russia. They were for the most part free to sell their products for whatever price these would bring, provided no extraneous profit accrued from the transaction; but even here such activities might readily be swept into those of a regular coöperative body. Peddling of articles, especially those from the farm or made in the home or village—or articles in general not produced in a regular factory—received a measure of tolerance in the Soviet land, though in later years they had rather to be confined to particular areas or to give way to the use of permanent stands or booths set up by the state (possibly to be rented by the users). Certain coöperative associations, particularly those created for the purpose, were likewise in position to sell their goods. This was especially true with regard to agricultural products.[1]

Facilities for the purchase of goods, wholesale or retail, became in time largely state-owned—in general in the hands of a state trust, commissariat, or similar state organization. Practically all manufactured articles except certain local handicraft articles were sold, if not through coöperative bodies, through such stores. Of all retail trade over one-half was at most times in the hands of the state, something like one-fifth with coöperative bodies, and the remainder in free markets.

Government stores, like regular private stores, were conducted for profit, but here the profit was for the state alone. They carried on advertisements of their wares, though not for the usual reasons—to compete with other stores—but to educate the people as to the desirability of the goods to be sold and to create a demand for them. Stores belonged to a general system—what in America would be called "chain stores." They were for the most part by the nature of the case what are known as "cash and carry." State shops of different grades were possible, some containing "extras," or goods not under rationing, or goods of better quality or wider variety than others, and open to different classes of customers or purchasers. Certain ones (some discontinued), perhaps having articles of luxury in stock (some of which came from former affluent citizens in exchange for more needed essentials of life), re-

[1] See *post*, p. 212.

quired all purchases in gold or silver, or in foreign currency, these being patronized in large part by citizens of foreign countries who were in Russia. Some of the larger industrial establishments and collective farms maintained stores for the service of their workers.

For the people in general there were two kinds of stores— those known as "commercial" and the ration stores. The former could charge relatively high prices, perhaps very high, open to all who had money to spend here. The ration stores were the low-cost ones, often with relatively little to be sold, some at times run at a loss. In later years attempt was made by the state to bring about something of an equalization in the matter, with the abandonment of the ration stores, and with all goods sold at the commercial stores at a single but somewhat higher price than had been the case with the ration stores.

Wherever state action might be wanting in the field of trade in general, there was something close to it in the coöperative associations in the country, something to which reference has just been made. These were as a rule not the independent undertakings under this name which are found in other lands, but in the Soviet Union a movement directly under the auspices of the government, and in fact an immediate link in the state business machine. Coöperative bodies here were in a sort of twilight zone between capitalism and socialism—on the one hand, with "shares" in the hands of individual citizens and with due participation on their part in accruing gains, and, on the other hand, with greater or less direction and control by the government, and with the exploitation of no person in their activities, or with the use of the hired labor of none. Such bodies received much encouragement and assistance from the state. In their mercantile operations they could expect materials of better quality to handle, lower wholesale prices, lower transportation charges, less difficulty in securing credit with lower rates of interest on loans, and lower taxes. Advantages of membership were constantly pointed out. (For a time membership of persons eligible was virtually compulsory.) There were some features not unlike those of labor unions, especially in recreational, educational, and cultural activities, but not on so wide a scale.

Coöperative bodies, especially of consumers, had long been known in Russia, and were something with which a considerable number of people were already more or less familiar.[1] In the new Soviet order they might be of consumers or of producers, including to an extent market dealers. Operations of some associations, especially of city consumers, which might more or less compete with the state stores, were in time liable to be transferred to the state, to be conducted through or as a state enterprise, though in later years they received certain encouragement. Greater indulgence was allowed to rural organizations; more of them could remain on their feet. In rural areas consumer coöperatives were the main means of buying goods. Despite the general advantages accorded to coöperative bodies, some of them, particularly some of the coöperative stores, seemed not to have been managed altogether according to businesslike principles, and ran into difficulties.

Consumer bodies were concerned with the purchasing of various articles, notably food products, a particular activity being the securing, preparing, and serving of food in public eating places. Considerable buying was on the peasant market. Producer bodies were in earlier days concerned largely with the disposal of handicraft articles (especially consumer goods, including articles of clothing, household utensils, etc.), and also to an extent with agricultural products, or with the processing of a commodity like lumber or brick; further examples were in fisherman or hunter groups. In later years, to increase general production in the country, a larger field for producers' organizations was permitted, the state even allowing the use of its machinery or material for the purpose. Coöperative housing was likewise for a greater or less length of time an important

[1] See *ante*, p. 71.

form of the movement.[1] Coöperative stores did at times considerable business. As a general thing the goods they sold were the cheapest of all. Prices set by coöperative bodies were to bear a definite relation to those of the state stores.

Private trading through middlemen was of course always legally barred. One could not sell the goods of another; nor could one rent the goods of another. Private speculation none the less in different commodities, or buying low and selling higher, perhaps with respect to articles procured at some cheaper mart, practically always persisted in greater or less measure even in this socialistic land. Nor is it to be thought that there was not illegal private trade of other kinds, as bootlegging or black market dealings. Improper housing transactions were far from unknown. At times middlemen through coöperative bodies were charged with taking advantage of low-paid workers. Some such practices as these would be almost impossible to prevent altogether in any circumstances. There were nearly at all times, now more frequently, now less frequently, operations of this nature. Illegal trading on the whole, however, was not often of great moment. Large profits were as a general thing not possible here. The government put forth strenuous and determined efforts to break up all such transactions. For them were imposed severe penalties. To meet a particular form of profiteering—that of taking advantage of a time of price inflation, with a shortage of consumer goods, and accumulating money while it rose in value—the state could take the drastic step of devaluating its currency. Such profiteers were disposed to hoard their money rather than put it into banks, as in the latter case they could be asked embarrassing questions as to how they came by it.[2]

By the Soviet state there were carried on various forms of insurance (life, fire, theft, etc.). There was practically nothing left in private hands. Any such insurance taken out was in ad-

[1] See *post*, p. 286.
[2] See *post*, p. 192.

190

dition to what the state had undertaken to provide of itself.

At the outset the Soviet country had to try the experiment of getting along without money—not altogether from deliberate purpose, but rather in consequence of the exigencies of the early days of its existence. It was then that barter became the generally prevailing means of exchange over the land. There was also at that time an issue of paper money, which quickly ceased to have value except in great quantities; and a period of inflation swept over the country, something not unknown to it from Czaristic years. It was recognized before long by the Soviet authorities that regular money was an essential factor in the workings of the new state, socialistic though it was, the temporary resort to the "new economic policy" having, for one thing, done so much to establish the use of money and put it into circulation. It remained true, however, that as a general thing money or "cash" had a slightly more restricted employment here than in the case of capitalistic countries in general.

When the Soviet Union took steps to meet its early monetary difficulties and proceeded to set up a currency system, it was a stable or balanced one that was brought into being, which in due time drove out the old depreciated currency. The system was a managed one, but based upon genuine intrinsic values, supposedly with little fluctuation. There was something like a gold standard (as was the case with Czaristic Russia), or a "hard currency," with a reserve of gold or other precious metals, to meet national or international obligations.[1]

It is a notable commentary on socialistic procedure in the Soviet Union, and at a time when it was trying its wings, that there was little place or sympathy with anything other than a sound money policy; there was no suggestion or consideration of any wildcat financial venture. For all its socialistic principles and convictions, the Soviet government in more than one way

---

[1] The chief coin, the ruble, was at one time 5.3 in terms of exchange for one dollar of United States money. Later the ruble was to equal so many grams of gold, with one ruble exchangeable for twenty-five cents of American money.

proved that it was not unmindful or unheedful of good business practices. It was not a rash adventurer in this field; it displayed business acumen and sagacity. It moved in general on solid financial ground. There was demanded a reliable, accredited financial system—a demand of no less potency than in a capitalistic nation—even though it had to fall in with the peculiar Soviet economy.

The Soviet state as a socialistic one had free and uninhibited powers over its currency system, and in times of financial crisis could move as was deemed best to meet it—for there could be financial crisis here no less than in capitalistic countries. A particular occasion was that following the Second World War, with heavy expenditures of money forced on the land, with a great increase in the amount of currency (some counterfeited by the Germans), with speculation possible through the accumulation of an appreciated money, and with an insufficient supply of consumer goods to be had in general, when it resorted to the expedient of devaluating its currency, requiring more of a given circulating medium to equal what had been the case before—calling in what money was outstanding and replacing it with a smaller number of monetary units.[1] Not only were hoarders adversely affected, but farmers and others who were inclined to use the savings banks but sparingly. In some respects this procedure was nothing less than an act of repudiation in financial matters, but there was something to be said for it—for one thing, the consumer could now for the most part get more for his money. Some such procedure has been followed in countries not communistic.

Importation and exportation of Soviet money was forbidden. In foreign trade and in financial relations in general with other

---

[1] Money on this occasion in hand, or "cash," generally was reduced to one-tenth of its original valuation. Money in savings banks of relatively small amount (as was often the case) suffered no change; higher amounts were reduced by one-third, and still higher by one-half. Government bonds were reduced to one-third, and earlier ones to one-fifth. Payments on account of such bodies as coöperative associations or collective farms were reduced by one-fifth.

countries Soviet Russia sought to live up to its obligations—despite the fact that debts incurred under the reign of the Czar were repudiated.

It was seen or taken for granted by the same processes of reasoning as called for a currency system, that banks were something that could not well be dispensed with even in a socialistic state, no more than in a capitalistic one. A general banking system was set up, with branch banks over the land, and having many of the features and functions of banking systems in capitalistic countries; but there it was under the immediate control and direction of the state, designed to promote its interests and to serve its general ends. Indeed, the so-called bank here might be regarded, not always as a bank in the usual meaning of that term, but rather as a necessary department of the state commissariat of finance. It was indispensable in settling accounts between the government and its various agencies, in making advances of one kind or another to them or in receiving payments from them. Banks could also be used for rent payments and other public services.

Even in Soviet land interest was possible on money that was lent out; such practice was neither tabooed nor abhorred in the practical, realistic life of the Soviet state. The procedure was for the gain of the state and of the individual citizen alike. Rates of interest appeared to be fair and reasonable, and pretty much the same as in capitalistic countries.

As in capitalistic lands also, the Soviet banks sought to make all the money they could, but only for the advantage and increment of the state. Among other activities banks could allow credit to different state institutions or agencies, or have subsidies granted to them. Savings banks, with interest on deposits (guaranteed by the government), were likewise part of the Soviet fiscal economy, and were available to and at the service of the citizens. By the banks something on the order of letters of credit could be issued, but with the use of what are known as checking accounts to hardly any appreciable extent. Loans might be made by the government or by its banks to state trusts, state factories, collective farms, coöperative associations, trade unions, clubs, local governmental units, or for the promotion of some state planning program. Under proper circumstances money might be lent to individuals, as for the building of homes.

The government could borrow money from its citizens. Money might be lent to it through the buying of interest-bearing bonds. In fact, there might be enthusiastic campaigns to induce the people to purchase bonds; what is more, certain pressure might be exerted upon them to this end—it might not always be safe not to do as expected here. Payment for bonds could be deducted from the wages one received, with at least ostensible willingness. There might also be offered bonuses in the matter. Some organizations in the state, as coöperative bodies, might be required to invest in state bonds. Lotteries were an accepted means for raising money by the state. During the Second World War certain gifts were made to the government by individuals and groups.

Government revenue was to be had from several sources, besides those just mentioned, and besides the direct gains from the early direct expropriation of property. First was a "turn-over" tax, something like the sales tax known in America, but with important differences. According to the Soviet plan, taxes were collected when goods were produced or manufactured—in the "make-up" of goods at different stages, or whenever goods changed hands in the process of production. After due consideration of the costs of production, distribution (including delivery), inspection, etc., the tax was added on—it was imposed after proper allowances were made for the cost of these several factors. This tax applied to industries in general. Its amount was based largely upon the abundance and character of the article in question, and upon its destination. It also depended in some degree upon what goods the government wished to encourage in production and upon what it wished to discourage. It was believed that this tax could help to re-distribute the balance between the costs of consumers' goods and the costs of producers' goods. It ostensibly served to reduce unnecessary personal consumption, and effected some saving on capital goods.

The tax was eventually to be passed on to the consumer; being a concealed tax, it was relatively easy to apply. The amount of the tax varied greatly with the nature and use of a given article—from one or two per cent, or even less, to three-fourths or nine-tenths, or almost all its supposed value. Articles of necessity or articles to meet basic needs could have a very low rate, perhaps only a nominal one; articles of luxury could have a very high one. The tax on vegetables was rela-tively low, to encourage alike their growth and their consump-tion. The tax on intoxicating liquor was, conversely, high. As, however, there was little in the way of luxuries or what we call creature comforts produced in the Soviet country, the actual revenue from this source proved slight, despite its nominally high rate. In consequence most of the returns from the turn-over tax came from taxes upon the necessaries of life of the general population, which could often amount to a stout sum. It has been described as a sales tax with a vengeance. It could cut deeply into the citizen's income. (This tax largely took the place of a former sort of trade licenses, together with certain scattered small taxes.)

It was the turnover tax that in general provided well over half of the revenue for the state. There could be with or in it a designated tax levied upon profits from state enterprises (a sort of excess profit tax)—state enterprises affording both a turnover tax and a profit. Part of the profits from state-owned industries were expected to go for replacement, expansion, or improvements, and for social welfare measures.

There were charges by the state for the use of tractors and other agricultural implements on farms. There were special taxes in the form of licenses on certain occupations to do business tinged with a more or less private character. There were also various excise and similar taxes, as those on royalties, insurance premiums, certain financial accounts, admission to entertainments, railway tickets, etc., apart from certain so-called luxury taxes. Included were stamps for certain business transactions or legal documents. Likewise there was a duty on exports, and a tariff on imports. There were duties on passports to leave the county, so high in fact as to be next to prohibitory if not entirely so.

Still another source of revenue to the state was the income tax. This tax might be little or but nominal, or nothing at all, for those with meagre incomes, but pretty high for those who were regarded in the Soviet country as relatively affluent. Income taxes could be applied in the withholding of wages. There were several categories of the population upon which the tax was specifically laid. One was producers of goods not otherwise covered, the tax here on the whole not being of great amount. Another consisted of professional classes, including writers or persons with no fixed salaries, the tax here being progressively steep, though not greatly more than in some capitalistic countries. A third category was of independent artisans or other persons who produced goods on their own account, or not members of some coöperative organization, with possibly a very high rate, unless happening to have meagre earnings from their occupations—the purpose here being frankly to discourage such private production.

There was also imposed what was called an agricultural tax, really hardly other than an income tax, on the products of farms, whether the collective or the homestead one. Though persons with unduly large incomes could be taxed accordingly, proceeds from the agricultural tax were as a general thing relatively small. There was also a certain tax on coöperative bodies. Receipts from the income tax were on the whole not great, there not being many in the land with considerable incomes.

There was a special tax on bachelors and on families with

few children. Taxes were reduced for those having dependents, especially families in which there were a considerable number of children or families widowed or orphaned through war. Largely or altogether exempt from the payment of an income tax was the bonus, honorarium, or public gift to national heroes, whether soldiers, scientists, inventors, industrial engineers, outstanding artists, or other persons who were regarded as having done well by the state. Tax need not be paid on deposits in savings banks or on the income from state bonds.

There was likewise for a time (later abolished) an inheritance tax or death duties—something supposed to be contrary to one of the cardinal principles of Marxian socialism—which was of progressive character, not applying to inheritances of small value and with certain things, as bank savings, exempt. Neither in character nor in rates was the Soviet inheritance tax greatly different from that prevailing in some capitalistic countries—something that was true to no small extent of the general taxation system of the Soviet state. Again this state showed the accepted understanding of fiscal matters.

A potential source of revenue to the state lay in the rent of houses or other forms of real estate—the state being the only lessor recognized in the land; in a large measure, however, what was not directly the property of the state, as a dwelling house, belonged immediately rather to a municipality, local Soviet, trade union, coöperative body, etc. (the supreme state of course remaining the ultimate possessor).

In remote regions or regions with limited economic resources the burden of taxation was more or less lightened. Receipts from taxation were duly apportioned or allocated between the several governmental levels. There might be particular taxation for the benefit of some local community, but fitting into the general scheme.

No property might be used in the hands of the individual for the production of further wealth. Accumulation of possessions that were not directly earned or were earned with hired labor was under definite ban. Ownership of private property was legally possible; it was allowed, but only to a limited extent, and then with qualifications—and never of a sort that would interfere with or halt the operations of the socialist state. The right of private property in land was formally abolished; it could not be sold, bought, leased, or bequeathed. A man could occupy his dwelling virtually as his own (provided it did not have more than a few rooms)—he could have an indefinitely long occupancy except that for reasons of its own the state might step in at any time and take over. He could not own the land upon which the dwelling was built—the land itself belonged altogether and outright to the state. It was capable of being rented, as the term is ordinarily understood, only from the state. Thus in a sense while land was not subject to private ownership, the buildings upon it were. With the house might go a garden plot, the products from which belonged to the occupant. A home or quarters in one might theoretically be rented, but there must be no profit involved in the transaction for the benefit of an individual, all being under careful state regulation. Speculation of any kind in matters pertaining to one's dwelling was rigidly forbidden. Special lease of used land might be permitted in the event of a natural calamity or in certain other special circumstances.

Private property was permitted in the furnishing of one's home, household articles, articles of personal use or convenience (or consumers' goods in general), and also in one's earnings and savings (including interest on government bonds), as well as in craftsman's tools for one's own use. Such things as patents and copyrights were likewise subject in greater or less measure to private ownership.

What was possessed by an individual could in general be bequeathed. There might be bequests or legacies not only to individuals, especially dependents, but to institutions and associations. Property could be passed on to one's children—that is, the right of inheritance was recognized. Dependents of a deceased person not provided for had prior legal claims to sharing what had been owned. Property could thus to an extent remain in one's family. Where there were no relatives, the property of a deceased person simply reverted to the state. Goods of an intestate were disposed of as in most other countries.

The products of one's own labor and efforts (without the compensated employment of another person) were his property; he could dispose of them as he wished, perhaps in sales—though he could not do this with what had been produced by another. One could have the usufruct of a tract of land of a few acres around his home for the raising of small crops or vegetables or livestock—such as could not be used for the creation of further wealth, or for the increase of one's possessions—or a garden or orchard or poultry yard.[1] One could also own small implements to be used on this homestead, or home tools and auxiliary husbandry articles in general—or tools employed in some small individual trade (as that of a shoemaker). Collective farms were in a particular sense the property of those organizations concerned with them; they were supposed to be leased perpetually from the state to the collective group. Such groups might also own equipment and appurtenances in their agricultural work.[2]

It was the rule in the Soviet country that none could exploit the labor of another; in the economic organization of this land there could be no employment of another for one's own profit, or in the production of wealth. Private economy was, however, allowed in a limited way. Hired labor might at times be permitted on a farm or in an industrial enterprise when for some reason those naturally expected to be engaged with it were not available. In some instances, as with producers' bodies, there might be under prescribed conditions employment of home workers unable to leave home because of disability or urgent home needs. Certain forms of industrial work were authorized

1 See *post*, p. 213.
2 See *post*, p. 208.

for private hands, as in handicraft operations, as we have seen. The production also of some homely commodity made to order, certain repair work, or the doing of certain tasks of a personal nature (as those of electricians, tailors, shoemakers, and the like) was likewise permitted. An extra penny might now and then in this manner be picked up, after the quota of one's state assignments had been met—provided that no "profit" was involved in the undertaking. Forms of private employment, all involving self-employment, included that of launderers, barbers, opticians, dressmakers, shoemakers, bootblacks, chauffeurs (or the more familiar drivers of droshkies). Repair work might be done individually or by coöperative groups, as with carpenters or painters. Personal services, as of secretaries or domestic servants, could under proper circumstances be had, without involving the creation of individual wealth, and with all due restrictions and regulations.

For services rather of a professional nature, or requiring specialized training for their accomplishment, as those of teachers or musicians, there might be payment made, but under appropriate state direction. In a profession like that of the physician or dentist private practice was theoretically possible, but in competition with an all but complete system of state medicine. Though one was entitled to free medical service from the state, he was at liberty to engage additional or special services at his own expense. Private practitioners could hardly be expected to provide their necessary medical equipment. In exceptional cases in private practice a substantial sum was nominally possible, but again within state regulations. Professional persons could on the whole expect little private work—only in the few odd hours when they were not in the service of the state, much of one's professional time having to be given to it—these extra or outside hours, furthermore, being those when one was not at his freshest. Trouble in general lay ahead if there was need of an assistant in their work, such hiring not being within legal authorization. Private practitioners must always be on the lookout for a special tax. They were also without the benefits attaching to trade unions or coöperative bodies. All such private activities were in keeping with general Soviet trends, possibly passing sooner or later into state or coöperative activities.

From the circumstance that there was in the Soviet land no formal limitation upon the amount of property one might own, together with the fact that the receiving of state interest might be included in one's income, and that in certain callings a relatively considerable sum of money might be earned, let it not be inferred that some of the Soviet citizens might have been on the way to the accumulation of riches or to the taking to themselves of an undue portion of the goods of the land. Total income could always in some manner be kept from exceeding certain limits, whether directly fixed by the state or not. (Reference to possible incomes is made in later connection.)[1] Taxes of some kind could, for one thing, be made to bear strongly upon one who appeared to be in the direction of amassing too much wealth or of approaching a state of too great affluence; state imposts could be made to have a fairly close relation to the size of one's income. In this land of Spartan virtue even the appearance of conspicuous wealth was discouraged. If there seemed in the possession of a citizen more wealth than appeared good or sufficient for him or than for him to live on in reasonable Soviet comfort, the government need not feel its hands tied or hindered from stepping in; it could without too great difficulty find a way to take appropriate restrictive action. Ways could even be found to circumvent the accumulation of money from such illegal practices as black market operations or speculation in the price of commodities (as had been the case in particular in the days of the "new economic policy" and following the Second World War). Devaluation of the nation's currency could always strike hard here.[2]

One's earnings could not be employed for the increase of

[1] See *post*, p. 246.
[2] See *ante*, p. 192.

one's wealth by any form of private enterprise. They could be used only in one of several specific ways—placing in government savings banks, investment in government bonds, or hoarded in one's domicile—unless expended at once for some particular article of consumption. Accumulation of wealth as such was not forbidden or directly opposed. But the essential consideration was that what one received in money must be used up; it must be absorbed into the general wealth of the state. Nothing was to be done to encourage the growth of a moneyed or "capitalist" class in the land. The state was determined to prevent the rise of any such class.

CHAPTER XII

The Soviet State and Its Farm Operations

THE whole issue of Soviet socialism might have had a more favorable outcome, with greater assurance in earlier days of success and stability, had not the rural situation in Russia had to be reckoned with. That country was essentially an agricultural land, with the bulk of its population, at least till the more recent years, living on farms and away from the cities. From practically the beginning the Soviet authorities were engaged in the proper "socialization" of this population, an undertaking bristling with difficulties and dangers of a kind unknown in the cities. The situation was made all the worse by what was told the country peasant at the commencement of the revolution and of the new order. He was told that the great landed estates were to be broken up and placed in the hands of peasant proprietors, a process in which he had himself already been more or less engaged. It was this announcement and this promise that largely won over the peasant masses and caused them to cast in their allegiance with the Soviet party, or at least not to make a decided stand in opposition.

Later the peasant heard himself listening to a different story. He was now told that the products of his farm, which he felt were mainly due to his bodily labor, were not to be his after all, for him to do with as he pleased; but that they might be appropriated by the state as it might think best. He also learned that the land which he thought was his was to be taken over and joined to others in a great state farm, upon which, more or less as a mere employee, he might be compelled to do whatever tasks were allotted him.

The great question in rural areas thus became of twofold nature: whether the peasants might retain their own farmsteads if they wished; and whether those who wanted to save up something and have something which they could call their own, to be sold at such price as they might see fit, might do so. Could the peasants in general come to favor state or collective farms over their own long-sought private holdings? Would they consent to have no direct possession or ownership over what they might produce with the labor of their own hands and through their own individual efforts—something that they and their fathers had been used to? Here was being prepared the great battleground on which in no small part was to be fought the issue of socialism in Russia. Was it a struggle at bottom against human nature, or against man's instinctive desire for the personal holding of land?

If collective or state farms should have been generally established, if they should have attained a considerable measure of success, and if the farming population as a whole had approved of the system, or at least had acquiesced in it without serious objection, then the Soviet state would have had a great achievement to its credit, and it would have proved to the world in no small measure its stability. But if this was to be brought about fundamentally through the use of force, the policy could not be written down as anything like a complete success.

From the outset the Soviet authorities had resolved that all peasant proprietorships of whatever kind must sooner or later go, and the sooner the better. They could not endure a "capitalistic" class in their new order, even among the humble farmers of the country.

But the collectivation or socialization of the farms was not to take place at once. It was to go forward by some sort of evolutionary process, with whatever of finesse or diplomacy was called for, if not by force as the eventual recourse, and with as much rapidity as was safe and desirable for all concerned. We have seen how in the early days of the Soviet state the peasant farmers were angered and embittered by having their products taken from them to feed the population of the land, especially the city population.[1] We have also seen how efforts were made to mollify and placate the peasant by the introduction for a time of what was known as the "new economic policy," which, a temporary relapse from strict socialism, so warmed the peasant's heart. After it the way was to be paved for state socialism on the farm, with the encouragement and facilitation of coöperative agricultural associations, something with which they were generally more or less familiar, as the principal step in that direction. An educational campaign was at the same time to be undertaken on the part of the Soviet authorities, to make the peasants see on their own account the value of collective farming.

The peasants were to be made to realize the oneness of the people of Russia and the need of their acting in harmony, with recognition of the interdependence of the country and the city dweller. In fact, there was felt to be not a little missionary work called for, not only to have the peasants get the proper point of view, but in the meantime to obtain necessary food supplies from them. Agents flocked to rural regions to explain the situation and to show the advantages of collective production on the farms. They were even armed with promises of special favors in case of compliance—and perhaps armed otherwise in case of non-complaince. Some proved themselves overzealous in the cause. All these elaborate and painstaking efforts were for the most part initially unavailing, though in certain areas or with certain groups they eventually proved more effective. The great number of the peasants, already not a little incensed against the Soviet powers, displayed anything but reciprocal good-will towards the overtures made to them; rather they incontinently repulsed them. There was little inclination on the

[1] See *ante*, p. 164.

part of the peasant farmer to surrender the property which he regarded as his own, to any outsider, even the Soviet state.

It was now that the Soviet authorities felt it incumbent upon them to take measures sharper and more drastic than attempts at peaceful persuasion. There was to be instituted a process of "liquidation" of peasant proprietorship, or of the pressing of all land into state or collective farms with the elimination of any who dared resist.

This new policy of violence was to encounter opposition that was of no less violence. Main resistance came from the "kulaks," a term not to be confined to more or less "rich" land owners, but to be applied to many who had simply been thrifty and relatively more skilled, and had become relatively well-to-do, including some who had lent money, rented out agricultural implements, or had engaged in other remunerative local enterprises. A considerable number of the peasants, even if not to be identified with the kulaks, were disposed to side with them, not being greatly impressed with the class distinctions so vigorously insisted upon by the Soviet agents, and in many cases being bound to the kulaks by ties of friendship if not by ties of blood. Some kulaks, on the other hand, had made themselves thoroughly obnoxious to the peasants. These had been quite harsh, exacting, grasping in their dealings with their poorer neighbors, had oppressed, and had exploited them. Such a kulak not infrequently bore down very hard on those peasants who were in debt to him, or whose property had become mortgaged to him. Payment for debt had sometimes to be made in cruel labor. Interest charges were at times exorbitant—real usury. The peasants could have little recourse to the law to help them out. Kulaks were too often mortgage holders or land speculators. The latter type of kulaks received little sympathy, no more than from the socialistic state itself.

Peasant farmers, whether or not kulaks, who were antagonistic to the Soviet demands were suspected, and often rightly enough, of storing or hiding the products of their farms or other possessions. Agents of the government who sought to take these things were fought off, and at times came off second best. To both passive and active resistance the hostile peasants resorted. They refused to sow or to reap. Sometimes they disposed of what they had as best they could; if nothing better was at hand, destruction was possible, of grain and livestock alike. (Over one-half of the livestock was destroyed.) Sabotage was perhaps a new weapon to their hands, but one they found they could effectively employ. A portion of them decided that there was no hope for them on the farm, and left for the cities.

Pressure of all kinds was exercised upon the obstinate, recalcitrant farmers; and finally force was employed to make them yield. For lack of coöperation severe penalties were imposed. It was made a crime to kill livestock. An early measure to deal with the kulaks was restriction upon the amount of land or of labor which they could use. In a supreme effort to bring about the capitulation of the stubborn farmers, there was effected a mass removal of uncounted numbers from their homes. Some were separated from their families; some had their families taken with them. In certain cases kulaks or other obnoxious farmers were exiled not only as punishment, but as a means of getting forced labor elsewhere. In this drastic process some were slain at the outset, others fell by the way as they were shifted over the country, and still others were deported or exiled to far-away regions where they were left to perish of cold or starvation or to meet other wretched ends—a tale hardly paralleled in modern history. The Soviet authorities never disavowed their willingness to sacrifice great numbers of the population to attain their socialized goal, and expressed no qualms with respect thereto.[1]

Thus the farms of the peasant proprietors were taken from

[1] By the Soviet authorities it was sometimes stated that the peasants in general "demanded" the deportation of the kulaks. The following is an illustration: "The millions of peasants, wholeheartedly supported the policy of the government." "Soviet Farming" published by the Soviet government at the time of its exhibit at the New York World's Fair, 1939, p. 13.

them the length and breadth of the land, whether voluntarily or not—and there were some who willingly and of their own accord submitted. Peasants with small property or with little to lose were more disposed and ready to enter a collective farm. Some, especially those of the kulak type, had no other resort; they were forced in. The collective farm idea, however, was not altogether a new or novel thing in Russia. We have already taken notice of the communal systems in use in pre-Soviet days.[1]

The peasant farms were mostly absorbed or incorporated into larger farm institutions or collective organizations, all in reality the creatures of the state. These new farms were in an ascending order according to the degree or extent of state control. There were three forms which involved a variety of collective ownership in the hands of a number of persons pooling their land and working in common, but with general state oversight, direction, or planning. The lowest form was a sort of limited coöperative association, with the members individually living in their homes, owning their own tools, and coming together for joint agricultural purposes. The second form was that of a group living in individual homes, but with the basic means of production held in common, and paid according to the labor performed by each. The third was a body where all lived and worked together, all property being held in common except personal property, and where all shared the proceeds of their joint endeavors—approaching more distinctly a real communal arrangement. There was also a fourth form, the highest of all, which, in fact, constituted the culmination of the system —a state farm directly in the hands of the government, organized and operating much on the order of a state factory. This last, however, appeared on the whole less advantageous and promising than the others, though it might be used to a considerable extent as an agricultural laboratory or experiment station or for specialized operations, or as a sort of model farm.

[1] See *ante*, pp. 42, 61, 78.

Only a relatively small proportion of the total number of farms were of this type.

The first form, where only land was held in common, was of a declining order. The second form, or that where land, buildings, animals, implements, etc., were jointly owned, but not the homes of the different workers, was regarded as the most efficient of all, and on the whole the most desirable one; it was the one most frequently to be found. This form, which was a degree less than a fully communal one or than one under full state control, would indicate a certain recognition of the value of a person's having his own home in which to live. A completely individually owned farm, however, would not fare so well. There would be various discriminatory practices directed toward it. It would have to face heavy taxation, difficulties in securing the use of tractors and other implements, it not being possible to purchase or rent farm machinery, and other obstacles. Loans would be hard to get. Livestock or seeds could not easily be procured. Certain small individual farms had, it is true, nominal existence, but in a steadily diminishing number, practically to a vanishing point. No individual farm could be leased.

Collective farms were under perpetual lease to the group in charge of them. With the payment of the tax a farm might theoretically be regarded as rented from the state. The land so used could not be sold; nor could a member sell his share if and when he left. In general a worker might withdraw from a collective farm provided there was no loss or disadvantage occasioned thereby to the farm or to the farm group, and always with the consent and approval of the state. A worker received "credit" according to the labor or time expended by him in farm operations. A minimum amount of labor was required of all (usually not less than 100 or 150 days during the year). Those doing the more difficult tasks could be allowed more "credit" days or more pay. Workers on a collective farm included not only actual farm operators, but clerical workers, bookkeepers, accountants, and others, besides engineers and various types of mechanics—these last named constituting a fairly large proportion of the total.

The worker on a collective farm occupied something of an anomalous position. He was a sort of cross between an owner and a mere farm hand. In his capacity as a member of an agricultural association cultivating a certain tract of land, he was in the position of owner; as a worker who had little choice in the operations, whose every action after all was at the behest of the state, and who had to labor as he was bidden, he was little better than a hired laborer under compulsion, perhaps a serf of a sort. Under the system no simply hired worker as such could be employed, though in later days this ruling was in special circumstances more or less modified.

The government always stood by, and was prepared to exert itself to aid in the farming of the land. It supplied tractors, harvest combines, and other agricultural implements. There were machine and tractor stations, each serving a given area. It sent out expert agents to educate and to advise as to proper and advanced agricultural methods. It bespoke the use of the most modern and most efficient machinery. For new and undeveloped regions it provided loans of money, seeds, livestock, and a certain amount of equipment. Compulsory insurance applied alike to farm buildings, crops, and livestock, no less than to an industrial establishment or town dwelling. It is needless to add that the government had much to say as to the scope and methods to be employed on farms of whatever kind.

The collective farms sometimes had troubles to be faced. In certain years there were serious famines in the country. In some places agricultural implements were not of the best, and, particularly in the earlier years, were far from adequate. Breakdowns and fuel shortages were by no means unknown. Farm implements in the hands of untrained peasants unfamiliar with them were liable to breakage or other injury. With time there was improvement in general.

With the invasion of Russia by the Germans in the Second World War much farm machinery as well as livestock was destroyed or removed. Many of the collective farms suffered heavy damage or demoralization. For a time thereafter some resort had to be made to the more primitive methods of earlier days.

On the farms as a general thing machinery came into ever increasing use, though no little had still to be done by hand. Employment of machinery was encouraged, and was provided for to the greatest extent possible. With the extensive use of tractors it was found that earlier and deeper plowing was possible, and with better and hardier grain. Growing of grain was extended to distant northern and to semi-arid regions. In certain areas a grain like rice was sown by aeroplane. In general, cereal as well as other productions greatly increased. There were notable strides forward alike in agriculture and in stock breeding or animal husbandry, though there was an admitted lag in the latter respect. More varied production was possible. New crops, especially in later years, were introduced in different parts of the country, as hemp, tea, and various fruits. In later years also there was undertaken a vast program of reforestation to check soil erosion and heat waves over parts of the land. In nomadic and semi-nomadic regions most attention was given to the breeding of animals. Collective farming on the whole, however, proved best suited for waving fields of grain covering acres upon acres; it was less suited for things like vegetables or poultry or certain kinds of livestock. So promising in fact had large-scale machine farming become in the Soviet Union that the farm population could be expected to become increasingly smaller, leaving a larger proportion of the population of the country available for industrial tasks in the city. Agricultural production, however, per person remained considerably less than in a country like the United States.

On the produce of the farms the government had the first claim. Besides the tax that had been levied, a designated part was required to be assigned to it, which as a general thing was at a price set below the regular market price. There were also charges for the use of tractors and other machinery furnished by the state, certain insurance costs, and administrative costs, including advice given or other special services rendered by the state. Before profits or dividends could yet be distributed to members of the coöperative body, there had to be further sums set aside for reserve funds, for new equipment, for permanent improvements, and for contributions for welfare work and mutual aid. What was now left was apportioned among the various member workers according to the work done by each. As with factories, there might be penalties imposed upon laggards, and bonuses or premiums or extra pay bestowed upon the more energetic and more useful generally. Profits to individuals were in part cash, and in part products of the farm. These products could be for the consumption of members and their families; or they could be sold to the state, to a coöperative association, or on the free local market.[1] One could sell his own produce, but not that of another.

With the passage of time the resentment and animosity on the part of the farmers toward the collective process were moderated somewhat; these gave way on the whole to more favorable reactions, with lessening objection to the pooling arrangements. This was in large part due to the increased productivity of the collective farms, with a larger measure of prosperity for all than had been the case before. There was greater appreciation in particular of improved agricultural methods, including the use of modern machinery, making available a more abundant food supply, with less likelihood of a food shortage for the country as a whole, with generally better diet and health for the farmer's family, and with less drudgery and back-breaking toil on the part of the individual farmer. With the tractor there was seen to be involved less expense and greater efficiency than in keeping one's horse for general farm work. With a larger and larger portion of the population it was realized that

[1] See *ante*, p. 199.

the returns from small isolated holdings in the hands of ignorant, starveling peasants could hardly be expected to be a
match for those of the large-scale farming enterprise; that a
tiny tract of a score of acres cultivated with rude backward
methods could hardly be pitted against a vast area of a thousand acres or of some thousands of acres equipped with the
latest and most scientific means of extracting crops from the
earth; that in regions where the harvest must be rapid only the
best mechanical equipment was to be thought of.

The peasants, moreover, were taught important lessons in
agriculture, both at agriculture institutes held from time to
time and directly on the farm—the value of proper seeds, in-
cubation methods, means of combating insect pests, scientific
stock raising, etc. Large-scale farming, furthermore, served as a
model in farming operations and afforded wider opportunities
for instruction in proper farm activities. Coöperation on the
farm was itself seen to have educational values.

A highly mollifying influence upon the attitude of the peasant farmers, it is to be added, was in the permitting of the cultivation about the home of a little plot of ground or garden or
orchard of a few acres, for the production of food for the use of
the family, together with one, two, or three cows and a like
number of pigs, a dozen or so of sheep or goats, a score of hives
of bees, and poultry and rabbits without limits in numbers, all
these altogether over the land amounting to a considerable figure. (A little homestead of one's own had been the case in pre-
Soviet days in connection with the communal farming system.)
No horses or other draft animals, however, could be so owned,
it being possible to employ these for the creation of individual
wealth. Small farm implements could also be objects of private
ownership on the diminutive homestead. In his home employment the peasant owner had always to do the work on his own
time. He could engage no hired help. Home products thus
procured, as vegetables, eggs, milk, etc., could, like the products
raised directly on the collective farm and not needed at home,

213

be sold to outside parties, in regular commercial transactions, in private sales, or as a market might be found, and without group interference.

To industrial workers garden space near their dwellings, even in cities where possible, might be allowed by the Soviet authorities.[1] During the Second World War "victory gardens" were widely promoted in the Soviet land.

The struggle, however, between the peasant farmer and the Soviet government was by no means over. From time to time it was charged by the latter that the farmers were not doing their part on the collective farms. It was said that too often they were found idling or trifling here, or that they were taking more than their share of the products, or that their homestead operations encroached on the collective land operations. They were not infrequently asserted to be more concerned with their own private operations than with the business of the state— to be giving too much time to their own garden or pigs. Some of the peasants were even declared to be renting out part of their limited domain—a restoration of landlordism even though on a small scale. Others were affirmed to be engaged in a sort of buying and selling of surplus land—a species of speculation of distinctly capitalistic hue. Still others were alleged to be hiring workers upon the tracts of land in their possession— a practice no less socialistically reprehensible. Some were accused of taking advantage of what was offered by membership in collective farms to escape taxation in some way or other. Because of too great a devotion to their own holdings on the part of the farmers, there might be occasioned an actual shortage of labor on the general farms.

On their side, the farmers claimed that the share of products demanded by the state was often quite too large, or that in some other way they were taken advantage of. Nor did they give up the belief, cherished by them from the beginning, that they were discriminated against in some fashion in favor of the

[1] See *ante*, p. 198.

214

city dwellers. Neither had they forgotten that in the devaluation of the country's currency, with their savings kept to themselves rather than entrusted to a bank, they were heavy losers. Some of the peasant farmers at one time or another were so dissatisfied or disaffected that they left the country of their own accord, usually going to the city to swell its population. Some were forcibly taken away in case of a sparse farm population in other regions or in case of needed agricultural workers in some place in the wide Soviet domain. From time to time there were charges of graft in some form or other misdoings in agricultural operations. There were more frequent charges of agricultural mismanagement in one or more particulars.

Although the collective farm under the general direction of the state doubtless became stronger with time in Soviet Russia, there were still many who harbored the old resentments. Perhaps it was too much to ask of human nature that it abandon all at once an age-old persuasion that a freehold, a moderate sacred space about one's home, should be immune from outside interference of any sort, even that of the state. Perhaps there was also the fear that an agricultural serfdom was somehow being established in the land. Finally, it was easy to recall the fate of those who at the beginning had protested against such things, and had to suffer so grievously in consequence. Should the peasants in general have had to resign themselves to the policy of farm collectivation or should they heartily have accepted it, they would probably demand a larger voice in government and in the disposal of their products.

The government itself, while desiring to see improved conditions among its farm population, was not without certain fears of its own. With the growing economic role of peasants, their political power would be enhanced, with somewhat unpredictable results ahead for it. The government realized the situation, and recognized its position and the need of caution in its treatment of the peasant farmers of the land.

CHAPTER XIII

The Soviet State and Its Industrial Organization

THE great economic aim of the new socialistic state in Russia was the industrialization of the country—its transformation from one so largely agricultural to one to a very great extent industrial, and able to produce in its factories as well as on its farms all the things that its people would require. The "anarchy of production" was here to come to an end.

In the Soviet state, as it got on its feet, and felt its oats, so to speak, great stress was placed upon state planning of production. With the conclusion of the "new economic policy," or after some half-score years of that system, it embarked upon a wide and far-reaching production program. There was no longer to be dependence upon foreign capital, which in any event it had never been easy to obtain, and which, besides, was not altogether in keeping with socialistic principles. A particular purpose, in addition to attaining national self-sustenance, was to catch up economically with the more industrial capitalist lands, or at least to reduce in some degree the inequalities hitherto existing between Russia and those lands.

All the capital necessary for the new venture was to be obtained in the Soviet country alone—something that could appeal to the pride of the citizens, and perhaps throw consternation into the hearts of foreign capitalists. Heretofore grain, lumber, and other products of the land had to be sent abroad to get necessary articles in exchange for it; no longer would such procedure be called for. It is true that for a time in early days machinery and technicians would have to be imported to provide essential equipment and facilities for the raw and untutored country; but very soon all this was to be done away with.

There was now set in view a really awe-inspiring, hitherto unconceived-of program, which was no less than the practical making over industrially of an immense backward agricultural country. It was an unprecedented attempt to render in a very short time a gigantic new-born state self-sufficient in the material things of life, and to set it on the way to success and prosperity for the general well-being of its people. There was to be a modern diversified industrial economy, sufficient to meet the needs of a growing, healthy population. With it there was to be created a happy, contented people, supplied with a large measure of the good things of life—education, culture, health, a place in the sunshine materially, which were to be available to all, and to be enjoyed by all. There was to be a raising of the levels of the people's life in all respects—to the utmost possible heights. The whole project was in its way the most ambitious scheme ever undertaken by man. There was never anything quite like it in human history.

To secure the necessary financial backing for the gigantic program in prospect, the people would have for a time to suffer serious deprivations; they would be called upon to make heavy sacrifices, especially in the immediate lack of consumer goods. There was no holding back of what was to be involved. The people were told what they would have to face in this great period of stress, and what the rewards would be on the attainment of success. All, it was strenuously insisted, was to be for their use, and for the private profit of none. The campaign was entered into with full energy, and with a certain enthusiasm— as though the people were marching forth to war, as in a sense they were.

The country took an inventory of its needs and requirements, and proceeded to adopt a design to meet them. Under this planning program, the quantity of goods to be produced was to be definitely ascertained, and industry geared accordingly.

217

In the process of achieving the goal, a balance was to be struck between consumption and production; there was to be no slump, no depression, no crisis, no waste. There would also be decided what community consumption was to be encouraged and what to be discouraged. An important incidental expectation was that, with increased production of goods, purchasing power of the people would be raised, and higher standards of living would eventually be available for them. In order to reach the desired ends within the alloted time, there were to be intense, even feverish efforts made to speed up production in the highest conceivable tempo. A country of ignorant, untrained peasants was to be changed into a skilled, progressive, industrial nation, and at top celerity.

In the efforts at the rehabilitation of the national economy, there were to be several governing principles. One was the location of industrial establishments near natural resources and near cheap power. Another was the development of backward regions, including regions in Asia, both industrially and culturally. There was in general to be better geographical distribution of industry, all with reference to the location of raw material, with in particular an eastward trend. Some sort of equilibration was also to be established between industry and agriculture; the production of each was somehow to fit into or complement the production of the other. Technical efficiency was to match that in capitalist countries; total output was eventually to surpass that in those countries.

For a time there would have to be attention to the production of goods that could be exported, and thus provide exchange for the obtaining of material needed for the initiation and promotion of Soviet manufacturing. There would also for a time have to be brought in foreign engineers and technicians till the country could have enough of these of its own.

There were set for successive five-year periods definite production goals alike for manufactured goods and for agricultural products (also with more or less allocations during a given year). For the first five-year period emphasis was to be placed upon capital equipment or producers' goods—articles that could be employed for the production of further articles, especially the so-called heavy industries—electrical power stations, power plant machinery, blast furnaces, foundries, oil plants, railways, waterways, coal, iron, and other mines, factories producing such goods as automobiles, tractors, machinery, chemicals, etc. At the same time there was to be an intro duction and expansion of collective farming on a large sca .

In the second five-year period emphasis was to be plac 1 rather upon consumer goods, to raise general standards of li v-ing, but with as little let-up as possible in what had been undertaken in the first five-year period. There was now to be produced more food, more clothing, more household goods, more building material, and more of other consumer commodities. Both factories and collective farms producing these things were to be increased and expanded. In addition, there were to be constructed more school buildings, hospitals, rest homes, r reation centers, club quarters, libraries; those already cc structed were to be developed and strengthened. Industrial ganization was in general to be promoted, and a marketi g technique put under way. Civil aviation was a particular matter that was to receive attention.

The third five-year period was, practically speaking, to be given to the extension and development of what had been embarked upon in previous periods, along both material and cultural lines. This was to be true in particular in respect to matters having to do with education. Things that were concerned with a generally pleasanter life or with more conveniences, including means of entertainment or sports and housing projects, would have enhanced consideration. At the same time, and in fact during preceding periods as well, no little attention had to be devoted to the matter of war preparations—an attitude that has remained in the land.

It is to be added that following the Second World War further and hardly less ambitious planning programs in keeping with those that had gone before, were set on foot, both industrially and culturally, together with a vast scheme of rehabilitation and reconstruction in general in the land—not only, it was proclaimed, to recover pre-war levels in all particulars, but considerably to surpass those levels. Emphasis was still upon the restoration and development of heavy industry (including transportation)—with much attention at the same time to war articles. Consumer goods on an extensive scale would have to have a further wait.[1]

The final planning periods, theoretically speaking, whether they were to materialize on scheduled time or eventually at some later date, were to witness the passing of the Soviet people to a state of well-being and happiness never before approached. There would then be flourishing industries, abundant agriculture, well-equipped laboratories, high levels of technical and economic development, and goods of all kinds produced in sufficient quantities to make a people comfortable and in pleasing circumstances. With the plentitude of consumer goods all would be freed of concern over the material necessaries of life. When all the proper and legitimate needs and desires of the people had been met, cultural matters would then have their full meed of attention. Higher education facilities would be broadened and made available to ever greater numbers. Creative work would be encouraged for its own sake, and for the enjoyment of all concerned. There would be none for whom there would not be means of self-expression. There would be labor for the sheer joy of it.

The country would now be ready for communism, and could step into it with little further ado. There would be in an order of abundance a transition from socialism—to each according to his merit—to communism—to each according to his need. The country would be well on its way to the complete establishment of a classless society, an unprecedented reign of happi-

[1] See *post*, p. 238.

ness and order—the earthly Elysium of which man had so long dreamed but had never been able to attain.

After the painting of the glowing picture of future communism in the land, there were certain practical, material, tangible matters that demanded attention, with the application to some extent of a measuring rod, with respect in particular to the first and second five-year periods—the third being interrupted more or less by war preparations and actual war. The general outcome of this most carefully planned program in the Soviet Union had a varied story to tell. On the whole there was much accomplished in the directions set—much that would otherwise not have been accomplished—and in a relatively brief space of time. In some instances there was a considerable measure of success attained, even though not all that was hoped for or claimed. In certain respects there were impressive gains for the new program. There were notable strides toward national industrialization.[1]

Industry was on the whole greatly advanced. Production in the factory and on the farm was augmented in a high degree. National wealth was much increased. There was an extension of arable agricultural areas, with more intensive cultivation in all. Swamp clearing, irrigation, soil conservation, reforestation had a place. There was a large expansion in the production of certain goods, including in particular goods of which the country was so sorely in need, such as agricultural implements and automobiles.

Certain forms of industry increased several times, especially among heavy industries or in producers' goods.[2] The Soviet Union became second among the nations of the world in pig iron production and machine production; it came near being first among the nations in production of agricultural machinery. Less and less machinery was now called for from outside. The

[1] The industrial population increased from 5 percent to one-third.

[2] Altogether trustworthy statistics regarding industrial operations in the Soviet state are not easy to obtain; but what is said here is believed to be reasonably correct and conservative.

country took great steps forward in electric power, and in steel, coal, and oil production, with an increase of several fold; it became one of the world's leaders here. In a greatly needed industry like boot-making was a very notable advance, which was also true as to chemicals and some textiles. In industrial output in general the country passed from fifth to second place among the nations. Well over half the national wealth was now in industry. There was also marked improvement in transportation facilities, including railway expansion and inland waterways. Road construction grew apace. Shipbuilding was embarked upon to an extent. Strides were made in aviation, both for transportation and for overhead scouting purposes. There was a great increase in technical and engineering skill, and in the use of machinery. There was heightened interest in scientific developments. Food and household goods in the end became more abundant; standards of living were on the whole eventually raised, at least to higher levels than had been the case before—without present consideration of war consequences. From its endeavors and experiences the nation received something of a moral tonic—or so it was regarded.

In its economic progress the country had special outstanding achievements, in particular in building up and developing hitherto neglected areas. This was particularly true with respect to the bleak and forgotten expanse of Siberia, stretching away from European Russia to the waters of the Pacific. A region formerly containing some six million people in all, a motley array of settlers, exiles, refugees, adventurers, criminals, it grew into one with a population practically quadrupled. Here was a "winning of the west," in reverse from that known in America. The new inhabitants came from various regions, including some fairly trained workers and farmers. Both farming and industry were here encouraged. Arable farm regions and urban centers were created. Vast areas were made into valuable agricultural lands. Siberia was enabled to grow its own food. Towns sprang up in Siberian wastes. Factories were constructed in one place and another, especially those that could have a part in war preparations, these being located well within the frontier from Europe. Mining, of which there had been for long a certain amount, was greatly increased, notably in iron ore and in precious metals. Of hardly less significance was the bringing of industry and agriculture to cold Arctic regions in both Asia and Europe.

At the same time there were in these planning programs certain less favorable results. Some products proved to be defective or of inferior quality. There was in not a few cases an advance in quantity at the expense of quality; the latter was sacrificed to the former, though quality in general improved with time. As was planned and expected, consumers' goods did not keep pace with producers' goods, though there were more of the former in later days. For a time standards of living had to be materially lowered, especially at the beginning, to allow the export of food in return for needed machinery from outside. (To some extent better machinery and motor vehicles could have been imported than those actually produced.) Industrialization of the land was in some respects attended with considerable waste. Because of the desire for speed, machinery and materials were often seriously injured. Machinery was driven hard, with not enough attention to its repairs. Some measure of inefficiency was to be expected, particularly in the lack of wide technical knowledge. Too often in the whole proceedings there was a superabundance of red tape. There were also charges at times of internal sabotage. In some instances results turned out to be little, or hardly worth the efforts that had been put forth. Various disappointments the people were called upon to endure.

Though speed was gained, it is true, it was not without the accompaniment of privation and distress and real suffering, and no little sacrifice. The whole project was declared to have been paid for by decreased consumption power in general, especially in earlier stages, together with the levying of heavy taxes. There was a cost also in the massed liquidation of kulaks on the farms.[1]

The production program of the Soviet Union had always a dark cloud hanging over it, under which it had to labor, and to which it had always to adjust itself, one that became darker with time. It could not fail to keep before it its powerful neighbor to the west, which was looking upon portions of it with covetous eyes. Much material and labor that could have been devoted to peace-time projects had to be turned over to war preparations. The war situation had a very important part in causing industries to be located east of the Ural Mountains, and as far as possible from the grasp of German arms. The Soviet Union capitalized on its tremendous advantages here— Siberia and the boundless east. But the country's development could only move under the shadow of German aggression. During actual war operations there were highly creditable large-scale conversions of peace-time industrial activities to those of war.[2] There was also tremendous loss in goods of all kinds. Following the Second World War there was continued production of war material, consuming a large part of the nation's industrial efforts—a disproportionately large part.

The question of state planning is a very large one, with some indubitably good points, and with some not so much to be commended. Our approval or disapproval will depend in no small measure on what we regard as sound economic principles or elementary economic laws, upon what we feel should or should not be left in government hands, upon our possible belief that in such procedure there are too many factors lying in the unforeseeable future. A socialist state is always in the best relative position to undertake state planning, for, like a gigantic, all-embracing corporation, it has under its control all the means of production, together with a directed general economy and a managed financial system. Besides, a socialist government is in control of the several organs of public opinion

[1] See *ante*, p. 207.
[2] See *post*, p. 240.

and of full means of propaganda, which it can make serve its own ends.

How far in general the Soviet nation was directly set forward in consequence of its ambitious program; how far scarcity in each particular field was relieved or prevented; how far the hardships and sacrifices imposed on the people were justified; and how far the whole matter was affected by the conditions peculiar to the country—these are matters that cannot readily be determined.

Certainly Soviet Russia's daring innovation, its initiation of its new policy in shaping its economic order, compelled the world's attention. Whether or not in its bold attempts production in this land, hampered no doubt as it was by not a few factors, may have lagged in comparison with that of some other countries, its achievements in its own bounds cannot be regarded as other than remarkable. The outside world may have been inclined to belittle or deride some aspects of the planning program, but the Soviet state experienced little disheartening; it went ahead, and apparently on the whole with genuine good to itself.

In the industrial development of Soviet Russia there was forced labor on an immense scale—to an extent that can only be surmised. The fact is that on account of the vast amount of work, including the various schemes of public work, to be carried out in that land (not omitting the enormous exertions in the making of war supplies and munitions), there were not always enough workers available or at hand. No small part of the population had to be drafted. Furthermore, because of the frequent inexpertness or heavy-handedness in the more or less technical operations, together with the lack of sufficient modern equipment, several laborers were required to do what one could do in a country like the United States. There was no place for idlers or loafers anywhere. (The matter of forced labor is also considered later.)[1]

[1] See *post*, p. 324.

In a sense, all labor was of a compulsory character; it was largely conscripted labor. The state saw to it that all essential jobs were filled, all essential services rendered. For persons of specified ages compulsory labor could be provided for by law. The state excused no one; it might assign labor much as it saw fit, whether on the farm, in the factory, or elsewhere, although such transfer of labor might often be referred to as "voluntary" on the part of the workers. Though a great portion of Soviet citizens had callings of their own choosing, there were large numbers of state employees engaged at allotted tasks, or at whatever was offered them, not all in earlier days with specific preparation or qualifications. Should they balk, they stood to lose membership in trade unions, social insurance benefits, and certain civil rights, besides having their names removed from labor exchanges. Under the circumstances there need have been little unemployment in the land. For long periods unemployment insurance was in abeyance because there was no unemployment. After a fashion a sense of industrial security could prevail over the land.

Though in subsequent years there might be a greater force of laborers available to the state through a high birth rate, it was still possible, practically speaking, without waiting, to augment the labor supply or to create a labor reserve. Women might be called upon to do various forms of work, some quite onerous, though this was something to which Russian women had long been inured. Advantage might also be taken of the provisions of the law as to apprentice work of children and youth; these provisions might at times be stretched, especially by mass training for a longer or shorter period, to permit regular manual tasks. Of later years what are known as labor reserve schools could provide a recruiting ground for youthful industrial workers. Boys from fourteen to seventeen and girls from fifteen to eighteen years of age who were to be so engaged were subject to a labor draft, being assigned or shifted to such industries as there was need, to an extent by voluntary action on their part, but through state direction or compulsion if necessary.[1] Following trade or vocational training, there was expected a period of four years in general state employment, after which there could be greater or less freedom in choosing one's future work in an industrial establishment or on a collective farm, or perhaps in preparation for a professional career. Evening or continuation schools might be made available for those desiring further education.[2]

To be added was convict labor in general. Further labor force was to be found in the considerable numbers of political offenders whose toil could prove useful in various forms of rougher work.[3] Much of the industrial progress of the Soviet Union is ascribable to forced labor—a heavy blot on its escutcheon.

Workers were theoretically free to move about over the land; but there was in reality no great mobility of labor. Workers were rather welded to their jobs, and could not well give them up. Attempt to change a job without authorization might land one in prison. Workers were, furthermore, required to keep record books with them as to their movements. These, remaining in the hands of industrial managers, and constituting a sort of internal passports, could readily impede steps inclined to rove; through them workers could remain tied down to their particular niches. Upon their work records depended the workers' standing in such matters as social insurance benefits. Moving about in the Soviet country was in general not an easy thing. One had to give a good reason for attempts in this direction and satisfy more or less inquisitive officials.

At the same time, despite the possible coercive measures to prevent the workers from seeking new fields of endeavor, there was for one reason or another a considerable turnover of labor in the land, especially in the seeking of the right man for the right place in the industrial order, or to meet needs at some

[1] See *post*, p. 259.
[2] See *post*, p. 260.
[3] On work in concentration camps, see *post*, p. 325.

particular place. Shifting the labor of a corps or body of workers from an industry of one kind to an industry of another kind was itself a far from unknown practice. In case of an actual shortage of labor in the city or elsewhere there could be a drafting of rural workers, rural areas perhaps being required to send a designated percentage of their numbers there. Recruiting officials could visit rural areas to make inquiries in the matter. Higher wages, more generous ration cards, or better living conditions in one place than in another could at times prove an effective means of enticing workers. There was also a considerable wandering about of certain would-be workers, especially of rural workers desirous of trying their fortunes in the overcrowded cities. It was even regarded as necessary at times to put a curb on these migratory tendencies, perhaps by the withholding of passports.

In general there could be said to have been a genuine exploitation of the workers in the Soviet Union. They were under the one employer possible to them; they could have no other master than the state. Regimentation of labor could be carried far, and with a stern hand. Whatever of hardship or suffering might have been inflicted in the process, including the liquidation of anything that might run counter to Soviet economic policies, there were no official records to indicate.

The industrial organization and operation of large-scale farms and factories in the Soviet Union had much in common. Both farm and factory were something more than mere producing units; there were added cultural and social features— health centers, education centers, recreation centers. With their particular productive work as a nucleus, the accessory parts could take on the appearance of a small village. Spreading out from the core might be to a greater or less extent clubs, houses of culture, schools, nurseries, medical centers, hospitals, dispensaries, theatres, gymnasiums, sport fields, libraries, stores, laundries, bakeries, eating places, housing units, power plants, flour mills, brickyards, sheds, stables, etc.—a community of its own.

In the Soviet language farms might be called grain factories or agronomic culture centers. Some went from the village to the farm to work, as had for long been the wont with peasants in Russia.

In the regular factories organization was carried to higher levels still. In all industries trade unions were to be found. They played a not unimportant part both in the factory and in the affairs of state; they had more than one role to fill. They were given every encouragement by the state; they were in fact never independent of it, but rather an arm of it. The trade union was a most valuable training ground for the inculcation of Soviet doctrine; it was a most useful instrument for state propaganda purposes. It also nurtured the worker in the service of his employer, which was the state; it was likewise an instrument of the state to help it in discipline with the workers. It was an agency for mediation between the management of a state factory and the employees in it. It could smooth relations between government and workers; it was a sort of buffer between them. It could have a large part in the handling of labor problems.

The trade union could lend a hand in the matter of production: it could stimulate production—it was a vehicle in increasing the productivity of industry, in redoubling its output, in promoting the efficiency of the worker. It could have a role in the planning of production, and thus feel that it was something of a partner in the process. It was at the same time concerned, on the one hand, with such matters as general working conditions, sanitation, safety measures, wages, hours of labor, and broad social insurance measures (seeing, for one thing, that there was no abuse in possible malingering on the part of workers), and, on the other hand, in such matters as education, recreation, health, housing conditions, care of the aged, rest homes, and general welfare measures. There might be maintained a coöperative store or restaurant or mutual aid facilities for the benefit of members. The trade union in the Soviet

Union had both material and moral effects and influence. It was by no means a superfluous or inefficacious institution. The Soviet trade union was in certain respects like the "company union" in the United States, but with important differences. The Soviet trade unions, with their prime aim that of increasing production, had actually less power than their American counterparts, which were mainly concerned with wages and the improvement of labor conditions. In the Soviet country the trade union remained the agent, the instrument of the state.

The trade union intertwined with the ubiquitous clubs of the country, which of themselves had a considerable part in taking care of the leisure time of the workers—for with the shortened workday of the Soviet land, actual or contemplated, there would be no little leisure time at their disposal or available for them. The trade union itself might be said to be concerned principally with industrial conditions; the club, with recreational and cultural activities. As with coöperative organizations in general, there were special inducements for joining the unions—membership being nominally voluntary—lower taxes, lower rent, cheaper tickets at entertainments, prior rights as to nursery attention or schooling for children, etc.—apart from full social insurance benefits. It was also much easier to get a job if a member of a union. For a short time at the beginning of the Soviet state membership in a labor union was, as we have seen, compulsory.

Legal rules and regulations governing labor in the Soviet Union were, as was to be expected, quite favorable to the workers. Measures for their protection, for their safety and comfort, were of a high order. There were early attempts to make the working week basically one of six days, or even of five days, but this only caused confusion; and the week was returned to the regular one of seven days, with one of the seven days free from labor and a day of rest for each individual. Work was for a time staggered, a process that permitted it to proceed regardless of the calendar, and regardless of the free time of one's fellow workers, but at the same time with continuous, unbroken production.

Maximum hours of labor per day were eventually fixed at eight, at one time at seven; in early Soviet days it was even less. For certain intellectual "white collar" workers it might be six. A forty-eight hour week was not uncommon. With reduced working time as the desired program in the Soviet state, production might appear to be more or less subject to retardation. It was expected that from time to time, in emergencies or as the circumstances might require, this schedule would give way to longer working periods. Overtime was in general to be paid for at one and a half or double time. Though overtime was not formally encouraged, it was permitted under due regulations. While much of this could mean relatively long hours, it could also mean extra pay, something by no means unworthy of regard. A special form of "overtime" work was the voluntary efforts at self-improvement in industry or the voluntary service of a "shock brigade" which deprived itself of some of its leisure time to lend a helping hand to some slow-moving producing unit—something later to be considered.[1]

Wages and hours varied according to the disagreeableness or the hazards involved in one's work. Toil that was grimy or very arduous or fraught with special peril might have topmost pay (mining being an example). Such labor might require only six hours, or even four a day. For particularly dangerous occupations more holidays were also to be allowed. Overtime work was restricted to three hours a day. For all a limited rest or vacation period was the privilege, a two-week holiday (sometimes a week or two longer) during the year with pay being the accepted order. Factories might have as part of their equipment, not only hospital and first-aid facilities, but general health and recreation facilities, including gymnasiums and athletic equipment, together with eating places and housing ac-

[1] See post, p. 249.

commodations; there might also be libraries and other cultural facilities, including those of the trade union or club.

There were not exceptionally high standards for child labor; it was in good part brought to levels approved by child labor organizations over the world. Children as a rule might not engage in remunerative tasks until they were sixteen years of age, though there might be exceptions in particular circumstances for those from fourteen to sixteen, in which case their hours were to be shortened (usually to four a day). Those from sixteen to eighteen years were to be regarded in the light of apprentices, with their hours also reduced (usually to six).[1] No overtime work was permitted children. None under eighteen could enter industrial work without having an elementary education; nor could such persons have part in dangerous trades.[2] Night work was similarly restricted. Children, however, might do much work around the farm; all could help at harvest time. We have seen that apprentice or labor reserve schools might at times be availed of to secure workers under the formal age.[3]

Women were not permitted to engage in certain very heavy or arduous or unsuitable tasks, though these might be of much more strenuous character than was the case with women in other lands.

Social insurance measures were liberal, being of non-contributory character, with the employer enterprise (the state or an agency of the state) paying premiums and costs of administration. Agricultural as well as industrial workers were covered.

---

[1] Admission to trade, technical, or vocational schools, requiring relatively high qualifications, and involving two or three years of training, was set at fourteen and fifteen for boys and at fifteen and sixteen for girls; admission to factory apprenticeship schools, of a more general labor character, and involving half a year's or a year's training, was from fourteen to seventeen for boys and from fifteen to eighteen for girls. After general training there was, as we have seen, required four years in state enterprises. See *ante*, p. 226.

[2] In war days there were some adjustments in labor standards, with restrictions lifted to a greater or less extent. Working hours were in general increased, though less so with respect to heavier forms of work. Vacations and holiday periods were reduced.

[3] See *ante*, p. 226.

The matter was largely in the hands of the trade unions. (The subject of social insurance is considered elsewhere.)[1]

Full provision was made for collective bargaining. The agreement here, as might be expected, was an elaborate affair, covering many matters, and with rigid regulations for the protection of the rights of the workers, which included wages, hours, general working conditions, overtime labor, rest periods, safety measures, inspection, etc. The agreement was between the labor union on one side, which was hardly other than an arm or branch of the state, and, on the other side, some agency or department of the government concerned with production—perhaps an odd, anomalous arrangement, but one not outside the logic of Soviet reasoning. The situation might become all the more peculiar because of the presence of a third party, the representative of the Communist party, who perhaps, still more strangely, might be serving in one of the two other capacities. As the government directed the whole proceedings, it might happen that the labor unions, despite their vaunted powers, were at times, especially when production was to be accelerated, hardly more than its bare instruments; in such cases there might not be too much scruple about disregarding some of the provisions of the labor agreement, the workers perhaps having no recourse other than to do the bidding of those in power. (The matter of trade unions is also considered elsewhere.)[2]

Labor discipline in factories, to keep production "rolling," might be very severe; it might be tightened according to the exigences of a particular situation. The plant manager had no little power vested in him to get full production; to foremen might be given amplified authority, possibly not far removed from dictatorial. Workers behind in their production quotas could be made to suffer accordingly. For spoiled goods the worker might receive no pay or have to make good. For waste, loafing, slacking, shirking, inefficiency, misbehavior, ab-

[1] See *post*, p. 284.
[2] See *ante*, p. 229.

233

sence or tardiness, a penalty could be imposed—public reprimand, demotion, dismissal, withholding of wages, liability for
possible damage done, loss of working card, forfeiture of trade
union, housing, or other privileges, fine, durance. Absence
from work without good excuse could invite eviction or dismissal from one's dwelling. Workers attempting to leave their
work without leave could be held by compulsion.

Those in charge of production operations also had stern
duties to perform; they were under no light obligations and
responsibilities in their tasks. Manufacture of poor goods, too
slow manufacture in general, or delaying the movements of
merchandise was regarded as a crime against the state. For an
accident occurring to a railway train those in charge might be
criminally liable.

Factory managers were chosen or selected for various reasons
—industrial skill, organizational ability, personal popularity,
party services, devotion to the communist cause. With them
sentiment could be mixed with hard business efficiency.

Provision was made for the adjustment or settling of labor
disputes or disagreements; and workers were supposed to abide
by the decisions rendered. Under the circumstances strikes were
seldom to be expected; persons engaged in procuring or fomenting them might readily be accused of sabotage, of spreading of unrest in industry, or even of "counter revolution."
After a strike was over, its leaders might be duly disposed of.
For permitting such conditions as might lead to or invite
strikes, labor unions or state officials might be charged with
dereliction in the performance of their duties.

There were factory councils and factory committees concerned with various matters—with economic considerations,
with cultural matters, and above all with increased production. As might be expected, production was held back from
time to time by what could only be designated as factory de-
bating societies or by long drawn-out committee deliberations.
Workers in factories were permitted to make suggestions as to

management and operations, a procedure that worked two ways —good and bad. Suggestions were often of a sentimental nature or were impractical. Self-appointed committees, even from outside, might descend upon a factory to see how things were going, at times helpfully, but possibly creating more or less disorganization and confusion in consequence. Matters in these respects in general improved with time.

All in all, things economic did not go as smoothly and as speedily in the Soviet Union as had been hoped for; some of the economic dreams of the promoters were quite far from coming true—though in all fairness it must be said that whatever unfavorable results there might have been were not to be laid wholly at the door of its peculiar economic organization.

Apart from what took place in the struggles with the peasant farms in the efforts at collectivation of the farms,[1] industry could not be said to have fared altogether happily in the Soviet land. Production in general proved much below what was needed for a country the size of Russia. Distribution of goods was often in a greater or less state of uncertainty and disorder. There were both shortage and delay with needed commodities. The quality of goods offered was not always of a high order, and frequently quite poor. Prices charged were at times exorbitant, and quite out of keeping with quality. Costs of production could be high—perhaps in greater or less part because of inferior industrial organization, low factory productivity, limited skill and technical education on the part of the directors or workers, or other similar factors.

Methods of advancing industrial processes were often crude and ill-digested. Some industries were badly integrated: there was not infrequent lack of coördination between one factory and another. At times raw materials or necessary parts of machinery were poor, defective, or unsuited for their destined use in the factory. Some factories were unable to get raw materials when needed. Possibly the sources of raw materials were far

[1] See *ante*, p. 207.

removed from a producing center, especially in earlier days. Supplies, machinery, etc., which were to be employed in manufacturing, might be slow in arriving; and there had to be shutdowns or a period of idle waiting. Flow of what was necessary could not always be counted on. Goods might be sent out only in a partial state of completion. Finished products were irregular and uncertain in delivery. There was often much waste of material on the way to the factory or in the factory itself. Valuable material might be left outdoors to rust. Goods were sometimes spoiled in manufacturing. There was considerable breaking down of machinery; for parts injured there might be no provision for replacement. There was frequent lack of lubrication. There might be rapid deterioration of machinery. There was often lack of new and modern machinery. Heating of factories in very cold weather was itself not always an easy matter. Capital in general to carry on modern industry was at times not available. Nor could essential credit always be readily obtained.

The railway system was in general inadequate. It was often overtaxed. Train service was not always reliable, and could not be counted upon. Trains often failed to arrive on time; they often failed to conform to schedule. Railway traffic was frequently crowded and congested; traffic could be blocked at one point or another; bottlenecks were far from being unknown. Freight could move slowly and clumsily. Goods could be piled up at freight stations, waiting to be hauled away. Goods were sometimes sent to the wrong address. Equipment was often in need of repairs; at times it stood idle. Roads or highways over the country remained in large part poor, with not too many of any kind—with little automobile travel outside the large cities.

Charges of sabotage by internal enemies were sometimes made; but this could not explain all the shortcomings and flounderings that beset the land in its industrial efforts. High costs and inefficiency of operations were often due, on the one hand, to confused, disorganized, muddled, garrulous mass or "committee" direction, and, on the other hand, to an interfering and domineering state bureaucracy. There were constant variations in plans for the operation of factories. There were frequent changes in personnel. There was insistence upon unimportant details. There was fear of assuming too much responsibility on the part of plant managers. At times these managers, in apprehension of punishment for delay or shortage in their production requirements, drove their machinery too hard, neglecting overhead or repairs. Occasionally excessive holiday time interfered with smooth and rapid operations. Want of technical instruction and technical experience was nearly everywhere all too obvious. Many workers were simply "greenhorns" at their tasks; relatively few were adept at handling complicated machinery. Lack of expert guidance and direction was along too many lines painfully in evidence.

In Soviet industrial activities, furthermore, there was a good deal of bookkeeping and accounting operations called for— much on the order of red tape—which more or less delayed proceedings, and required a due contingent of functionaries and clerical staffs.

There were in the land recurrent charges of waste of material in production, of maladministration in industrial operations, including failure to meet quotas, of concealment of important details in these operations, of malingering on jobs, of failure to make proper tax returns, of too many office workers in both industrial and agricultural operations.

As in capitalist countries, a troublesome situation could assert itself from technological progress, from the constant effort to substitute the machine for human hands—to get rid of muscular toil so far as this might be possible. It is to be said that labor-saving devices in the Soviet Union were not in general looked upon with disfavor. They were regarded in a very practical light: they could produce more goods with less labor. A practice on the order of "feather-bedding" could receive little sympathy and could have little place in the Soviet economy.

If, however, this substitutionary use of the machine should be carried very far, and if redistribution or readjustment of human labor should not properly be provided for in the process, would there be enough jobs for all? If, furthermore, to afford more jobs, hours of labor should be reduced very far, would there be assurance of sufficient production? And, finally, how far could an efficient productive force be guaranteed if living levels were not on a sufficiently high plane? Such questions as these the Soviet power had to ponder. Communism could have industrial difficulties of no mean order in the production of goods no less than could capitalism.

Standards of living in the Soviet country in general remained low. The masses were often in serious, even in distressing need of consumer goods. The demand for such goods was often beyond the power of the authorities to meet; they at times were simply not to be had. Rationing was by no means an unusual occurrence in times of peace; in some spheres it was for long an all but continuous order. Queues, sometimes of considerable length, were to be found on the streets in consequence of the shortage of some article of merchandise. There were sporadic bootlegging and black market operations in respect to food and other goods. Largely because of the rapid movement to the cities, housing became a prime problem. In many of the homes of the people there was great overcrowding; numbers had to live in barrack-like structures.[1] Rent or what had to be paid for shelter, all things considered, probably came nearest to reasonable figures; it could as a general thing fairly readily be adjusted to the size of one's budget, perhaps requiring as little as one-fifteenth or even less thereof. It was an article like clothing that very often could cost the most. The price of food in general was in some part kept within bounds, possibly by stringent government measures. Food production was at times below what could be expected; food shortages were too often

[1] See *post*, p. 285.

accepted occurrences—actual famines were not unknown. Modern home conveniences were few and far between. There was little of what could be called luxuries in the land. A much needed article was one like soap. There were not many automobiles, radios, or telephones in private hands. Railway facilities were limited. There remained on too wide a scale primitive conditions of living. There was too much of a monotonous daily diet, too much of shabby clothing, too much of shoddy goods in general, too much of multi-family one-room apartments. Following the Second World War there was in general a rise in living costs.

Improved housing conditions were hampered at one time or another by lack of forest cutting machinery as well as by lack of adequate transportation facilities from the forests. A further very important factor in housing construction as well as in the production of both producer and consumer goods was to be found in the outlay for war preparations, which took a heavy toll in the resources and in the productive energy of the people —a condition that has strongly continued.[1]

Such was the situation on the whole which the Soviet people long found confronting them in their attempts at the industrialization of their land. To a large extent the situation was taken philosophically and with good grace. With a considerable portion of the population it was the only thing after all to be expected; nothing else need to have been looked for. Under the circumstances in which the new industrial program was inaugurated in a land quite unready for it, there was bound to be more or less confusion and disarray. The country had been undergoing the pains of a new industrial order—a country that had hardly been prepared or qualified to undertake and carry on large industrial undertakings. The task of making Soviet Russia over into a great industrial nation could not be contem-

[1] Soviet soldiers in occupied lands to the west following the Second World War were guarded against too great acquaintance with or exposure to commodities or articles in use there, for fear that they might make hurtful comparisons with what was to be found at home, or might spread invidious reports on their return home.

plated as an easy one. New types of machinery and new methods of production had to be put into operation or use not before known in the land. Workmen lacked mechanical competency. In speeding up production, or at times even in carrying it on, technicians and engineers had to be improvised or too rapidly trained. An industrialization which usually required a space of many years was to be rushed through in the space of a few. The country could not do otherwise than stumble and grope in its novel industrial enterprise.

Never to be forgotten in later days was the staggering, overwhelming, appalling setback received in consequence of the German invasion in the Second World War. One-third of the productive area of the country was occupied, and that the most productive part. Industrial plants were systematically demolished or stripped of machinery and materials; grain and livestock were destroyed or removed; collective farms in occupied areas were demoralized or rendered useless; mines were flooded; oil refineries were gutted; homes and other structures were levelled to the ground; means of communication were shattered. There arose a heavy shortage in horses, tractors, etc. Consumer goods were greatly depleted. The Germans denuded the land of all they did not demolish. Standards of living, such as they were, were heavily hit. The Germans made a clean sweep, a thorough job of destruction. The country was crippled on a tremendous scale; it had been dealt a body blow—to get back on its feet would require mighty efforts.

The exertions of the country to deal with the wide disorder that had befallen it reflected great credit upon it—both in war years and in post-war years. The movement of industries, especially war industries, to the east, away from German depradations was a notable feat, accomplished with speed and efficiency. Even though aid from the Allied Nations in supplying war material was very considerable,[1] the Soviet Union produced a great deal itself. Provision of food for both the mili-

[1] See *post*, p. 350.

tary and civilian population was itself a tremendous task. During the war numbers of men and of horses were taken from the farm. At the same time there was a constant inflow of refugees to be cared for. Following the war, recovery and reconstruction proceeded as rapidly as circumstances would permit. The whole story constitutes a great tribute to the spirit and energy of the Soviet people.

The Soviet country from its early days was not hesitant or dilatory in recognizing the industrial situation it had to face. It made no denial of its seriousness; rather it repeatedly proclaimed it to the people. The Soviet state and the Soviet people were alike far from satisfied with the situation. From the beginning they resolved to do something about it, and to better it. This task they set about in grim earnestness, and with a certain enthusiasm.

A very considerable portion of the people of the country sought diligently and assiduously to adapt themselves to the new conditions and to the new tempo on which they had so ruthlessly and rudely been thrust. They took their inconveniences and privations and hardships in stride, perhaps not altogether without some grumbling, but, all things considered, in good part, in some cases with a measure of cheerfulness. If they could not expect immediate benefits, they could look for better returns in the days ahead. They proved themselves willing even if slow learners. They steeled themselves to pay the price for their vast industrialization program.

The Soviet people ever insisted upon high levels of production in their land; they kept demanding more and more of the satisfactions of life. They constantly exhorted themselves to increased output. Every incentive and inducement was put forth, no expedient was neglected, to this end. The matter was conceived of and spoken of in military terms—"attack," "industrial front," "shock troops," "labor brigades"—all soldiers in the common cause. The story might be told by wayside posters. There might be public processions with banners to show forth the importance of the matter, perhaps with the announcement of the breaking in some place of production records. There was loud applause when production quotas were exceeded. To help the good work along, moving slogans were invented. Songs could have a part in the inspiring program. Bonuses and prizes were glitteringly placed before the eye. Newspapers might devote space to proclaim production failures and production victories. Nor were the Soviet people averse or reluctant in earlier days to call in experts from outside, particularly from the United States. America was taken pretty much as a model in industrial production, notably in work with such things as railways, steel production, and automobile manufacture. There was throughout little reluctance in encouraging mechanization in both industrial and agricultural production; this was carried out as far as circumstances would permit.

There was also insistent demand for better quality goods. The people were not satisfied with inferior goods if something better was possible. They clamored not only for more things but for better things. Complaints were loud and caustic over the production of inferior goods as well as over scarcity of goods. Factory managers proved responsible could have condign punishment meted out to them.

With the years matters industrial in the land began to manifest improvement. There was steady engineering and technical betterment; general industrial efficiency was on the upward trend. There was increase in the productivity of labor. There was gain on the part of factory managers and factory workers alike. And the wealth of the Soviet people grew in greater or less measure. It is never to be forgotten that the production of war material caused reckonable trouble and delay in the production of other goods—nor that damage in war created something like havoc.

There was undeniably considerable material advance to the people. Apart from conditions created by war, somewhat better and more food, somewhat better and more clothing, somewhat better and more house furnishings, far from seemly or satisfactory though these things were, told something of the story. For the population as a whole standards of living became higher, especially with respect to manufactured goods, though still remaining low as compared with some other nations. The people could have been better off still if more consumer goods had been available for their purchase. There was a slightly more varied diet on the table than in earlier days, something for which the people of Russia had long been waiting. There were more shoes for their feet, for which they had also long been waiting. There was a certain increase in such things as telephones and radios. There were more new houses, and more light in them, including electric lighting. Most of the larger towns now had electricity. There were handsome public buildings and public ways and works of an attractive order brought into existence. There were more paved streets, and cleaner streets, with better night lighting. The people as a whole were appreciably better off than in Czaristic days—always with the results of war kept in mind. After all, perhaps credit is to be bestowed chiefly when consideration is directed to the depths from which the country had to arise. Nor ever to be overlooked is the frightful damage to the country through war, with its heavy setbacks and bitter pills.[1] No less to be kept in mind were the effects of war preparations upon industrial output.

Wages paid in the Soviet Union were on the whole higher than they were in Czaristic Russia. This circumstance was, however, more or less counterbalanced by the higher costs of living—without allowance for the several forms of state aid to the workers, or the several forms of social insurance (accident, health, old age, etc.), besides shorter work days, vacations with pay, admission to rest homes, and other welfare measures. Costs of living were at the same time not a little affected by the dues to be paid to trade unions, by the turnover tax on con-

[1] Following the Second World War the resources of the Soviet Union were measurably increased by what was removed from occupied countries, including German war reparations.

sumer goods, and also by the practically required purchase of government bonds from time to time.[1]

Actual wages received by the workers were an uncertain quantity; they involved elements and factors peculiar to Soviet ways and processes of reasoning, and perhaps a bit puzzling to the outsider.

The preferred method of work was piece work. The wage here might be increased or supplemented to a greater or less extent by extra payments or rewards, by bonuses, premiums, progressive piece rates, etc., for particular efficiency or for acceleration of production in some way. By the Soviet authorities it was claimed that the various public services rendered by the state—medical treatment, education, recreation facilities, etc.—were to be regarded as augmenting or reinforcing or expanding wages—though such a conception of "socialized wages" as a ground for giving reduced pay would have little acceptance in capitalist countries in general. Social security benefits, it is also to be remembered, were largely contingent upon the character of the official records of the workers. It is to be added that the coöperative eating places, which were on so broad a scale in the land, helped to lessen the cost of food, while the efforts of the government to keep housing charges down were not without effect. The situation was further complicated by the circumstance that the prices prevailing over the country for a time were not always the same; they might vary at different selling places.[2] There was also in general more or less price fixing in the land. In consequence of the Second World War there was an increase in the volume of money in the land, but a decrease in the amount of consumer goods, with a decline in the purchasing power of money as a result—something that called for government action, as we have seen.[3]

Actual income in the Soviet state was likely to be determined in greater or less degree on the basis of general family income,

[1] See *ante,* p. 194.
[2] See *ante,* p. 188.
[3] See *ante,* p. 192.

rather than on that of the individual worker—to a wider extent than was the case in most other countries. All the members of the family engaged in some form of remunerative labor could contribute to the total family income, which was thus enlarged. At times it was possible for one to pick up an extra penny or two by doing some job on the side.

In comparison with the days before the Soviets came to power, some of the "white collar" workers were appreciably worse off, something to which Soviet philosophy might not be expected to be altogether averse; on the other hand, certain persons of this description, particularly intellectual and professional workers rendering recognized useful service, fared better under the Soviet régime. There was certain effort to wipe out or bridge over the distinctions between intellectual and manual labor.

All in all, there were considerable variations in income in the Soviet state. With time the number of persons in the higher income groups increased. There may even be said to have developed a sort of middle class on a mild scale in the land, especially among a group who held important industrial and professional positions, together with the fairly large bureaucracy. Certain of those in the professional ranks, particularly artists (including musicians and actors) and writers, were likely to receive the highest incomes; it was such as these who on the whole came off best. In the upper brackets were also persons on the order of highly trained engineers and technicians, experienced and capable industrial managers, and to an extent scientists in general as well (some of whom might also receive bonuses). Persons of competence and skill, and known for their efficiency in industrial administration or in some field of public service, were more and more finding appropriate material reward, with opportunities for promotion and advancement. There appeared to be a considerable measure of freedom in the opportunities here afforded.

There were conflicting stories that came out of the Soviet

Union as to what workers actually received for their work. It was far from easy to determine just what were "real wages" (measured by the extent and character of the goods or services to be purchased from one's earnings). Soviet claims were regarded by some as confusing and misleading. Whatever, moreover, might be obtained as earnings, there were reports at times of inflated, perhaps inordinately high prices, which had to be paid for consumer goods. According to this measurement, wages might, it was affirmed, approach something not far above a pittance, occasionally on the order of starvation wages. On the other hand, much brighter pictures were painted, with workers getting what at least could be called fair net wages.

Just before the Second World War average wages in the Soviet Union, as expressed in United States money, were quoted by some as hardly more than $40 a month, by others as something like $75 or $100. In any event a wage of $90 a month was regarded as an extremely good wage or a very high wage. Following the Second World War general wages were raised somewhat—to what extent we cannot be altogether sure—but not always sufficient to keep up with rising prices for goods. In specialized employments there were persons receiving $400 or even considerably more per month. To none were paid what could be considered very large or excessive salaries. There was no evidence of swollen fortunes anywhere. There were few signs of a real leisure class arising in the land.

At all events we can have few doubts that even if standards of living were above those maintained in pre-Soviet days, they were appreciably below those in many capitalist countries. The main question in the Soviet land was whether this was necessarily to be the case, or whether the matter could be put in the way of being changed.

In the wages or salaries paid to workers in the Soviet land there did not exist a dead levelism; nor was any pretense made that there did. No economically equalitarian society was set forth—though in beginning Soviet days there were closer efforts in this direction. In no inconsiderable degree among the citizens there appeared gradations of income. In hard-headed Soviet reasoning it was held that if the skilled and the unskilled, the good producers and the poor, received the same wages, there would be little incentive for the unskilled to become skilled, or for poor producers to become good. Not only was industrial efficiency to be recognized and rewarded, but responsibility in industrial endeavors was something to be taken into account. In time there arose increasingly sharp distinctions between different categories of workers.

Actual payment for work might be determined by the quantity or the quality of the work done, or by the measure of competence and experience of the individual worker, as well as by the contribution of each to what was regarded as the social value of the article produced, or by general social considerations. To a greater or less extent wages in theory were to be commensurate with the utility and general worthwhileness as well as with the innate character of the work performed; but practical considerations were allowed to have due or full weight. Even agricultural distribution could be according to the work done by each worker on the collective farm. There could also be different wage scales in different industries.

Piece work rates, bonuses for special industrial assiduity, and the introduction of labor-saving machinery might all find justification in the conviction that greater production for the community as a whole was thereby achieved. All this was looked upon as nothing less than common sense, at least at the existing juncture, and not in violation of any fundamental socialist doctrine. Such forms of speeding up were not only permitted; they were encouraged.

There could be progressive rises in pay for piece work after the completion of the established quota, perhaps in time doubling or tripling. For industrial managers such could be the case according to the excess of production beyond the planned assignment, or the measure of the fulfillment of one's quota, or the extent of completion of the allotted tasks ahead of time.

Rewards to industry might be expressed otherwise than in monetary returns. For those in possession of needed skill in the economic endeavors of the state, or for those with marked ability in directing industry or in increasing production at lower costs or with greater efficiency, or for those displaying superior workmanship therein, there might be recompense of more or less tangible nature, though not necessarily in the coin of the realm. To such persons, as to favored or privileged groups in general in the Soviet land, there were certain perquisites possible. There might be access to or discounts in better-class stores or restaurants, assigning of more comfortable or more convenient dwelling apartments, lower rent or lower lighting or water charges in one's dwelling, prompter and better medical service, longer holidays, farther, pleasanter, and speedier railway traveling, cheaper rides on street cars, more or less occasional use of state automobiles, more desirable seats at the opera or play, more expeditious or less expensive recourse to sanatoria or rest homes or claim to better accommodations therein, more generous expense accounts in state undertakings, and other material or cultural concessions. There might also be write-ups or pictures in the newspapers. On the other hand, workers who were found dilatory, supine, lackadaisical, or slackers, or not manifesting sufficient zeal or eagerness in the operations of industry or in the activities of labor unions or coöperative associations, or otherwise not measuring up to proper Soviet standards, might discover themselves in disfavor, discriminated against, or penalized in some way or other.

Under a system named after a Soviet industrial hero (Stakhanov), an extraordinarily skillful and rapid worker, there were special efforts to speed up work without causing detriment or impairment to it, and to set patterns for the workers of the country. Particularly capable workers were placed in different plants as pace-setters. These picked workers who were to be so used were given the best tools, with equipment always at the right spot, with a flow of materials without interruption, with unnecessary or superfluous movements of the workers eliminated, and with freedom from petty or minor details. Through all this there could be established a record, which was to be regarded as a model if not an example. There were to be notable gains from the process: better division of labor, greater skill and efficiency for all concerned, general saving of time, and enlarged output.

While much praise was lavished upon this development in industrial operations, evils were likewise to be pointed out. Its essence was claimed by its opponents or detractors to be simply a more or less disguised way of speeding up or of the efficiency expert concept, with all its undesirable connotations. Those engaged in it were declared to be mainly out for a "record" in output. In it emphasis could be placed upon quantity rather than upon quality. It was said at times to result in attempts at excessive speed, in intense feverish driving of the workers; it was asserted to lead to something on the order of sweating. By means of it hours of labor for some might be increased, or there might be permitted a lowering of sanitary standards. Accidents were more likely to happen in disregard of proper safeguards. The process was alleged to be unduly hard on the machines. Finally, with it the rate of pay, it was stated, might be reduced for the general workers, or the more expert of the workers might simply be getting unduly good pay.

In the economic life of the Soviet state there was one phase that was somewhat of idyllic nature. There was preached, and to a greater or less extent practiced, a principle of mutual help or of voluntary, unpaid labor for the cause. Notably meritorious or outstanding services or activities in industrial operations were requited by public recognition or honorable mention. This industrial public-spiritedness or social emulation might be manifested in one of several ways. Upon men (and women) who had produced more than was expected of them or more than others, or who had broken records in production, or who had shown superior skill or aptitude, or who had brought to light improved methods of production, or who had made the earliest delivery of products, or who had taken their own time to expedite business, or who had displayed the highest degree of coöperation, or who had the best balance sheet—upon these "heroes of social toil" was bestowed the benediction of the state. To factories in front there might be prizes or awards. There might also be "wall newspapers," upon which were rolls of honor for those who had performed extraordinarily well in industry—and possibly also corresponding rolls of dishonor.

Appeal, furthermore, might be made to the sporting instinct, or to the spirit of competitive sportsmanship—in a new kind of game or play. Special voluntary efforts were made to increase efficiency and to eliminate waste. An hour of overtime might be given to improve one's industrial skill. Factory, farm, or office groups might be pitted against each other, with challenge to see which could in "social emulation" accomplish or produce the most. Thereupon the winning team could go over to the losing and find out what the trouble was, point out shortcomings and defects, and show the way to improvement, lending perhaps not only advice but direct manual assistance—all for the weaker sisters that had not done so well. In substandard establishments the workers might get together and discuss the reasons for their low estate. Shock brigades might take it upon themselves to make up some shortage in the industrial structure, on the farm, in the factory, or on the traffic ways, or to meet some emergency therein, giving without cost their time and energy. (There was something here not altogether unlike an American corn-husking bee.) For a group whose quota was incomplete others might rush in and finish it up. Possibly there was taken under "patronage" some particular unit. Holidays might be surrendered to make sure that a particular task was moved toward early fulfillment in the interest of the state. Some organization as a school could "adopt" a factory to coöperate with it or to make it more efficient, or vice versa.[1]

Very efficient workers were not only publicly extolled; they were sent from place to place to inspire other workers by precept and by example, constituting a sort of "pep" squad—to stimulate to ever greater exertion, to stress the importance of increased production, and to proclaim and expound the doctrines of communism in general.

Finally, toward labor was taken a new attitude. Its dignity became no idle abstraction. Labor was not to be regarded as drudgery on the part of an inferior, but something to be shared by all, in honor and in joy, and in service for the community.

Such was the shining picture, such the thrilling story that came to us out of the Soviet Utopia. So far as there was recognition of things so fine and admirable in the daily doings of men anywhere on this earth, we can only bestow our blessings upon their heads. With respect to Soviet Russia, before we can commend them fully to the rest of the world, we should feel entitled to hear much more about them. We should want to know more of their spontaneity, their artlessness, their penetration, their breadth, their persistence. Just how far was this intensification of labor, this special overtime procedure, this form of pace-setting or of speeding up a government scheme for increasing production? Just how far did there exist outward compulsion from the state? And were those who engineered these ventures motivated by some more or less material reward? But, however far these expedients were simply state-induced means of redoubling the production of goods in the land, it can hardly be doubted that there was involved in them no little voluntary effort, no little sincerity and enthusiasm. In any event the Soviet Union deserves well at our hands for having given us the conception that some of these things are worth thinking about in our industrial society, and of having given them practical application.

[1] See *post,* p. 258.

How far the economic outcome in general in the Soviet Union was to be ascribed to inherent efficiency or inefficiency of state socialism, or to the kind that had been shown there, or to the character and condition of the country in which it had been essayed, or to circumstances not entirely propitious for its introduction and continuance, there is none as yet to tell us. Even if the land was good soil for the trying out of socialism, there should have been a much longer time for its preparation. It must always be remembered that with the tempo imposed there was involved a gigantic attempt to transform a backward agrarian state into a modern industrial one, and one largely standing aloof in its policies and practices from other nations.

CHAPTER XIV

The Soviet State and Its Educational and Cultural Activities

HARDLY less pronounced than the economic revolution that took place in the Soviet Union was the cultural. One of the most hopeful and yet one of the most disturbing things in the whole Soviet undertaking lay in the system of education that was to be instituted there. This had to do alike with the vast amount of illiteracy that had existed in Russian territory and with the purposes and methods of instruction that were now to be pursued.

The problem of illiteracy or of extremely limited or of the barest education, inherited as it had been from the old Czaristic régime, was of a seriousness which it is difficult to exaggerate. It may be said with a large measure of truth that in the situation as to education all of the troubles of the old and of the new Russia had their origin. It cannot be repeated too often that a large part of the Russian people, with all their noble and generous qualities, had for years been sunk in a mire of illiteracy, that whatever education had been offered them had been of a very restricted and meagre character, and that the knowledge of the masses of the people with regard to the great world outside their borders was hardly to be counted.

In such circumstances, with a vast portion of an immense population singularly backward in education, with enormous distances separating the inhabitants, and with roads poor and often hardly usable, the wiping out of illiteracy and the creation of an educated citizenry became a gigantic task—gigantic enough for the most intelligent and progressive government, and for the ablest educational generalship of the world, supplied with abundant financial resources, manned with the most skilled teaching force, and with a program extending over a long period of years.

Be it said to the high credit of the Soviet state that it was fully alive to the seriousness of the problem, and never wearied in bringing the problem to public attention. It was doing materially more in the way of attack than was the case under the old Czaristic régime—which for many years had been slow to realize and deal effectively with its great problem.[1] Possibly no other country of the world came to render relatively more generous financial support to education than did the Soviet Union. There was awakened in the land a genuine and far-reaching thirst for knowledge. In a sense education may be said to have become a passion in the land, well-nigh a master passion. The "liquidation" of illiteracy was the alluring slogan for its doing away with. There were "down with illiteracy" societies created. In the inviting campaign were marshalled all classes. Each of the organizations in the Soviet network had a place in the heated program. Factories, farms, trade unions, coöperative associations, clubs, all had their enthusiastic part. Without a modicum of education soldiers might not leave the army. Prisoners in their prison houses had education as a part of their prison discipline. Ready means of instruction for all the people were at hand in such vehicles as the radio, the motion picture, the theatre, the museum, the public billboard. We were being treated to the spectacle of a nation rising in massed attack upon its ancient foe. Seldom in the world's history has there been presented such a drama, or has there been so great a tribute to education.

In its general educational policies the Soviet government faced in one respect a relatively easy and simple task. As with

[1] See *ante*, p. 83.

everything else that came into its hands, it had quite a clean slate to work upon, with no leftover ways or measures to clog or impede its operations, with no traditions or ancient customs to get rid of, with no opposition or critical element to put obstacles in its path or to find serious fault. Whether its principles and procedure were good or not, the Soviet government had a rare opportunity to put into practice the latest theories or ideas in education, and to avail itself of the latest expert pronouncements upon the subject. No nation had ever been given, at least in modern times, such *carte blanche* as to what it should do in the instruction of its children. Russia might have provided a vast educational laboratory for the enlightenment of the rest of the world, though in not a few respects the country was hardly the fittest one for such experiments.

All in all, there was an almost unparalleled reduction in illiteracy, perhaps in the time consumed unapproached in recorded history. In many areas of the land in previous years illiteracy had embraced a very considerable part of the population, in a few almost the entire population. After a score of years under the Soviet régime it was in general reduced to one-tenth or even less. In time there were scarcely any under thirty years of age who were altogether illiterate or without some rudiments of knowledge. Of the entire population at one time practically one-fourth was said to be in school or in a class of some kind for instruction. We are not informed, however, just how "literacy" was defined in the Soviet Union.

As compared with the countries of western Europe and the United States, educational standards in the Union of Socialist Soviet Republics were not for the most part to be regarded as of the highest. To a great extent in what is to be called "pure" education it fell somewhat short of the levels in those countries. Professional education was as a general thing of less intensive character than in them. With time Soviet standards tended to advance.

Education in the Soviet commonwealth was from the start

to be free and universal. (For a time this did not apply to certain classes, as children of former Czaristic officers.) Schools might be established not only in cities, towns, villages, and rural hamlets, but in connection with or as appurtenances to factories or farms. Higher education and professional or advanced technical education were mostly under the aegis of the central state government, with lower forms entrusted to political subdivisions or to local units, always with more or less supervision from the general authorities. Teachers colleges were duly provided for the training of teachers. (Teachers of special classes received higher pay.) Co-education of boys and girls was after a time abandoned except in higher education and vocational training.

The attendance of children at their schools grew better with the years, except for situations consequent upon war conditions. In some regions attendance was better than in others, often depending upon the density of population in different sections. Compulsory education laws were in general from seven to fourteen, in some rural areas for a time from seven to eleven. It was hoped later to make the upper limit eighteen. These laws appear to have been enforced more effectively in some places than in others. In some areas school equipment was meagre; in some there were overcrowded classes. Inroads of German armies had taken a heavy toll of school structures. In some regions there were transportation difficulties; in others, teacher shortages. In some places only a part of the children were in school, and education could not have its fullest effects. A considerable number did not have sufficient schooling because of being called out prematurely to aid in the industrial tasks of the nation.

The child in the Soviet Union began his education at a very early age, in fact, he stepped into it from the nursery—or rather he might be said in his early years to have one foot in the nursery and one in the school. Formally, the first three years of the child's life were in the crèche, the next four in the kindergarten, under the health and under the educational authorities, respectively. A more or less incidental result of this early start in education was to dilute the allegiance the child owed to the parent and to turn more of it to the state—to loosen the influence of the home in the building up of the child's life and character, and to vest more of these things in the control of the state.

The educational process followed the most advanced theories. There was no end of educational experimentation. Children were put to all manner of tests; rarely have they been so much used as "guinea pigs." There were introduced certain "short cuts" to education. On one hand and another was there displayed opposition or reaction to what the Soviet authorities were pleased to call formalism in education. There were some features that experienced educators could hardly regard otherwise than superficial, even though dressed in more or less pretentious language. Perhaps educational processes were moving at too fast a pace. Perhaps there was in them something a bit exotic, something a bit unreal with respect to human nature, despite certain undeniably good points in the Soviet educational system.[1]

The guiding principle in the schools was largely self-expression on the part of the child. Self-government had a definite part in its work; children helped in maintaining discipline. The much-loved committee conceptions of the Soviet people reached even to children in their schools, especially in the earlier years of the Soviet régime; they were to have a word to say, along with their teacher, as to what and how and by whom they were to be taught.

Physical chastisement had little place in the educational process; rather there was resort to methods of encouragement and reward—punishment involving the loss of privileges. The child in school was to observe, to question, to judge for himself. He was to learn by doing. Fairy tales were not given unless

[1] On later changes in educational attitudes, see *post*, p. 381.

suited to communistic purposes. Dramatics, drawing, music, with the museum, were definite means of instruction; there were visits and trips outside the classroom both for contacts with nature and to have close-up views of Soviet institutions. Schooling was designed as a laboratory within and without the classroom. As nature study was stressed, so were the natural sciences in general. To children believed to be gifted or talented was offered special encouragement. Teachers from the school could come to the child's home to have further part in its development. There was an organization on the order of parent-teachers associations.

Nor was it to be forgotten in the schoolroom what the country was, what it stood for, and how great it was. From childish throats shrilled chants of praise to the "Red Commonwealth" where they so happily lived; to children in less favored lands were stretched out childish hands of sympathy or of pity. In Soviet teaching about other lands there was not always the strictest adherence to the truth, the plain, unvarnished truth. History of other countries could be flagrantly distorted.[1]

A notable feature in Soviet instruction was the combination or correlation of vocational education with intellectual education. Schools were largely semi-technical institutions, manual labor and intellectual instruction going hand in hand, or linked together in striking fashion. To play was given a utilitarian side. It might include instruction in making useful things or employment at useful toil. Toys might be in the guise of tools, models, mechanical devices, all designed to lead to creative labor or to other occupation that would be of advantage to the state. In the Academy of Pedagogical Sciences there was a branch concerned with children's toys. Technical education received paramount attention. Science and industry were closely interwoven. A thing like electricity could demand early study.

To promote pleasant relations, and to create a sense of unity

[1] There were training manuals for teachers to show how children were to be indoctrinated with proper Soviet conceptions of morality, discipline, patriotism, etc.

between the schools and different Soviet organizations, a school might be "adopted" by a factory or collective farm; while the school in turn might "adopt" an army unit, a trade union, a machine tractor station, or a hospital.

After the kindergarten there came four years of elementary schooling, followed by three years of what might be called junior high school. If a full high school course was to be had, three more years were required. At a "technicum" (technical high school) four years were necessary. At fourteen or fifteen was reached the age when was to be decided in what direction the child's future educational training was to proceed—in high school towards a higher education if properly qualified therefor, or in a trade or vocational school if not so qualified and if such training was desired. Decision lay theoretically in the hands of the child, though he was to be amenable to considerable persuasion from the state authorities.[1] College education was of a highly practical nature, of limited "liberal arts" character. It was largely preparatory to the future professional career that was to follow—"pre-medical," for example. "Postgraduate" work was mainly for those expecting to be college professors or full-time scientists. There were also higher technical schools.

Because of the returns that were to be expected in the service of the state, and because not many were able to pay the expenses of a college education, there were for a time government subsidies or stipends for higher education. In later days tuition fees, though of moderate size, were imposed to help meet the costs of high school or college education, though not for war veterans or choice youth.

There were set up in the land something like eight hundred institutions for higher education or advanced technical training, including a score and a half of universities. In certain regions there had previously existed none. The total number of college students, however, was not great—hardly over one-half

[1] See *ante,* p. 227.

of one per cent of the population really to be so called, a proportion considerably less than that in the United States, but not comparing unfavorably with the situation in some European countries.

To promising students was lent encouragement to go through college or advanced technical school, aid perhaps coming from an organization like a trade union. Encouragement was likewise extended to workers in different lines for their educational improvement. To some industrial establishments were attached facilities for vocational education, with counselling features.

But education in terms of intellectual values was not all. Physical education, physical culture had a notably high place. Elementary hygiene was given a conspicuous niche. Not seldom were opportunities seized upon to give lessons in such matters as sanitation, table manners, and general etiquette to children, and to their elders as well. Public posters could even be used for the purpose.

It is to be added that education in the Soviet Union was not without its military bearing. Practically from the lowest grades on through college certain subjects, as mathematics, geography, physics, chemistry, etc., besides physical training, could have a definite tinge in preparation for the possible work of the soldier who might be called upon for defense of the communistic Fatherland. There were a number of special military schools for youth, particularly for the sons of military commanders and for certain orphan children (not altogether different from some under the Czar).[1]

Adult education, also to no small extent of vocational or utilitarian character received ample consideration. Continuation schools, evening schools, correspondence courses had their part in the educational process. Technical and agricultural institutes might be set up in different places for workers. In the factory, on the farm, in the trade union, in the club, education in some form was glaringly presented or continued. Stress was placed

[1] On military training in connection with youth organizations, see *post*, p. 321.

upon "polytechnization," technical education with broad, lib eral bearings.

Matters as to education in the schools and elsewhere in Soviet Russia were marred by the attitudes or peculiar slant toward it. Education as set forth by the authorities of that country was, strictly speaking, hardly to be called education at all; it was made a political thing. Communist indoctrination was constant, unceasing from earliest life; few religions could have surpassed it in persistence and fervor. Schools were in no small sense organs of the state for the promotion and dissemination of its tenets. In the institutions of higher education, and also in lower ones, there was unremitting attention given to the so-called class struggle.[1] In the Soviet scheme of education what was so denominated was in large degree primarily and fundamentally an ideology—the inoculation of particular propaganda or the moulding into a particular pattern. In the whole undertaking were dogmatic attitudes which permitted no gainsaying, no deviation.

Besides the formal means of education in the schools, for the inculcation of communistic principles, there were other agencies set up for political instruction and indoctrination, and of a peculiarly Soviet order. There were in particular certain youth organizations, each appealing to youth of different ages, and with a certain educational program for each group. (These are described in a latter connection.)[2]

Education in the Soviet Union not only took a wide range, but was to bring into use special instruments for its greater effectiveness. A Latinized alphabet was planned eventually for the entire country. In bringing education and intellectual activities to some backward national groups in the vast Soviet territory, it was sometimes necessary first to provide an alphabet or a grammar. Groups that had no written language were

[1] To help keep alive memories of the days of the Revolution, there were given to localities of historic significance such names as "Place of Fallen Heroes." There were holidays to celebrate outstanding events in Soviet history. Statues were erected to, and cities named after, great leaders.

[2] See *post*, p. 320.

helped to acquire one—some groups had even been without a script. At times it happened that in a given language there were no technical or scientific expressions to be found; special efforts were called for to meet this inadequacy. Each country or nationalistic group kept its own language, but Russian was taught as a second language in all.

Education in the Soviet Union went far beyond the school room. In a sense the whole population was seething with the new-found article. Desire for knowledge swept up and down the land. Printed matter of all kinds poured from the presses. Newspapers found avid perusers. Metropolitan papers might have local editions over a greater or less part of the country; there were also editions in non-Russian languages. Newspapers increased vastly over Czaristic days; there were said to be over seven thousand printed of one kind and another. Relatively few were dailies. A considerable part were of professional or trade character, with some from factories, farms, or other Soviet institutions—not less than a half were to be called "house organs." A special kind of newspaper, and a special means of education, was the "wall newspaper," or "billboard newspaper," which was to be found in factories, collective farms, and elsewhere in the land. It contained a certain amount of news, but even more of an appraisal of the work of the employees. There were both party and official government papers. When the size of the population of the country is considered, the number of newspapers does not appear large.

Besides newspapers, there were published periodicals of various sorts, some well prepared, possibly illustrated—but largely propaganda for the Soviet cause. Without special government authorization no foreign newspaper or other publication was allowed in the land.

From the presses there flowed a constant stream of new books. In one year there were said to appear one or two score thousand. Bookstores or book bazaars were everywhere. Newsstands sagged under their heavy loadings. More books were perhaps published here than in any other country. (It should be added that a large portion of books were cheaply printed, and paper-bound, as was often the case in some countries of Europe.) These books were in general of the more serious or more worthwhile kind, dealing particularly, apart from matters of socialism, with science, travel, adventure, or genuine literature. The people devoured scientific literature. There was relatively little of the frivolous; there was relatively little of crime for its own sake. Compared with what was to be found in some countries, newsstands were notably free from gross or dissolute presentations. In the novels issued there was often an important Soviet moral. Not a few books, devoid of an anti-communistic slant, were brought in from foreign countries, including the United States. The Soviet people were quite curious in some ways to know about the people in other lands.

No books could be printed, and none could enter the country, unless with the approval of the authorities. In fact, there could be no printing press or printed matter, or printing material, in the land without the express authorization of the powers in the seat of government. This was all state-owned or in the hands of state-sponsored organizations.

Public libraries were scattered over the land, with a very large number particularly for children. There was constant stimulation for local libraries. There were travelling libraries for rural regions. In many of the clubs of the workers, which occupied so prominent a place in the life of the country, reading rooms were a necessary adjunct. There were an abundance of museums—not a few of a high order, and in general well attended—educational, scientific, agricultural, industrial, cultural. There were special museums for children. There were museums of the "Revolution." There were Tolstoi, Tschaikowsky, and Pushkin museums. There were Lenin museums here and there over the land. In the larger cities there were what were known as central houses for arts education of children.

By the Soviet authorities there were promoted all manner of

excursions and tours—to museums, to factories, and to other places. The people were encouraged to travel about. There was abetted a sort of local "Chautauqua," with study courses, lectures, concerts, and so on. Always the motion picture, the theatre, the radio were instruments for education, of wide scope and of great power, and within the reach of all. A recognized and much used part of the scheme of education were public posters, placards, notices, slogans, catch words. No known medium in fact was neglected in the education of the masses— or perhaps in spreading Soviet communistic teaching.

Whether or not as a sort of frenzy over the new education now open to the possession of all, or over the general blessing believed manifest in the Soviet state, there were everywhere, in the country and in the city, unceasing meetings, speeches, processions.

In all the various forms of education in the land, it is never to be forgotten that nothing might be uttered or printed or otherwise disseminated that did not have the imprimatur of the authorities. All means of diffusing knowledge or of expressing public opinion were in the hands of the government. To all forms of education, there had to be a communist approach, a communist firman.[1] History and even general literature were to be written to suit Soviet ideas.

Public discussion followed in the wake of the new and wide concern in education. It was now a sort of national pastime. With it there was almost constant mass instruction in civics, or in the affairs of the Soviet state. The pointing out of public abuses or evils—the laziness of a factory foreman or the incompetence of a railway director—or a sort of state self-criticism, was an indulgence vivaciously participated in by all. Our

---

[1] "All publications in the U.S.S.R.—periodical and non-periodical—are supervised and censored for their political and ideological content. Counter-revolutionary matter, writing which incites to nationalistic or religious fanaticism, and pornographic writing are banned." "The Soviet Union Today," 1946, p. 67. "The party 'interferes' in particular in literary affairs when it sees that tendencies alien to the spirit of the Soviet people, manifestations that lower the social role and aesthetic significance of Soviet literature, have appeared in it." *U.S.S.R. Information Bulletin,* March 25, 1949.

commendation of this nation-wide public forum was to be tempered by the consideration that in it there must be nothing beyond what was prescribed by the authorities. There might be finding of fault with details, but never with the system. The only real public opinion was to be the official one.

Newspapers, be it said to their credit, did not stress or play up personal crimes or scandals or vulgarities or social trivialities, unless the state should in some way be concerned. There was no particular effort at mere amusement or entertainment for the reader. Comics and "funnies" had no great place. Not a little space, it is also to be acknowledged, was devoted to scientific and cultural discussions, and to more and better industrial production. There was always room for official communiqués. Magazines as well were in good part of serious order. There was little of what could be called advertising, the state not requiring such a medium for the disposal of its goods— and there frequently not being any too large a quantity of certain consumer goods after all for sale—though advertising could be availed of at times to get rid of some excess or surplus goods; such advertising as there was was largely for educational purposes, as with respect to health or living conditions. Advertising did not fail to laud the Soviet state.

Citizens were encouraged to criticise internal policies or arrangements or ventures, which they did with great gusto, sometimes in a sharp or in a severe vein. On the other hand, in the Soviet press there might be almost complete silence with respect to something that did not speak so well for the Soviet state or for the governing powers; a serious railway wreck or a devastating famine might largely escape newspaper notice. Foreign correspondents in Russia were not always permitted to know the whole truth about some internal matter. Foreign news was often of a misleading character, with emphasis upon or exaggeration of unfavorable events; there was almost continuous distortion of conditions existing in capitalistic countries. No little space was given, and with no little relish, to such matters as strikes, unemployment, "colonial" wars, and other of the troubles to which such countries were heir. A "straw man" was often made of conditions in such countries, with vigorous onslaughts thereupon. News was seldom looked upon with full objectivity; it was mostly in relation to state policies. Newspapers served in large part as purveyors of government propaganda. They were to a greater or less extent mouthpieces of the state—or shall we say of the Communist party?

With such attitudes toward the governmental powers, there was constant laudation, a sort of public glorification with regard to the aims and procedures, the potentialities and achievements of the Soviet state. There were grandiloquent boasts and claims. No opportunity was passed by for proclaiming one or another enterprise of the state as the "biggest" or the "grandest," its programs as "enormous," its success as "unqualified"; Soviet scientific discoveries were "unrivalled." There was no end to pointing out the benefits and advantages inherent in the Soviet state. Official outgivings could hardly be outdone by those of an American chamber of commerce or hotel association as to local attractions.

Perhaps attention was no less called to the wickedness of the outside world which had the temerity or ignorance to question or to belittle or to find fault. Everywhere were depicted or emblazoned the shortcomings, the derelictions, even the horrors of the capitalistic state, and the virtues, the blessings and the glories of the socialistic—on billboards, in cartoons, in art galleries, over loud-speakers. There could also be almost continuous honey-mouthed adulation of the Soviet leaders. Whatever of bareness or drabness might be found in the Soviet undertaking could be made up for in some degree by the glamorous descriptions with which it was invested.

Scientific research, be it further said to the high credit of the Soviet state, was sponsored on a far-reaching scale, though at times with a little too high-sounding language. There appeared a determination to wrest from nature her last secret. There were created endless institutes—of chemistry, biology, physics, agriculture, genetics, archaeology, literature, aviation (aerodynamic), electricity, medicine, machine building, promotion of workers' welfare (including one on hygiene for occupational diseases)—agriculture alone having a wide variety. There were scientific institutes in many cities, academies of science in different regions.[1] Whatever the depth of the foundation underneath—and it often went down deep—there was a certain furore over science in the land. Popular participation in it was encouraged for its own sake and for what it could do for the country. Scientists as well as creative workers in general enjoyed exceptional prestige; they were afforded full facilities for their work. To scientists making notable contributions of worth might be given prizes or emoluments. Outstanding inventors and explorers were "heroes of the Soviet Union." The incitement of scientific experimentation and exploration on the part of the Soviet government in some fields won the admiration and gratitude of the world. Long will be acclaimed the epics that had their seat in the frozen Arctic.

But the world could not forget that scientific research, if dealing with matters pertaining to the socialist state, and its vital concerns, could not always be expected to be strictly objective or "pure"; it might be here given the hue that the Soviet state wished it to have. There might even be issued a fiat as to what was and what was not to be regarded as scientific truth. Censorship and propaganda even in the holy domain of science were not asleep. There could be such a thing as "Soviet science,"[2] or "Soviet mathematics." Science was to be used only

[1] By the national Academy of Sciences there were issued over a score of specialized journals and an even larger number of annual tracts, besides certain large specialized volumes and general summaries.

[2] "Science in the Soviet Union is based upon the teachings of Karl Marx, Frederick Engels, Nicholai Lenin, and Joseph Stalin." From official publication of Soviet Union at World's Fair. in New York, 1939. "Soviet science possesses a qualitative singularity." *U.S.S.R. Information Bulletin*, April 22, 1949. With respect to biological inheritance, upon which divergent views were entertained by Soviet scientists, there could be employed such characterizations as "reactionary Weismann biologists," "reactionary Weismann-Morgan school . . . bankrupt in theory and practice," "pseudo-scientific doctrine of Morgan-Mendelites." *Ibid.*, September 8, 1948.

for service to the Soviet state. There was no place, furthermore, for the non-communist scientist. Science was a closed province here—there could be no dealings with scientists in other lands. Contacts with scholars and men of learning in general over the world were increasingly discouraged, and restricted, and denied.

Not only upon worthy scientists, but upon men of note in the world of literature or the arts, the Soviet state did not demur in conferring honor, and also in material reward, as in pensions or in the remission or reduction of taxes, or in such things as passes on railway trains; it did so with gladsome acknowledgment. Competition in the creation of individual wealth might be under ban, but it was freely allowed and encouraged in general industrial production and in scientific and cultural achievement. At the same time intellectuals whose productions proved obnoxious to the communistic state were made to suffer dishonor or lost caste; they could disappear from sight —they could no longer be accounted for.

Education in some respects in the Soviet land was a peculiar, anomalous thing. In it was not included accurate knowledge of the outside world; as to this the people were kept in heavy darkness, getting only what the government wanted them to get. With all its zeal for education, Soviet Russia did not let the people know all—something that might betray a want of complete faith in what we rightly call education.

In this country education was not merely a means of dealing with youth; nor was it merely a system of popular education. Through education here as a universal force man was to be made over—that is, into a good communist, with all that communism signified or connoted in the construction of a commonwealth based on its principles. Its program of education was not concerned with education purely as such; it was designed and carried out so as to make the people of the land of a distinct political and economic complexion, one so deep and lasting that they could never depart from it or wear it off. The

Soviet Union was educationally engaged in nothing less than the most stupendous task ever set before a nation. In this it took far-reaching strides alike in matters of culture and in matters of political economy—so great that there has been nothing similar to it in human history.

Education according to the Soviet understanding of the term did not stop at the country's borders. There was carried on an extensive and efficiently conducted campaign of propaganda in other lands, particularly with very attractive publications and superb motion pictures.[1]

In the field of art, whether in the sphere of education or of general culture, the Soviet government had another claim to our consideration and respect. Art in its broadest and fullest sense was preserved in Soviet Russia in a highly creditable manner— "preserved," for art had always had a high place in Russian life; and Soviet Russia was but upholding the national traditions. Not only collections of art, but places of historic interest were made available for the people, who were encouraged to visit and have enjoyment of them. The priceless collections at the Winter Palace and the Hermitage in Leningrad and at the various institutions maintained in Moscow and in other cities, as well as the numerous museums in all the larger cities, attested the appreciation of this form of education or of art on the part of the Soviet government. Intact were kept as far as might be possible various estates, buildings, and monuments of the former régime, for the eyes of the newer generation to see, and perhaps to compare. For its work of preservation and care of historical and archaeological monuments in general this government deserved the thanks of lovers of art, of culture, of history the world over.

To every form of art, of expression or of ornamentation, was given encouragement, including native arts and crafts throughout the wide Soviet domain. Nor must mention be omitted of endeavors in city planning or of attempts to combine beauty

[1] See *post*, p. 333.

and utility in the rebuilding of the land. Special consideration was given to areas injured in the war with the Germans. Landscaping received measurable attention, as did outdoor art in general. Nearly all the cities of consequence were marked with handsome public buildings. In certain of the cities, notably Moscow (once called a "great Asiatic village," and now to be made a model city), where towering modern structures touched elbows with quaint reminders of far-gone days, narrow ancient lanes might emerge into appealing spacious vistas or gardenlike squares lined with goodly trees or arrayed with flowers. Worn-out parts were to be destroyed, and new attractive parts to be created in their stead—there were in time to be no slums. In Moscow there radiated impressive boulevards from central foci. On the principal center was to be erected the 250-story high "Palace of the Soviets," surmounted with a statue of Lenin— designed to be the biggest and tallest structure in the world. And it was Moscow's subway, or Metro, which declared that none other in the world had been constructed with so much attention to what was pleasing to the eye, to say nothing of vying with it in general usefulness to the citizens of the city. Here station platforms were multi-colored, with noble pillars, and with the ceiling decorated with gold and blue mosaics; some flashed with archways of stainless steel. In this city there was expressed the hope that eventually the subways would be so far-flung and convenient as to make unnecessary surface lines for transportation.

In dramatic production the Soviet state was living up to the conceptions and performances of old Russia. Here it was maintained in gallant, even in heightened fashion. Not often elsewhere was the stage of such order; not often elsewhere were skill and labor and money so freely lavished to attain lofty standards. Excellence of execution, gorgeousness of display, efficiency of technique, cleverness of movement all shone forth in increased brilliance in the newer Russia. Nowhere else was the ballet so pretentious and so correctly conducted; the ballerina was a highly popular figure in the land. All this was not, however, the doing of Soviet Russia; it was in part the doing of the Russian people, unchanged intrinsically whether under Czar or under communism. It was the Soviet state that enlarged and improved the drama, and made it essentially of popular character, for all to take part in or to see. The Soviet people proved themselves fond of dramatic entertainment. There was relatively little on the stage that could be called deliberately vulgar, smutty, or risqué, though here as well as elsewhere the people were accustomed to plainness of speech. There was little of the horrendous or morbid on display. There was no great amount of gunplay except in war scenes.

Dramatic productions were carried on under different auspices, besides those of the state directly. Schools had any number, as did the many clubs of the land; in fact, nearly all the organizations of the Soviet state had greater or less concern in the matter. Children's theatres were a notable part of the dramatic program of the country—theatres for presentations for their particular enjoyment, and theatres in which they did the performing. Even more than with adults, these theatres were for the twofold purpose of entertainment and education; they fitted into the educational scheme of the state no less than into the dramatic. Marionette shows, some of them excellent, had a definite place. The larger theatres might contain training schools in dramatics.

There were few cities of any size that were without a theatre of some sort. Provincial theatres were stimulated and promoted; theatrical troupes or stock companies went about the country. High-class performances were frequent, not seldom of the classics, whether of native or of foreign origin. Strongly as was the theatre for the uplift, diversion, or amusement of the people in general, it had didactic purposes no less; such purposes were often obvious. The theatre, as was to be expected, was a very important vehicle for conveying and promoting communistic conceptions and aims. All artists were

271

held to the party line; there could be no deviation from communistic ideals in their presentations.

Motion pictures in Soviet Russia were often to be described as superb, at times with a certain naturalness or realistic qualities to a remarkable degree. The state took pains to see that it had something like the last word in the production of motion pictures. Historical pictures had a place of their own, and were the best of all. Educational aims here were quite manifest, and along divers lines. The motion pictures, too, could be counted upon as a powerful means of Soviet propaganda.[1] The Soviet state took delight in its dramatic productions in contrasting conditions of old Russia with those of the new. On both the screen and the stage there could be gross misrepresentations in respect to disliked foreign countries.

It is needless to say that the radio had wide use in the Soviet land, as was in time to be the case with television as well.

Music likewise had a high place in the cultural program of the land. It was to be cultivated, whether on the part of the performer or on the part of the mere listener. There was to be musical training both for the specialist and for the masses. For city factories and rural communities there were aid and encouragement in dramatic productions and orchestral renditions alike. There could, however, be no "bourgeois" music, either in words or in sounds.

Other forms of art, including painting and sculpture, had their meed of recognition; there was none neglected. Through trade unions, coöperative associations, and other bodies some form of culture was promoted and brought to the people, or was presented for their benefit. But nothing in art was to be derogatory of the Soviet state. There could not even be permitted such a thing as "bourgeois" architecture.

Creative art, whether amateur or professional, whether in the drama or elsewhere, received encouragement on every hand;

[1] The cinema "aims at depicting the truth of socialism and the heroes of the Revolutionary age." U.S.S.R. Handbook, 1936, p. 486.

stimulus, often ample, was given to those who had artistic promise in any direction, no matter under what conditions or under what economic barriers one might live. Expression was to be denied to none, so far as the state could do anything about it, with financial aid where necessary. Talented children were nurtured, as we have seen. Not only material assistance was granted to persons with capacities or endowment in some field of art, but appropriate recognition of other kinds as well. Actors and musicians, no less than writers and scientists, were singled out for honors and prizes. Stage or screen stars, on the other hand, though perhaps glamorous personages, could hardly become the pampered darlings of the nation.

For different industrial, national, or other groups there were festivals or some like form of entertainment or merry-making or show organized from time to time. Outdoor mass gymnastics could be well executed. Pageants were usually dignified, impressive spectacles. In Soviet public entertainment there was relatively little of "jazz"; such things as beauty contests were largely absent.

In its wide program of cultural promotion the Soviet authorities saw to it that nationalistic genius, talents, or gifts in various parts of the Soviet territory were not passed over; all possible was done to promote and advance them. Any local or regional traits or historical or legendary storehouses were to be afforded suitable notice and consideration, and if possible a due outlet. There were attempts at revivals of national culture in different areas, perhaps in folk lore or fairy tales, perhaps in folk dances, perhaps in arts and crafts, perhaps in some other phase of distinctive local tradition. Institutes might be held to further such activities. To evoke artistic expression in some more or less backward region, prizes were bestowed. Among the monuments to national heroes over the land, there were not neglected those of local bearing or significance.

Culture, art in its various manifestations, was to have an important and distinct place in the lives of the people; it was to

273

be woven into these lives. It was no longer to be an exclusive possession of aristocratic circles; it was to be something in which all the people might share. It was to be democratized and made accessible everywhere in the Soviet domain. No efforts were spared to bring it to the masses, and to make them in greater or less degree appreciative. Most of the larger cities had their "palaces of culture."

In the matter of culture, however—an expression so freely used in Soviet Russia—some of the finer values that had been associated with the term were lost. In the use of high-sounding phrases, in which the Soviet state excelled, probably no term was so overworked or misemployed as was the term "culture." Under it were covered a multitude of matters, not excluding some rather pertaining to particular forms of personal behavior or etiquette. It was as though culture were a hot-house plant to be quickly coaxed into bloom; or as though culture were something to be summarily thrust down the throats of the people. In addition, and more importantly, in the promotion and encouragement of that consideration, the single authoritative agency was the state. It remained the sole arbiter in determining what was and what was not to be recognized and regarded and denominated as culture, and to what extent and in what measure each different form was to be promoted and encouraged. As everywhere else in the Soviet state, nothing was permitted in this field or in this category that might bring harm to or cast doubt upon the communist cause.[1] There was hardly any such thing as art for art's sake. Objective presentation of art, of literature, of science was hardly to be expected. There was no sphere in which the Soviet state did not set itself up as supreme arbiter and dictator.

[1] "Practically the whole professional art field, with the exception of the cinema, is under the aegis of the All-Union Committee on Art Affairs. . . . The Committee's supervision covers every phase pertinent to these fields: art education, theatres, circuses, music halls, museums and galleries, price of tickets, repertoires, royalties, awards of titles, advertisements, wage norms, recordings and artistic radio programs, manufacture of equipment, erection of monuments, etc. The Ministry of Cinematography has similar comprehensive control over movies." "The Soviet Union Today," 1946, p. 61.

There was appearing in the Soviet Union an ever more drastic control over all forms of intellectual life—over all things in the spiritual life of man. There was no phase of any of the factors that have been mentioned that was not employed to mould Soviet society into one particular definite pattern—to fix in the people the conviction that the Soviet communistic system was superior to any other in the world, and that all others must in due time give way to it.

CHAPTER XV

The Soviet State and Its Social Welfare Measures

IT was possibly to be said to the credit of the Soviet state that it endeavored to provide entertainment and recreation for all its people—and on a scale not even conceived of in Czaristic days. It was quite conscious that with the vast machine production coming under way, there would be an increasing amount of leisure time for the people; it strove to be able in some measure to meet and forestall this great need. It aimed to have no region in its vast empire untouched. Remote villages could at least be brought within the reach of the motion picture and radio, and perhaps also of some other means of diversion.

There were abounding "parks of rest and culture" not only in cities but on collective farms, which were to make an appeal to all classes of the population. This form of amusement or entertainment or instruction or repose or relaxation—perhaps all combined—could range all the way from a circus or Coney Island roller coaster and all manner of games (not excluding games on the order of ping pong or on the order of chess), to theatricals, motion pictures, folk dancing, festivals, lectures, concerts, art exhibits. The parks might contain giant flower beds—or fashion shows—or general exhibition halls. They might have track and field sports and athletic facilities, with setting up exercises for all. There might be water sports, indoor dancing, parachute dropping from a high tower. Payment might be required for the use of what had been provided, but seldom too large for a modest purse. If there was an entrance fee for children in "children's villages," they could have for it all necessary care and attention. The activities of one of the numerous workers' clubs over the country might read like those of a social settlement or of a paternalistic industrial establishment in America.

In profuse array throughout the land throve sports, athletics, physical culture exercises, and for all seasons. Clubs for such purposes were practically everywhere. A stadium was to be found in every city of considerable size, and perhaps as well on a large collective farm. Sport organizations were encouraged and promoted, generally by the various clubs or youth organizations in the land, and also by trade unions and other bodies, possibly as a part of their regular functions. By some industrial establishments facilities were provided for sports or physical culture. After the Revolution certain new sports, including football, were introduced into the land. There were spirited contests and matches. At times there were efforts to stress the inherent values of play apart from the matter of competition.

Mountain climbing, skiing, various aquatic sports all had their devotees. Wrestling was a sport in which the Russians had long excelled. In the larger cities there was horse racing (with betting), usually once a week throughout the year. The circus was always a popular institution in many parts of Russia. Vacation periods, which were a regular feature in one's year round employment, together with holidays, which were always important days in the Soviet calendar, had ample provision included for play and sports. Traveling about and around was itself a happy diversion whenever possible.

It is to be added that in this land joy-giving, health-giving sport and recreation were not commercialized. All was on an amateur basis; there were no full-time professional athletes, no sport entrepreneurs. Sport and recreation were promoted and conducted for the financial profit of none. There was no personal or private gain from any aspect of Soviet life. It was asserted, however, that certain outstanding athletes were granted

277

non-monetary perquisites or emoluments in some form, or were given more or less nominal employment, with possible occasional subsidies for training purposes, to further their athletic prowess.

It is also to be added that the activities that could come under the name of "sport" in the Soviet land were more or less state-planned or state-directed or state-instigated—or at least nothing could be done along these lines without state approval and endorsement; the consent of the state must in any event be secured for the use of the necessary facilities or apparatus which belonged to it or to some organization under its sponsorship.[1] There was not much room or opportunity for the play of private intiative or enterprise, unless immediately or rather closely linked up with what the state wanted or demanded. Public spectacles, particularly in sports or in marching exhibitions, could be well-nigh perfect examples of regimentation; ostensibly they were to be looked upon as spontaneous demonstrations, but they could exact hard and prolonged rehearsal.

What was true here was true of other matters. "Clubs" for sports, for entertainment, for some form or aspect of culture, for educational progress, for civic improvement, for social reform—for young and for old—which swarmed over the land, and which nominally might be "private," told the tale: behind the scenes was the Soviet *deus ex machina*. Persons with common interests could band together in a more or less formal association for various purposes—for congenial discussions, for mutual enjoyment, for convivial gatherings, for athletic contests, for scientific inquiry, for study of literature or art or other cultural benefit, or for the advancement of some other particullar object; one could be free to join as he wished. What were termed "voluntary" committees or organizations might make provision or set up facilities for the accomplishment of their pur_ poses; they might manifest concern or take action with regard

[1] "The All-Union Council of Physical Education, a state organization, supervises and plans the entire system of physical culture and sport throughout the Soviet Union." U.S.S.R. Handbook, 1936, p. 489.

to whatever matter was before them; they could go about the country or from place to place in the interests of better health, better education, better industrial methods, or better something else, conducting campaigns and holding public meetings— there was a fairly numerous list of such public-spirited bodies. But over all these reached the long arm of the state, perhaps unseen but always felt. There could be little of which it did not know and did not approve. Any organization of a political nature whatever was of course out of the question—outside the only organization of that character permitted, which was the Communist party. "Private" bodies must all be duly registered. All meetings and programs must have received official sanction beforehand. Toleration or the showing of the head of any activities or plannings that might conceivably be antagonistic to the Soviet régime could hardly be expected. Should private gatherings be too frequent or with too large an attendance, the matter would soon reach the attention of the authorities; it would be speedily looked into. Ostensible or nominal private organizations were really in no small part state-made or state-controlled or state-inspired, or at least without or beyond state objection.

Any action or procedure, furthermore, which was requested or directed by the state was duly forthcoming on the part of private bodies.

In the Soviet land there was a general tendency toward standardization of the people's lives—moulding them into a state-created pattern according to which they were to live. Nearly everything of any consequence affecting the individual citizen had in the background the definite concern of the state. There seemed on nearly every hand a certain artificiality, an absence of complete individuality or spontaneity—one's actions were to proceed with one eye on the state authorities. In the life of the citizen there could, furthermore, be a bit of overorganization—plentiful red tape in one direction or another—in forming a society of some kind, in securing a book from a library, in arranging a railway journey. There was little in the lives of the men and women of the country, beyond minor personal items, that did not suffer regimentation in greater or less degree —sport, education, culture, industry, one's very life. There were some who heartily approved all this; there were some who enjoyed it in a sort of boyish glee or blissful irresponsibility. There were some who found it onerous or tedious; there were some who looked upon it as confining or enslaving.

In sport, in education, and in all other forms of state activity stress was placed upon physical development or physical culture. Health examinations, proper exercise, instruction in the building up of able-bodied, sturdy, robust citizens—systematic physical training for all classes—were no small part of the Soviet program—in some respects almost to the point of worship—though possibly in actual results with little more achieved than in certain other countries of the world. Many factories as well as clubs and other organizations had their own gymnasiums or other facilities for bodily exercise. The land teemed with youth movements, abounding in energy and enthusiasm, all with their "strength through joy." Young workers were to have "healthy lungs, strong muscles, steady nerves, sound hearts"—something to which youth might well aspire in all lands. The health and vitality and soundness of the people were regarded as necessary for the welfare of the state.

In the Soviet Union there were praiseworthy far-flung efforts to cope with disease—in a country where such efforts had long been desperately needed. A great problem in general public sanitation was found in respect to a country never known for its cleanliness—a problem that would require prolonged and intensified attention. The Soviet authorities were not slow in meeting and attacking this gigantic problem. Broad programs were set on foot, including a popular educational campaign through lectures, pictures, exhibits, posters, pamphlets, motion pictures, radio. In every possible way the matter of health was brought home to the people. There was mass health education on a scale and of a depth perhaps never before equalled in any country. The people were made to know that the health of one was the concern of all. To youth organizations was given the slogan: "I protect my health and that of others." In foremost regard was placed the matter of the prevention of disease or illness. No people could be more health conscious.

The general shortage of physicians that had long prevailed in the land was remedied as fast as conditions would permit. With the years their number was several times that of the old Czaristic days. The number of hospitals likewise increased several fold. There were set up half a hundred medical training schools (several times as many as before), besides dental, pharmaceutical, and other like institutions. Great medical skill or protracted medical training, approaching that of countries to the west, could not as a general thing be expected for some years; but there was steady progress in the matter, and there arose here and there some notable practitioners, as well as some distinguished specialists. To help out in the general medical shortage, there were a number of what might be called sub-physicians, or persons prepared to attend to less serious ailments or to assist regular physicians in their work. Physicians were granted a month vacation during the year. Rural physicians were allowed refresher courses at times.

Some of the hospitals established in the Soviet Union were well appointed and quite up-to-date. Of other hospitals not so much could be said. Some overcrowding or other unfavorable condition was in greater or less part the consequence of wars during which both soldiers and civilians had suffered. There were some fairly good nurses, though not a great number of fully trained ones. There was a network of more or less inter-related organizations having to do with the problems of health in the land. Medical and public health vocabularies bulged with such terms as prophylactic and epidemiological institutes, medical centers, health stations, medical supplies industries, medical laboratories, ambulatoriums, sanitariums, sanitation centers, clinics, maternity homes, dispensaries, polyclinics, health resorts, medico-therapeutic facilities, health museums, scientific research agencies, child health centers, nurseries, brain institutes, prophylactoriums. Scattered over the land were a considerable number of rest homes, health resorts, and sanitariums, some with attendants, medical specialization, laboratories, etc. The rest homes at hand were not able to provide sufficient accommodations for all who might enter; some were crowded—there were often waiting lists. Those admitted had usually to pay something under one-half of the expenses. Some rest homes which had belonged to the former nobility were not altogether suited to their present purposes.

There were in addition the general health benefits of the social insurance provisions of the land;[1] through them was to be had free medical attention and treatment to a greater or less extent.

Medical treatment was to be made available for the entire population so far as this was possible, extending into rural areas, no less than into urban centers. (There had been a medical center in Czaristic Russia.) There were roving physicians and traveling clinics to go about the country. From medical centers nurses went out to visit homes where there was illness or where health conditions needed attention. There were postnatal vacations for mothers. There were health centers or medical stations ("polyclinics" in Soviet language) not only in the cities and larger towns, but in many of the larger industrial establishments and larger farms. There were continuing nutrition studies. Restaurants and other eating places were to give due concern to dietetic principles and values. There was virtually no place in the land that did not have inspection of the health conditions surrounding it. Despite all these efforts, the problem of health and sanitation remained a serious one in many parts of the country.

The Soviet state, be it said to its credit, was greatly concerned

[1] See *ante*, p. 232.

with scientific medical procedure. It had little sympathy with quack doctors or medical nostrums. It constantly sought to dissuade the people from resorting to them. It is good to be able to say that on the way out were the medical fakers, soothsayers, and witch doctors that had so heavily infested the land in the years of the past.

Large claims were made for the advances in Soviet medicine, some doubtless more justified than others. Some were truly of a high order; some would have to await later verdicts by medical men of authority.

Care and treatment of the so-called defective classes were likewise given a full place. Mental disturbance or derangement was believed to be to a great extent due to economic environment or to the economic organization of a particular locality; through proper economic adjustments, especially through freedom from troubles and worries of an economic order, was to be accomplished a good deal for the restoration of mental health. Frequent psychiatric examinations were encouraged; to some extent they were provided for. There were a number of what were called neuro-psychiatric institutes, as well as of small hospitals for incipient cases of mental trouble. There was no little resort to occupational therapy in the matter. Special study was given to the possible connection between mental and physical disorders. In the program of medical treatment to be afforded, general institutional provision had some place, though not a relatively large one; it was reserved mostly for acute cases. The rest homes over the country could have some part in dealing with the less serious cases.

The treatment of classes like the deaf and the blind, though following the form or mould to be expected of this communistic state, was not of a particularly high order. Attention did not seem always to be based on the soundest principles, though it was called most progressive, and even ultra-modern. There seemed to be a little of the superficial about it. The number of institutions for these classes increased somewhat over the number in Czaristic days. The work here was related to the Institute of Defectology, a branch of the Academy of Pedagogical Sciences. Vocational rehabilitation work for the physically handicapped had made definite progress, though such things as artificial limbs were far from sufficient for those needing them. Persons in general incapable of labor were to be duly cared for; there was a constitutional right to maintenance in case of disability as well as of old age.

Standards of general social welfare measures could not as a rule be ranked quite on a level with those of the most progressive countries of the world; but they were constantly improving, and bade fair in some respects to set an example. The trained social worker, as known in the United States, had made an appearance only to a very limited extent, outside of medical nurses. Probably what came nearest to organized "social work" in the land was done through clubs or trade unions. Social work of a sort, and sometimes of a fairly good order, could be found in connection with hospitals, clinics, nurseries, prisons, the Red Cross, etc. Palaces of culture were often on the order of what we often know as community centers. Children in evil plight received some attention from communist youth organizations. Children's vacation periods, parties, or holiday activities could be looked after by such organization or by some club or trade union. There were numerous summer camps for children, toward the costs of which parents might make a small contribution. Certain social welfare work was promoted through social insurance funds. There was less place in the land for what is called private charity, the state undertaking to provide for all, though giving was always possible between friends and neighbors.

Social insurance provisions were on a wide scale, though not so very much more so than in most countries of Europe before the recent wars, where the system had been in use for a greater or less number of years. Covered were death of family breadwinner, permanent and temporary disability, accidents, illness, old age, maternity (and theoretically unemployment). The matter, including rest homes and vacation outings, was largely under the direction of the trade unions.[1]

Great attention had to be devoted in the Soviet Union to the matter of housing for the people. Following the First World War and the subsequent civil wars, and with an ever increasing population, there was a very serious housing shortage in the land. With the general birth rate high, something encouraged by the state, and with migrants from the country pouring into the cities, it was not easy to catch up with the housing situation. Nor was the matter helped by the constant creation of new cities. (During Soviet days the urban population increased from one-tenth to one-third.) The situation was rendered more acute in consequence of the Second World War; conditions were greatly worsened. No small part in the matter was played by incoming war refugees.

The matter of providing a sufficient number of dwellings for the people to live in ever proved one of the pressing and primary considerations in the affairs of the new state. Apartment overcrowding and room overcrowding, often including the taking in of boarders, both constituted in themselves no small problem. The housing construction which was undertaken, and of which there was really a prodigious amount, was not of a high order as a general thing; too often it was of cheap or flimsy character, with relatively few modern conveniences, largely because nothing else was possible in the circumstances. Lack of building material played no small part in the matter, especially in later days. A beginning was made with prefabricated houses.

Complaint was sometimes voiced that much of the money that went so prodigally into club or public building construction and facilities could be put to better use in the erection of actual dwellings for the people. It is needless to say that in some areas war played sad havoc with many structures that

[1] See *ante*, p. 229.

housed the people. With time, apart from war-created conditions, housing became considerably better. But under generally more favorable conditions proper housing could not be expected directly or at an early date. Even with the rather make-shift housing, which at times was all that was possible, the housing shortage in the land had little chance of being entirely or fully met. Inadequate housing or relatively poor housing seemed likely to continue long for a large part of the population.

As would be expected, there were full housing regulations, an elaborate housing code dealing with many particulars, in the Soviet state. Some had to do with the size of the building to be constructed, the space about it, the distance from the street or from other houses, materials to be used in construction, joint family arrangements, accessibility of playgrounds for children, sub-letting, and so on. The amount of space to be occupied by an individual person might be specified. Dispossession or eviction from one's dwellings was carefully safeguarded. This could be only after due notice, and not accompanied with undue hardship. Nor could it be for mere non-payment of what was owed. When a family was evicted, other quarters had usually to be found for it.

A dwelling might be secured through some general state department or agency, usually a local community or municipality, or through some coöperative association organized for the purpose. In addition, there might be dwellings provided by some industrial establishment or other state enterprise for its employees. For a time coöperative housing, which was something to be looked for in the communistic scheme, and which was permitted and even encouraged in earlier days, later fell into more or less disfavor with the governing authorities, and became of somewhat diminishing order. There had been complaints of loose and unbusinesslike procedure and of certain abuses, including a measure of profiteering by some members over others—there were charges at times of covert unlawful transactions in housing dealings; some of the associations had also failed properly to comply with legal regulations.

In connection with the matter of housing there were committees to pass upon sanitation, eligibility of applicants, the amount of rent to be charged, proper use of premises, etc. (even including recreation and cultural facilities). There was also often created a sort of local government with its own court, to settle possible controversies between apartment dwellers, and to avoid disputations and bickerings, these local bodies having considerable power with regard to general housing arrangements.

With time there was, even in this socialistic commonwealth, greater inclination to encourage outside congested areas in the cities the construction of small individual homes for those who were to live in them, with possibly greater or less state aid. The land for the purpose was theoretically perpetually leased from the state. Such a dwelling could also be directly rented from the public authorities. In the city, however, there remained, as in other countries, a trend toward large-scale apartments, perhaps directly rented or otherwise procured as above explained, rather than individual homes, the better in the city to provide for a larger population and to afford greater or less measure of communal living. Dwellings could be sub-let under careful and rather strict regulations, and provided that no profit accrued to any party in the transaction. Any kind of speculation here was of course under heavy Soviet ban. No dwelling might be taken over oftener than once in three years.

The birth rate in Russia had for long years been a very high one, in some regions the highest among the Caucasian peoples, and at times approaching what had been regarded as the maximum for the human race. In Soviet Russia the birth rate slackened a little, though it remained about twice as high as in some other white countries. A high birth rate was favored and encouraged by the government, in part to meet and to develop the vast resources of the country, and in part to provide an army strong enough to hold off all future foes—though thought would have to be given to the potential agricultural production and other resources sufficient to support a large population. To this end, bounties were offered to families with a large number of children; family allowances increased sharply with the increase in the number of children born; they began with the third child; they were particularly high for children after the sixth, and higher still for later ones. Mothers of ten living children, with due regard for war dead, were called "mother heroines." The "glory of motherhood" first-class was conferred upon mothers having nine children, second-class upon those having eight, and third-class upon those having seven. Large families could expect better living quarters, or better or cheaper nursery accommodations. Women were encouraged to marry young and to have children. Birth control preventives were frowned upon, if not forbidden by law to a greater or less extent. Contraceptives, however, always had a greater or less extended sale in the land. Special taxes might be laid upon bachelors and upon childless marriages.

If the birth rate in Russia had been high, so had been the death rate. With the general lack of medical attention and of broad sanitary measures, nothing else was to be expected. Under the Soviet régime mortality rates showed a decline, steady though not rapid. There were appreciable reductions in the death rate from such affections as tuberculosis, venereal disease, cholera, smallpox, scarlet fever, diphtheria, and malaria, and also in the infant mortality rate (cut one-half). There was a notable decrease with trachoma, a serious eye affection in some areas. After the German invasion there was an increase with some diseases. Death from disease in general was accentuated during the war among both soldiers and civilians. In time the death rate in several large cities compared well with that of some other European cities. A factor that was not without bearing upon the death rate in the Soviet Union was the massed killings of a portion of the population directly or indirectly through its internal struggles and dissensions, and through fatal mistreatment of inhabitants in various civil uprisings and economic disturbances. Famines also took their toll of the inhabitants; at times several million were lost in a single year. Death was often the case with those whose fate took them to concentration camps. Wars cut heavily with both soldiers and civilians.

Despite conditions in Russia to hold down population, whether in old Russia or in the new, population in that land generally increased, at times at the rate of several millions a year. The population was in great measure a young one; the median age was around twenty or twenty-five—half was under that age.

In the matter of the family, or in the regulations pertaining to marriage and divorce, Soviet Russia for a time went far. (It is to be remembered that under the Czar there had been a rather liberal attitude here in some respects.) The earlier laws permitted marriages to be contracted mainly by registration at some government bureau of the persons concerned, with perhaps a witness; qualifications were few; few questions were asked. When either party became weary of the marriage relation, or perhaps when a new union was sought, little was called for beyond a similar registration, with a small fee, with few reasons to be advanced, with a postcard notice to the other spouse—and all was off. Some citizens were able to point to a considerable line of ex-wives. Marriage might be contracted not only from matrimonial desires, but with an eye to practical utility, or for the aid a wife could render in one's muscular tasks. Rural dwellers at times entered in to the married state to get needed help on the farm at a busy season; when the heavy work was over, they could turn to divorce.

The only concession that might have been made to what were regarded as the decencies of life in some other countries was that one spouse might have been required to make contributions to the support of the other, with aid also for possible children of a previous marriage. In the earlier days of the Soviet state abortions were legalized, and were numerous. They were permitted later only when necessary to save the life of the mother, or when a hereditary disease might be involved. With somewhat stricter laws on marriage women were more inclined to complain of possible cruelty on the part of husbands.

Marriages were legal, whether registered or not. Only civil marriages were recognized—religious ceremonies were only a work of supererogation. Illegitimate children were of equal status with legitimate; for a time any potential father might be held responsible for the support of a child.

The age-long problem of prostitution, which according to Soviet philosophy was almost wholly the result of economic conditions, was glibly declared to be solved through medical treatment in special institutions of those who had practiced that profession, through their training for jobs, and through careful education of the public as to the possible physical ills involved in the practice. For the wealthy, especially among foreigners in the land, there was admittedly exceptional procedure. It is to be added that the situation was somewhat affected by the early age of marriage prevailing in the land, which was encouraged by the state, by the wide employment of married women in industry, and by rather loose relations still existing among some elements in the population. On the whole the evil was considerably less pronounced than in Czaristic days.

Married women were related to the state directly, and practically as *femes soles,* and not through any supposed partnership arising from their marriage. A wife might retain her name, and might have a different domicile from that of her husband. Names in general could rather readily be changed.

With the idea of lightening the physical labors of the housewife, of expediting the industrial work of the country, of effecting general economies, and perhaps at the same time of more or less blunting the edge of too strong individual home ties, there were promoted and encouraged the setting up of communal kitchens, dining rooms, laundries, etc., together with wide sales of ready-prepared food. "Kitchen factories" was a term that had an established place in the Soviet vocabulary. One-half of the industrial population is said to have been fed in greater or less part collectively or in large communal dining halls. A notable activity of consumers' coöperative societies was the providing of public kitchens, bakeries, and restaurants.

Family life in Russia, particularly in the earlier days, existed under greater or less difficulties. Both husband and wife could have diverse interests outside the home; it could not be expected to be the chief center of attraction to either. The things to have an influence upon one's life were mostly outside the home. Breaking of bread together might not be a common occurrence—in fact the chief meal of the day was usually taken away from home. Being perhaps at home no great length of time during the day, a married couple might on the whole see little of each other. Friends, furthermore, could be met conveniently outside, with less need of their calling at the home. Nor did crowded apartment living, particularly in the earlier days, and also in later days, conduce to wholesome family life. At the same time it was declared that Soviet married women, released from much of the drudgery they had been used to, could now have greater love for their husbands.

An ever pronounced competitor with the home was the ubiquitous club, with its various conveniences and alluring recreational and cultural features; it was in a measure the pet of the Soviet régime. The youth organizations, too, had their own facilities of somewhat like kind, which could serve to draw the children and young folks away. All this might be said to be in line with the general Soviet attitude or philosophy toward the family and the state. Children might love their parents; but their first love was to be for the state; it was the state that was to be paramount in their affections as well as otherwise.

Though Soviet Russia, true to communistic principles, declared marriage to be a personal matter, and not within the special purview of the state authorities, there were those there, as in certain advanced circles in other lands, who at times expressed something like ridicule or contempt for the institution; what were regarded as old-fashioned notions on the subject could become ready topics for satirization. In connection, furthermore, with the mass bringing up of children, and the almost immediate care of them by the state, the family, the one natural institution lying between the individual and the state, was not looked upon by some as of the greatest concern. Many of its functions, it was said, were being lost to different state agencies. Only limited respect for it in early days was formally enjoined upon either the child or the citizen.[1]

In the rearing of the child the state was to have a marked hand—to accept responsibility to a greater or less extent—through a chain of advisory centers, milk stations, kitchens, crèches, infant nurseries, nursery schools, and kindergartens, or until the period of formal schooling was well under way. There were certain "institutes for the protection of mother and child," including a museum. Whether engaged at work or in attendance at some form of diversion, the mother might look to some means provided by the state, as in a nursery, for the care of her child, or where she might "park" her child, perhaps in connection with a factory, coöperative association, collective farm, town section, or some other unit of the Soviet organization. At some railway stations there were special children's rooms. The mother need keep her child only a month or two after its birth. She was not required to place it then with a state agency of some kind; but if she did she could have more time as a worker or citizen. Leaving the child in a crèche or in some other state-initiated child-caring agency was supposed to confer certain definite benefits: the proper care of the child while so placed; opportunity for instruction of the mother as to how to take care of the child to the best advantage, or ad-

[1] On later attitudes toward the family, see *post*, 376.

vice in child hygiene or psychology—with attention to food and nutrition to be had both before and after birth; release of mother for some task of industry, visits with friends, or attendance at some entertainment or cultural affair. A not inconsiderable portion of the children spent their early years principally at their nurseries, especially if living at some distance away, perhaps visiting their parents from time to time. Children at their earliest years were taught the art of living together; they were also taught the art of self-help.

Parental control of the child was co-existent with or was shared with that of the state. Punishment of the child was for the most part denied to the parent. On the other hand, a child might report to the state authorities any supposed derelictions of the parent, especially such as might affect the state's well-being. Around fourteen the child might be in position to choose his name, his occupation, his religion. At the same time there was a reciprocal legal obligation as to support by child or parent.

Where necessary, guardians could be appointed for children in need. Placement and adoption of children in foster homes was provided for. There were a considerable number of institutions over the land for orphan or otherwise dependent children.

One pathetic result of the weakening of the home and of the family life was the army of children wandering over Russia in the earlier days, many of whom died, and others had to be placed in special homes or institutions or colonies (some being farmed out in private homes). These homeless, vagrant children were often diseased, tough, swaggering, cunning, nimble-footed. They roved over the country, prepared to steal, and if need be to kill. The situation in respect to them, however, was partly ascribable to general conditions in the land after the initial war ordeals. In the days of the Revolution, furthermore, and in the days just following, many parents were killed; or children got lost from their parents—apart from those who were of illegitimate birth. There was a somewhat similar problem after the Second World War, though it got out of hand to a less extent, the Soviet authorities having anticipated it and made some provision for it.

In no country did the "emancipation" of women, or equality between the sexes, proceed so far or become so established a principle, as in the Soviet Union. Women, in a wretchedly low position in old Russia, in certain parts of the empire having been traded as brides or forced into marriage under age, were now placed on a level with men legally, politically, socially, culturally. Perhaps the part played in the matter by biological laws was to be more or less an after discovery—working hours, for one thing, were to be changed in their behalf. The fact of marriage might leave a woman as free as before in her occupation, activities, interests. Not only were suffrage and office-holding before her, but equal vocational training and equal entry into the occupational pursuits of the country. Not only did large numbers of women come into manual labor and professional callings, but relatively large numbers were engaged as skilled workers, engineers, technicians, administrators (as heads of collective farms or of certain industrial operations), legislators, judges, executives, in research and laboratory undertakings, and in general government service. An especially large number were in medicine and allied service, in some areas not less than half the physicians being women. The number of women in the professions in general, as well as in attendance at the universities, steadily increased, reaching in time almost one-half. Women constituted hardly less than one-third of the industrially employed. (In pre-Soviet days something like half the women in employment were in domestic service.) Women in Russia had long been inured to hard physical labor. During war days women, as in other countries, assumed many tasks. Women entered sports and athletics on a wide scale.

Women, however, were found to vote and to hold office to a less extent than men. In general the political and economic fields that had been thrown open to them were not completely filled. Interfering factors were, as in time was to be discovered, household duties, a certain measure of economic dependence, lack of particular interest or lack of sufficient training. Women in Soviet Russia were somehow still women.

The legal system of the Soviet Union was more concerned with the affairs of the state as such than with the affairs of its individual citizens—more interested in the protection of the former than of the latter. Law and justice were conceived of only on a socialist basis. Aside from the matter of enforcing communistic state regulations, the law courts in Soviet Russia dwelt more with criminal matters than with civil; there was as a general thing more of criminal law, and less of civil law to be dispensed. Private litigation, because of the relatively small amount of private business in the land, was of no great moment. It was possible, however, with regard to such matters as domestic relations, and also with regard to certain property rights, including patents or copyrights. The matter of contracts could receive measurable attention, in large part with a state administrative agency or business enterprise as a party concerned. Citizens could be involved in trade regulations, housing matters, wage adjustments, work conditions, etc.

What in America are known as inferior courts (magistrates' courts, justice of the peace courts, police courts, etc.) were in Soviet law called people's courts—the great hopper for the reception of all sorts of cases of minor and less serious character. There were also higher (regional) courts for the more important cases; they had both original and appellate jurisdiction, in some instances being empowered to review proceedings of lower courts. There was as well a supreme court in each of the republics of the Union, as well as one for the entire Union. There were, in addition, more or less informal "comrades' courts" in connection with the larger apartment dwellings or smaller individual homes, whose task it was to dispose of minor local disputes and troubles; if they could not settle the difficulties, these were passed on to a regular court.[1] Local arbitration courts or grievance committees were encouraged in industrial as well as in other controversies. For those living or working together there thus might be a sort of communal court.

Judges in the courts had as a general thing no long legal training (perhaps only a few months); nor was there necessary any considerable experience at the bar. They served for relatively short terms. They were subject to recall. Along with the regular judges were "lay judges," or a sort of jurors from the panel, chosen for the occasion by the workers—an unusual combination of judge and jury. (There had been something not altogether different from it in old Czaristic days.) An official, as a rule called procurator, whose duty it was to protect the interests of the state in general, conducted the prosecution; he was given wide powers, usually including the work of preliminary investigation—though for the most part no broad detective work might be called for except in political cases, where the secret police could have active part. Arrayed under the chief prosecutor were regional and local officials. Voluntary assistance from citizens was also to be availed of.

Private lawyers for the accused, ostensibly to see that his rights were duly protected, could be engaged or were provided by the state. They were more likely to be found in the higher than in the lower courts. The accused could have counsel or an "advocate" of his own choosing, and at his own expense; he might even act for himself. In trials of a political nature the lawyer for the accused must move gingerly, not being willing to incur too much of the state's displeasure for his defense activities. Cases were handled not so much by individual lawyers, as by one or more of a group of lawyers, perhaps a coöperative association of lawyers, or by a "college of advocates" (quite different from a "firm" of lawyers). Free legal advice was often possible, especially from trade unions, coöperative bodies, clubs,

[1] See *ante*, p. 287.

etc. In some places there might be an institute of criminal research to study the offender.

Simplicity and informality were the distinguishing characteristics of the Soviet courts. As a rule there were few formal-
ities or technicalities in legal procedure, with little drawn-out
litigation. Bail was usually possible except in the case of political offenders. Judges took an active part in the proceedings, and
had no hesitation in asking questions of the accused and others
(following English procedure in this respect rather than American). Judgments were rendered not so much according to
legal precedents as according to the general sagacity and the
predilections, including communistic predilections, of the
judges, communistic principles always having due regard.

In criminal proceedings justice was supposed to move simply
and with celerity, as it often did. At times, however, especially
in political trials, it could be held up by various incidents in
and out of the courtroom, including perhaps certain all too
ready "confessions" or what appeared to be bizarre or more or
less fanciful self-accusations. (Confessions were at times said
to be secured by some form of torture.) It could at times have
too many of the elements of theatrical display. There could be
in it a note of tragedy, or a note of whimsicality. In state trials
witnesses for the defense need watch their step: their very role
invited suspicion. Verdicts of guilty in political trials were
sometimes foregone conclusions; such verdicts could win enthusiastic applause from the communistically inclined.

Juvenile delinquency, of which the Soviet Union had its due
share, was supposed to be attended to chiefly through the processes of education. No child under fourteen years of age might
be brought before a regular court. When a child gave trouble,
a committee of counsellors was formed to deal with it, consisting usually of a teacher, physician, and lawyer. Children from
fourteen to sixteen could come before a court only in extreme
cases, and when a committee was not able to handle them satisfactorily—in such cases family, friends, and others being

called upon to take suitable action. Probation was employed to a considerable degree in juvenile cases. Procedure here was in some respects not unlike that of American juvenile courts, though hardly with the type of probation officers known there. There were certain institutions on the order of junior republics for youthful offenders, where they could in a miniature social order learn the ways and feel the responsibilities of good citizenship.

Nothing could perhaps so well illustrate the extent of the concept of "socialization" in the Soviet state as its attitude toward the criminal. Like so many other things in this state, crime was believed to be mostly if not entirely of economic causation. The profit motive or the lack of employment, held so largely responsible for crime in capitalistic countries, could have no place in it. Here relation was principally to the real or potential ill done to the state. Crime was to a considerable extent indeed defined as the actual or attempted "undermining, weakening, or overthrow" of the economic functions, or of the power and authority or the general administration, of the state, perhaps under the name of "counter revolution." Political offenses were not precisely defined. Sabotage or obstruction in industry could be so regarded.

There were no criminal classes—only "socially dangerous classes." Injury to state property was a particularly evil deed. Stealing of property from the state was a far more heinous thing than stealing it from an individual; in fact, the two forms of theft belonged in two quite different categories. For even petty pilfering of state property, of which there were alleged fairly recurrent instances, there could be exacted harsh satisfaction. For those inculpated in the misuse of state funds or in peculation in state factories, of which there was considerable complaint at times, there could be condign punishment. For sabotage or wrecking by workers in industrial operations or for falsification or juggling of figures by managers in industrial plants, of both of which offenses there were charges from time to time, there could be ample retribution. Bribery, graft, defalcation, corruption in government circles were by no means unknown; the communistic state was by no means immune to such practices. But these things when discovered on the part of state officials could evoke drastic castigation. There might be impressive penalty for failure to run a factory properly, for permitting waste in essential materials, for inadequate or unsatisfactory production of goods, for carelessness at work, for neglect to provide proper housing, when such was one's duty. For such deeds as secreting food in certain circumstances or killing livestock the death penalty might be possible. Violation of the law by members of the Communist party was liable to draw a particularly stern penalty, as such persons should have known better, and should have set a proper example to the people in general.

In dealing with offenders against the Soviet law the "punishment" concept was not supposed to be present—except in the case of political offenders, who might receive punishment of the most severe or even abhorrent kind, perhaps worse than was generally known in Czaristic days. For other offenders there was to be no "punishment"—but only "measures of social defense" or "social protection," or "social detention," or "social rehabilitation." In proceedings for the treatment of the law-breaker in general, the declared object was his reclamation. What was aimed at was the "cure" of a "sick man." The correctional rather than the punitive treatment of the non-political offender was the underlying principle in Soviet criminal legislation. Criminals were to be trained to live in society by the therapy of socially useful toil.

In taking steps with the offender the Soviet Union had an advanced penological program, all of which might prove of interest, and some of which might prove enlightening, to the penologists of the rest of the world. There was notable medical and psychiatric attention to the offender. A high place was given to what corresponded elsewhere to probation or parole, though with probation or parole officers of a rather voluntary character. The indeterminate sentence was also in effect—the prison term to be reduced in consequence of good behavior or "good time." There was to be no imprisonment for non-payment of fine. The formal term of imprisonment ranged from one to ten years, perhaps averaging something like three. There was no life imprisonment imposed except for political offenders. Discipline was effected chiefly by denial of certain civil rights and privileges, or by the issuing of plainer food. There was little of solitary confinement or forced labor (except for political offenders); there was no corporal punishment administered.

Besides the old prison structures inherited from the Czar (some of which were destroyed), there were a number of penal, or rather correctional, institutions, which were much on the order of what are known elsewhere as reformatories. Some were agricultural colonies; some were industrial settlements; some were hardly other than correctional labor camps. Some of the newer institutions were well constructed and met high sanitary requirements in general. The worst structures were reserved for political offenders who were regarded as deserving nothing better.

Imprisonment (excepting as to political offenders) might to a considerable extent be characterized by absence of restrictions or restraints except during hours of actual labor—if possible without absence of family ties. The place of confinement was called a "place of inhibited freedom." It maintained liberal policies with respect to those in its care or custody. Prisoners were allowed much latitude, and within certain bounds could do pretty much as they pleased (including smoking). Self-government was encouraged and promoted, with the establishment of special courts for those infringing upon discipline. Recreation facilities were provided, with no omission of that feature in which Russians excelled wherever they might be— dramatic production. Education had a high position, and was a notable part of the general scheme for the liquidation of illiteracy. The "wall newspaper" even had a place, with the privilege of making criticism of prison conditions if one so desired. Health was duly taken care of; some came out better off physically than when they went in. There was the enlightened procedure of affording occupation with pay; for extra good work there might be offered rewards. Opportunity was granted for the discussion of better means of production or of increased production of goods, just as in the regular factory outside. In not a few cases the so-called prisoners could be said to have been kept in confinement for a brief industrial training, and then sent back into society.[1]

In dealing with the problem of alcohol the main recourse was education, including the public ridiculing of the drunkard, together with medical attempts at cure. Drunkenness was regarded as largely of economic causation: with better living conditions there would be less desire for alcoholic stimulation.

Capital punishment was as a rule to be applied to no person under eighteen years of age (though at times it was alleged to be). As a general thing, especially in earlier years, it was reserved for political offenders, or for those who endangered the present social order—that is, the communistic state. In addition, hopeless criminals were said to be eliminated in some way. When executions took place, they were liable to be surrounded with a considerable degree of mystery and uncertainty. The names of those suffering it might not always be made public; bodies of the executed might not always be delivered to relatives. Sometimes a condemned person might be called from one place to another, in prison or camp, and while on the way, whether suspecting or not, might have a bullet fired into the back of his head from an unseen hand.

In the Soviet Union there were various miscellaneous forms of punishment for particular cases. Among factory workers there might be censure, suspension or removal from job or

[1] On later attitudes with respect to crime and punishment, see *post*, p. 382.

position, deprivation of certain civil rights, prohibition of work in certain callings, compulsory labor, exile, etc. Disfranchisement could cause loss of employment, social insurance, and opportunity for higher education.

For persons guilty of or charged with political offenses little mercy need be expected; the authorities knew how to make it hard for such. On appeal to higher tribunals, and at their discretion, a court trial might be allowed, perhaps an ostensibly open trial. Offenders could suffer public reprimand; loss of occupation, citizenship, or civil rights; compulsory labor; fine; confiscation of property; imprisonment, perhaps in a concentration camp; expulsion from one's community or exile or deportation to a distant place; death. Those under civil disability could be deprived of various priviliges, including voting; they might be allowed only a limited amount of clothing; they might be charged higher prices for what they had to buy. Those actually exiled had generally a bitter and cruel time of it, often in an isolated region; they might not be allowed to visit certain areas, especially their home territory. They might have to leave home after a secret trial, and upon short notice. Enforced absence might continue three or five years, or more, with long hours of heavy, usually disagreeable toil. Possibly one's family might be permitted to accompany the exile if they were able to do so; but the journey might be long, difficult, and tedious. When the exile finally returned—if he did—he might find few of his old friends, and difficulty in adjusting himself in the community, and above all in finding a job.

With some political offenders there were experiences of tragedy and of horror. Men could be taken away and never heard of again. Not a few of those who had gone to Siberia or Arctic regions to help and build up the territory had not gone there voluntarily; some never returned.[1]

As part of the measures for the defense of the Soviet state, there was a special form of punishment, no less to be called one

[1] On concentration camps, see *post*, p. 325.

of oppression or persecution. This lay in the forbidding, under penalty of death, of one to leave the country, or perhaps a particular part of it, without permission. The citizen's country could now become to him a sort of fortress. In those cases where there might be a formal requirement for a passport, the cost was for the most part prohibitive. Besides, the seeker thereof would be asked questions of more or less embarrassing nature.

From time to time there came out of the Soviet land reports, with what foundation few could say, of excesses under the color of bureaucratic power, or powers of the secret police, powers inherited from the Czar. Now and then unhappy stories crept out of some proceedings more or less on the order of torture. Punishment of an offender might extend to one's family; it might be visited upon one or more of the members.[1]

[1] "In the case of desertion from the army over the Soviet frontiers the adult members of the deserter's family are under given circumstances liable to criminal responsibility." U.S.S.R. Handbook, 1936, p. 497.

CHAPTER XVI

The Soviet State and Its Attitude toward Religion

IN orthodox Soviet reasonings there was not much standing given to what were looked upon as bourgeois moral concepts. Moral principles having their birth in capitalistic countries need have no corresponding validity in socialistic countries. Such a conceit as a "moral law" was considered to have little sound or realistic basis. All such notions were regarded in greater or less measure as rather puerile, antiquated things, needless and having little place in the irreconcilable class struggle which was essentially of economic bearings. They were perhaps to be smiled at, especially on the part of youth. In their stead was to be only what was held to be in the interests of the Soviet state, and to be physically or hygienically desirable for its people. As we have seen, the conception of crime generally centered about the possible injury to the state in what was done. The chief wrong in suicide might be the loss of an economic producer to the state.

In the Soviet vocabulary there was not given a large place to such old-fashioned personal concepts as "character" or "principle" in themselves, or at least little beyond what might be connoted or involved in allegiance to the operations of a particular political and economic order. There were no eternal or unchangeable ethical standards. What could be termed morality was a product of all social relations and of the class struggle. A Soviet code of ethics was to be worked out in the interests of the working classes. In consequence of this line of reasoning there tended to prevail, especially in earlier days, a certain attitude of "wide-openness," though this perhaps was less in evidence in practice than in theory.

If it be said that "private" morals were not deemed worthy of great formal regard in the new socialist state, it is to be remembered that among the Russian people views upon certain matters had for long not been altogether the same as in more western lands, but that among them as a whole there existed a common honesty that compared well with that of many other countries. Among the Soviet people there was no little openness of speech upon such matters as sex, but there seemed to be relatively no great number of crimes of this nature. In early Soviet days there was a certain looseness or licentiousness in these matters which called for reproof and rebuke from the state authorities. There was little printed in the land which could be called erotic or off-color. To the children in the schools, especially of later years, there were taught civic virtues; to them was given a system of precepts for the benefit of the state, including some which could well pass as moral, or could be given in an American Sunday school or to a boy scout group— courage, discipline, cleanliness, purposefulness, obedience, self-restraint, truthfulness, comradeship, initiative, courtesy, respect for elders.

In Soviet Russia, moreover, there was a notably stiff attitude toward public morality, or with respect to the conduct of those in public office. Here an unquestionably high position was taken; there was a holding of them to rigid standards, at least theoretically, and to no small extent quite sincerely, with the enunciation of a strict, in part almost puritanical, code of behavior. Such practices as graft or corruption in government or in the business of the state, or even the taking of tips, particularly in the earlier Soviet period, were held in peculiarly stern reprobation.

With respect to certain conditions in capitalistic lands regarded as unwholesome or noxious, a severe attitude could be taken. Fingers of scorn or sarcasm could be pointed at them, not only for their non-communistic practices in the sphere of economics, but for alleged political corruption in large cities and elsewhere, and for alleged delinquencies and looseness in the field of general morals.

A powerful factor in causing Soviet Russia to lose the sympathy and good-will of other countries, and in creating a sort of feeling that the land was morally diseased, and one with which there should be few dealings, and these only at arm's length, was its attitude toward and its attacks upon religion. It cannot be denied that for a longer or shorter period there was a steady, bitter, unrelenting, uncompromising warfare against religion, a campaign blatant and ruthless, an outspoken "godlessness" actually gloried in—for the most part if not under the immediate direction and with the authorization of the state officials, at least with their permission and sanction. It seemed that the undermining of religion was sought through the apparatus of government. This was unlike anything the world had ever previously witnessed.

In this land, with its superstructure of superstition, and here and there with something bordering upon pagan magic overlaying a religion with many noble qualities in itself, and with some in the old Russian church having little education and venal (with others high-minded and tender-conscienced), with the upper clergy in considerable part politically servile and aloof from the masses, with the church in large part believed to be the tool, hand-maiden, and mainstay of the old régime of Czar and nobility and wealth—with all these things assaults upon religion in the Soviet order were anything but difficult; and the Soviet régime was not slow to take advantage of the situation to deal religion a blow as unhappy as it was hard. Russia was in fact an ideal country for the making light of things religious, especially on the part of those of communistic tendencies. The attitude of the new state was what could be expected from those who had accepted radical socialistic conceptions. It had a certain resemblance to the social democratic

306

parties of some countries of western Europe; it more nearly took on the stamp of Bakunin doctrines or something inherited from the Nihilists of old.

There were certain happenings, moreover, when the Soviet party assumed power, to enkindle or intensify its hostility to the Russian church. The church had objected to the sale of costly religious objects and treasures to meet the famine situation then in the land. There was also in view the great landed estates and other property in the ownership of the church. A considerable portion of the Russian clergy had displayed not only unfriendliness toward the new order, but a positive willingness to take sides and line up with its opponents; to some extent there had been shown open rebelliousness against the new Soviet power. The church had already in general been allied with the old reactionary elements of the land, and had manifested its antipathy toward socialism, having spoken against it from the pulpit and in specially prepared pamphlets; the church had told its followers to obey the Czar and fight his enemies.

To the church under the Soviet régime came oppression and persecution. On one hand and another its liberty of action or movement was circumscribed, impaired, or denied. Its property in many instances was summarily, perhaps ruthlessly, taken over or confiscated; it was deprived alike of its land and of its treasures, including canonicals, sacred vessels, ikons, and vestments; from many churches bells were removed. Church edifices here and there were torn down, more of them in the city than in the country, possibly on some pretext or other: the building was on some public way, or the space was needed for some public purpose, perhaps the widening of a street. If the church edifice was not destroyed, it might be severely damaged; it might even be converted into a glamorous club or inviting museum, or a sort of community center. A certain number of monasteries were "liquidated."

Churches had to be "voluntarily" turned over to the state by its members; few could withstand government demands. Religious organizations had to be licensed; they must be duly registered, with the making of due reports. Each must have a minimum number of members (perhaps a score), announcing themselves as sponsors. There must be set forth the objects, the time and place of meetings, and the names and addresses of those concerned in the undertaking. Members must depend on themselves alone for the support of their organization. Church buildings had to be rented or their use authorized by the state. Collections could be taken only at regular meetings, and only of free-will character. Churches were subject to heavy taxation. Charitable work or material relief of members in distress was not permitted. There could be no libraries or recreation facilities. Soviet clubs were ostentatiously open at the same hour as the church meetings, the better to draw away attendance from the latter. The church lost its control over marriage and divorce. Religious ceremonies at weddings were permitted, but were not recognized in law. Baptisms and funerals had less and less place in it. Even if religion was not forbidden, one obstacle after another was placed upon the organization work of the church or its effective functioning.

Upon the clergy restrictions bore hard. Great numbers were placed under arrest, sometimes, it is true, on the substantiated charges of activities inimical to the Soviet state. Not a few were banished, exiled, imprisoned, or executed. Voting was denied them. Limitations were placed upon where priests could live and where they could go. They could not use the mails; they could not receive free medical attention for themselves or their families; they had difficulty in getting bread cards. They were subject to embarrassing questions as to the occupations in which they were engaged. In the event of the death of a priest it was not easy to get a new one.

Priests were continually derided and vilified. They were depicted as having been grossly well fed and as having lived upon the fat of the land. It was shown how they took advantage of poor peasants to get the possessions of the latter, or how they extorted money for their services or denial of services. There were representations of how science had been fought by the church. Bodies of miracle-working saints were sometimes demonstrated to be something else; preservation of the bodies of some was proved to be due to the character of the soil in which they had been deposited, and to no divine influence. Religion was set forth as little if any better than witchcraft.

There were direct and deliberate efforts to stifle religion. There were anti-religious societies and anti-religious schools. There was a League of Militant Atheists. There were anti-religious museums, sometimes set up in a former religious structure. There were pictures which were horrible travesties upon religion. There were anti-religious cartoons and posters, sometimes carried in procession. Some of these were disreputable and ribald, some with caricatures of the Deity. It was declared that kings had been pulled down from their earthly thrones— such was now to be the fate of the heavenly King of Kings.

What was of religious bearing or of religious significance was, if allowed to stand, belittled or demeaned. Even when expression of religious sentiment had been suffered to continue, it was made to appear that this was rather a sop or by way of indulgence to the weaker and inconsequential elements of the population. Whatever of contempt or ridicule could be thrown upon religion was thrown. It was openly and studiedly insulted.

No religious literature could be printed in the land or imported into it; and limitations were placed upon what was to be availed of. No religious paintings or objects could be made. Christmas trees could not be sold. Santa Claus with the Christmas tree and gifts at Christmas became Grandfather Frost at New Year's. In the schools there was definite and widespread teaching against religion; children who were to be the future citizens of the state received a full measure of anti-religious instruction. Instruction with them of any kind took on an anti-religious slant. Children were taught that while religion may have been necessary with primitive man, it was now an obstacle to his progress, that it was a relic of the past dislodged by scientific knowledge. In the schools "religious explanations of natural or social phenomena [were] inadmissible."[1] More than one university had a chair of atheism. All the agencies of education besides the school—the press, the museum, the theatre, the motion picture—gave forth fervid anti-religious indoctrination if not direct anti-religious tirades. Anti-religious books poured from the presses, and numbered their readers by the millions. Trade unions, coöperative associations, clubs, and other organizations of the Soviet state had for the most part an anti-religious bias. Youth organizations were loudly anti-religious. It was hoped that religion would die of itself with the coming generation.

With religious instruction not only barred in the schools, but anti-religious doctrines energetically taught there, the only religious instruction possible for children was that through a parent or special teacher; but no class was to contain more than four pupils. Religious people were anyway in general too poor to provide their own schools to any extent. Besides, there could be no distinctly religious schools, as education was a recognized state monopoly. If children felt that undue religious instruction was being given them at home, they could appeal to the authorities.

Against religious adherents or church attendants was practiced discrimination in various forms. They were under various legal disabilities. Suspicious movements of such persons could quickly draw upon them some direct or indirect penalty. In seeking to get employment, bread cards, social insurance benefits, etc., to say nothing of holding office or receiving public honors, they found themselves a marked group. Even persons allowing use of their property for religious meetings or assemblages could be made to answer. Religious youth could be barred from membership in communist or pro-communist or-

[1] *U.S.S.R. Information Bulletin,* February 11, 1949.

ganizations. Atheism might at one time have been one of the tests for membership in the communist party, though not officially so proclaimed—religious qualifications being said to have no place here.

The campaign against religion in Soviet Russia was gross, rampant, violent. It was a systematic, organized one. There was constant propaganda against religion. Religion was held to dull minds as to earthly evils. For a time on a wall near the Kremlin was an inscription—"Religion is the opiate of the people." The campaign was, moreover, often in part apparently of official character or with official endorsement or promotion. The state did not appear even neutral; it seemed quite definitely to take sides. Some of the most active and violent anti-religious leaders were members of the government, though it is to be said that by some in the seats of government the movement was believed to be going too far, and there was effort to check it. Atheism was, practically speaking, made a state doctrine. It was a dogmatic atheism that here ruled the day. It was evidently the aim and purpose of some elements of the Soviet state to weed out not only religion but all semblance of religion from the hearts of the people who dwelt within its bounds. It might be said that on the part of some who appeared anti-religious they were not so much opposed to religion as such, though indifferent to it; they were rather opposed to anything standing in the way of their communistic order, viewing religion often in this light. A considerable portion of the communists were hostile to religion on the assumption that it sided with capitalism.[1]

Not in the days of the Czar had there been such massed intolerance. Something that will be held against the Soviet power in future pages of history will be its fearful, stark, stupendous efforts to root religion from the lives of human beings. It is not easy to determine how far the attacks upon religion in the So-

---

[1] On later changed attitudes toward religion, see *post*, p. 377.

viet land alienated a large part of the world, or hurt communism in its economic, social, and political bearings.

Partly as a sop to the religiously inclined of the country, to win over in greater degree the people, especially in the rural areas, and to avoid too great disaffection in the matter, the Soviet authorities for a time sanctioned if they did not promote what was known as the "Living Church," which was something of a cross between the old church and the new communist faith. The new church bestowed its approval upon the Soviet régime, even though it declined to endorse its anti-religious campaigns. It was intended to combat the old church, and perhaps to take its place in the hearts of the people. The "Living Church" was tolerated in the land, but it had little practical influence or effect. In time it died out.

The anti-religious campaigns of the Soviet Union were confined largely to those of the Christian faith and to Jews. At first there was a certain tolerance toward Protestants, but after a time they were under no less hostile eyes than were the Orthodox and Roman Catholic bodies. The Soviet authorities did not care to trouble or antagonize or have conflict with the vast Moslem population in the southeastern parts of its dominion or in Asia in general, nor with Buddhists or other religious groups in that Continent with whom they had contacts, and among whom relatively few outright communists could be expected to be found. It did not feel it altogether safe to interfere with the ancient beliefs, customs, and practices of these peoples to the east and have in turn their animosity and ill-will toward it; it decided to leave them pretty much alone in their religious attitudes.

The Soviet authorities, try as they might, were never able to efface or eradicate religion from the Russian soul. Nearly everywhere in the land there was a remnant holding out, in some areas of no insignificant proportions. Secret meetings it was impossible altogether to prevent. The strenuous anti-religious campaigns, especially the anti-religious parades, were largely

312

staged by the anti-religious element in the population; they were recognized mainly as communistic propaganda; the great mass of people were interested only to a limited extent. Neither the indoor nor the outdoor anti-religious lectures were always well attended. Many of the people became tired of the constant anti-religious cavil and invective. Membership in godless societies and subscriptions to atheistic publications fell much short of what had been expected or anticipated. The great number of the Russian people proved themselves not ill-disposed to religion; vehement anti-religious feeling was mostly confined to rabid communists.

It was the country peasant who proved most tenacious of his religion, and resisted most strongly the attempts to separate him from the faith he and his fathers had so long known. It was the inhabitants of the large cities who were most ready to throw off the old religion of Russia, many having already practically done so before the Revolution. In nearly all the backward regions of Russia the peasants retained their ikons; even in the other regions a decided majority did so. In a census a few years before the Second World War by the Soviet authorities two-thirds of the rural population was found to be holding on to their religion, and one-third of the urban population.

Though religion as it had for the most part been understood among men was officially looked upon in the Soviet state as an obsolete institution, and something no longer worthy of respect, this state fairly well proved that religion was after all something that its people could not get along without. For that which had generally been accepted as religion there was substituted not only adoration of the communist heroes, their apotheosis, but in addition a trusting, confiding faith in what the communist state could do in more or less distant years—almost approaching a mystic exaltation. Their worship was truly of the state; it was not less than state idolatry; before it there should be no other gods. Marx-Engels-Lenin-Stalin—such was the apostolic succession in the Soviet ecclesiology.

Along with this there was a singular exuberant infatuation with science, or even with the machine—in part doubtless because of the new force in the lives of the people, or in a sort of childlike veneration thereof.[1] Science as the all in all of life might be regarded as quite satisfactorily taking the place of what was once known as morals or religion. Through it was salvation to be attained. In their ideology the Soviet people went beyond socialism; it was science in the socialistic state through which they were to get control over nature, and make it serve them; through science and socialism in combination they were to obtain a new heaven and a new earth. In all this castle building there may have been something fantastic or grandiose, something of wistful yearning, and also something that sought to express itself only along material lines, whatever the price in other respects.

[1] Henry Ford, the industrialist, not the capitalist, was their American hero.

CHAPTER XVII

The Soviet State and Its Political Structure

TO whatever Soviet Russia might or might not have attained
economically and culturally, there was one thing at which
it had hardly seemed to have arrived. This was democracy—
as it had hitherto largely been known in the world. Perhaps we
should rather say that what had come about was in great part
the negation of this thing; organized government in Soviet territory did not appear to function in that capacity.

The secret of the power of the Union of Socialist Soviet Republics, or of the reason for its holding control as it did, lay
primarily in the remarkable organization that had been effected, an anomalous, ingenious scheme of government that
might be said to be without counterpart in the history of the
world. The conduct of affairs rested with what was known as
the Communist party. This was not a real "party" in the sense
that that term is understood in other lands. In the Soviet Union
this party represented only a small minority of the population
—only a few millions out of the country's close to two hundred
millions. The rest of the people were unorganized, and were
without recourse before it—at its disposal, practically speaking.
The defense of this one-party system was that it was the only
party of the proletariat or the working classes of the land, there
being no other classes here, and that consequently no other
party was called for.

The party organization as a whole was a highly centralized
one. Membership was exclusive, limited to a select group. Its
heart was originally composed of those who had gone through

315

blood and fire in the old Czaristic struggles, "professional revolutionists" who had won a certain degree of skill therein. The
initial chieftains or "charter members," and those later inducted
into its guarded circles, formed a carefully picked body, in general under iron discipline, austere, contemptuous of frivolity,
zealous, devoted, perhaps personally impeccable or above re-
proach, perhaps of Spartan virtue. They constituted themselves
the "keepers of the conscience" of the Soviet state. Their general purpose was to guide the infant commonwealth in its untried voyages, with the masses of the people to be regarded as
not yet having sufficient education or sufficient preparation
for managing the affairs of state, or not sufficiently immune to
the blandishments or objurgations of an anti-Soviet world. Like
the guardians in Plato's Republic, they were to hold the reins
of government in their hands as rulers with the best education
and with superior, outstanding ability; and their rule was to be
absolute. Members of the Communist party were chosen mainly
for their qualities of leadership. A second and practically as
important a qualification was that they be distinctly of the proletariat. First bidden were those who had had some experience
as industrial workers. Those aspiring to full membership must
pass through a sort of screening process; they must be on probation for a year or two. No member could recommend a new
member till he had been in the organization for at least five
years.[1]

Upon members was charged constant and diligent study of
Soviet principles and practices. They were carefully trained in
their duties, which were principally, apart from attending to
the party's internal structure and planning, educational propaganda among the people, with whatever harsher measures
might at times be found necessary. Through these means control over the country was to be secured and maintained—and
the masses eventually moulded into the desired Soviet pattern.
One of their tasks was to keep informed as to public sentiment

[1] There was a department of propaganda and agitation.

in different parts of the land. The party maintained its own newspapers and other publications as distinct from those of the government itself. Members of the party had to pay regular dues, in greater or less part coming from their government salaries. A high degree of regimentation was enjoined in the party, a pattern which was to apply to the country in general.

Party principles and party discipline were alike strict. Woe to him who was not orthodox in his following! If not otherwise brought to light, wrongful acts or attitudes might be discovered by roving commissars in their peregrinations. Expulsion at least loomed up for disloyalty or corruption, or for breach of rules or for general inefficiency in party affairs, or for those who might not see eye to eye with the supreme party authorities. All cases of guilt were duly taken in hand, and sooner or later properly disposed of—if need be through elimination or "liquidation." Stories of party "purges," seemingly periodic, sometimes of tried and true members from earliest days, on charges of "betrayal of the Revolution," so far as they reached the ears of the outside world, sometimes shocked or distressed it, or left it aghast. In the so-called trials was not always satisfactorily proven how far there might have been plots against the Soviet state or only uprisings against a particular ruler or chieftain or functionary then in power. It was not always proven how far personal ill feeling or antipathy for an individual official of government or of party was really treason to the country. Attempt at overthrow of the party or of some of those in control of it might well be taken for attempt at overthrow of the government or of the state. By the ruling forces it was claimed that party purges prevented the rise of fifth columnists. After a purge the new claimants upon power were believed to be sufficiently imbued with proper communistic conceptions.

The organization of the party proceeded on a line fairly parallel with that of the Soviet government. Leaders or officers in one were in general leaders or officers in the other. There was no little overlapping between the two. In every place and angle of organization in the state was to be found the party man in the seat of power. Party captains occupied responsible economic and political posts. With key positions of the state in its hands, the party was in rare and impregnable position for ruling the land. In rural areas an important strategic place was control of tractor or other machine centers—the machine gave the government a grip over the peasant farmer. At a vantage point in industry might be installed a party representative to watch over proceedings. Such a one might accompany the army on its march to keep an eye on its officers and also to inspire due patriotism. Party members were everywhere at hand in the Soviet land to prevent deviation from communistic principles, to provide "pep," and to secure efficiency in all Soviet undertakings.

The government might be said to have been composed of hand-picked party men. In a sense the government was a sort of figure-head, something of a facade for the operations of the party. In public processions, in newspapers, in dramatic productions praise could be lavishly bestowed upon the "Party."

Representatives of the party were found, as a sort of nuclei or "cells," in all the reticulation of organizations criss-crossing over the land, and serving as tools or constituting cogs in the gigantic machine of government—trade unions, state farms, factories, coöperative associations, army units, village officials, state trusts, universities, educational bodies, newspapers—all thus being inextricably bound up with the party.

Local units elected party representatives up to an All-Union Congress for the entire country. There was a general meeting of this party congress every year or two, perhaps twice a year, besides frequent meetings of the controlling officials. The permanent official standing or central committee, elected by the congress, had charge of affairs and activities between regular sessions. Sessions of the congress were usually short, and more or less perfunctory, being in fact little more than the registration of the will of the leaders—and generally with few dissenting votes. Members then went home, leaving actual operations with the high-up officials. By the standing committe was chosen a secretariat or politburo, of somewhere around a dozen men, which formulated policies and in which rested the final springs of power. There were also a bureau for organization and administration dealing largely with the matter of personnel, and a bureau of party control, to see that members were kept in line, and in charge of party purges. At the apex was the all but omnipotent secretary-general. Matters could thus gravitate into the hands of a tiny body of men, a mere handful in the total population. (Joseph Stalin was secretary-general of the Communist party, as well as chairman or premier of the Council of People's Commissars in the Soviet government, besides being made commander-in-chief of the armed forces—"commissar of defense.")

It was the members of the Communist party not only in whose hands was vested the might of the state—most of the office-holders were members of that party—but who constituted a sort of upper crust, a privileged class in the affairs of the Soviet state. Party members were in possession of highly coveted powers; nowhere else could there be such wide and sweeping exercise of power. Theirs was also the joy of piloting a ship sailing uncharted seas under their peculiar banner. Perhaps these things might compensate in some measure for the thrill that in other lands comes from the struggle for the mastery of tangible wealth.

There were no less material perquisites in the hands of the Communist officials that were by no means to be lightly valued—rewards attaching to membership in the party that were anything but inconsequential. Not only did they hold in general the offices of the Soviet state; but it was usually these office-holders or government functionaries who could come off best or could get the best of nearly everything in the Soviet storehouse. They had distinct emoluments; they had privileges or prior claims in respect to housing, entertainments, rest homes, shops, travel accommodations, medical service, and other matters appertaining to the Soviet set-up. Advantages in higher education could be disproportionately large for members of their families. It was they, too, who had the chief voice in making appointments to government positions. It is to be added that there were always some who did not take advantage of their position for their own gain.

In addition to what was granted to members of the Communist party in general, there was a certain favoritism displayed, especially in the earlier days, to the industrial workers of the city, the real proletariat; it was they who received the first smiles of the state. For a time suffrage was allowed to them on a slightly more liberal basis and on a wider scale than to the country peasants.[1] They might also have had prior rights in such matters as the granting of ration books. The peasant farmers were a bit slower attaining their rights and coming into their own. In the organization and functioning of the Soviet government it was the city worker that had so large a part. In no small measure it was to his domination that was attributed the state's ability to carry on as it did. It was his group that was so much behind the scenes, always aware of what was afoot, and with ability to act most effectively. Over against his group was chiefly the backward, unorganized, scattered peasantry. The city worker could expect to be accorded greater privileges and powers because he was believed to be the more enlightened element of the country, and in better position to advance the cause of communism.

The Communist party was not content with having adults in its councils or among those who were to have part in moulding the new state. To have a firm and complete grip upon the entire population, it turned to account the younger elements of

[1] In the earlier days of the Soviet state, where there were different stages in voting, from higher to lower, there were fewer in the case of the city dweller. The city groups were thus somewhat over-represented. With more direct voting the two groups tended toward equality.

its people, proceeding to ever lower levels, and finally near to the foot of the ladder of life. It organized in efficient battalions its youth and its children. Each of these groups had its own function to perform in the communist organization.

For those of high school, college, and professional school age, there was the Young Communist League, in preparation for membership in the Communist party itself, and which was to be in active service to it. It had among its civic duties the setting of an example in good citizenship, inculcating of discipline where needed, encouraging of students in their studies, and promoting of physical training, Soviet culture, and productive efficiency in general. It might take charge of such matters as athletic events and Soviet entertainments or celebrations. It might have as one task the explaining of socialistic principles and programs over the country, as well as collecting opinions as to how the socialistic order might be improved. A by no means unimportant function lay in its military training activities, with its members as a potential core in case of war. In a sense it was the oil that kept the communistic machine in high gear.

Below it, and ready to pass into it in due time, were the Young Pioneers, of grammar school age, performing tasks somewhat like those of the Boy Scouts of America, or a sort of "big brothers," but with a most communistic leaning and color. A particular assignment might be the encouragement of the proper performance of home and school duties. Both these bodies engaged in certain welfare work for children in need of special attention. At the bottom of the fabric were those of elementary school age, who bore the significant Soviet title of Octobrists, and who in their budding ways found communistic work to do. They took upon themselves the rendering of various little services, performing odd jobs, all for the benefit of the cause.

In all its activities the Communist party brooked no rival, no competitor, no opponent, no adversary. There could be no effective counter to what was projected or devised or set on foot in its council chambers. Yet in no inconsiderable measure the party had its ears to the ground over the country. The general sense and drift of public sentimet and public opinion was to an extent eagerly sought. Members of the party were often good "mixers" (perhaps somewhat on the order of an American district leader); they sought to stand in well with the people. There were genuine efforts to feel out and sound out the public with regard to the policies of the party and of the country, a sort of public opinion tapping. Local committees made report as to local feelings. Discussions and consultations on general public measures, especially those that affected the country internally, were in some degree encouraged and smiled upon. Airing of grievances was with proper circumscription given leeway. Though there may have been a dictatorship in the land, there were strings of some sort between it and the thought of the country. The people could talk of, and make suggestions about, the economic and social life of their land, and could have part in such things as committee elections—with respect to farm operations or factory operations or with respect to some local set-up or arrangement—there was here democracy of a sort, but duly hedged in. It may be added that in the newspaper "letters to the editor," a sort of complaint bureau, a certain expression of public opinion was permitted.[1]

All such harking to the sentiment of the country on the part of the Kremlin leaders must be taken with distinct provisos. It was clearly and fully understood that nothing in the discussions in the land, especially as to general communistic tenets and ways and as to the handling of international matters, must go beyond definitely known bounds. Any expression of opinion must stop at a certain point; it must not proceed too far below the surface. Criticism of general government movements could be only nominal, if even that. The government, furthermore, was under no obligation to listen or to pay attention to any

[1] See *ante*, p. 265.

comments made, to say nothing of being influenced or having its policies affected thereby. The attitude of the government in inclining an ear was more than a mere gesture, perhaps, but it was not so very much more. Every one in the country was quite aware where the ultimate authority lay, and was careful to act accordingly. In the minds of none did question of it ever arise; the powers residing in the Kremlin were known of all to rule supreme and unified. It was only such monolithic oneness that could guarantee the communistic state against possible capitalistic inroads.

Compulsion by the state, or the regimentation of the people, so far as it existed, was sometimes described or referred to as "disciplinary measures" or as "administrative means"—as something necessary for the sake of the socialist state, and for its protection, and no less for the ultimate improvement and advancement of the life of the individual. It may or may not have been recognized that such was the essential doctrine of the totalitarian state in which democracy or the real rule of the people could have little part. It could be the ready language of any despot, benevolent or other.

However constituted, whatever its principles or details of organization, and wherever the promulgation of its rulings, the Communist party in the Soviet state was a most remarkable institution, whether or not it contributed to democracy. As a sheer organization, it probably never had a parallel elsewhere, certainly never an equal.

The Soviet state in its internal fabrication was a close officialdom, with a far-reaching bureaucracy—something apparently inherent in socialism. For the enforcement of its edicts there was a powerful standing army, far better equipped and far more capable than that of any of the former Czars. It could be expected to give a good account of itself wherever and under whatever circumstances it might be placed; it could do this best in defense of the homeland—something ever the wont of Russian armies, whoever their rulers might be. The Soviet army constituted the first charge upon the public treasury. Its life was relatively the most attractive and the most secure for the young men of Russia. There were special privileges for the army and for its officers.

Along with that of the army, and under a different setting, was the power of the state police, including the long known, omniscient, and ever active secret police. The existing system was forged from that of the old Czars. The first mandate was the protection of those in the seats of Soviet power. Few of the higher ranking officials of the most absolutist states had to be so carefully guarded by the police. Citizens in their turn could not expect to escape careful and unceasing scrutiny. Going about the country, they must carry with them identification papers or passports. No one was immune from the perennial (shall we say inherent or inevitable?) informer system. Even one's letters were subject to opening by the authorities. The eyes of the secret police were everywhere, and never slept.

A primary purpose of the police was the suppression of "counter revolution" or the weeding out of the "socially dangerous" or "hostile" classes in the land. It could strike one down pretty much as seemed good to it. By some of those under suspicion there might be expected at any hour the swooping arm of the law, a holding with little semblance of trial, a perfunctory court appearance with undisclosed sentence, perhaps ending in a concentration camp, in faraway exile, or in cancellation of life itself. The process of the liquidation of internal enemies, actual or potential, was not difficult; it could be by progressive stages—economic or civil discrimination, deportation, shooting. (Means of punishment of political offenders has already been considered.)[1] Of the labor of many such persons use could be made for the benefit of the state. The number of those in this forced labor was great—believed to be several millions.[2]

[1] See *ante*, p. 302.

[2] "There can be no reasonable doubt that in the Soviet Union several million workers are employed under police discipline and receive only miserable wages for

The Soviet state kept its own counsels as to the number and condition of those in its concentration camps. Visitors seldom entered to bring reports back. By that state it was claimed that outdoor concentration camps were better than regular indoor prisons; that persons confined in them were regarded as offenders against the state and as criminals to be punished, from whom labor was as a general thing to be expected; and that in a state based upon such revolutionary principles as was the Soviet state a relatively large number of political prisoners was to be looked for or taken for granted. By the Soviet authorities such places were called "correctional" institutions.

The Soviet state also sought to keep its citizens from leaving the country—they were confined somewhat as in a gigantic prison house. We have seen the difficulties in securing exit passports, with their excessive costs.[1] But this was not all. No country had its borders so closely guarded, or could apply such stern punishment to those discovered seeking to escape. Perhaps there was fear that those getting away might engage abroad in activities hostile to the Soviet régime, or that they might carry with them not the happiest stories to tell, or that the way might be opened for undesirable comparisons. At the same time refugees coming into the land from foreign countries were looked upon with greater or less suspicion, and had to offer satisfactory proof to the authorities. Emigrés from the land, whatever their manner or means of departure, could only remain in a constant state of foreboding and apprehension and anxiety; they knew not what fate might befall family or relatives left behind. For themselves they could feel better off away. Around the Soviet

their labor [estimates sometimes being in excess of five million]. . . . The population of these camps is drawn from political offenders, nonconforming engineers and intellectuals, kulaks, recalcitrant peasants, former industrial and other officials, and deviating communists of the Right and of the Left. . . . In later years the reserve of forced labor was increased by national groups believed to be hostile and populations residing along the many borders of the Soviet Union in Europe and Asia." "Communism in Action"—United States H. R. Document, no. 754, 1946. To be added were prisoners of war and displaced persons.

[1] See *ante*, p. 196.

land was a great towering wall with gates that opened out-wardly and inwardly on groaning hinges.

In such a country as this any direct expression of the will of the people was pretty much out of the question. Any possible opposition had no opportunity or chance to present its views or claims. There could be little ascertainment of the actual will of the majority. Definitely barred from suffrage at the outset were such persons as hirers of labor for profit or capitalists (de-pending on income not received from their own labor), mer-chants and traders, clergymen, the aristocracy, the landed gentry, officers of the old Czarist government and army, crim-inals, and the mentally affected. Suffrage was later extended to clergymen and former Czarist officials.

All who voted in the Soviet Union must vote the regular "ticket" or "slate," if they knew what was good for them. As a result elections were all but unanimous. Candidates for office were for the most part hand-picked party men. "Party and non-party blocs" could be expected to follow party lines with little deviation. At times special efforts were made to select non-party men, to some extent for the sake of appearances.

Not only did any attempt at expression of opinion contrary to the views or wishes of those in authority spell danger, but all means of expression were strictly reserved to the govern-ment or to the party—were in their hands alone. In the old days of the Czar, before the Revolution, things were not like this. In the time of the duma in particular there was a certain measure of electoral freedom; and there was afforded a place for the expression of grievances and protests. Newspaper editors might have to exercise a degree of caution in their comments upon the activities of government; but they were not called upon to offer a continual extolling. In various matters there was allowed a large measure of liberty. In Soviet days pronounce-ments contrary to the ideas of those in power could be nothing less than evidences of corruption or disloyalty. Seriously adverse criticism of official policies could be denominated treason, betrayal of the state, or counter revolution. Here as well as elsewhere eulogizing of those in position of authority could without great difficulty pass into something like fulsome adulation. In public processions could be carried large pictures of the leaders almost as demi-gods.

Just after the Revolution, and again a few years later, a preliminary or tentative constitution was promulgated by the Soviet authorities. After the lapse of a score of years, during which period the people of Russia were presumed to have had a due period of tutelage and discipline, and when full-blown socialism was supposed to be nearer at hand, the powers in control saw fit to entrust them with a new constitution, which might or might not be a momentous event in the history of the country, and which might or might not be a step in advance or toward democracy, though truly a striking tribute to it. There was at least gain in the wide reading and discussion of the document. On the whole, a somewhat more liberal attitude was displayed in it than before.

To an extent the Soviet constitution was rather a setting forth of the aims and policies of the state. The present one, a fairly elaborate instrument, and with not a few lofty and admirable sentiments, may be regarded as the last word in respect to the socialist state, the modern form of the Communist Manifesto. It was the apologia, the confession of faith of communism. While propounded as the organic law of the Soviet state, it did not neglect the opportunity to proclaim the virtues of the socialist form of government, and to extol and glorify socialism. It declared that through it the "exploitation of man by man" had been abolished (the first constitution including the expression, "the complete elimination of the division of society into classes"). It presented a temporary version of the socialist formula: "From every man according to his ability, to every man according to his toil"—the proper phrase "according to his need" to be introduced when a more advanced stage of communism had been reached. In the constitution there was direct mention of "dictatorship of the proletariat."

In the new constitution suffrage was universal for all eighteen years of age or over, regardless of sex, property holding, race, education, or present or past station in life. Balloting was asserted to be secret; but would it be well to vote against the government even thus? Elections were later made more direct. As in the United States, there was a tripartite separation of powers of the government—legislative, judicial, executive—though separation of powers was more nominal than real, the several powers rather shading off into each other. The judiciary which was established was declared to be independent; it was to a greater or less extent an administrative body—to see that the established communist order was maintained—to protect the Soviet state. A parliament was duly set up, though an opposition, or an effective opposition, was hardly conceivable. Proceedings were cut-and-dried, mostly the reflection of the views of the rulers. A republic was given the right to secede from the Union if it desired, but any attempt in this direction might be construed as something on the order of counter revolution on the part of the instigators. Though allowed certain rights, none could deviate basically from the will of Moscow.

Provision for the Communist party did not escape reference —as the "more enlightened and energetic element" from which candidates for office might be selected; occasion was taken to extend a eulogy upon this party, which was called the "vanguard of the toilers in their struggle for the strengthening and development of the socialist order, [which] represented the directing kernel (leading core) of all organizations of toilers, both public and state."

Both the rights and the duties of the citizen were recognized. New rights of man were established—to work (with payment, which was insured by "the socialist organization of the national economy, the steady growth of the productive forces of the Soviet society, the elimination of the possibility of economic crises, and the liquidation of unemployment"); to rest (includ-

ing limitation of hours, vacations, and use of state rest homes);
and economic security (with social insurance in respect to old
age, illness, or incapacitation, besides free medical attention and
the use of health resorts). It was not stated that the right to
labor might include forced labor—such labor as the state might
see fit to impose. Military service was also to be expected of
every citizen.

To education was paid a high tribute—it was to be universal,
compulsory, and free—and to include higher education and
education in the shops, on the farm, and elsewhere. It was not
added that this education was to be only through communist
channels and to communist ends. Full and equal rights, with
disqualifications of no kind, were given to women. Freedom of
asylum, or the right of refuge, was granted, but only to those
concerned "in the defense of the toilers," or in scientific activities, or in a struggle for national liberation, all according to
the Soviet viewpoint. Rights of organization (industrial, cultural, etc.) were guaranteed. It was not stated that all organizations had to have the approval of the government. Toleration
was enjoined toward different national and racial groups; forbidden were any limitations of citizens because of exclusiveness
or hatred on such grounds. But all such attitudes, it hardly
need be asserted, were in practice to be extended only when the
communistic state was not thereby to be endangered.

Certain old freedoms were reaffirmed—but they were not
absolute, and were to be exercised within restrictions believed
to be necessary for the preservation of the socialist state. Im-
plementation was lacking for the protection of the several freedoms or rights enumerated; there was no assurance of appropriate court action in this regard.

Under freedom of the conscience, the state and the school
were declared to be separate from the church; while freedom
of religion was permitted, its teaching might be only in the
family; freedom of worship was assured—and so was freedom
of anti-religious propaganda. Religion might not make full use

of the press or radio. An important consideration in the Soviet philosophy was freedom *from* religion, as was the case with respect to some other freedoms.

Freedom of speech, of the press, and of assembly (and also of public processions and demonstrations) was incorporated into the constitution; but such freedoms must be exercised "in the interests of the toilers, and with the object of strengthening the socialist system"—a circumscription that made them of no great value in the eyes of the rulers of this particular state. Above all, there was no freedom to change the form of government—the touchstone of democracy. All freedoms were conditioned upon the assumed needs of the working classes. Printing and publishing facilities were to be exclusively "at the disposal of the working classes"—in contradistinction to what was believed to be the practice in capitalistic countries, where such facilities were regarded as in the hands of those possessed of wealth. Under this conception there could be wide, practically unrestricted censorship of printed matter as well as of other means for the expression of opinion. In the Soviet view personal liberty was of no moment or consequence as long as one might be in economic need or distress or subject to economic exploitation; under capitalism there could be no real economic freedom, the workers being compelled to accept only what was offered them. The great issue thus seemed to be whether man's political rights—which in some other lands he had been accustomed to esteem more or less as the prerogative of his innermost or highest self—were to be given a lower rating, an inferior status, to his economic or material concerns —even on the assumption that such concerns were better looked after in the Soviet country. At any rate the Soviet constitution laid stress upon economic as well as upon political matters; possibly it was to be a pioneer here.

"No humiliation of human dignity," no vengeance in punishment, the "inviolability of the person and of the home," freedom from arbitrary arrest, and from arbitrary investigations in one's home or in one's correspondence, fair and open trials for those charged with breach of the laws of the land—such expressions or their equivalent found a place in the instrument. These were all fine-sounding phrases, but understood not to apply to political offenders or dissidents. Freedom from arrest might without too great difficulty be overriden by the procedure of the secret police. There was no promise of what we know as habeas corpus or of prompt and open trial by jury.

As to the guarantee of such things as freedom of speech or of the press, world opinion would have to wait upon their practical manifestations. Soviet Russia would have to prove that it understood in some measure what civil liberty meant. Men ask of what use is the secret ballot, a free press, and all the rest, when the party in power holds them in the hollow of its hand, and shows no inclination of letting go. Freedom was largely as the Communist party ruled; there was no other authority to determine the matter. Dictatorship, officialdom could remain, constitution or no constitution.

It is to be recognized that there had never been democratic backgrounds or traditions in Russia. The Soviet state saw no need and felt no obligation to help in their creation. It had had no practical experience with democracy, and could not be expected to understand it fully. It was inured to close rulership. Russia had long been nurtured on the principles and tactics of absolutism. An announced dictatorship of the proletariat had succeeded a proclaimed dictatorship of the Czar of all the Russias.

The Communist party not only was in the seat of power in the Soviet Union. It was ostensibly the head and front of all the Communist activity of the world. Moscow was the ideological capital of the Communists of the globe. It was in principle the center for an uprising of the workers of all countries and for the adoption of communism everywhere. In a large sense the International Communist Party (the "Comintern") was for a time its mouthpiece. Communists of all lands looked to the Executive Committee of the Communist party of the Soviet Union for light and leading; they even owed a certain allegiance to it. It was this Party, and not the formal government of the Soviet Union, that guided and largely financed it.[1]

The Communist International was formally set up in 1919, a year or two after the inauguration of the Soviet state, at a convention called at Moscow, with half a hundred delegates present from a score and half nations.[2] Here was created the Third International—at which was adopted a new or modern Communist Manifesto. At the time there were revolutionary uprisings in several countries, notably in Hungary and Italy, with Germany apparently on the verge. In 1920 there was a second congress, with over two hundred delegates from two-score lands in different parts of the world, with rather strict rules for admission. It was not, however, an extreme leftist meeting, but one which agreed to coöperate with parliamentary governments so far as might be necessary, in attaining certain objectives, and with discussion of agrarian, colonial, and other questions. In 1921 was held the third congress, with over six hundred delegates on hand from half a hundred lands. Revolution not having raised its head generally over the world, it had less confidence in the outlook, and was prepared to take rather a defensive attitude. It was largely concerned with means to repel and fight off counter revolutions, and with practical measures to deal with fascism. Congresses were also in 1922, 1924, 1928, and 1935, after which there were no more. In that of 1928 there was abandoned, at least for the time being, the idea of world communism, and efforts in the Soviet Union were con-

[1] After half a score years of the Soviet Union plans for worldwide communism were largely abandoned in Russia, Stalin winning out over Trotsky. Socialism was to be built up at home first.

[2] Reference has been made to what has been called the First International, which began in 1863 and continued for a few years. The Second International was created in 1889, only to fall to pieces at the outbreak of the First World War in 1914. In 1923 there was attempt at its renewal, with comparatively moderate tendencies. (From 1921 to 1923 there was a relatively mild "International" at Vienna, known as "One and One-Half.") In the later years of the First World War there was organized in Switzerland what was called the Third International, and on the achievement of the Revolution in Russia its headquarters were removed to Moscow.

centrated on making a success of the Soviet venture at home. At the same time there was advocacy of "popular fronts" in all countries against fascism and nazism. (It is worthy of note that the Axis powers—Germany, Italy, and Japan—were now calling themselves anti-comintern. Strong efforts were made by them to evoke anti-comintern feelings in all nations, particularly in Spain and certain South American countries.)

In 1943 it was ordered by the Executive Committee of the International that the Third International cease to exist; and it was accordingly disbanded. Moscow thus formally severed connection with communist bodies in other countries of the world. World revolution as the term had usually been understood was now ostensibly abandoned. The Soviet Union was no longer officially bound to the conception of global communism. Force and violence, furthermore, were no longer formally regarded as the only means of attaining the ends of communism. There were recognized the possibilities of the development of socialism along different lines in different countries.[1] But the con-

---

[1] As has been brought out in connection with efforts at education in the Soviet Union, these efforts did not stop at its borders; they included propaganda directed to other countries in its favor. This propaganda was of determined character, and generally in able, skillful hands. Some emanated from Moscow in the language of the country affected. Literature published in or for the United States was for the most part well gotten up, and of quite attractive character, often illustrated. The best foot was always put forward in the interests of the Soviet Union. (The propaganda here was much less clumsy than that once carried on by the "German Library of Information" and other pro-German agencies prior to the entrance of the United States into the Second World War.) From the Soviet Embassy in Washington certain literature was available as to conditions and activities in the Soviet Union, including a special Information Bulletin, issued at frequent intervals. In different countries, including some in South America, Soviet embassies were centers of propaganda, especially with their "institutes of culture." There were several organizations in the United States ostensibly designed to promote friendly relations between it and the Soviet Union, which published more or less literature. There were also several magazines of like character. Much of the material thus issued was of valuable nature, objective and in the main presenting a fair picture of conditions and events in the Soviet Union. A portion was manifest propaganda as to progress there, industrially and culturally. This type was decidedly *ex parte*, setting forth only what was favorable to that land. The bibliographies that were prepared contained no great amount of what was adverse to it. There was continuous extolling of its policies and practices, which were always unexceptionable. There might be harsh or bitter attacks on those who opposed or criticized. There were strong pleas for American friendship, but only on Soviet terms. Soviet motion pictures, in general excellent, and in part superb, had practically unrestricted showings in America (with English titles). A

ception of world communism had not departed from the Soviet heart.[1]

given motion picture theatre might be a center for Soviet propaganda. There was also propaganda through youth and labor organizations.

[1] In 1947 there was set up a Communist Information Bureau ("Cominform") by the Communist parties of the Soviet Union, Poland, Rumania, Bulgaria, Hungary, Czechoslovakia, and Yugoslavia (Albania then being a satellite of Yugoslavia), with representatives also from that party in France and Italy.

CHAPTER XVIII

The Soviet State and Its International Outlook

FOR a time after the creation of the Soviet state there were disquietude and apprehension in certain quarters as to what this state might mean to the peace of the world. In its international outlook it was believed to be just possible that, with its peculiar economic and political indoctrination and attitudes, it might be casting covetous eyes at least upon certain nearby countries, control of parts of which would, among other things, add greatly to its strategic strength. In these lands themselves there were genuine anxiety and misgiving, and even tremor; they were never quite sure whether their taking over by Russia might not conceivably, in lieu of moral suasion, be through the exercise of more material impulsion.

The rest of the world indulged in questionings chiefly during the formative period. It was in the days of the "Revolution," and in the days just following, that there was the strongest doubt and the deepest concern lest a land dedicated to communism, convinced of the desirability of world communism, cognizant of the blessings to be bestowed by its rule, and, indeed, highly conscious of its obligations to bring about such an order with the least possible delay, might come to the decision that the surest and quickest method after all was by force of arms.

But with the passage of time these fears were in great measure allayed, and were departing. It was increasingly felt that if communism was to advance and gain greater and greater possession of the earth, it was to do so by the more or less rapid

335

conversion of the proletariat of other lands to the Soviet way of thinking, by peaceable means, including perhaps propaganda and incitement to unrest—by general preparation of the soil for the seeds of communism. A certain economic penetration was also possible in the exportation of cheap manufactures and other goods to capitalistic countries. (The Soviet authorities made little attempt to disguise their sympathies with the "Reds" in other lands.) But all here was to be accomplished without the physical weapons of war. In international matters the world had almost come to forget Soviet breach of faith in breaking with the Allies of Russia in the First World War.

The Soviet state was, furthermore, too much concerned and too much engrossed and involved in its own affairs, in the building up of its own house, to think of warring upon other lands—apart from the consideration that its supposedly pacific philosophy forbade any such procedure. From that state came pronounced asseverations of its devotion to the cause and ways of peace. It would think of engaging in battle with no nation, save in the event that its own borders were invaded and attempts made to destroy its economic and political system. However Soviet Russia was looked upon, whether it was regarded in its domestic policies with a friendly or with an unfriendly eye, the conviction grew among the peoples of the earth that it could be counted upon on the side of peace, and that the world's peace was more secure in consequence thereof. When note was taken of the part played by it in the work of the League of Nations at Geneva, there were added hope and encouragement.

The ruling powers in Soviet Russia were believed to be particularly anxious to preserve peace while they could build up socialism at home, they having reason to fear that war might cause considerable political disturbance, perhaps counter revolution; with a long peace the infiltration of socialism into other lands might also be more of a possibility. Finally, the people of Russia had long been known as a peace-loving people, little inclined to and little to be provoked into war, except upon strenuous instigation.

The world came to conclude that communism had at least one good thing on its side, one good thing to be said for it— its consuming hatred of war, or at any rate war that could be held as of aggressive character. It would have nothing to do therewith. It was above such an outrage upon humanity; the slaughter of human beings had no place in its program. Such things belonged to the capitalistic and the imperialistic nations, and were to be left to them.

This soothing hope and belief the nations of the earth came largely to accept. Around the world it crept. Peoples were in greater heart; they began to live in a higher degree of assurance of the peace-mindedness of the Soviet state. That land was even hailed as a powerful defender of the peace of the world. Soviet Russia, whatever its internal merits or demerits, was to contribute to peace among men. The attitude of the world was kindly disposed toward it, at least in one respect.

After their Revolution, however, the Soviet people proved to be a sensitive and suspicious people with respect to other nations. They could long harbor, and even nurse, their enmities and piques and grudges, or what they regarded as their grievances and the wrongs done them. They had not forgotten the activities of the Allies in their civil wars following the Revolution, though there was something to be said for the Allies here. They were quite unable, or unwilling, to see the point of view of the Allies. They seemed unconcerned with the fact that by their separate peace treaty with Germany, with their consequent abandonment of the Allies, the Allies were left to bear the brunt of the conflict, which originally was as much that of the Russians as of the Allies. They did not seem to realize that in consequence of their going back on the Allied cause Germany came very close to winning the war. The Allies suffered heavily as a result of Russia's defection.

What is strangest of all, the Russians seemed not to see that

if the Allies had not fought to the end and had not defeated
Germany in the First World War, Russia could not have with-
stood that power, but would have succumbed to it, and for long
would have been kept in thrall by it, as a sort of subsidiary or
vassal state. It was truly the Allies that saved Russia. Russia
might well have fallen on her knees in gratitude to the Allies
for what they did. But no such thing. It never acknowledged
the vast debt it owed. Instead, it only displayed ill humor and
engaged in high words. It had only fault and blame to find
with the Allies. What it remembered and never forgave was
the allied intervention in Russia in the days following its
Revolution.

Whether politically and militarily wise or not, the Allies had
some grounds for what they did in the months after the defection of Russia, which had hitherto been a comrade in arms.
They were moved by several considerations, certain of which
are not to be dismissed lightly. In the first place, in the desperate struggle with the Germans they were anxious to see an
eastern front maintained or reëstablished against the enemy, the
Germans always realizing the danger when between an eastern
and a western front.

In the next place, there were large and valuable military
stores in Russia belonging to the Allies which they wanted to
repossess. Moreover, the Allies were much concerned in keeping Russian resources, especially food stuffs, besides certain minerals, from German hands. Though with the complete defeat
of Germany these several factors became of less account, there
remained exasperation and resentment—a part of which had to
do with the cancellation of Russian war debts. Even though
Germany had succumbed, there remained a strong feeling of
indignation and wrath over the withdrawal of the Russians
from the Allied side. They felt themselves decidedly aggrieved.
Had Russia now not deserted them, betrayed them, let them
down? Had she not released powerful German armies to
heighten the difficulties of the Allies in the west? With or

without regard to her particular governmental theories, was she now to be looked upon or treated otherwise than a potential foe? Was she a power that could altogether be depended upon, one worthy of trust, one from which they could feel themselves entirely safe? Did they not have reason to be concerned over the direction of her future activities? Without doubt they had occasion to be confused over the situation. There was no question at the same time that the Allies were fearful of and hostile to the régime of the new communistic order. It is to be remembered that it was much more difficult to know what was best to be done in those days of strain than it was in later days.[1]

But the Soviet people or their rulers did not see matters in this light. They appeared quite unmoved by the grave, deadly injury they had done the Allies in the hour of crisis, or by the moral implications of their breach of faith with their former war comrades. Rather, they saw only what they regarded as the deliberately hostile acts and efforts to strangle the newly created state at its birth, and felt highly affronted and outraged over it. With the passing of the years they held in memory only what they regarded as their grievances and wrongs, and with unabated bitterness. The future historian will probably record that if the Soviet people had the right to harbor resentment and animosity, the Allied nations had no less a one.

The Soviet state seemed quite forgetful or unmindful of another form of "intervention" on the part of America in this connection. This was in the desperate beginning days when the new nation was sorely beset with internal dissensions, famine, and hunger, and America came to its aid with food and other relief, from both public and private sources, and in no small quantities.

---

[1] It was declared by generals of the White armies that if they could have received Allied recognition, they could have defeated the Soviet armies. The Allies declined to lend encouragement to a Polish proposal for a quick march upon Moscow or Leningrad, which would probably have resulted in its capture.

As the Soviets proceeded with the building of their new economic and political order, they came to believe that they stood pretty much alone. They felt that they were fighting single-handed the battle of communism, with a hostile world looking on and ready to deal a death blow if it could. They considered themselves isolated within the confines of their own land. They looked upon themselves as friendless, a sort of pariah, among the great nations of the earth. They felt that every man's hand was raised against them. They were in position to keep alive their sensitiveness and suspiciousness.

Doubtless the Soviet country in the early days had some reason for its misgivings and apprehensiveness. In view of the whole situation it could afford to be distrustful of certain foreign countries. Be that as it may, these other countries had reason, and perhaps reason no less strong, to be distrustful of the Soviet Union. They could not for one thing overlook what they regarded as communistic penetrations in their lands, inspired from Moscow. Great Britain for its part could not well close its eyes to the interference of the Soviet Union in its domestic affairs, including at one time incitation to strikes with some of its workers. There were bound to be mutual suspicions, in part based upon ideological differences in governmental policies that had existed since the Union's emergence as a socialist state. The suspicions now existing on both sides, and becoming firmly planted with the years, were to be aggravated by what was to transpire on the European stage— in the tensions created by Nazi Germany, of whose activities and plans both Russia and the western nations were in increasing concern and fear.

An event was now at hand which was to throw more or less light upon the Soviet Union's general disposition. This was the predestined war of Nazi Germany which was to loose itself upon Europe. As the clouds were gathering, both the Soviet Union and the nations of western Europe were sharply eyeing each other. It has been charged that each was hoping that the

340

other would come to grips with the Nazi power, and that then these two would be engaged in killing each other off.

In the preliminary but fruitless negotiations regarding the Nazi demands upon Czechoslovakia and regarding its proposed dismemberment, it was possibly a mistake on the part of the Allies not to have consulted the Soviet Union to a greater extent, and to have come to a fuller understanding with it. But this want of action was primarly due to a more or less justified suspicion of the designs of the Soviet Union, and uncertainty as to what could be counted upon from it at the present juncture. The Soviet Union at the same time, while decrying the policies of the Allies, did not itself come to the aid of Czechoslovakia in its critical hour, and gave no conclusive word that it was willing to join hands with Britain and France to check Germany, on any but its own terms. It announced no intention of coming to Czechoslovakia's assistance in any event in case of attack by Germany; it in fact made no move in that direction. It is true, as the Soviet Union could claim, that Great Britain and France themselves failed to come to the aid of threatened Czechoslovakia; it can be said for them only that those countries declined to act because of the powerful and insistent peace sentiments in their home lands, and because of the failure of the people of those countries, as well as of other countries of the world at the time, to realize that there was no such thing as Nazi appeasement. (If the United States had been a member of the League of Nations at the time, things might have been different.)

In the sober light of history it seems that the feelings of Britain and the Allied nations towards the Soviet Union had better justification than the feelings of the latter towards them. In particular were they unwilling to accede to the Soviet request that its armies be allowed to enter the Baltic states and Poland, and have a free hand in them, against the wishes of those countries—something that would hardly have been possible with nations that had respect for democratic theories and principles as well as for the rights of smaller nations.

The case for the Allies becomes much stronger in the light of subsequent events. They would never, on the failure of acceptance of or acquiescence in their own terms, have done what the Soviet Union did on failure to win its terms or secure its demands. While emissaries from Britain and France were in Moscow seeking to secure at least some understanding with respect to future joint operations to meet the ever increasing danger from what all recognized to be the common foe, Germany, the Soviet Union stunned the potential allies by announcing, in a sort of cynical glee and scorn, that it had just signed a mutual aid pact with Germany—had joined hands with that country in what was for certain purposes hardly less than collaboration, hardly less than a practical alliance. Through it Germany, in return for machinery sent to Russia, was to get war materials and supplies for its aggressions upon states of Europe that were strenuously seeking to avoid war. Germany was also to give credits to the Soviet Union for commodities which it wished to have. (It may be noted here that at one time German officers had been engaged to train soldiers of the Soviet Union.) Under this pact Germany was to have a free hand in its actions as to Danzig and Poland in exchange for a free hand for Russia in its actions as to Finland and the Baltic states. Each of the contracting parties agreed to give no support to any power attacking the other.

In defense of her dealings here it was maintained by the Soviet Union that the non-aggression pact with the Germans was signed only for the purpose of gaining additional time to build up the Soviet strength and to fortify its defense areas. This exculpation never went far outside of Russia. If the Soviet Union secured additional time to prepare itself against the expected German attack, it also allowed the Germans more time to conquer western Europe, and eventually to put them into position for the attack on Russia. (It is to be remarked also that Great Britain with France had given Poland guarantees

that they would come to her aid in case of attack by Germany.)
There was something about the whole procedure so cold-
blooded, so callous, so indifferent to the principles of fair dealing and honor that it could not be washed clean by all the
labored apologies, explanations, and counter charges on the
part of the Soviet authorities.

What the Soviet Union really did was to give Nazi Germany
a clear signal to go ahead, and to open the flood gates of the
Nazi horror. It had turned aside from the overtures of those
countries which wished and strove to coöperate with her in
checking the coming Nazi onslaught on the world's liberties.
and the inconceivable suffering that was in time to be visited
upon Russia itself.

Within a few weeks after the making of this pact there was
launched the German attack upon Poland. That country had
previously refused to allow Soviet troops upon her soil, ostensibly to defend her against Germany, a refusal that seemed
quite justified in the light of what was to happen when Soviet
troops were upon the soil of the Baltic states. Within a few
weeks after the Nazi invasion from the west, there was a Soviet
invasion from the east, these two powers by agreement now dividing up Poland between them. Russia's action was accompanied with a declaration that Poland had been "abandoned to
its fate"—though this was only through Russia's collusion with
Germany. It was claimed by Russia that the part taken over by
her was then in a state of anarchy, and required to be placed
under orderly government. It was also claimed by her that this
part had once belonged to her (though some territory was
taken that had not so belonged)—that Poland, taking advantage of her weakened condition after her internal Revolution,
had possessed itself of this region. The boundary line, however,
that had been established had been recognized by formal treaty
between the two countries, which was hardly entitled to be
broken by unilateral action. Besides, whatever may have been

the just claims of Russia in the matter, this was indeed no time for their assertion.

Not long afterwards the Soviet Union, with the acquiescence of Germany, seized air and naval bases in the Baltic states, with the arrival there of Soviet troops in considerable strength—despite the fact that the Soviet Union had recognized the independence and statehood of these countries with due solemn treaties, which had subsequently been confirmed with non-aggression provisions. Before the lapse of many months these countries were declared to constitute a threat to Russia, and were accordingly taken over and absorbed into the Soviet Union. (They had been a part of the old Russian Empire.)

In the meantime Finland was attacked and a portion of her territory contiguous to Russia was wrested from her. In vindication of her actions here, the Soviet Union declared that she was being merely realistic and far-sighted; she was simply making her defense against the day of the inevitable German attack; she was only making herself better able to resist. Her sufficient justification in her own eyes was that she needed territory to ensure her protection—she pointed to the few short miles that lay between Leningrad and the Finnish border. Somewhat later when Europe was in the throes of its war, an ultimatum was issued to Rumania to cede to the Soviet Union certain areas which had once belonged to it (and a little more besides).

By its action in seizing territory of neighboring states, especially of Finland and the Baltic states, while the rest of Europe was engaged in a death struggle with the Nazi legions, and when much of the Continent had succumbed, the Soviet Union forfeited no little of the trust and faith placed in it, at a time when the world was coming to have increasing regard and friendliness toward it. The attack upon little Finland, its weak but courageous neighbor, in particular drew the indignation and resentment of the world, with sharp and strong expostulation and castigation, and causing its expulsion from the League of Nations. Nothing that the Soviet Union had so far done turned the world so fully from it or alienated so much of sympathy from it. Whatever the legitimate apprehension of that country with respect to the danger at its border, the world could not condone its actions when, striking to serve its own ends, it disregarded treaties it had made.

Not altogether convincing were the charges that the affair was to be laid at the door of Finland's "ruling classes"; that Finland was a spearhead and a gateway for a long-planned attack by "capitalistic" and "imperialistic" nations, with the Soviet government acting in the nick of time; that Finland had engaged in "provocative" acts, had been "insolent," had made "hostile refusal" to all the Soviets' well-intentioned requests, and had offered "brazen denial of facts." In response to the reproaches levelled against the Soviet state, it became only the more incensed. It bristled up against those who had presumed to find fault. It added to its bitter store of memories with respect to the outside world.

Upon other nearby nations on the Baltic sea the Soviet Union under military threats made such demands as it might have seen fit to make, if not by way of territorial aggression, at least for greater or less power over their land, and in greater or less degree over their ways of life, that were hardly less than direct invasion of their soil, and that involved impairments or compromises in their sovereign rights as nations.[1]

In its dealings with weaker neighboring peoples the Soviet policy grew ever bolder and more arrogant. In bringing such lands within its orbit of control, or in more or less rapidly overcoming or subduing them, a certain technique may be said to have been developed—possibly in different stages, possibly along different lines. The orders issuing from Moscow to those

[1] There were undoubtedly certain elements in Finland and the Baltic states who were friendly to Germany or who had pro-German leanings. But with the people at large there was lack of sympathy with the Soviet Union and general fear of it. Finland, bitter over its reverses in its first encounter with the Soviet Union, was unfortunately too much inclined to go along with Germany in the Second World War, to get revenge and to recoup its losses.

lands might be more blunt or less blunt, some couched in polite-sounding diplomatic language, and some not so. Not too heavily camouflaged were promises of quick, stern, and adequate military measures if compliance or obedience was not forthcoming—though possibly attended with assurances of the protection of the "security" and "independence" of the threatened countries.

In order to gain a sufficient foothold or a position of sufficient authority, the command from the Soviet capital might call for a demobilization of the armies of those nations or for their general demilitarization. A somewhat more elaborate procedure might consist of a declaration that these other countries were incapable of defending their neutrality, present or future, in the event of war; to see that this was properly attended to, was the added request that Soviet troops be permitted to enter certain areas, or that certain military or naval bases be turned over (or perhaps "leased") to the Soviet authorities—all possibly with an agreement of "mutual assistance."[1]

More prompt and expeditious and more thorough-going action was to be had in charging the government of the other countries with fomenting or permitting secret plans or activities hostile to the Soviet state, or with conniving or conspiring or contracting alliances with certain "imperialistic" or "capitalistic" nations, or with engaging in intrigues that were counter to the well-being of that state. In such a case a new and stronger agreement might be insisted upon, perhaps with the bidding that there be installed a pro-Soviet government, the better to attend to the mutual assistance pact, and with the admittance of an increased number of Soviet troops. Now was the time for the organization or promotion of an effective local communist party, if one had not already come into being, which

[1] The Baltic states were said to be "declining" economically (and also culturally). U.S.S.R. Bulletin, "The Sixteen Soviet Republics, 1945. There was "retarded industry . . . enterprises closed down . . . more and more workers condemned to join the mass army of the unemployed . . . years of impoverishment and ruin of small holders." *Ibid.*, Aug. 11, 1948. See *post*, p. 397.

was betimes to assume the reins of government. Next in order might be the voicing of vigorous protest respecting the "horrible" or "intolerable" conditions prevailing among the working classes or peasants. A variation of the theme might be that friends of the Soviet land were undergoing mistreatment or persecution, or that the authorities were not sufficiently cordial toward those who would cultivate closer ties with that land, or that attempts were being made to suppress agitators favoring such closer ties; in other words, the government of the other states was to desist from any efforts to check the disloyal elements within their own borders. Strong representations were now to be expected from Moscow that relations with the Soviet state were imperilled by such actions. The Soviet state, it was solemnly proclaimed, was duty-bound to protect its friends, faithless plotters though they might be against their own state.

At this point the stage was set, the time was ripe, for the creation of a puppet Soviet government, and its being placed in the seats of power. The formality of an "election" was gone through—but with only one ticket in the field, with soldiers at the ballot places, with the voter required to produce official papers indicating his right to vote—and with only one result possible. Those who were "elected" immediately set up a movement for annexation with the U.S.S.R. Formal petition in the name of the peasants, workers, and soldiers was made to Moscow for union, the new state now to participate in the activities and share in the blessings of the Soviet order. Moscow did its part with all due solemnity in carrying out this mockery of free and democratic institutions. By it, and as was to be expected, the whole proceeding was loudly acclaimed as having practically unanimous popular endorsement. All this highhanded procedure, the delivery of a weaker neighboring state into the hands of the Soviet Union, was all for the "security" of that Union.

With the absorption of the helpless victims of Soviet power into its body, or their joining up, as it was called, the initial step in introducing the new order was likely to be the nationalization of banks, industries, and the larger farms; small farms with a limited amount of livestock were for the time being left in the hands of individual owners or occupants, to await the complete nationalization of the country.

To make sure of the unanimity of the expression of popular will, the most active or the most determined of the enemies of the U.S.S.R., or those least inclined to see the light, were whisked away—were banished or otherwise disposed of. After the taking of the ill-fated land into the Soviet state, the latter could declare that it had been greeted "with tears of joy, with delirious exultation, with speeches, flowers, songs." It could show pictures of all this jubilation, it is true; but how could these helpless folk, if not a picked group, resist the order for their display of rejoicing?

All these things proceeded, with Moscow proclaiming, as was its wont, high ethical and humanitarian considerations and standards—finding exemplification in its international transactions no less than in its domestic ones, and all in the name of the one true democracy of the world. It is not to be forgotten that about this time the Soviet state had had little compunction in aligning itself to a greater or less extent with a powerful, militaristic dictator state—few qualms, when the occasion arose, in making common cause with the enemies of the democracies, to the heavy injury of these democracies, and in the end to itself.

There was also in evidence the application of force, something already applied within the land to recalcitrant elements, next to be applied without as well—to lands whose people preferred their own ways, including more democratic processes.

Marxian socialism was not to proceed after any such fashion. The U.S.S.R. was to go it one better. Charging other nations with "imperialism" and with "imperialistic designs," disclaiming any such appellations or motives for itself, and rendering unctuous lip homage to democratic institutions, it hardly ap-

348

peared the "bulwark against war and aggression" that some of its ardent admirers then declaimed. Under the plea of safeguarding the working classes in other countries, of thwarting the designs of "capitalistic" nations, or of providing "security" for itself against the machinations of states that were envious of it or would be content only with its destruction, it might not be slow in finding apologies or offering extenuation for the "protection" or "liberation" of oppressed peoples in lands not its own.

When the Second World War finally struck Russia,[1] the one free opponent of Nazi Germany in Europe was Britain—the United States not being affected for some months yet. On the invasion of Russia Britain immediately signified her willingness to do all in her power to aid her new eastern ally, and proved this by her deeds. Russia's gigantic war efforts, stupendous losses, and unbelievable sacrifices and sufferings affected her allies profoundly. In the strongest possible terms they expressed their sympathy and their gratitude; they were never weary in extolling the unshakable courage and determination of the Russian people. They extended material aid without limit and without stint.

On the side of the Russians the picture was somewhat different. They remained largely sensitive and suspicious, as they had been from the beginning. They could not see far beyond themselves. They were never fully generous to the efforts of their allies; over these efforts they were often querulous. They magnified their own efforts; praise of the efforts of others was of a begrudging sort. For long among their own people they claimed to be practically the sole combatant against Germany, and their victories over Germany the only victories that counted; they were the saviors of Europe and of the world. (They made somewhat similar statements as to Japan, against which they began action late in the day, and then only at a

---

[1] There were reports that Hitler broke off with the Soviet Union in part because of its demands for too great power in southeastern Europe.

price and on their own conditions.) They insisted upon a "second front" before the allied general staff was ready for it or thought it wise to attempt it. They forgot that they failed to help with a second front when in earlier days so many of the nations of Europe were in desperate need, and would have welcomed beyond words a second front in the east. They were slow in letting allied airmen have bases in their own territory. They refused bases in Siberia when America was keeping Japan off the back of Russia. They failed fully to realize how far German troops were being kept busy in different areas of the world battlefield. They failed fully to realize how Britain's activities in Greece and Crete held back at a critical time Germany's invasion of Russia. They failed fully to realize what the Allies were doing in Africa and in Italy; what the Allied airmen were doing to German munition factories and transportation systems, and in keeping German aeroplanes from Russia.

There were in general tardy acknowledgment and sparing recognition of what Russia's allies had done in sending war and other supplies to her in her hour of pressing need—though it is always to be remembered that Russia herself provided the larger part. There was failure in particular to realize the deprivations and hardships which Britain had to suffer that Russia might get through. The major portion of the population of Britain (over sixteen years of age) was directly engaged in the war effort. New factories were created ahead of time to speed up the production of goods largely destined for Russia. Immense quantities of aircraft, trucks, tanks, and the like were dispatched. The food and general comforts of the people were severely reduced—stores and houses were drained—so that there might be immediate delivery of these things to Russia. Britain lent large sums of money, hundreds of millions of dollars. The British people made donations to the Russian people of a value of millions of dollars, despite the heavy taxation they were compelled to bear. Within a few months after the invasion of Russia Britain sent great quantities of rubber, tin, and other necessary material for Russian military weapons, shiploads of wheat, thousands of tons of sugar (something its people themselves so much needed); within this period it also sent hundreds of railway cars and locomotives; in less than a year it sent several million pairs of boots, of which the Russians were in such need. In addition, much material was shipped to be made into clothing on Russian soil. Great quantities of drugs, surgical instruments, and other medical supplies were transmitted.

The goods that left British shores in general reached Russia intact, and for the most part ahead of schedule. To accomplish all these things, a large part of the already overworked British navy as well as merchantmen that were needed elsewhere, had to carry cargos through the bitter cold of the Arctic north and by way of distant parts of the earth—around Africa to the Persian Gulf, or perhaps across the Pacific. Goods destined for Russia could be sent more safely overseas by way of Persia, but this required a journey of twelve thousand miles, with continued possibility of attacks from U-boats, and thence an inland journey of almost a thousand miles through a country of primitive conditions, with slow-moving camel trains, with a poor one-track railroad in continuous need of repairs, with mountain roads that had really to be built. In the Arctic voyage the cold was generally far below zero, and was attended by fogs, blizzards, and icebergs, with large squadrons of aircraft having to fly overhead. From the fjords of Norway U-boats lay in wait, while landing fields there could send out aircraft to menace the British convoys. Of all these things the Soviet people were largely unmindful or forgetful.

From the United States there went huge quantities of war equipment and material, of clothing, of food, of money—provided from public and from private sources alike; lend-lease arrangements were made fully applicable to Russia. Over eleven billion dollars worth of war material was sent, including fifteen million pairs of army boots, not far from half a million motor vehicles, fourteen thousand airplanes, and vast quantities of other things.[1] In America there were loud-crying communists who did all possible to impair and hinder its war efforts, and who declared that "the Yanks were not coming" —until Russia was itself invaded. Without let or hindrance they carried on Soviet propaganda, through literature, motion pictures, and what else they could—though for such activities conversely in the Soviet Union there would have been the punishment which it knew how to mete out for all such doings.

After the Second World War was over, and the stricken, crushed world was seeking to get on its feet again, to restore itself in what measure it could and to establish some order of peace, it was confronted with spreading Soviet influences in bordering and neighboring countries. From the position of ascendency and authority of the Soviet Union here, there came to be asked certain questions regarding her purposes and designs, about which there was not altogether clear or sure understanding, and about which there was over the world more or less misgiving and disturbance. Was the Soviet Union, more or less clandestinely, imposing her will in countries which her troops had occupied or which were regarded as within her "security" orbit, infringing upon their rights and dignities or

[1] More specifically (in round numbers), there were among supplies under lend-lease from the United States some fifty thousand jeeps, seven thousand tanks, eight thousand tractors, four hundred thousand trucks, two thousand locomotives, ten thousand freight cars, half a million tons of rails, one hundred thousand tons of railroad wheels and axles, thirty-five thousand motorcycles, seventeen million tires, one hundred merchant ships, one hundred and thirty-five thousand machine guns, eight thousand aintaircraft guns, two hundred torpedo boats, one hundred submarine chasers, one hundred thousand submarine guns, eight thousand marine diesel engines, three hundred thousand tons of explosives, six hundred thousand tons of chemical products, sixty power trains to supply war factories, seven hundred diesel engines to furnish power, four hundred thousand field telephones, a million and a quarter miles of telephone wires, several hundred centrifugal pumping units, one hundred and fifty million yards of cotton and of woolen cloth, several million tons of steel and other metals, a like quantity of petroleum products, a billion dollars worth of machinery, fifty thousand square feet of aircraft and steel landing mats, several million tons of foodstuffs. There were some twenty-six hundred shiploads of seventeen million tons. There were entire factories sent in cargo lots. Over one-half of Russian highway-borne supplies in the last months of the war were carried in American-made trucks. Some eighty million dollars was contributed in relief from America.

upon their territory as sovereign states, even though the while charging her capitalistic allies of former days with these very things? Was she engaged in direct or indirect aggression? Was she making them more or less her satellites? Was she endeavoring in organized fashion to indoctrinate them with Soviet communism? Was she looking to their eventual incorporation into the Soviet Union? Was her control over them based fundamentally on her military establishment? Was she in violation of her agreements with her former allies imposing upon them governments of her own choosing?

Was she displaying little reluctance in intervening in internal or domestic affairs and policies for her own advantage and gain? Was she more or less dictating programs of action? Was she employing some political subterfuge or more violent procedure to work her will? Was she more or less covertly interfering with democratic processes, or with rightful representative government? Was she taking advantage of outward forms of justice, or legal or constitutional technicalities, to seize or usurp power? Was she able to have a small, vigorous, unresting communist minority demand recognition in a coalition government, especially in police and communications or information departments, there to be not only in a highly strategic position, but also in a position where could be muzzled or driven out opposing factions? Was she getting up "fatherland fronts" as hardly other than screens for communist control?

Did she if stronger in a country turn to tactics of intimidation and suppression, or to tactics of stark terrorism? Was she resorting to strong-arm methods in disposing of opposing leaders—was she railroading them to prison or exile or more dread punishment still? Was she forbidding or dissolving antagonistic political parties? Was she disfranchising contrary elements on trivial or trumped-up charges? Was she infiltrating into labor and other like organizations, gaining power therein, perhaps doing away with leaders who were proving unfriendly or uncoöperative? Was she planting communists in

other parties to mislead them or to win them over? Was she
making the police a party instrument? Was she using the police to subdue enemies by threats to themselves or to their families? Was she infiltrating into the army and seeing that officers were staunch party men? Was she charging with "conspiracy" any who were standing athwart her path? Was she
"liquidating" individuals or groups for their "reactionary" attitudes, or because of their "coöperation with foreign imperialistic interests to impair the sovereignty of the state," or in consequence of "plotting" along these lines?

Was she through schools and other means of indoctrination
and by appropriate government and party organizations, making satellite countries conform to the Soviet pattern?

Was she employing food rationing to make people yield to
her wishes? Was she overawing through troop concentrations?
Was she securing control of the means of communication and
information, especially through the press, radio, and moving
picture, so as to have exclusive use of them for her own ends
both in the countries concerned and for the outside world?
Was she in possession of the paper supply of a country, forbidding its use by opposition newspapers? Was she forcing
journalists to join unions of her own direction?

Was she bringing in her own people to take possession of
farms or industries in occupied countries? Was she importing
trusted communists to take positions in countries under her
sway? Were some of the principal officers really Russians under assumed names?

Was she inciting border disturbances to wear out enemies
beyond the border? Was she encouraging surreptitious border
violations? Was she compelling neighboring countries to enter
military alliances with her against the possible day of war with
non-communist countries? Was she threatening or seeking to
intimidate nearby nations on the ground that they were col-
laborating with or preparing to give aid to her potential enemies or were harboring "war criminals"? Was she in more

or less distant countries engaged in stirring up political trouble or in promoting subversion or conspiracy against their government? Was she conducting a war of nerves?

Was she seeking to build up air-tight economic union with satellite countries, to get further and further control of their business economy? Was she in her powers of occupancy, or by claims of reparations, or by acquiring majority interests in a country's resources, aiming to divert national commercial channels into her own economic orbit, to incorporate them into her own economic system? Was she exerting pressure in the taking over of certain resources of these countries, particularly food and other consumer goods? Were her armed forces living upon the resources of the countries overrun or occupied when these countries were having extreme difficulty in meeting the needs of their own people? Was she taking materials, perhaps choicest capital goods, including machinery, from these countries, possibly under guise of war damages or war reparations, with or without the concurrence or consent of her partner nations? Was she draining them of some of their natural resources? Was she going so far in certain occupied countries as to deprive them of means of industrial recuperation? Was she forcibly taking away both skilled engineers and common laborers for work in her own land—in a measure enslaving them? Was she bringing in deportees from occupied lands for her forced labor camps?

Were refugees from her own land or from lands under her domination, whom she sometimes called "fascists" or "war criminals," proving themselves unwilling to return to their homes if in such areas? Was she ready and anxious to use compulsion to get them there? Was she disinclined to allow them material assistance while they maintained these attitudes? Was she taking advantage of the situation to attempt communistic propaganda through them? Was she moving masses of people away from their own homes when she thought it would be safer for herself if they were elsewhere?

Was she always faithfully and unequivocally carrying out the agreements made with her former allies? Was she sometimes demanding a policy of appeasement or humoring as the price of her coöperation or participation in joint action in international matters? Had she taken advantage of the need here to secure unfair advantages for herself?

Was she deliberately delaying reconstruction in conquered countries in the hope that through confused and disordered conditions there she would be more likely to gain her ends? Was she in consequence of her peculiar political system incapable of applying democratic processes or majority rule to international matters, perhaps on the ground that her own security would thereby be endangered or impaired? Was she unwilling to have her soldiers and other nationals come into contact with those of western countries, fearful of possible effects on her own?

Was she seeking her own ends or the ends of communism in claiming to be the champion of weaker nations, in claiming to be the friend of the oppressed peoples of the earth, ever striving for their liberation, protection, security? Was she sometimes found fishing in troubled waters for the advancement of her own interests? Was she promoting or encouraging the creation of economic or political chaos in one land or another so as to be able to reap the fruits there? Was she trying to keep the world in ferment and turmoil to hasten the communistic revolution? Was she seeking to terrorize other nations?

Was her real objection to any sort of supranational control over weapons and implements of war (including the atomic bomb) based upon unwillingness to have foreign powers bring prying eyes upon her internal conditions or to have foreign contacts for her people? Could it be that the loud charges of "war-mongering" and "capitalistic imperialism" on the part of other nations was designed primarily for home consumption— to inflame the home people and to create a belligerent spirit or frame of mind among them, perhaps so as to keep leaders in power who might not feel altogether secure on their thrones or sure of their places, and who, as has happened more than once in human history, felt it incumbent upon themselves to resort to fears of attacks from without for their own preservation or for the preservation of their own political systems?

Was she making herself the nucleus or center of a vast empire, with her satellite states about her, reducing or forbidding contacts between them and other nations of the world, with Moscow planned as the eventual capital of all communistic lands?

Was she, if not instigating or egging on communistic aggressions against non-communistic countries, at any rate giving assent or sanction to such aggressions, at the same time brazenly charging these countries with aggression? What meaning was there to her pleas for peace and denunciations of war when in her general policies she frankly displayed a willingness and readiness to resort to force and violence to attain her ends?

The Russian people are themselves not and never have been a war-minded people. They have for the most part been rather a peace-minded people, whatever the propensities of particular rulers. They may be said on the whole to be peace-minded by nature. Apart from given rulers at times, one of their characteristics had been rather a leaning toward pacifism.

Besides, have the Russians not had enough of wars? Have they not suffered long and keenly from the horrors and depredations and devastations of war? In their condition after two depleting and exhausting World Wars, has there not been an agonizing cry that they be freed from the thought of war, and afforded an opportunity for the restoration of their torn, wasted, and uprooted land? Have they not devoutly and fervently hoped to be let alone, and not be disturbed or distracted in their mighty task of rebuilding? Have they not had enough to do along these lines for long years to come? Have they not needed all their manpower for the production of needed goods?

No country could want or demand peace as could the Russians. They would be the last to desire a resurgence of war.[1]

In addition, Russia would have in general little reason to be at ill-will with the rest of the world, or to have necessary antagonisms for it, apart from any possible clash between conflicting ideologies, and beyond more or less natural envy toward certain countries with wide dominion or of great wealth, or perhaps making greater strides in the arts of peace. Possibly Russia could find herself at times a trifle irked over the prevalence and relative abundance of consumer goods in capitalistic countries like America—though a land declared to her people to be hamstrung with constant strikes and labor troubles in general, and filled with angry, despoiled masses. Russia has a wholesome regard and respect for the industrial and engineering genius and achievements of such countries, perhaps considering them as rivals which some time she hopes to equal if not surpass; she is aware that war with such countries would mean a terrific strain upon her and her resources even if she felt any considerable chance of winning. At the same time with her powerful armies and her immense territory, she knows that it would be most difficult to defeat her or really to conquer her. Finally, she must realize that what she needs above all is not war, but the aid and coöperation of other nations in her rebuilding and progress.

But with all these considerations there are other factors in the situation regarding potential Russian attitudes. The Russian people, while of pacific disposition in many ways, do not have anything like the abhorrence and destestation of war *per se* that a people like the Americans have. This may in part be because, as some think of them and as they often like to think

[1] Russia is said to have lost something like fifty million lives in connection with the First and Second World Wars and intervening famines and plagues. In connection with the Second World War there are said to have been between five and six million military deaths and even more civilian deaths, with five or six million fewer births in consequence. Material losses were virtually incalculable—sometimes said to be two-thirds of a trillion dollars. Two-thirds of the pre-war wealth of the invaded regions is said to have destroyed. *U.S.S.R. Information Bulletin*, Sept. 22, 1948.

of themselves, they are a more forthright, "tougher," more realistic people, more children of nature, with less of the embellishments, trappings, and conventions of modern society; they are of the more rough and ready type, of more homespun character, more like the old American pioneers. They are not inclined to indulge in wishful thinking with regard to war or anything else. They are more likely to look upon war as at times a matter of necessity, as in the course of human events, something to be expected with human nature as it is, something to be faced frankly, rather than covered up with pious objurgations as a horrible evil beyond the thought and action of civilized man. While always preferring peace to war, as do nearly all peoples, and while anything but a bloodthirsty people or people finding delight in war, they are not so "squeamish" upon the subject as are people like the Americans.

Was not the Russian country without natural barriers to check advancing foes—though more than once in her history her illimitable plains had well served the purpose by engulfing such foes? Had not the Russians for centuries seen their soil reddened with the blood of embattled hosts? Had not the pages of their history been from time to time so dyed? Had they not in later as well as earlier days witnessed if not participated in sanguinary combats, not only with foreign foes, but among their own people in internal clashes within their own borders? Were they not more or less inured to war both in theory and in practice? Could they not stand the thought of it better than some other peoples?

Apart from definite or "formal" wars, the Russians had been acquainted with wholesale shedding of blood. Deeds of violence had seldom been absent from their story. Under the Czars they had seen an endless line of political executions, singly or in numbers. During the Revolution and in the days of its aftermath they had beheld killings by the thousands, by the tens of thousands, by the hundreds of thousands. In those times, as we have seen, the new Soviet power had showed that it could be quite as skilled and adept, and as little finical, in the art of human slaughter as its predecessors in the Russian government. In those days were not blood baths a necessary and a recognized part of its procedure in its successful revolution?[1] Highly fanatical, intolerant of foes within and without, of any who did not see eye to eye with it in its political and economic outlook, had not this power urged, had it not exhorted the people to give no quarter to their enemies—particularly such as were of capitalistic leanings or were wearing capitalistic colors? Had it not told the people to strike down, to make away with these enemies, or with "the enemies of the people," without mercy and without compassion? Had it not told them to smite hip and thigh? Was not liquidation—a word to which the Soviets had given a peculiar and sinister meaning—to be the portion of all in the land who did not outwardly, and inwardly so far as it was possible to ascertain, conform or subscribe to the tenets of the Revolution? This liquidation was a sort of sincere madness, a consuming passion, looked upon as a sheer necessity for the existence of the embryonic Soviet state. Shooting down those who favored any other régime was for a time the order of the day. The Soviet state was in danger, the people were warned, from internal as well as from external foes; it was to be saved from destruction only by the destruction of its enemies. Early leaders boasted of their intolerance toward their foes. Their slogan was one of fighting and overcoming their enemies, and in a truceless war. Nowhere had the world seen such flaming, fearful intolerance, such gross, inordinate intolerance, such fantastic, frenzied intolerance. Never was there such combative fanaticism on so huge a scale.[2]

As a weapon in this intolerance, the Soviet power was pre-

---

[1] See *ante*, p. 174.

[2] "Suppression and the use of force by the state are still essential during the transition period." A. Y. Vyshinsky, "The Law of the Soviet State," 1948, p. 3. "The Court [social justice according to Soviet principles] accomplishes [its ends] by destroying without pity all the foes of the people by whatever form they manifest their criminal encroachments upon socialism." *Ibid.*, p. 498. See also Communist writings, *passim*.

pared to use force, without bounds and without stint. Force was made a cardinal doctrine and a cardinal arm in its movements. It felt that the employment of force required no justification, no extenuation. It inherited conceptions of force that went far back in Czaristic history. It was habituated to force; it could think fundamentally in terms of force. Force could operate variously—by threats, by the laying on of violent hands, if necessary by execution; there were few punctilios as to deportation, individually or en masse.

All these factors were of intensified order under the particular economic and political doctrines which the Soviet power had espoused and embraced, and in which it was immersed. Fierce dogmatism and bitter intolerance had now redoubled strength. It was here more than anywhere else that danger to the world lay—not so much in the economic and political aspects of the system in themselves. A considerable part of the population— how large no one can know—was so obsessed with the supposed benefits and needs of the new order, so fearful that it might be overthrown or undermined by envious or antagonistic forces without or within, that it could ascribe no good motive to those who differed. Nor is it to be forgotten that the Soviet Union was not only dominated by, engulfed in, her communistic theories, but regarded herself as having a distinct mission in the world therewith. It was her deep-seated conviction that there was no hope for the masses of men otherwise. It was her abiding faith that the wave of the future was hers—an irresistible tide.[1] According to her notions virtually all the economic ills and mischiefs of the world stemmed from, were traceable to, capitalism—it was the sum of all evil. Communism was something held as a passionate religious convincement, with a bitter consuming hatred for all dissenters therefrom. It admitted no alternative, no rival to itself. It was steeped in a philosophy of its own, with an ample supply of dialectics.

---

[1] "In our time all roads lead to communism. There is no power in the world that can prevent the death of capitalism." *U.S.S.R. Information Bulletin,* April 28, 1948.

Communism had worked itself into a mighty, boundless passion.

Communism was not only profoundly intolerant; it was highly aggressive. Communism was nothing if not militant; it constituted itself a relentless drive. It was essentially a missionary religion, something that it was the express and solemn obligation of the Soviet state to carry to darker regions of the earth. That state was dedicated not only to the perpetuation of communism, but to its spread. It was her definite belief that by the nature of the case communism could not eventually be confined to one nation; it was not possible forever for a single country. She was persuaded that the world could not remain half communistic and half capitalistic. It was her conviction, whether well-founded or not, that a communistic state could exist only in a wholly communistic world. Her internal and her external policies were to be predicated upon the eventual adoption of communism as the exclusive political and economic system of the world.

Was it not then incumbent upon her to speed the new gospel, and by whatever means were possible? On mere moral grounds under communistic conceptions there need be little withholding. Preferably, if Soviet communism was to gain possession of the world, it should be by propaganda, by direct appeals, by indoctrination among a sufficient portion of the population to be affected, when enough persons had been made to see and approve the Soviet way and the Soviet program.[1] But was it justice to the communist cause to say that this was or need be the exclusive method? Never was there on so mighty a range the promulgation of the doctrine that the end justifies the means.

The Soviet people were fed upon the alleged evils and dangers of capitalism. Over and over were they told that the workers of the world without communism were to be crushed to earth by black-hearted capitalism, were to be broken to pieces

[1] See *ante*, p. 269.

under its malevolent heel; that their only refuge, their only salvation lay under the protecting banner of communism. Capitalistic countries were war-mongering, and were already seeking the overthrow of the Soviet state—the people must be on constant guard and prepared to make any sacrifice for its protection. It was sometimes added that capitalism had had its day, and that its doom was sealed, that capitalistic countries (meaning in particular the United States) were already facing an economic crisis to be delayed little longer, and that their collapse was now nigh at hand. The capitalistic system, already under death sentence, needed only a knockout blow for its demise—something the communistic state should be prepared to deliver.

Not only was the Soviet communistic system lauded to the skies as the only possible conducement to happiness and prosperity among men, the only proper pattern for the existence of human beings, the only decent social order, the only one worth having on earth, but uncandid, disingenuous stories were set loose regarding conditions in other lands. There was a deliberate campaign of misrepresentation of these other countries. Their shortcomings were harped upon without ceasing, and not without ample exaggeration. There was considerable departure from the truth in what was set forth. There was unending scoffing at bourgeois democracy.

The American people in particular were painted as frivolous, uncouth, barbarous, decadent, soulless, greedy, money-mad—and plotting the destruction of the Soviet communistic commonwealth; the American land was the citadel, the last stronghold of the capitalistic enemy. There was incessant pointing out of its lurid or unsavory features or its vulgarities. There were caricatures of America in its different aspects and ways of life. The bourgeois philosophy of life was declared to be bankrupt here as elsewhere.

To crown all, the people of the Soviet Union were under a government that would permit no expression of opinion contrary to its established policies. It was nothing less than a dragooned public opinion that existed there. With respect to foreign or international situations, the government prepared, usually after the event, a digest for its people or for its different agencies for the dissemination of information. They were not allowed to take in what could come to them from outside their own country except through governmental intermediation. News from other countries was either banned or was admitted in curtailed or distorted form or out of its proper setting, or "doctored"; it could come only through definitely designated channels.

In consequence of all this, the people were literally bottled up. They were purposely kept in the dark. Discussion could proceed only along prescribed government conduits. Opinions as to "capitalism" were funneled into one conception—that which the government directed for it. Capitalism was a monster of so frightful a mien, a virus of such utter malignancy, an enormity of such proportions, an evil so accursed beyond words—the one paramount iniquity of the present day, the arch enemy of the human race—that the people were under no circumstances to be exposed to it. To the Soviet state the outside world was an unconscionable realm of capitalistic guile and oppression. It was a fantastic picture in which the orbit of capitalism was painted. In combating so dreadful a bane, in the Soviet opinion the supreme battle of the ages, there were no means, no weapon, that could not demand a place in their panoply of arms.

No country ever had the political education, the political indoctrination that Soviet Russia had. This indoctrination was not only one-sided, *ex parte,* without thought of a hearing for opposing parties, but it was something in itself fierce and rampant. By all the facilities of education possible in the land, to young and to old, were pointed out the actual or potential evils prevailing in enslaved capitalistic countries. Against them all the agencies and vehicles for Soviet propaganda were put into requisition. At the same time no criticism or fault-finding with the general policies of the Soviet state was permissible. There was no such thing as free public opinion—in its formulation or in its expression. The Soviet people lived in a darkened house through which the light could filter only through colored glass.

The Soviet state was not content in having its own people know of the blessings of the communistic order and the horrors and dangers of the capitalistic. It would have these important considerations known to all the world—to the countries within its political orbit and to the capitalistic countries, the latter being the ones who perhaps most needed to know. It conducted a vast campaign to this end—by printed matter, the radio, the motion picture.[1] Its mission was to educate the world on the subject.

As there was restricted freedom of expression in the Soviet state, so there was restricted conception of civil rights or of the rights of the individual citizen, a perverted conception according to the notions and ways of western democracies. Full conceptions could hardly have a definite place in the communistic scheme of the Soviet government. As was to be expected in totalitarian lands in general, all was for the state. There was no ground upon which the individual could stand as such. The only rights that were valid were those of the state—here the Soviet state.

The Soviet state loudly affirmed its adherence to democracy; it declared that such was its foundation and fountain head. It asserted that its brand was the only true one—though it was a democracy that was nothing less than controlled voting within the communistic framework.[2] The democracy here was predicated upon the principles and aims of communism. According to Soviet claims, its democracy was not only the better form; it was the only genuine form. Soviet democracy was a "new and higher type of democracy." With little variation such was the

---

[1] See *ante*, pp. 264, 272.

[2] Stalin has been quoted to the effect that a fairly elected government "in any of these [eastern European] countries would be anti-Soviet—that we cannot allow."

theme forever harped upon. All who spoke of it ran true to form.[1]

A peculiar source of danger to the tranquility of the world has lain in the Soviet conceptions of "security"—security for herself and her communistic state—conceptions made all the more serious for the no little amount of sincerity in them on the part of the government and of a very considerable portion of the population. Instead of building up her house through amity, good-will, coöperation among the nations, she had preferred to surround herself with a cordon sanitaire of her own making—a circle of satellite states, hardly more than mere puppet states, which could act only as they were bidden by her; towards them she has assumed an overawing attitude, a position of domination. The "security" of other states had no place in her conceptions.

Towards foreign countries, especially those that had dared to remonstrate or reprehend, she has often adopted a surly, ill-tempered, even truculent, tone; she has not greatly sought after a spirit of mutual understanding. With nations once in alliance with her she has displayed little willingness to share military secrets or even to indicate her military status, though she has keenly resented a like attitude on their part. She has shown no reluctance to ascribe unworthy motives to those who have not agreed with her. She has been prone to charge other nations with objectionable intentions and practices which she herself has appeared to contemplate or to have engaged in. She has even prompted her people to put the blame for their poor diet and hampered housing, even their lack of luxuries, upon the

---

[1] "One of the major factors that make the Soviet democracy a true democracy is the fact that no one can use private property to exploit others. That is also the main distinction between Soviet democracy and bourgeois democracy. For it is obvious that there can be no real equality between an employer and owner of the means of production and the worker who is at his economic mercy." *U.S.S.R. Embassy, Bulletin*, Nov. 1946. Peoples adopting communism are on "the shorter and straighter road to democracy"; they have taken "the course of progressive democracy. . . . The substance of progressive democracy consists in the fact that it liquidates the landlord class . . . that it concentrates the economic key positions (banks, large-scale industries, railways, etc.) in the hands of the state." *New Times* (Moscow), May 15, 1946.

world plutocracies. She has accused certain nations of criminal activities in war preparations without convincing the world that her own actions here were altogether blameless. She has loudly—perhaps in fiery language—announced that she alone was a peace-loving nation, though peace was to be only on her own terms. She was ready to declare as "provocative" displeasing words or acts of other nations when they were merely asserting their own rights. She has accused other nations of "ganging up" on her. She has charged other nations with desire and striving for world domination; she has declared herself not to be intimidated by them. She has used strong, even vituperative language in speaking of other nations; she has shown herself here not unacquainted with the barbs of sarcasm. She has not hesitated in her government-inspired press or otherwise to call to account other nations or citizens of other nations who have ventured to express disapprobation of her actions or movements. She has not hesitated to impose such terms as "fascists" or "reactionaries" or "imperialists" or "war-mongers" or "war instigators" or "spreaders of anti-Soviet slander" upon those whom she has not fancied. She has without hesitation or reluctance applied the term "criminal" to actions of other nations displeasing to her. She has indulged in words of virulence, at times with no little departure from the truth, in her charges against other nations. She has had no compunction in leaping over international boundaries in naming names in making out her catalogues of those whom she has regarded as the desirables and those whom she has regarded as the undesirables, with respect to her conceptions of economic and political matters; or to stamp upon their foreheads her brands of approval or disapproval.

In matters of international consociation and fellowship the Soviet Union has been a somewhat slack participant. Though she has joined with other nations in efforts for a world organization for the peace of the earth, she has been found from time to time to put obstacles in the way of smooth and rapid progress or to employ obstructive tactics, now and then standing alone or with her satellites in some claim or demand or showing willingness for compliance or agreement only on her own terms. In matters of an economic order she has proved herself slow in coming to an understanding with other nations; she has made difficult the setting up of financial arrangements with her.

Shut in upon herself, locked in from outside, dwelling in a chilled reserve, a self-imposed isolation, nursing her suspicions, believing herself in danger of encirclement by openly or secretly hostile nations, the Soviet state has developed an ingrained dread, misgiving, distrust toward foreigners, particularly those with capitalistic leanings; these she has regarded as her natural, inevitable foes.

There has thus remained the extreme suspiciousness of the Soviet country with respect to other nations, which to some extent might be regarded as childish except for the fearful earnestness in which much of it is conceived. Finally, from among men there could not easily be removed the feeling that back in her mind was the unsleeping thought and expectation of world communism, whether sooner or later, whether to be attained by the ways of peace or by other ways.

The great problem before the nations of the earth today is somehow to rid the Soviet land of those conceptions lying in her which cause uneasiness and disturbance in the minds of the rest of the world—to acquaint the Soviet people with the truth as to the rest of the world. In particular that land must be prevailed upon to prove that she is not proceeding covertly in her relations with other nations, especially those in which it is hoped that communistic growths may be nurtured, that she is not acting unfairly in seeking to advance her cause, that she is not anywhere attempting to gain her ends by compulsion or force, or to restrain or thwart the free expression of the will of the people. The Russians have too many good qualities, are able to contribute too much to the well-being and progress of humankind, for them to be led elsewhere than in the ways of peace.

No less must the Soviet state be convinced that the nations of the world outside her orbit do not wish her ill, are not basically unfriendly to her, are not in collusion to destroy her and her economic and political system. Unless she so wills the contrary, there is no reason why communism and capitalism may not lie down as the lion and lamb together. She must somehow be made to understand that there is room on this globe for both—that the only worthwhile precept or golden rule by which international life may be lived or endured on this earth is that of live and let live.

Of vital, utter necessity is it that there be free, unfettered communication between the Soviet Union and the outside world. Happenings and feelings of the outside world must somehow be gotten, be brought home, to the Soviet people.

Great help in this direction is to be expected from the wide exchange of goods, or freehanded commercial intercourse between the Soviet Union and the rest of the world. America in particular might well adopt a liberal attitude with respect to the exportation of goods to Russia (if not for definite war purposes), as well as with respect to the importation of goods from Russia, thereby encouraging and promoting commercial interchange between the two countries, and improving their general relations.

The American people could likewise help no little in the matter by not deriding or disparaging or making light of the Soviet attempts at industrial advancement and of her present levels of living. It is to be remembered that, all things considered, the Soviet Union has some remarkable things done to its credit, some at no small sacrifice on the part of its people —and that the country has gone through a terrific war of devastation. It is to be kept in mind also that there are other countries not under the red banner of communism whose industrial progress and general standards of living are considerably below those of the United States. Nothing is to be gained for America or for world peace by seeking to decry or detract from what has been accomplished in the Soviet Union.

Nor is there benefit or advantage to be won in appearing to gloat over, or to engage in what might sound like gleeful comment upon, financial or other difficulties in the Soviet Union, or to seem to relish some misfortune befalling that land, or disparagingly to point out shortages in some necessary or convenience of life which it is desperately trying to overcome. Such conduct, which is really beneath Americans, only serves to exacerbate and needlessly sting the feelings of a people already acutely sensitive and suspicious. While America must be on armed guard for all possible eventualities, it must ever make known its ardent and profound desire for world peace. As a prime and paramount consideration, America, in formal conjunction with other nations, must see that peace is preserved over all parts of the earth, with immediate suppression of any attempt at aggression anywhere. In international matters as elsewhere, order is heaven's first law.

We shall even have to bear with the Soviet country in the matter of invective and vituperation, unmannerly, discreditable, and vulgar as it may be. We cannot afford to meet her here, especially when she can choose her own terms and her own levels: we cannot outdo her. We must use all our powers of self-restraint. We can present the truth as to conditions in Russia and elsewhere, can supply facts for that country and for the world—indeed, we are under obligations to do so—but always in moderate, dignified, and objective fashion—and then leave the affair to the world court of public opinion.

Indeed, there are definite obligations resting upon a nation like the United States in the whole matter. This country has before it the solemn responsibility of putting her own house fully in order, removing whatever of economic or political defects are to be found therein. She must initially see that within her borders there are none oppressed or exploited. Apart from elementary considerations of justice and fair dealing in general, she must for her own security and protection with all dispatch concern herself with the great problems of human want and distress, and address herself to the task of alleviating them or extracting their causes so far as it lies in her power—if by different processes and through different economic and political channels from those offered in communism. She must recognize the implications of mass destitution in whatever lands it may show its ugly self. She must devote her most earnest attention to those forces in human society that breed or give rise to a thing like communism. She must understand that communism has its spawning ground in and feeds upon misery, made acute by hopelessness, and perhaps lashed by deliberate fomenters of unrest, that widespread wretchedness makes a social order quite ready for communism—that communism capitalizes upon human economic misery—that communism is often but the counsel of despair—a cry from the depths—a symptom, a dread symptom, of fierce disturbance underground. She must take full cognizance of the giant of poverty which stalks over so large a portion of the earth and can bring in its wake stupendous upheavals in the affairs of men which may redound to anything but their good. She must recognize that when destitution, illiteracy, oppression co-exist anywhere in the world, conditions are ripe for revolution of some sort, and that no region is safe from danger while they continue. If communism is to be effectively combated, this is possible only by striking at its roots.

Together with other nations of enlightenment and good-will, America must address herself with all haste and diligence to the gigantic task of meeting the economic maladjustments among the peoples of the earth—to cleaning up so far as may be possible acrid festering economic sore spots wherever they subsist. She must make herself conscious of the grievances that may lead to economic and political revolution. She must strive with all her might to put an end to those forms of

social injustice that foster discontent and unrest, and must create conditions favorable to a wider sense of security among
men. By all the enlightened and far-sighted thought and study
of which she is capable she must seek measures to supplant with
something better, any order which is sunken with a burden of
human woe, and from which there may be developed among a
greater or less number a philosophy of nothing to lose and possibly something to gain, inviting violent overturn of the existing order—a situation of which a determined, perhaps purblind, perhaps unscrupulous minority may take advantage, even
climbing or leaping thereby to the seats of power in a state,
with possibly catastrophic injury to all.

It must be recognized that through ever expanding channels
of information and communication the peoples of the world in
ever increasing measure are learning of the good things that are
being brought into existence in one place or another, of the
higher levels of living prevailing in some areas, and are asking
if they may not have a larger sharing therein.

This country must apply itself to the raising of low living
levels both here and abroad—over the world in general. If she
believes that her economic and political system is the highest
and best for the purpose, she must make that thing known
everywhere, and not merely with words. She must give practical assurance that the productive capacity of this system is
unchallengeable; that it can produce in sufficiency, with possibly eventually a more fit distribution of the goods that are
produced; that an order of abundance is achievable with her
system—in many ways the big question before the world today.

This country must make it clear that man can thrive best
and the human race advance most favorably under the banners
of democracy—that the world is much worse off with anything
less than democracy; that democracy even with capitalism is
better than communism with its totalitarianism, and can give
man more, both spiritually and materially. America must "sell"

democracy to the world, democracy together with a future of promise for human well-being. She must eschew any policy that would appear to support "imperialism" or "colonization" in the world.

A supreme obligation resting upon America is to see to it somehow that there are no illegitimate, inordinate, or unfair accumulations of wealth in the hands of any individual or group in the land, and that in government there is no place or standing for graft or corruption or unequitable dealings. America must acclaim these things to the rest of the world by way of precept and by way of example.

Finally, it is incumbent upon this country to convince the world that her only activating motives are justice and equity and righteousness, together with the establishment and maintenance of liberty and democracy; that she has no thought or intention or desire of exploiting other nations or of using them for her material advantage; that with respect to other nations she is inspired only by considerations of peace and good-will. She must give evidence that her chief ends are not the piling up of wealth, that she is not a worshipper of mammon, that she does not regard plain living and high thinking as old-fashioned or outmoded. She must demonstrate that her concerns are not alone with material things, but that she has concern as well with things of the spirit. She must make manifest that her ideals are those of service to the world; that she seeks only to be a good neighbor in and to that world. America has a leadership in material things, and a potential leadership in things of the spirit, never before vouchsafed to one nation among the nations of the earth. Let it not fail them.

CHAPTER XIX

The Soviet State and Its Changes with Time

A S the years passed under the Soviet régime, especially the latter years, there were certain changes in attitudes of the country—towards the nation, the family, religion, education, general social life, political economy, international relationships —a rather considerable range. After greater or less actual experience with the socialistic state there came about in greater or less measure alterations and modifications in keeping with what was found necessary or desirable in the carrying on of its day-to-day life, some of which were notable and significant. Realism was a characteristic of the Soviet state. It was prepared to adjust itself to the practicalities it was called upon to face, but with the entailing of as little departure as possible from orthodox Marxism. There might be plenary planning for a new world order based upon communistic philosophy, together with a desire for sweeping changes from the past; but there were recognized to be essential matters requiring consideration in the immediate present.

After a time the wildest or most pronounced radicalism seemed to have spent its force; the swing to the farthest "left" seemed to have passed—it was slowing up in howsoever slight a degree. On different sides was to be observed a somewhat remarkable spectacle—or was it one after all to be expected? In its rush after new things, in its eagerness to experiment in so many directions, Soviet Russia had traveled far. But with time there set in a certain reaction, even if not on the widest and fullest scale, a reaction perhaps more or less inevitable.

There came about a little less ecstasy over the "Revolution," and a little more sobering second thought.

Perhaps first comment is to be made upon the changes in nationalistic sentiments—though strict Marxism is opposed to such considerations. Whether or not there was less international profession along communistic lines, there was certainly more regard for Russia in itself—present-day Russia and the Russia of the Czars as well. There was a fervid patriotism steadily rising or asserting itself in behalf of Russia the Fatherland.[1]

Old heroes of capitalistic and Czaristic Russia as Alexander Nevsky and Peter the Great were revived and adored anew. A good word could even be said of Ivan the Terrible for what he did to defend and strengthen the land. Some of the old Czaristic military commanders, known for their able generalship but sometimes used for the suppression of democratic tendencies or uprisings in some part of Europe, were not outside the Soviet pantheon. Scientists of former Russia received acclaim—not a few discoveries and inventions were ascribed to them. The old Russia, once vilified by communists, was found to have some worthy points after all. The conceptions of homeland and country were proved to have a really deep hold on the Russian people; such things were no longer to be derided and sneered at; they were to be honored and cherished. Russians were still Russians, still Slavs. The socialist revolution, furthermore, was to a greater extent thought of as a Russian affair, at least for immediate days; its international aspects and bearings did not now loom quite so large, whatever might be the issue in years somewhat more distant. The "International" need no longer be the only national anthem. There was restrained con-

---

[1] In the invasion of Russia in the Second World War the Germans were not a little surprised and disappointed to find the Russians disaffected to so slight an extent as not to be disposed to side with them. Doubtless at the same time the cruelties and inhumanities of the German armies aroused the Russians to a higher pitch of hostility and resistance. There seems to have been a certain number who were inclined to coöperate with the Nazi forces. In the Napoleonic invasion of Czaristic Russia in 1812 the whole population appears to have turned against the invaders.

cern in revolutionary ideology, and a more realistic approach to national necessities, for the present.

Family life was becoming a little more secure. Stabilization of family relations was felt to be necessary. Family obligations were regarded more seriously. Greater emphasis was placed upon family affection and cohesion. Loose marital relationships were more and more frowned upon; they were declared to be socially and politically unwise. In later divorce proceedings both parties must sign documents; notice of contemplated divorce must be given to the other party within a reasonable time; greater efforts were made to collect contributions for support of former wife or of children, with payment of alimony harder to dodge. Still later, divorce was to be allowed only after public notice, after a regular court decree, after the presentation of satisfactory reasons for the action, and after attempts at reconciliation of the parties, while the fees for divorce proceedings were considerably raised. In divorce cases in general children were becoming a more important consideration —they must be provided for by both parents. For children there was to be closer association with and less separation from parents, with greater respect for them. Parents were given increased disciplinary power and authority over their children. Fuller and more careful measures were also made with respect to the adoption of children.

In Soviet Russia the marriage bond was in fact tightening; life-long unions were upheld as desirable from all points of view, including that of the state. An educational campaign was conducted to strengthen the family. Such return as there was to the ideal of the family was due largely to the fact that there had been too many family desertions, too many abortions, too many illegitimate children requiring state care. Another very important factor was the desire for a high birth rate to insure a large population for the country, and to insure a large army for its protection, advancement, and enhancement. It was also discovered that husbands and wives could truly and deeply love each other, that both could devotedly love their children, and that children were quite capable of responding in like manner. It was even discovered that some families preferred their own kitchen to a communal one. Warmly cherished was the little plot of ground as a homestead; it riveted family relationships, and made the home something dearer. In proclaiming the activities of the state in behalf of its citizens, stress came to be placed on loans for "private" homes.

The importance of the family as a social unit was having renewed emphasis. The family was found to be an institution and a force that could not safely be dispensed with. The discovery was made by the people themselves, and then to be endorsed by their rulers. It constituted in some respects one of the highest tributes to human marriage in the history of the race.

Of not less significance and importance was the changed attitude toward religion. There was less professed enmity to it, and less open attack and onslaught; greater tolerance, and even encouragement of it of a sort. There was marked let-up in the noisy, ridiculing assaults upon it. While it is not to be thought that anti-religious sentiments had died out altogether among all groups, or that deep-seated animosity and flaring impatience did not remain with a considerable portion of the population, the attacks were no longer the open, glaring things they once were. The jeering and the mockery no longer had any large place; they were ceasing. The government itself showed a much more liberal and favorable attitude toward religion.[1]

There were a number of ways in which the Soviet state made concessions to religion, or by which religion in the land may be said in some measure to have come back, especially in the days of war. One bar after another was removed. Rights of the clergy were less restricted; they could now vote. There was moderation in the treatment of believers, with diminishing discrimination against them. Anti-religious propaganda was de-

---

[1] Reference is not made here to conditions in Cominform countries outside Russia.

cidedly on the decrease. Activities of the godless societies were curtailed if not stopped; the League of Militant Atheists was disbanded. Anti-religious papers quieted down. Anti-religious museums were less in evidence. There were no longer anti-religious processions. Blasphemous or offensive broadcasting or plays or motion pictures were toned down if not largely suppressed. Scornful and obnoxious reference to religion played a less decided part of the teaching in the schools. Christianity was admitted to have done some good works in the past.

Religious literature was permitted within general Soviet restrictions. There was no longer prohibition of the manufacture and sale of ikons and other religious articles. Churches and some religious shrines were permitted to be reopened. The patriarch was restored after an absence of two hundred and fifty years (though with decreased authority). There was resumption of the ringing of church bells. To the church was restored some of its property. Special taxes on religious organizations or property were reduced, if not removed. There might be public solicitation of funds for religious purposes. Some social services by churches were permitted. Church attendance was made easier; labor laws were relaxed so as to permit attendance in fuller measure at church services and religious affairs. There was more turning to the church for marriage ceremonies. A seven-day week was recognized, with Sunday as the accepted day of rest. Space was allowed in the newspapers for the role of religion in the Soviet state. Orthodox priests were allowed among soldiers in the army who wanted them. The Soviet state insisted that Roman Catholics were able and were permitted to practice their religion in regions where they lived. Church members, including theological students, were more welcome at state universities. The setting up of theological seminaries was authorized. A distinction was pointed out between religious "teaching" and religious "worship," with increasing tolerance for the latter. Religious instruction was allowed to larger numbers outside the home (within Soviet restrictions).

378

Bureaus were created to deal with religious organizations—one with the ancient Orthodox Church, and one with other bodies. At the same time a less indulgent attitude was taken toward some of the Moslem practices in Asia—they were made less of an exception.

Even through all the religious persecutions and attacks there were still always, as we have seen, some faithful in the land; in fact, a very considerable portion of the population.[1] Religion was hard to kill off altogether. It was always burning steadily underneath; in time it was bound to flame forth. In a land of quondam godlessness there proved to be a remarkable vindication of religion, one of a kind hardly ever known before in human experience.

There were a number of reasons for the changed attitude towards religion. One was undoubtedly the unconquerableness of this thing in the hearts of the great mass of the people, particularly in rural regions. Another reason lay in the reaction against the measures and the tactics of the extreme anti-religious groups. These groups had overplayed their hand. Their excesses, their violent attacks, often unfair and repulsive, had aroused indignation and resentment, and had even won back adherents of religion. Still another factor lay in the circumstance that a large portion of the soldiers in the army came from homes, especially rural homes, where religion was still held in reverence; they brought with them in considerable measure this reverence—and it was something by no means to be ignored or insulted in those desperate days. It is quite possible, furthermore, that the effects upon other nations of a kindlier attitude toward religion were something worth considering in war times.

The war situation had much to do with the whole matter—a circumstance the Soviet government was quick to recognize. Along with an outburst of renewed patriotism in the land, there was a certain allegiance to the religion of the land. The

[1] See *ante,* p. 313.

church and its followers had stood out boldly against the German invaders, and had suffered along with all the rest of the country. The church had urged the people to withstand the common foe and to uphold the government, communistic though it was, that was fighting the battles of the Russian people. The church had contributed greatly to the defense of the nation in its hour of dire need. The church was behind none in its patriotism, in its devotion to the Fatherland.

The government was deeply gratified over this response and sought to show its appreciation. As the church had bestowed its blessing upon the Soviet state, so the state was all but ready to bestow its blessing upon the church—and in a fashion did so. Each found that it could help the other. The war served greatly to mitigate the hostility of state authorities to the church and to a considerable extent win their favor. In fact, in later days church authorities went so far as to minimize the persecutions of the church in earlier Soviet days. For its part, the government even took pains to proclaim its friendliness for the church. In a sense the church was being adjusted, if not assimiliated into the new state; or at least it was finding a place in it, whether or not a secure place. Was there ground to expect that the church could retain its spiritual independence and integrity, that it would not become an arm or tool of the government as was the case in Czaristic days? Though the church might be called free in some ways, it was understood on both sides that it was not to engage in matters affecting the state, was to have nothing to do with "secular" affairs.

It is not to be thought that the Russians as a whole were becoming religious or were turning to religion. The official attitture was one rather of toleration than of approval or of heartfelt friendliness. The old bitter enmity toward religion continued. Soviet leaders still regarded religion as an error which was to be combated. It was a hangover, a set of superstitions from days of ignorance, and was to be dispelled in the full light of Soviet knowledge. Hardly more than the forms of religion were to be tolerated. If the Soviet state did not directly persecute religion, but only insisted upon the rigid enforcement of its laws on the subject, the effects might not be greatly different. How far Soviet youth, so thoroughly indoctrinated against religion, had been permanently weaned from the church only the years could tell.[1]

In the schools there was less of pupil self-government, less of the abnegation of authority, less perhaps of a reign of laxity, less of a succession of educational experiments upon innocent children. There was appearing somewhat more of objective teaching, somewhat more of discipline and order and system. Perhaps there was slightly more attention given to spelling and the three "R's." Schools were now opened to all, even to children of former officers of the Czar. Higher education was no longer the free thing it had been at first; for those to be benefited by it certain charges were imposed.

In general cultural matters, however, there seemed to be something of a tightening up of regulations regarding literature and art, with greater restraint upon what was produced here, and with less patience with what was of "bourgeois" order. There appeared more pronounced and more determined efforts to mould the Soviet people into the one true pattern, the communistic, and to permit no departure or deviation therefrom.

Class distinctions were increasingly in evidence in military life as in economic life. In the army there was just a little less of "democracy," a little less of camaraderie between officers and men, in the interests of military efficiency; there was more of saluting; there was in general an appreciable stiffening of discipline. The accompaniment of political commissars with army units, to keep up the proper communistic spirit and attitude, as well as to keep officers on a level with the soldiers, became less a necessity, also in the interests of military efficiency. "Commissars" in the government become "Ministers."

[1] On the greater amount of "moral" teaching in the schools, see *ante*, p. 305.

In the treatment of criminal offenders there was in some respects a trifle more severe or rigorous or hard-boiled attitude; there was to be discerned a little less patience with certain evil-doers, especially those whose wrongdoing did not necessarily involve the state, as robbery, assault, etc. The conception of improvement of one who had done ill to the state and was now up for confinement was giving way just a bit to the older and sterner conception of punishment. Imprisonment for some might not prove so pleasant an outing experience as before; its maximum term, furthermore, might be lengthened somewhat. There was a tendency to transfer older children's cases to the regular courts. In dealing with delinquency there came to be recognized other factors besides economic ones. In the law of the land in part there was a trifle less of "sociological" theory, with less attention to the criminal and with more to the crime, and a certain return to the basic conceptions of European law, but always with due socialistic postulates. On the other hand, in some respects there was greater leniency or a more moderate attitude displayed towards certain types of offenses, especially those of milder civil character. To an extent party castigations or liquidations seemed to have become of less severe or drastic nature. Capital punishment was formally abolished for non-political offenders, a prison term of twenty-five years being made the maximum punishment.

As in the causation of crime, so in the causation of mental disturbance or derangement it was being more or less seen that economic considerations were not the only ones to have a part.

Law itself was found, even in a socialistic state, not to be a matter of extreme simplicity and brevity, but something that was to undergo expansion and development in keeping with human experiences.

In entertainments and amusements of the people there was more of moderation; the school-holiday attitude was giving way just a bit to less confused conceptions of recreation and sport. There was greater indulgence in some of the bourgeois

382

enjoyments and pastimes of life; there was less of the ascetic attitude toward dancing academies, café dining, and like more or less innocent diversions. Ballroom dancing was slowly gaining over the old national dances. There was a trickle of "jazz" entering the large cities—possibly coming from America. There was perhaps a bit more levity in the land, but not overmuch—the Soviet state still took itself very seriously.

The moulding of sartorial fashions to one pattern was found not altogether in keeping with what human nature craved; in the shops there was a little more concession to human vanity. Fashion plates could have eager observers. There could be such things as a style show or beauty treatments. There was a little more attention to perfumery making. There was a little more regard for social etiquette; there was more formality in social life, with greater recognition of titles and decorations. Officers in the army were more smartly attired; there was more wearing of epaulettes and gold lace; more decorations for valor adorned the breast. Personal cleanliness was found to have values in itself; the virtues of soap need not be foreign even to the most militant revolutionary—Soviet authorities could prove themselves zealous in urging measures of sanitation. There was in general a little more recognition of the amenities of life.

It could be hoped, however, that changes here would not go too far or in all directions—that a certain simplicity and absence of display and vaingloriousness which had marked some aspects of early Soviet life might not be surrendered or abandoned altogether.

In the sphere of political economy, the sacred precincts of Marxian socialism, there were changes in attitudes, even though somewhat less profound. A slightly modified form of socialism seemed to be under way in the land.[1] It was seen and in large measure accepted that incomes were not wholly to be disso-

[1] That Soviet Russia in its early days did not go entirely to the left may be indicated in some measure by its refusal to follow Trotsky in his views as to the necessity of prompt world revolution and as to more vigorous handling of recalcitrant peasant farmers in the matter of the collectivation of land.

ciated from individual earning capacity. In some areas there were rather steep differences in incomes, corresponding in greater or less degree to the practices of capitalistic countries. There was less insistence upon communal living or upon equal sharing as the only equitable or just system of social living. *Quasi*-ownership of a homestead of a few acres with some domestic animals was found to make better citizens, and to give strength to the state. There was realization that a modicum of private ownership or control over one's domicile and personal effects, as well as over a few local consumable products among peasant farmers or the sale of surplus products distributed among members of a collective farm, with goods to sell in a more or less open market, did not come amiss in the socialist commonwealth, but was rather a stroke of good public policy, as well as of sound political economy. Attention was called to the providing by the state of booths and storage facilities for peasant markets. Mention has been made of the willingness of the state to make loans for private homes.[1]

A cardinal principle of Marxian socialism which would permit no inheritance of property was abrogated, with the later recession of even a tax thereupon. The circumstance that certain professional persons like physicians could carry on, at least theoretically, a measure of private practice was pointed out as an example of the liberal attitude in such matters on the part of the socialistic state.

There were other changes and deviations from strictly Marxian concepts or generally accepted socialist theories. "Refinements" and "interpretations" could go a considerable way in helping the Soviet state over any technical difficulties. It was no longer claimed with such boldness and finality that labor created all values. It was rather indicated that the value of an article might measurably determine the value of the labor put upon it. To different workers were ascribed different degrees of competence. Some were recognized as skilled, others as semi-

[1] See *ante*, p. 194.

skilled, and still others as with little if any industrial equipment—all factors to be considered in the allotment of pay. If there were the same pay to each, there would be little incentive to the equipment of skill. Some factories, too, were recognized as having better technical organization, with larger or superior output, than others, and accordingly entitled to receive appropriate greater rewards for their products. The hour or day of work of different persons was found to be different in its worth to the total production of a given article, with payment to correspond to what had been actually accomplished in that time. The labor of different individuals had thus different values; and in the general laws governing production there must be differences in wages.

It was further set forth that part of the products of social labor were to be devoted to an accumulated reserve—a portion to be withheld as capital surplus which was to be expended for new equipment, facilities, tools, etc. Accumulations of capital goods, it was maintained, were to an extent proper and legitimate. It was even allowed that some operations in the Soviet state might be conducted for profit, even if for its eventual profit.

While the price of some articles, moreover, was to be fixed largely by the state, there were other articles whose price was to be determined more or less by the law of supply and demand. This was recognized in no inconsiderable degree in whatever free markets were permitted in the country, particularly where there was to be sold one's own portion of farm products or articles made by oneself. This law was perhaps to have an increasing part to play in the economics of the state. To it price control must at times to a certain degree give way. Market prices and market competition could in a measure be justified. A "free market" was possibly to have a slightly larger place in the general national economy. There was "competition" of sorts both between state establishments and coöperative bodies and between the former and rural open selling.

("Social competition" in the production of goods was something different.)

Community production, exchange, and the use of money were asserted to have preceded the use of capital, and to an extent to have paved the way for it. Primitive conditions in production had in time to yield to such newer methods, which would allow more room for the development of effective production forces. Capitalism could be regarded as a necessary step in the pathway of social progress, and could prove its usefulness, at least for the time being, whatever might be the future working out or evolution of that system. There were largely absent the pungent invectives and anathemas towards capitalism so far as it was an essential part of the domestic program—that is to say, state capitalism—though these things could be quickly evoked when resentment toward disliked capitalist countries was to be aroused.

There was perhaps discernible, furthermore, a slight though less marked change in attitudes towards democratic principles —not so much perhaps in the promotion of democracy in the home land, as in a fuller understanding of its significance and of its operations in other lands—except so far as the matter might be affected by altercations with those other lands, or so far as what was to be practiced in satellite states. Even in the home land there was some reduction in the requirements for suffrage. On all hands there was displayed at least lip service to democracy.

In later days in connection with the Second World War Soviet attitudes towards other countries, particularly those of its allies, underwent a certain change, at least for the time being or for the war emergency. A friendlier or less hostile and suspicious eye was now cast in their direction, and their war operations and their general merits were better understood and given a more sympathetic hearing, even though to no great extent. Their efforts against a common enemy were for a while a little more graciously and more fully valued and appreciated.

There were temporarily in some respects less intolerant views of other lands. The country was in general becoming more sensitive to public opinion in outside lands—an attitude that has not grown less with time. Soviet Russia was also beginning to see that it could not quite get along without other nations, at least in war days, even though their political and economic structure was so different from its own, and that joint operations were not only feasible, but could be more or less succesful and for the good of all concerned. There arose with some an enlarging vision of the values as well as of the obligations and needs of a certain measure of international understanding and coöperation and concert—even with "capitalistic" nations —while these nations on their part could become more ready to listen and to learn from the Soviet power. That power, as we have already seen,[1] had formally announced its turning from the "International," with Moscow as its center. There was being abandoned, at least overtly, the conception of world communism as an immediate goal, or of global communism to be obtained forthwith through force and violence. As we have also already noticed, the immediate international outlook was giving way to one more definitely nationalistic.

Such were the attitudes arising in times of war. Perhaps in times of peace the Soviet Union might find all these things no less manifest—something that would bode well for all concerned, and to the high gain of the human race. As the days following the war sped into the past, however, a change in reverse seemed to be coming over the Soviet state here. Whatever of friendly and coöperative attitudes had existed appeared to be giving way in greater or less degree—whether or not to be of long standing or permanent—to the suspiciousness, aloofness, ill-will of former days.[2]

All in all, in the Soviet state there seemed a little less effort at adhering in all particulars to an uncompromising Procru-

[1] See *ante*, p. 333.
[2] See *ante*, p. 337.

stean, preconceived program of action—with the possible exception of issues involving relations with other nations. There were on the whole fewer experimental innovations in one direction and another. There was more getting down to business, to more realistic thinking in the conduct of human affairs.

This backward swing in general must be taken with all due consideration and qualification; it must not be thought that the pendulum was moving otherwise than very slowly, or that all points in the Soviet compass were being affected. But it seemed that certain of the most most marked of Soviet Russia's extreme measures, or of what some might call its arbitrary or capricious flings and frenzies, had been reached. What was in later days developing could not be called a "return to normalcy," according to the standards of most countries; far from it. Yet without doubt an appreciable if not considerable transformation appeared to have taken place in the Soviet land. Perhaps it was the old story of the assertion of human nature. They were coming to do in the Soviet Union only what all mankind has been compelled to do from the beginning—to reckon with naked realities, and to learn from the endless series of human experiences. The Soviet state found, however belatedly, or however faintly, that certain time-honored or time-proved values and principles might not be held lightly, or tossed aside as chaff or outworn substance, under the impetus of a régime that in the fortunes of men had come to the seats of power.

At all events, matters in the Soviet land had not moved forward to the promised goal of communism; that advanced and final stage beyond socialism was admittedly not immediately at hand, not on the point of realization. Despite the considerable number of years that had elapsed since the Revolution, the transition period was still under way. In certain respects, as we have just found, it would appear that the current had been rather in the other direction.

Yet whatever the changes or modifications that might have

been made in the Soviet system, there were no signs of departure from the basic principles of socialism that had been implanted in the country. What were to be regarded as its essentials remained. There was in general no private property employed in the production of wealth. Ownership of the means of such production continued paramountly in the hands of the state. One might not be in the pay of private employment. Nor might a private citizen receive income from the trinity of evils in the Soviet index expugatorius—rent, interest, profit. Socialism was still the foundation and the undisguised ruling force in the land.

What is more, there was increasing effort to·harden the people of the land in the principles and conceptions of communism, to mould them into a rigid pattern—one of intolerance and aggressiveness.

CHAPTER XX

The Soviet State and Its General Appraisal

LET us set down without reservation the things that have been done to the credit of the Union of Socialist Soviet Republics. All this is to be considered quite objectively, regardless of the political complexion of a particular state, whether communistic or not, but without forgetting to what extent in the process the people here were deprived of individual freedoms or were put into a rigid vise of state control, or to what extent the actual progress and well-being of the state was tarnished, blighted, or vitiated by its advocacy of force and violence in the attainment of its ends, or how far trust in and exercise of these things might eventually prove fatal.

This country secured some sort of order in a land thrown into deep confusion and chaos. Without previous experience, it showed a surprising grasp of the principles of government organization, as well as a practical sense in handling an extraordinary and extremely difficult situation at its beginning. It moved the capital back to Moscow—a rare stroke of policy. It made the country a union of self-governing states within their own confines, instead of a highly concentrated government at a distant capital (except as to general national policies). It lent encouragement to backward peoples, and helped develop their local resources. It provided a government for them adapted somewhat to their present cultural levels and to their political maturity. It sought to preserve and promote national cultures among different peoples (and without patronizing attitudes). It greatly diminished racial prejudices and animosities in the land. It put an end to Jewish persecutions and pogroms. It took a stand against anti-semitism (except so far as internationalism or cosmopolitanism was concerned, or so far as amalgamation with the general population was retarded). It promoted a movement toward an equilibrium or better distribution of the population of the country, in particular getting large masses to hitherto sparsely settled areas.

It showed a highly pioneering spirit, and in more than one direction. For it no scheme appeared too audacious. It went after the long-sought northeast passage (northwest to Americans), to get around the world via the Arctic Ocean; it sailed the top of Europe and Asia in this frozen sea. It sent out explorers, colonists, settlers to unpeopled regions. It set up modernized industry in hitherto lifeless towns on frontiers or in inhospitable climes. It created steel mills in the wilderness, and made crops grow in frigid zones. It displayed a restless energy along all lines, industrial and scientific. It recognized the importance of research in all fields of human activity, and was never weary in encouraging and promoting it.

It attempted in the boldest sort of way the industrialization of the land, and in what hitherto had been overwhelmingly agricultural land, and a very backward agricultural one at that. No country ever made so full a survey of its natural resources. It broke records in its efforts to advance production of goods to the capacity of the nation, production to the uttermost within human limitations—to make two blades of grass grow where one grew before—affording the world a valuable object lesson here. It insisted upon the highest possible productivity in the land, in industry and agriculture alike. It took up the industrial rehabilitation of the country methodically and determinedly, which it caused to proceed at a rapid rate. It called attention to the possible values of state planning in respect to the production of goods. It introduced new and more efficient methods of winning the harvest from the soil. It took

391

up the systematic development of its vast natural resources, seeking their discovery and their use to the farthest possible degree. It caused great industrial structures to rear their heads over the land, and had some genuine engineering triumphs to its credit. It made important extensions in hydraulic power. It achieved considerable progress in irrigation, with the lessening of the effects of droughts. It put forth vigorous effort to check erosion in its land, and in some areas to withstand the effects of scorching heat waves. It procured reforestation and swamp drainage. It demonstrated the advantages of coöperative attitudes in agricultural production. It called attention to the possibilities of the reduction of costs of production through the elimination of competitive advertising and the middleman. It set forth a social motive in the production of articles to be consumed by the people.

It brought about the stabilization of the currency of the land, and thwarted the prostration of its money and banking system, under remarkable and hitherto untried conditions. It proved itself capable of carrying on the fiscal matters of the new state in a businesslike fashion. It also proved itself capable in times of emergency or crisis—to tide it over, to keep its life going— to resort and adapt itself to certain non-socialistic practices. It likewise permitted the existence of certain elementary forms of property and services in private hands to an extent, even though to a limited extent. It sought diligently and earnestly to eliminate extravagance and ostentation from government, and to eject graft and corruption therefrom.

It highly and strongly recognized the importance of education, including vocational education, and sought to bring a measure of education and of culture to all the people. It made a massed attack upon illiteracy, and tremendously reduced it— a massed attack possibly in range, energy, and relative monetary outlay being without parallel in the history of the world. It multiplied educational institutions of all kinds. Along with education, it promoted reading habits of the people in far degree. It encouraged the expression and appreciation of art in all its domains and in all places in the land. It declared that a modicum of culture was a part of the good life for all. It sought to make graduates of its institutions of higher education realize the obligations resting upon them to serve the public. It reformed the calendar, adopted western systems of measurement, and promised in due time to take over the Latin alphabet. It set the habits of the people toward self-discipline and coöperation. It sought to provide recreation and entertainment of some kind for the masses. It sought physical health and efficiency for the people, and the cultivation of the hardy virtues. It made the people conscious of the value of sports and athletics, offering a wide program in this respect. It recognized the importance of providing for leisure time activities in a machine age.

It sought to introduce humanitarian conceptions in some of the policies of the state. It instituted a noteworthy program of prison reform. It provided rest and recuperation centers for part of its population, particularly worn or disabled workers. It sought in notable measure to give labor a dignity not merely in words, but also to show values in it not entirely to be measured by the quantity of goods produced—goods perhaps produced with mutual help—and it rendered public honor for service rendered here. It gave all a chance to share in the wealth of the land in return for some labor. It gave women a new and more notable part in the life of the state.

There arose to a greater or less extent throughout the land a certain fellow feeling, a certain comradeship, if not in fullest measure, at least in very considerable degree, and even if approaching a pale uniformity, or dipping towards a deal levelism —something at least to take the place of the old hateful system of a handful of nobility living on the fat of the land and the vast masses writhing under foot—so it was declared.

Possibly the greatest thing that came to the people of Soviet Russia since the old Czaristic days was the changed outlook upon life. Instead of the partially paralyzed masses of former years, there came into being to a greater or less extent a people interested in the life about them, alert, stirring, charged with very considerable energy, animated with a genuine enthusiasm for many of the undertakings in which they were engaged, with a greater respect for themselves, and with a wistful but determined hope for better things for their land and for themselves. They felt themselves participants in a great national drama—or at least in a great national dream—of their own origin and execution, and for the benefit of their state and of themselves alike. The question was as to how widespread or deep-seated was this feeling or attitude, or how long it was to last, in a state exercising full compulsion over its people, to whom were denied some of the essential freedoms of man.

A very important contribution which Soviet Russia made to the thinking of the world in general, and which might have no less application there, lay in its theories of progress. The Soviet state had unlimited faith in the possibilities of human betterment. If success, it declared, was to attend its efforts, and if it was to move toward a truly communistic state, use would have to be made of all of the science, art, technique, and experience of the human race. To the affairs of men was to be given the full and untrammeled application of science. In particular vast trust was placed in the power and efficiency of the industrial machine—including constant technological improvement and wide progress in electrification over the country—in the production of wealth and in making possible a "good life" for all the people. In contemplation of such results it was taking cognizance of the amount of leisure time which was to be at the disposal of the people, and sought to make provision for putting to account this leisure.

Soviet Russia surprised the world by showing, not that its policy was largely a negative one, but that it had a positive and highly constructive program. For not a few matters it demonstrated quite a statesmanlike attitude—apart from consideration of the matter of force and violence. While some of the industrial operations often displayed crudity or haste, others displayed resourcefulness, or even ingenuity; in nearly all there was ample zeal. Those who were in charge of Soviet affairs at the beginning gave proof of their intellectual acumen and of their intellectual training; a very considerable portion of the original leaders had had university training, whether in Russia or outside.

All the more credit is to be given in view of the situation which had to be faced. There was the immense, almost incalculable difficulty of adapting socialism to a large agricultural country like Russia, with its great number of peasant proprietors naturally averse to the extension of the policy to their holdings. There was widespread poverty in the land, with little capital to start any sort of operations. There was little enlightened engineering counsel or guidance, especially for the organization of industry. For great undertakings there had to be employed a labor force of little technical experience and with little discipline. (Soviet Russia, however, did not have to start out industrially altogether from scratch; it had left over from Czaristic days a small number of technicians, some factories, and some acquaintance with such matters as agricultural coöperation, factory regulation, and social insurance.) But whatever Soviet Russia accomplished, it had to accomplish alone; it could expect little of encouragement, of coöperation, and of fellow feeling from other lands.

Always to be remembered as a most notable accomplishment was the introduction of a backward nation of the seventeenth or eighteenth century into mass production technique of the twentieth century. Both industry and agriculture were called upon to make a leap over several centuries, with a corresponding evolution from primitive social conditions to the conditions of a modern industrialized state—and with corresponding changes in the attitudes and modes of thought of a vast people.

Great care must be exercised in appraising, from the economic standpoint, the concrete, material results of the new venture, but it may be said in general that, compared with former times, in Russia there was a definite improvement in industrial and living conditions—without failure to recognize war conditions and consequences. If actual wages paid into the hands of workers might not have changed so much for the better, it is to be remembered that a great deal was being done for them by the state which otherwise, if secured at all, would have had to be had at the expense of the individual. It must be remembered, too, that while in the midst of its industrial development, the Soviet Union was struck by a frightful, devastating war.

What success, however, was attained in Soviet Russia, or whatever credit was to be set down for it, is to be tempered by several circumstances. In the first place, the Soviet government had a relatively clean slate to work upon—one that only an autocratic government could have at its disposal. There was no serious opposition which had to be taken in hand. There was very little to stay the execution of whatever policies the government felt called upon to adopt. To make matters the easier for it, the people over which it ruled were at the outset in general singularly unenlightened and unresisting. Never was there such an amorphous mass ready for the moulding. The Soviet state was, furthermore, in position to use forced labor in almost unlimited quantities to carry out its industrialization program.

It is by no means certain that whatever improvements or reforms or beneficial developments took place in Soviet Russia could not have been undertaken and carried into execution just as well under a different form of government, and quite possibly with more solid results. Russia after its Revolution was part of a world engaged in general reorganization and development. Whatever occurred in Russia under Soviet direction, with its socialist bearings, was made to appear of spectacular nature, and was heralded with loud acclaim. In Turkey, by way of example, there were instituted some far-reaching reforms without any such fanfare. Certainly, also, in the quondam neighboring states that were carved out of old Russia—Finland, Lithuania, Latvia, and Estonia (and to a less extent Poland)—great developments took place, and ones of notable kind. Here was abundant evidence of the progress of independent, enlightened nations. On all sides there were to be found industrial and agricultural development, the promotion of markets, the building of schools, social welfare legislation, coöperative societies (especially consumers' societies and agricultural societies), government-promoted housing for the people on a wide scale, and so on. Some of these lands had in fact high achievements to their credit. Their record of progress in more than one respect was truly an inspiring one. But what they did was not with the flourish or with the high-sounding language of Soviet Russia.

It is to be remembered, moreover, that some activities of a socialist nature in Russia were different from those in other countries in degree rather than in kind. In nearly all the countries of the Continent there was state socialism practiced to a greater or less extent. This included government ownership of means of transportation and communication in general (railroads and waterways, as well as telegraph and telephone facilities), besides a large part of the forest reserves and other natural resources. These things were taken as a matter of course, and there was virtually no organized opposition to them.

One of the best tests as to the possible success of the operations of the Soviet state is to be found in the attitude of the people of other lands, especially adjacent lands, towards it before the Second World War, and in the extent of their desire to secure a like government. In the states that were created out of old Russia, and that became independent of it at the time the Revolution was effected there—and succeeding the First World War—there was to be discovered no great leaning toward or hankering after its political and economic system, or any pronounced yearning to repeat Russia's experiments in their own territory. The condition of the industrial and farming population in these countries was on the whole probably a bit above that in Soviet Russia; and probably no large portion would have favored following in its footsteps. As a matter of fact, from the time of the Revolution, the great hope and prayer of the people in general in neighboring lands may be said to have been that Soviet Russia might not, by the exercise of military power or otherwise, be permitted to overcome them and impose upon them its political and economic system. In later days when those countries had been overrun by the Soviet Union, and were behind an "iron curtain," we could not even surmise their present sentiments. Over Europe generally the cause of communism could hardly be declared to have gained ground in consequence of the experiences in Russia directly after its Revolution.

In the setting up of the Soviet empire there was a marked likeness to some of the things that were brought into existence in Germany, especially the Nazi Germany—though one state was intensely communistic and the other announced itself as determinedly anti-communistic. To an extent there were parallel movements in both lands. By the Soviet Union there were doubtless owed to German statesmen, as well as to German philosophers, not a few of the concepts of the socialist state. At the same time it can hardly be doubted that in some respects it was the other way about: Nazi Germany took more than one point from the Soviet Union. Each could learn from the other.

In numerous regards the Soviet state pursued policies and practices that had a place in the neighboring country to the west, at times going that country one better. In more ways than one it seemed to have taken Germany as a model. It took over, greatly extended, in a sense perfected, and clamped down harder the program of state socialism there found. It appeared to have acquired important lessons in government authority or bureaucracy from what Germany had in that regard.

As with Germany, the Soviet Union sought to transform the

land from one largely agricultural to one largely industrial, but with the fullest possible development in both directions. They both hooked up production in greater or less degree with the needs of the state, including military needs. They gave education of school children a military touch. They both were prepared to utilize national manpower for state ends as the occasion might require. They both made business largely a state-controlled matter. Each had a word to say with regard to the possible pecuniary returns of the citizen, though one much more than the other. Both had control of the productive forces of their respective lands; both had a greater or less part of their work carried on by forced labor.

The Soviet Union had social welfare measures very similar to those in Germany, including general care of the physical well-being and health of the people. It likewise sought a strong physical stock. It provided public services for the people, including such things as medical aids, housing projects, nurseries for children, sport clubs and athletic fields, and facilities for culture and entertainment. It attached high value to the museum and similar means of popular education. It integrated technical education with general education. It sought to introduce alike play conceptions and instruction along practical lines. It stressed early education in connection with doing. It made the school a powerful tool for inculcating complete subservience to the will of the state. It created youth organizations, the better to have present youth and future citizens properly conform to the state pattern. Each began with young children in creating a military frame of mind. Both urged large families. Both urged simple, frugal living.

The Soviet Union placed immense if not infinite faith in science, something so characteristic of the German nation. Like that nation, it bestowed honors upon men of science, as well as upon those who had otherwise in the eyes of the rulers contributed to the good of the state. In one country there was such a thing as a German science; in the other, such a thing as Soviet science.

Above all, in both the Nazi and the Soviet state was adopted a discipline that was of iron. Both had a terror-inspiring secret police. Both could resort to force or violence in gaining their ends. Both could use strong-arm methods in putting down domestic dissidents. In both could be set up concentration camps for political offenders. In both there were frequent military displays for the massed effects at home and abroad. Soviet Russia and steel-thoughted Germany were not separated by a wide gulf in their attitudes towards absolutism in government, or in what is sometimes called totalitarianism—the state as all in all. In both there was a fervent, frenzied, almost idolatrous adulation of the leaders. In both was imposed a rigid censorship upon what was to be seen, read, and heard—upon the organs of public opinion. To the citizens of one country as of the other was denied any wide degree of individual freedom. Neither the Nazi nor the Soviet state had use for religion.

In each country there was expectation that through its peculiar political system it was to become the most advanced country industrially and culturally in the world. Each felt that it was its mission to carry its system, by force if necessary, to other countries; its system was the only one that could have a place upon the earth. Each country was to become the core or nucleus of a vast world power organization. The capital city of each was to become the political, economic, and cultural capital of the world. In each love of country (or of its political tenets) was to go hand in hand with sweeping, purblind antagonism toward its adversaries. By each there was subversive propaganda conducted to affect and weaken other countries. Each loudly asserted its desire for peace, but always on its own terms.

In both lands, citizens were to become well-cared-for masses, if not a sort of wards of the state, at the expense of their personal freedom; possible protests of the spirit were to be stifled by material well-being. In both there was a sole, exclusive, all-powerful political party, only slightly behind the scenes, which was the real ruler of the land.

Of the final outcome of the socialist undertaking that had birth in Russia, no one could say with certainty. The time may not have come for the complete painting of the Soviet people in their communistic kingdom. But the fair pictures and the intriguing stories put forth by the Soviet authorities or their agents to the outside world, ever putting their best foot forward —the Soviet Union has always had an excellent intourist bureau and very efficient propaganda organization—leave much to be desired. They were decidedly over-drawn so far as they related to existing conditions, especially before the Second World War—portraits and stories depicting a "land of hope" or of "blessedness," with a happy, smiling, contented, well-dressed, well-conditioned people of all classes, in the van of which were always singing youth. Homes were portrayed as of culture and with all modern conveniences; industrial operations, as most efficient and of a high order. There was quite too evident here the hand of the promotion engineer, the salesman who wished to "sell." Too obvious was the desire to make a "front," to create an impression in the world without, to cover or to hide whatever there was of bareness or of unattractiveness within—so much window dressing. Did there not seem to be an overdoing, an overacting? Was not the painting in too florid colors? Was not the trumpeting with too great a flourish? Did not this self-praise to some extent defeat itself? Somehow one could not rid oneself of the doubt whether the enthusiasm and the fervor reported so loudly and displayed so rapturously on behalf of the Soviet state was not in some part a made-to-order thing, a state-concocted thing, a thing inspired in greater or less measure by a hand within the Kremlin.

Of promises of a better life in the Soviet Union there was no end—promises of greater wealth for the state and for the individual, of an abundance of the things for creature comfort and for the enjoyment of the mind, of a fuller measure of culture and of knowledge of the arts, of play and fun, of the practical bestowals of science, of the achievements and general heritage of the human race. Among a portion of the people—whether an increasing or a decreasing number cannot be known—there were certain private doubts of the realization of these promises within an early period of time, or within any period that could readily be measured. Some were frankly fed up with promises, and were asking, even though not audibly, about the possibilities of fulfillment. By a very considerable portion of the population these promises were heartily believed. These were firm in the faith that to whatever extent modification or adaptation of socialist theories to actual conditions was needful, the net result would be nothing but a great improvement in their manner of life, and that large things were possible and in store—in the offing—under the Soviet order. There were some who were assured that a new heaven and a new earth were about to manifest themselves in the Soviet land.[1]

[1] A volume needs to be written on the Americans who visited Soviet Russia during the days of what may be called its prime. One of the sufferings which that country had to experience—though with financial profit to it—was the flocking upon it of tourists of varied descriptions. While some went with serious purposes in view, and with a genuine desire to understand and to know, there were a great many who went for the excitement, as to a sort of frolic or circus. A trip to Russia was regarded as a sure-enough adventure. With some no small concern was the meeting of other Americans at Moscow. There were some who were radicals or "pinks," and who regarded Soviet Russia as their long promised land. There were some who liked what they thought were the free or unconventional or anti-religious attitudes in that country. Some went to make a sincere scientific study of the really worth-while and truly remarkable things that had transpired there. The views and opinions of a large number were subjective and personal; they usually found there what they wanted to find. Many who went were credulous at the beginning, and remained so to the end. Many were incredulous from beginning to end. Not a few wrote of their experiences, and perhaps of what fellow Americans they met at Moscow. The Russian people did not in these visitors always see America at its best or in its most wholesome aspects; those who reflected most credit upon America were usually the quiet unobtrusive sort, who went about their way unseen but seeing. With the procession of American visitors the Soviet intourist bureau proceeded to make hay while the sun shone. Whether favorably impressed or not with those who came to visit, it had a golden opportunity to show off their country to the best advantage. It incidentally was able to get much needed foreign currency, while the tourists got their money's worth in an abundance of marvels, thrills, and shocks. The bureau was a businesslike affair, knowing what it was about. It handled the matter capably from beginning to end. It made a business of educational tours to it, and invited all and sundry to come

In the Soviet state was the vast experiment of which the world had dreamed and for which it had waited so long—the possibility of a coöperative society, a state order, in which the profit motive and the profit system were not to be controlling factors in the affairs of men, and in which the competitive spirit among them was to be done away with. There were envisaged some of the noblest ideals that have ever taken possession of the human mind, ideals perhaps approaching the conceptions of the brotherhood of man. A society was to be organized in such fashion that those foremost considerations of human existence, wealth, leisure, and the general means of happiness—what the philosophers have denominated the "good life"—should not be left or confined to a small, limited section or class of the population, but should be shared in by all, including the masses, and including more particularly those who perform useful labor, labor that is essential for the life of the people and of the state, and that supplies the human element for the creation of wealth—while this labor, because of a steady increase in production, would become less and less necessary, there in time being enough of the good things of life within the reasonable reach of all.

The socialist state after long years of parturition had arrived among men—in the form presented in the Soviet Union. The experiment here, if it may be so regarded, was of necessity a startling one. No such experiment of anything like such dimensions had ever before been attempted in human society. It was, furthermore, to be tried out full-blown in a vast, unwieldly land, in very many ways the last place on this earth of ours for such an undertaking.

If the issue of socialism in the Soviet Union had been con-

and behold in operation at first hand its gigantic socialist experiment. The guides who conducted the visitors over the country were a chosen, well-trained lot, speaking a variety of languages, including fairly good English. They moved at top speed, firing statistics as they went—from hotel to factory, from clinic to crèche, from museum to college. They showed the tourists what they thought the tourists ought to see; they had carefully arranged tours, designed to present the country at its best. Many of the tourists listened wild-eyed. Many were pretty much spoonfed; many were gullible; many could have only superficial impressions. But from many a throat was ejaculated: "How wonderful!"

fined to the large cities, and there had been no outside com-
plications, it might be said that the new state had proved unquestionably a going concern, had turned out to be a considerable success—at least for a measurable period of time. When
reference is made to the whole land, rural as well as urban,
the story may be somewhat different, no little depending upon
events in country regions. Whether the roots of the new undertaking went down deep enough in the soil of human nature
and world conditions to insure a propitious issue for the future,
or how far in general policies or procedures were built upon
solid foundations, were questions to which answer could not at
once be at hand. How far, furthermore, the people who lived
under the new system were better off from the economic point
of view alone than they would have been under one of less
radical conceptions and of less radical bearings, was likewise a
question to which reply could not be immediately forthcoming.

So far as the state had been built upon principles of force
and violence, it might be asked if these things were not in the
end to prove its undoing, to be the source of its eventual undermining.

But so far as had appeared, the people of the Soviet Union,
speaking for themselves, had in large but unknown numbers
been behind their Soviet undertaking; as we have seen, they
had to a considerable extent quite abundant faith in it; they
believed that they would make an unmistakable success out of
it, if they had not already done so. In no small part they had
regarded all that the Soviet state was and had as their very own.
Never to be forgotten was the steady, unremitting indoctrination in communistic principles and conceptions which the
youth of the land had undergone from beginning of Soviet
days, an indoctrination that could not help bearing some fruit.

The people in fair measure seemed persuaded that their state
system provided the greatest good for the greatest number;
that it was superior to any other in affording in the long run
human contentment, self-development, and material advance-

404

ment. It was asserted that despite serious setbacks, some heavy ones, the gravity of which they did not pretend to deny, there had been on the whole steady, substantail progress toward the aspired-after goal, which was now not far over the horizon. It was declared that their great experiment had so far, all things considered, worked well, but had not been completed—that the country was not yet ready for the transition from socialism to the desired consummation of communism. If the state so far showed few signs of withering away, it was largely because it had to live in an environment of hostile capitalistic nations. At any rate it appeared that the new undertaking had not gotten beyond an embryonic stage; even at best there was little evidence of its approaching the classless order, the end of orthodox socialism. There remained some, still an unknown number, who could ask pointedly just what they were getting out of the great experiment, materially no less than spiritually. Some might have been of the opinion that their local or their general state boss was no better than the one to be found in private employment, and in the latter case with perhaps more individual freedom.

In the Soviet Union was to be found one of the two extremes possible in men's governing of themselves—here the absolutist or totalitarian, with complete state control—the uttermost "left"—the farthest in this direction that man on any considerable scale had ever gone. We might ask if the notion of collectivisim among men had not been carried so far that there was no longer room for the conception of the individual man as such or of individual operations on his part. Did the fine conception of fuller coöperative undertaking among men in their economic life have to reach an end like this?

Aside, moreover, from the matter of communism, we might also ask if there had not been effected too much organization here, if there were not overorganization and a certain top-heaviness thrust to such lengths as really to hamper the effective workings of a state. Or did communism permit no alternative?

A fair inquiry, furthermore, would be whether, practically speaking, communism meant too violent a conflict or break with the spirit of individual private profit—whether in the present state of the world large-scale communism could be expected to work—whether private profit, with its competitive spirit and system, is too great an incentive for carrying on the business of the world to be discarded. A cognate inquiry would be whether communism is sufficiently in keeping with the general feelings of men or with innate human nature. Such inquiries will probably have to await long-established evidence in one direction or another, whether in Russia or elsewhere.

Possibly a backhanded contribution of the Soviet Union to the progress of the world lies in the question it has posed, and in terrific form—in asking the world to concern itself with the possibilities of a more equitable distribution or sharing of the wealth created by the hand of man—whether this can be done by any method of joint endeavor or social coöperation among men, without impairing or crippling or wrecking the system known as capitalism with its demonstrated efficiency in the production of wealth, and with its affording, even though perhaps for some more than for others, the highest levels of material human existence that have been known to the world. Is it possible for private enterprise, with its peculiar qualifications, with its connotations of energy, initiative, ingenuity, keenness, resourcefulness, aptness, worldly wisdom, calculation, circumspection, sure-footedness, and general temper, to be consonant with supreme regard for the fullest humanitarian concerns or the widest general welfare programs? How far was unlimited, entirely free private enterprise compatible with considerations of the well-being or the security of the people in the mass? Could a happy balance be struck between the two? In many respects in the posing of this question has been posed the principal question of the present age.

The issue has now been joined. There have been brought face to face the two great opposite systems for the production of wealth, each arrayed against the other in the full panoply of at least economic war, each set upon its survival or its victory. One or the other must prove to an eagerly observing world its superiority—in human progress, in social welfare, in general culture, in making the wealth of the world of the greatest abundance, of the widest intelligent sharing, and of the highest levels, and also in the extension of democratic institutions, and without restriction upon the dearly bought freedoms of man. It is possibly the greatest issue ever put upon this earth of ours.

At this place a pointed question rises to the surface. Was there required such an earth-shaking explosion to bring mankind to the recognition that all was not well in the nether regions of society? Was there needful such a thundering tone of violence as has obtained in the Soviet undertaking to make the world face the necessity of something being done in respect to its economic maladjustments and its wells of human distress reaching to so large a portion of the population of the earth—even if the remedies and solutions proposed in the Soviet Union did not supply the answer, and even might bring calamitous results to the world in the costs entailed, in the setback of democracy and human freedoms if in nothing else.

It is highly unfortunate that the great communistic experiment in Russia had to be attended with the violence it was. In the eyes of thoughtful men its cause has been weakened and there has been estrangement from it thereby—its ready and deliberate resort to physical force to gain its ends. It has kept the system in its economic and political bearings from being considered on its merits in other respects. Or is there no alternative for communism?

The world would be stupid if it failed to realize and appreciate certain quite notable achievements in the Soviet state, and if it failed to take notice of or to put to account whatever steps forward in human progress have been brought to pass there, or whatever contributions might have been made to world advancement there—noting at the same time the evils and dangers that have been incorporated into the fabric and the outlook there, and also noting that a large part of the world— particularly those parts of the world with low economic and cultural levels—is watching with keenest interest the developments and results there.

In more than one matter the world in general might to its gain take a leaf from the Soviet notebook. With respect to more than one consideration the Soviet experiment could offer a chal-lenge to the rest of the earth. In particular the world should be mindful of and take to heart the serious, whole-hearted efforts put forth there to make the life of the masses more tolerable, with a larger measure of prosperity among them, with a broader sharing of the things afforded by nature or produced by human exertion—to abolish or eliminate what have been known as privation or indigence among men, the age-long state of a great part of the human race—to secure somehow "freedom from want," which has become an acknowledged quest among the enlightened of all lands, and indeed a present world demand. The very contemplation of the removal of these things from among men, even if regarded as visionary or chimerical, or even as but grandiose thinking, is in itself enough to win the consideration of the wise everywhere.[1]

---

[1] In an article in the "Saturday Evening Post" (June 14, 1947), entitled "The True Meaning of the Iron Curtain," it is stated: "The feeling that the 'Communists have got something' is prevalent throughout Europe today. . . . It is the most important single impression . . . brought home from a three-year sojourn in Europe. . . . Communism offers a powerful ascendent doctrine . . . perfectly fitting solutions of every one's ideological, political, and economic problems. The temptations to slip on this thing, to walk around happily ever afterward is greater than most Americans . . . can imagine." In an Encyclical Letter of the Lambeth Conference (Anglican) in 1948 is the following: "[We] cannot ignore certain lessons which are to be learned from the unquestionable fact that communism has awakened a disciplined response in the minds of many both in the West and in the East. . . . To them communism appears as a protest against social injustice. It seems to them to have inherited a concern for the depressed and downtrodden." In the report of the World Council of Churches (Amsterdam) in 1948 are these words: "Christians should ask why communism in its modern totalitarian form makes so strong an appeal to great masses of

If the Soviet order should be found wanting, and the order prevailing elsewhere was to win the day and constitute the future pattern for man, the world would do well to give itself to heart-searching examination in the light of Soviet effort and experience, and to learn better therefrom what it lacked, and how it might take measures for its improvement and reform. From the spirit evoked and from the methods or machinery employed in the Soviet land, there was much to be gleaned by a world largely of non-communistic mind, something for its advantage and something by way of warning. If resort is not to be made to the antithesis of capitalism, which is communism, for the production of goods required and desired by man, or for the way of life he is to follow in his earthly journeyings, and if a society based upon the principle of what is called free enterprise is to remain, there cannot be too much study of what has been attempted and of what has been accomplished in the great Soviet undertaking.

We could admire the zeal of the Soviet state in the wide educational program that has been provided for its citizens, even though we did not regard its methods and its aims as always the soundest, even though we felt that it ought to be purged of its political bearings, and even though we were struck with anything but happy feelings at making education a political thing. We could not be otherwise than moved by the efforts of the Soviet state to have education of such wide range and effectiveness, and its people of such enlightenment, as to enable them to understand and appreciate the various factors lying within socialized living, and to fit them to face intelligently the problems of a present and a future society—while deploring that this education had to be with the warping and discoloration arising from its amalgamation with a political

people in many parts of the world . . . a revolt of multitudes against injustice that gives communism much of its strength . . . [they] should realize that for many, especially for young men and women, communism seems to stand for a vision of human equality and universal brotherhood . . . who see in communism a means of deliverance from poverty and insecurity."

system. We could not but be happily impressed with the paucity of the scandalous and sensational on the printed page in the land. We could look with interest into the educational uses to which the advertising of goods for the consumer might be put. We could appreciate the importance given to technical education in respect to the conditions of modern life. We could express our gratification over the high place bestowed upon scientific research along so many and so varied lines. We could not but applaud the relentless energy given to inquiry in the realm of science—but grieve that upon that realm were imposed state-inspired conceptions. We could esteem the realization of the increasing amount of leisure time being made available to the people through technological advance and the importance of making some provision for the proper use of this leisure time. We could rejoice that in sports and games there were to be cultivated other values besides merely beating an opponent, and could view with some satisfaction an approach or attitude towards sport or athletics other than one of commercialization, though we must shudder at the thought that such things were simply matters in the hands of an all-directing state.

We could commend the attitude displayed toward backward people and peoples hitherto denied so large a portion of human consideration, with whatever advance toward the brotherhood of man was signified here—however it might appear that in reality people under the domination of this land were to become subject people to a dictatorship. We could think well of the simplicity and frugality of those who held office (as a general thing, or at least in earlier days).

We could also think well of a land that held in such disapprobation and repugnance such things as graft and corruption in government—even though it had to admit that it had not proved altogether successful in keeping them out.

We could voice hearty approval of the spirit of a land that did not regard the possession of great wealth as the safest and most desirable measure of success. We could speak highly of a land where there was on the whole no vulgar or vainglorious display of wealth, though in part for the reason that there was little wealth of any kind for display, or a land where there was engaged in little wasteful, riotous existence or squandering of the substance of the land (despite the more or less frequent practices of certain of the state chieftains). We could not but admire an attitude generally favorable to plain and simple and not sumptuous and ostentatious living. We could feel that there was something here that was most refreshing as a tonic in human affairs—if we allowed ourselves to forget other considerations.

We could applaud the efforts to have a people physically hearty and sound, and as far as possible free from illness and frailty. We could view without disfavor notable humanitarian conceptions introduced into various phases of public service. We could say a good word for the encouragement of coöperative attitudes among the people in the doing of their tasks and in the building up of the country—in a coöperative undertaking on a scale and of a breadth such as the world had never witnessed—even though lamenting that this coöperation was not altogether of the free will of the members, but was something largely at state instigation and under state compulsion.

We could not do otherwise than commend a stress upon socially useful toil. We could not withhold our approbation for the envisaging of a scheme for the economic security of the masses, even though we were somewhat doubtful of the means employed to this end. We could extend praise for the insistent demand for the maximum production of goods in the land, including the furthest possible development of the country's natural resources, so that as many as possible might enjoy the satisfactions of life—with efforts involving heavy strain on muscles and nerves alike—an undertaking without parallel in human history. We could sympathize with and applaud the use of every possible means, every possible resource for the ut-

most production in the land, though we were entirely without
this feeling when we call to mind the brutal, inhuman practices of forced labor, of the labor of the concentration camps.
We could view without dismay the breaking up of the old
landed estates (largely the work of the peasants themselves),
though we might not look with equal complacency upon a gigantic state farm estate created in their place. We could offer
our benediction for the dignity that was at least theoretically
bestowed upon labor in the organization of human society,
even though we could doubt if labor in its practical bearings
had fared altogether well in the Soviet land. We could not be
without gratitude that there has been called to the attention of
men a possible social order where the wealth created should
be more widely and more equitably shared.

But we could not refrain from asking at the same time if
whatever things were good here might not have been approached in circumstances that would have held in honor some
of the finer values of human existence, such as had been cherished by man as essential to his real progress, and in circumstances that would not have done violence to his free spirit.

However much we might appreciate what the people of
Russia had gone through in the long bitter past, and could realize the truth of the ancient saying that where the wind was
sown, there would the whirlwind be reaped; however much we
could understand how a people so wrongfully used, so grievously and cruelly downtrodden would in due time be moved
to secure the just rights of men; and however much we could
comprehend natural efforts toward a better political, economic,
and social order—yet notwithstanding all this, a large portion
of mankind could not help being disturbed, dismayed, and distressed at some of the excesses that too often seem to have taken
place in Russia in the name of these things. Even if that country were found to have made notable advance or to have attained a measure of success in her political, economic, and so-

cial undertakings, we would still be constrained to cry: At what price this advance or success if it be such!

How many unhappy peasant proprietors were uprooted from simple homes, driven to freezing Arctic climates, maltreated and tortured, possibly even paying with their lives—perhaps for not much more than a love for their little farms which they wished to cultivate themselves, and the fruits of which they wished to enjoy for themselves and their families, or perhaps for an unwillingness to be dispossessed of what they regarded as their rightful belongings, at the bidding of an all-powerful hand at the seat of authority? How many citizens were compelled to toil at forced labor, with insufficient food, hounded or misused by secret police, or herded into wretched concentration camps, perhaps stood before a firing squad—perhaps for little more heinous than some infraction of a meticulous, sumptuary, arbitrary code or government behest, perhaps mere disagreement with government authorities, or as an object lesson for those who might think of disagreeing too far or of resisting at all—perhaps for lack of sufficient enthusiasm in certain government projects? What was the extent and the meaning of the periodic blood purges—of own party members in government officialdom, perhaps of those once in positions of influence and authority? Could it be that in the new Russia political prisoners were subjected to greater hardship and cruelty than in the old; that there were more mass killings now than then? Could it be that we were to have in these respects something, not better but worse, than what we knew of the Russia of the Czars, which was said to be an absolutism tempered with assassination—ruthless violence from above countered with ruthless violence from below?

What is to be said of a land where those in power were there only because of the force or threat of force in their hands, who could find support only by physical coercion? What is to be said of a land that, to carry out a particular economic or political program, had to make use of such compulsion that human beings had no alternative but to live by it if they were to live at all? What is to be said of a land that in the name of communism boldly and frankly repudiated the hard-won conceptions of democracy, and set up a dictatorship of power and force in the hands of the few for the government of the many, not even rendering lip service to the principle that all governments derived their just powers from the consent of the governed, or that the individual citizen had certain rights deserving of respect, even from government? What is to be said of a land that had so little esteem for human personality, for the integrity and dignity of the individual human being that it could compress its citizens into a machine of one gigantic mould? What is to be said of a land where upon art, literature, science was exercised more or less undisguised coercion —where these things, things of the intellectual and spiritual life, were mobilized, were deliberately set to work to make impregnable the power of a particular order? What is to be said of a land, with a philosophy narrow and dogmatic, where culture, recreation, and much else must suffer in the way of regimentation?

What is to be said of a land that, under the guise of reconstructing its institutions and of building up a new social order, could give itself to the setting up of a structure of so materialistic a content? What is to be said of a land that had few qualms or scruples as to the end justifying the means, whatever the fair-spoken and sonorous phrase or whatever the moving slogan employed, or however much there might be involved of oppression or violence in the means employed? What is to be said of a land that stood ready to use naked force to secure its way of life with weaker neighboring peoples, perhaps the while professing desire and intent for their protection or liberation? What is to be said of a land that by sheer might would drive its communistic order down the throats of nearby lands or lands somehow under its control? What is to be said of a land that would threaten the world with its plans of violent conquest? Was it to be by methods of terrorization?

Was state compulsion at home lessened or sweetened by claims that the exercise of authority was simply a measure of discipline or of administration, not only for the safeguarding of the Soviet state but for the eventual advantage and betterment of the people—a totalitarian conception quite flouting democracy or the will of the people? And how does it come that a state may take all wisdom to itself—that those few in its seats of power may become all-knowing as to what is good or desirable for the individual man or for the mass of men under their sway? And was the ultimate question arising that of a police state versus a free society?

Even though there was a constitution set up for the land, how far was there constitutional government beyond its trappings as long as its foundation rested upon the guarding and perpetuation of a particular party system, and permitted no deviation from strict party lines? How was actual democracy in such surroundings more than a tinkling cymbal?

Was there in power in the Soviet land a relatively small band, which in other days might have been denominated an oligarchy, a tyranny, at least a benevolent despotism, some sort of dictatorship—even confessedly of the proletariat—which was the elect of a particular party, holding in its tight grip the reins of economic and political authority, bolstered by an internal armed force of such might that none would dare provoke it? Was there at the seat of government an authority with all the power of its country gathered to itself, the mightiest ever known among the sons of men, with supreme, unquestioned will over its own people, and perhaps looking to a time when the will of the system it represented would hold all the world in thrall? Did whatever counsels that might prevail behind the darkened screen there with respect to national and international policies remain its own occult secret? Did there within the recesses of the Kremlin abide a dread uncertain power, an

415

inscrutable force upon which the light of political day shone only in dimmed rays? Was it this which ruled the land, and would rule the world?

Was there not something about the whole Soviet undertaking that rang hollow, something that was of mechanical structure, that ran counter to the deepest aspirations of the human spirit? Was there not in it something made of iron into which the freedom of man could never be moulded, could never be fitted? Was there not something brought into being that was stifling to what was enthroned in man's heart, something that warred against the innate pride of man's soul?

It must be kept in mind always that the real question here lies not so much in communism as such—however considered by many as a faulty and undesirable economic policy—as in its political totalitarianism, its aggressive intolerance, its willingness and readiness to resort to force and violence to attain its ends.

Men of intelligence and with humanity of heart must reject the doctrine that only the play of economic forces, however tremendous it is after all, is the sole or the main determining factor in human conduct or in the affairs of man, and that nothing else need be reckoned with. Such doctrine can only shrivel if not destroy the soul of man. That, furthermore, the evils of the world can be traced or attributed to a particular economic order, and that with its ending and the substitution of another, all will be well, is something not readily to be accepted. Nor can we look with favor upon the conception—no matter what the brave languge used to establish it—of a "mass-man," so far "socialized" that he no longer has an individual personality, worthy of respect and regard, and without the qualities and aspirations to which man is everlastingly the heir.

Even granted that man is better off economically, materially, in an environment such as that afforded in the Soviet system—supposing this to have been proved—was he for the attainment of such a state to sacrifice the things for which his spirit has to do, paramountly his freedom? Was a promised repast of fleshly pottage to be at the price of what he has held to be his inalienable human birthright? Was he to become a half-slave in order to be physically well cared for? Were the political rights of man—which may be regarded as the assertion of his truest self, of his spirit—always to be held subordinate to, and on a lower plane than, his economic interests and material well-being—assuming that in the Soviet state the latter could be counted upon with the greater assurance? Was bare economic security, conceding it was to be found here, preferable to one's innate liberty? Did such considerations necessarily have priority over all else in the life of man? Was this the great issue now put before the human race?

However grave and pressing the evils in human society, including the admitted evils of a capitalistic society, whatever their depth and their breadth, is it not possible to find a way to remove them and thus effect a better estate for man, to separate the good from the bad and to concentrate our attacks upon the latter—without indiscriminate destruction of what experience has shown to be of value in the present order, and without the possible creation of new evils and greater perils?

The state should somehow forever remain the servant of man; it should never emerge with such strength in its hands as to become a Frankenstein and make men cower before it. And when such a state is not implanted upon genuine democracy, but upon something else, there is multiplied peril alike to man and to the possibilities of his advance.

Socialism, so far as it is an economic doctrine, and as such entitled to a respectful hearing among the possible programs offered for man's economic well-being, should be free from all such unworthy attitudes. If socialism means greater insistence and greater reliance upon the conceptions of human brotherhood, this is all the more reason why the spiritual values of life should not be set at naught, esteemed lightly, or thrust under foot, or that there should be any limitations imposed upon the expression of the thoughts arising in the mind of man with respect to his way of life or his governance. Perhaps Soviet Russia with its experiments on so gigantic and so moving a scale will have given to the world an awesome lesson—one that will stand it in good stead for long years to come.

BIBLIOGRAPHY

LIST OF BOOKS ON RUSSIA

(Not included are very brief works or pamphlets or books primarily of technical or military character or dealing largely with foreign affairs.)

Before 1917

R. Myall, The Character of the Russians, 1823

R. Pinkerton, Russia, 1833

E. P. Thompson, Life in Russia, 1848

A. de Gorowski, Russia As It Is, 1854

G. de Lagnay, The Knout and the Russians, 1854

N. V. Gogol, Home Life in Russia, 1854

E. J. Brabazon, Russia and Her Czars, 1855

S. Edwards, The Russians at Home, 1861

H. Morley, Sketches of Russian Life, 1866

H. Barry, Russia in 1870, 1871

H. Barry, Ivan at Home, 1872

E. D. Proctor, A Russian Journey, 1872 (1894)

E. C. G. Murray, Russians of Today

A. Rambaud, History of Russia, ed. 1879

J. Geddie, The Russian Empire, 1882

N. K. Dole, Young Folks History of Russia, 1883

G. S. Bloomfield, Reminiscences of Court and Diplomatic Life, 1883

E. C. Locker, All the Russias, 1884

E. Noble, The Russian Revolt, 1885

J. C. Hare, Studies in Russia, 1885

W. T. Stead, The Truth about Russia, 1888

W. E. Curtis, The Land of Nihilism (Russia), 1888

L. T. Khomtrov, Russia Social and Political, 1888

G. Brandes, Impressions of Russia, 1889

G. Kennan, Siberia and the Exile System, 1891

E. M. Vagüé *et al.*, Tsar and His People, 1891

C. A. Stoddard, Across Russia, 1892

E. J. Dillon (E. B. Lanin), Russian Characteristics, 1892

F. J. Whishaw, Out of Doors in Tsarland, 1893

J. Murray, Handbook for Travelers in Russia, etc., 1893

A. Leroy-Beaulieu, The Empire of the Tsars and of the Russian Peasants, 1894

S. Stepniak (S. M. Kravichinsky), Russia under The Tsars, 1894

S. Stepniak (S. M. Kravchinsky), The Russian Peasant, 1894

I. F. Hapgood, Russian Rambles, 1895

J. A. Logan, Joyful Russia, 1897

P. Kropotkin, Memoirs of a Revolutionist, 1899

E. Noble, Russia and Russians, 1900

H. H. Munro, The Rise of the Russian Empire, 1900

M. S. Emery, Russia through a Stereoscope, 1900

F. H. Palmer, Russian Life in Town and Country, 1901

J. A. Norman, All the Russians, 1902

W. R. Morfill, History of Russia from Peter the Great to Nicholas II, 1902

F. H. Skrine, Expansion of Russia 1815-1900, 1903

G. Drage, Russian Affairs 1904

A. J. Beveridge, The Russian Advance, 1904

N. Appleton, Russian Life and Society, 1904

H. Ganz, The Riddle of Russia (The Land of Riddles), 1904

W. D. Foulke, Slav or Saxon, 1904

C. Joubert, Russia As It Really Is, 1904

E. Von de Brügger, Russia of Today, 1904

W. Von Schierbrand, Russia — Her Strength and Her Weakness, 1904

V. Berand, After Russian Empire and Czarism, 1905

G. H. Perres, Russia in Revolution, 1905

E. Singleton, Russia as Seen and Described by Famous Writers, 1905

A. Ular, Russia from Within, 1905

K. Zilliacus, The Russian Revolutionary Movement

W. D. Wallace, Russia, 1905 (1916)

L. Decle, The New Russia, 1906

G. Gapon, Story of My Life, 1906

A. M. B. Meakin, Russia, Travels and Studies, 1906

P. N. Milyukov, Russia and Its Crisis, 1906

W. R. Morfill, Russia (Story of the Nations), 1907

J. F. Fraser, Red Russia, 1907

B. Pares, Russia and Reform, 1907

E. A. B. Hodgett, The Court of Russia in the Nineteenth Century, 1908

W. E. Walling, Russia's Message: The People against the Czar, 1908

H. W. Kennard, The Russian Peasant, 1908

V. O. Kluchevsky, History of Russia, 1911

J. Prelloker, Russian Flashlights, 1911

M. Baring, The Russian People, 1911

R. K. Wood, Tourists' Russia, 1912

G. Dobson et al., Russia, 1913

R. Reynolds, My Russian Year, 1913

N. O. Winter, The Russian Empire of Today and Yesterday, 1913

G. Alexinsky, Modern Russia, 1913

A. S. Rappaport, Home Life in Russia, 1913

H. W. Williams, Russia of the Russians, 1914

J. Mavor, Economic History of Russia, 1914

M. Baring, Mainsprings of Russia, 1914

S. Graham, Undiscovered Russia, 1914

N. Jarintzoff, Russia, Country of Extremes, 1914

K. Baedeker, Russia, etc. (Handbook for Travelers), 1914

S. Graham, Changing Russia, 1915 (1913)

J. Hubbach, Russian Realities, 1915

C. C. Young, Abused Russia, 1915

D. Garstin, Friendly Russia, 1915

S. Graham, The Way of Martha and the Way of Mary, 1915

H. Bury, Russian Life Today, 1915

L. Wiener, An Interpretation of the Russian People, 1915

P. Vinogradoff, Self-Government in Russia, 1915

A. Lethridge, The New Russia, 1915

M. and A. R. Lethridge, The Soul of Russians, 1916

W. Stephens, The Soul of Russia, 1916

R. W. Child, Potential Russia, 1916

C. E. Bechhofer (Roberts), Russia at the Cross Roads, 1916

J. Foster, Russia of Today, 1916

R. Reynolds, My Slavic Friends, 1916

E. A. B. Hodgett, Glorious Russia, 1916

C. Sarolea, Great Russia, Her Achievements and Promise, 1916

C. Sarolea, Europe's Debt to Russia, 1916

S. E. Howe, One Thousand Years of Russian History, 1916

1917

I. F. Marcosson, The Rebirth of Russia

R. L. Wright, The Russians: An Interpretation

A. J. Brown, Russia in Transformation

S. E. Howe, The Real Russia

L. I. P. Souviny-Seydlitz, Russia of Yesterday and Tomorrow

A. Kornilov, Modern Russian History

A. B. Ruhl, White Nights and Other Russian Impressions

F. B. Reeves, Russia Then and Now

H. de Windt, Russia As I Knew It

R. C. Dorr, Inside the Russian Revolution

S. Graham, Russia in 1916

M. J. Olgin, Soul of the Russian Revolution

I. D. Levine, The Russian Revolution

J. D. Duff, Russian Realities and Problems

C. Sarolea, Russian Revolution and War

1918

C. E. Beury, About Russia

O. Gilbreath, Russia in Travail

B. Beatty, Red Heart of Soviet Russia

A. J. Sack, Birth of the Russian Democracy

J. Pollock, War and Revolution in Russia

R. Beazley et al., Russia from Varangians to Bolsheviks

M. Buchanan, Petrograd, City of Trouble

C. E. Fanning, Selected Articles on Russia

E. A. Ross, Russia in Upheaval

P. Graevenitz, From Autocracy to Bolshevism

J. Calino, Scenes from Russian Life

H. Brenner, Sidelights on Russia

C. E. Beury, Russia and Its Revolution

M. Baring, Year in Russia

E. Poole, The Village: Russian Impressions

E. Poole, Dark People: Russian Crisis

C. E. Russell, Unchained Russia

L. Bryant, Six Red Months in Russia

E. J. Dillon, The Eclipse of Russia

A. N. Drew, Russia: a Study

S. E. Hume, Real Russia

E. Vandervelde, Three Aspects of the Russian Revolution

J. L. Haughteling, Diary of the Russian Revolution

F. L. Harper, Runaway Russia

1919

J. Pollock, Bolshevist Adventure

E. P. Stebbing, From Czar to Bolshevist

R. C. Long, Russian Revolutionary Aspects

W. C. Bullitt, The Bullitt Mission to Soviet Russia

T. G. Masaryk, The Spirit of Russia

R. Power, Under the Bolshevist Reign of Terror (Under Cossack and Bolshevist)

A. F. Kerensky, Prelude to Bolshevism

A. Bullard, The Russian Pendulum

H. V. Keeling, Bolshevism

A. S. Rappaport, Pioneers of the Russian Revolution

J. Reed, Ten Days That Shook the World

R. Wilton, Russia's Agony

J. M. Goldstein, Russia, Her Economic Past and Future

A. Ransome, Russia in 1919

O. M. Salyer, Russia White or Red

E. H. Wilcox, Russia's Ruins

J. Spargo, Bolshevism: The End of Political and Industrial Democracy

1920

J. Varney, Sketches of Soviet Russia

M. G. Hindus, The Russian Peasant and the Revolution

J. Spargo, The Psychology of Bolshevism

J. McBride, The Barbarous Soviet Republic

W. E. Walling, Sovietism—A B C of Russian Bolshevism According to Bolshevists

W. Hard, Raymond Robins' Own Story

B. Russell, Bolshevism in Theory and Practice

Memoirs of General Wrangel

P. N. Miliukov, Bolshevism an International Danger

G. Lansbury, What I Saw in Russia

W. T. Goode, Bolshevism at Work

W. A. Born, Jr., Groping Giant—Revolutionary Russia

C. L. Malone, The Russian Republic

M. W. Davis, Open the Gates to Russia

R. W. Postgate, Bolshevik Theory

C. R. Ballard, Russia in Rule and Misrule

P. S. Crosley, Intimate Letters from Petrograd

E. Antonelli, Bolshevik Russia

F. Anstey, Red Europe

G. E. Raine and E. Luboff, Bolshevik Russia

A. R. Williams, Through the Russian Revolution

J. D. (Grant) Cantacuzene, The Russian People

1921

H. N. Brailsford, Russian Workers Republic
H. G. Wells, Russia in the Shadows
M. Hillquit, From Marx to Lenin
S. Gompers and W. E. Walling, Out of Their Own Mouths
M. E. Harrison, Marooned in Moscow
J. Spargo, The Greatest Failure in All History
E. A. Ross, Russian Bolshevist Revolution
D. R. Francis, Russia from the American Embassy

C. Sheridan, From Mayfair to Moscow From a Russian Diary, by an Englishwoman
A. Schwartz, The Voice of Russia
C. E. Bechhofer (Roberts), Through Starving Russia
L. Pavolsky, The Economics of Communism
J. F. Biddleyey, Russia in the Eighties
M. P. Price, My Reminiscences of the Russian Revolution
F. McCullagh, A Prisoner of the Reds
A. Ransome, The Crisis in Russia

1922

B. L. Brasol, The Balance Sheet of Sovietism
H. Kehler, Red Garden
A. A. Heller, Industrial Revival in Soviet Russia
P. N. Milyukov, Russia Today and Tomorrow

C. R. Buxton, In a Russian Village
K. Laites, Recent Economic Developments in Russia
P. Dukes, Red Dusk and the Morrow
A. I. Denikin, Russian Turmoil (also memoirs of other generals in Russian civil war)

1923

L. Bryant, Mirrors of Moscow
E. A. Ross, The Russian Soviet Republic
F. A. Mackenzie, Russia before Dawn
G. S. Eddy, Russia, Warning and Challenge
E. Goldman, My Dissillusionment in Russia
M. S. Farbman, Bolshevism in Retreat
S. A. Korff, Autocracy and Revolution in Russia

M. A. Paine, Plague, Pestilence, Famine
O. Keun, My Adventures in Bolshevist Russia
G. Buchanan, My Mission to Russia and Other Diplomatic Measures
M. E. Harrison, Unfinished Tales from a Russian Prison
S. S. Masloff, Russia after Four Years of Revolution

1924

R. Eaton, Under the Red Flag
A. L. Strong, The First Time in History
E. Goldman, My Further Disillusionment in Russia
M. S. Farbman, After Lenin
M. Marx, Romance of New Russia

C. Sarolea, Impressions of Soviet Russia (also 1948)
P. O. Sorokin, Leaves from a Russian Diary (also 1949)
E. R. Shapleigh, The Specter (an American Woman in Russia)
E. T. Blanc, The Coöperative Movement in Russia

1925

S. Graham, Russia in Division
E. W. Hullinger, Reforging of Russia
N. Makeev and V. O'Hara, Russia
A. Berkman, The Bolshevik Myth

S. F. Platonov, History of Russia
G. Shelley, Speckled Domes
G. Shelley, Blue Steppes (Adventures among the Russians)

M. Eastman, Since Lenin Died
British Trade Union Delegation to Russia, etc., Official Report
A. Rado, Guide to Soviet Union (leading cities)
V. Figner, Memoir of a Revolutionist
Soviet Union Year Book (also later years)

1926

M. G. Hindus, Broken Earth
L. H. Guest, New Russia
M. Gordin, Utopia in Chains
M. S. Miller, The Economic Development of Russia 1905-1914
A. Porter, A Moscow Diary
S. N. Harper, Civic Training in Soviet Russia

J. Colquhon, Adventures in Red Russia
S. P. Milgounov, The Red Terror in Russia
S. Zimands, State Capitalism in Russia
E. Elnett, Historic Origin and Social Development of Family Life in Russia

1927

J. F. Hecker, Religion under the Soviets
A. Karlgren, Bolshevist Russia
S. Nearing and J. Hardy, Economic Organization of the Soviet Union
M. Spinka, The Church and the Russian Revolution
L. H. Bury, Russia from Within
L. Lawton, The Russian Revolution
A. F. Kerensky, The Catastrophe

B. Wrangel, From Serfdom to Bolshevism
M. Baring, What I Saw in Russia
J. N. Rosenberg, On the Steppes
H. H. Fisher, Famine in Soviet Russia (1935)
R. F. and M. S. McWilliams, Russia in 1926
A. R. Williams, The Russian Land

1928

L. W. Wilson, New Schools in New Russia
J. Mavor, The Russian Revolution
G. London, Red Russia after Ten Years
A. Wickstead, Life under the Soviets
J. Smith, Woman in Soviet Russia
R. P. Arndt, Soviet Russia and Her Neighbors
H. N. Brailsford, How the Soviets Work
K. Borders, Village Life under the Soviets
I. L. Lee, Present Day Russia
W. J. Brown, Three Months in Russia
R. W. Dunn, Soviet Trade Unions
A. J. Haines, Health Work in Soviet Russia
G. M. Price, Labor Protection in Soviet Russia
F. A. Mackenzie, Russian Crucifixion

A. Rado, Guide Book to Soviet Union
M. H. Dobb and H. C. Stevens, Russian Economic Development since the Revolution ("Since 1917," 1938)
E. A. Walsh, The Fall of the Russian Empire
E. M. Newman, Seeing Russia
R. N. Baldwin, Liberty under the Soviets
D. F. Buxton, The Challenge of Bolshevism
S. Chase et al., Soviet Russia in the Second Decade (Joint Survey of Technical Staff of 1st American Trade Union Delegation)
B. Pares, History of Russia (and later years)
G. P. Fedotov, The Russian Church Since the Revolution

1929

W. C. Emhardt, Religion in Soviet Russia
H. J. Greenwall, Mirrors of Moscow

A. L. Strong, Red Star in Samarkand
D. Thompson, The New Russia

A. V. Bailaloff, In the Land of the Communist Dictatorship

A. O. McCormick, The Hammer and Sickle (Russia Enters the Second Decade)

M. G. Hindus, Humanity Uprooted

T. Dreiser, Dreiser Looks at Russia

W. R. Batsell, Soviet Rule in Russia

J. P. Trainin, Soviet Democracy

J. Dewey, Impressions of Soviet Russia

E. M. Kayden and A. N. Antifero, The Coöperative Movement in Russia during the War

A. P. Pinkevitch, New Education in the Soviet Republic

E. Ashmead-Bartlett, The Riddle of Russia

G. M. Gooden, Russia under the Red Flag

A. Meyendorff, Background of the Russian Revolution

L. Kyaksht, Romantic Recollections

P. Gronsky and N. J. Astrov, War and the Russian Government

G. T. Marye, Nearing the End in Imperial Russia

Soviet Information Bureau, the Soviet Union

Soviet Union, Facts, Description, Statistics

A. Badayev, Bolsheviks in the Tsarist Duma

1930

J. Douillet, Moscow Unmasked

E. J. Dillon, Russia Today and Yesterday

W. H. Chamberlin, Soviet Russia Living Record and History

P. Haensel, The Economic Policy of Soviet Russia

J. G. Fletcher, Two Frontiers

H. von Eckhardt, Russia

K. Foss, Black Bread and Samovars

Union of Socialist Soviet Republics, The Soviet Union Looks Ahead

Illustrated History of the Russian Revolution

S. G. Bron, Soviet Economic Development and American Business

A. Yugov, Economic Trends in Soviet Russia

A. T. Vassilyev, Ochrona the Red Secret Police

G. V. Vernadsky, History of Russia

B. Edelhertz, The Russian Paradox

E. J. P. Benn, About Russia

G. T. Grinko, The 5-Year Plan of Soviet Union

N. Farson, Seeing Red Today in Russia; Black Bread and Red Coffins

G. S. Counts, A Ford Crosses Soviet Russia

E. Burns, The Russian Productive System

L. Fischer, Soviets in World Affairs

H. Barbusse, One Looks at Russia

N. R. Hamilton (Rowan-Hamilton), Under the Red Star

N. Petrova, Twice Born in Russoia

M. J. Larson, An Expert in the Service of the Soviet

S. de Chessin, Darkness from the East

1931

W. A. Fairburn, Russia Utopia in Chains

P. Istrati, Russia Unveiled

K. Breshkouskaia, The Hidden Springs of the Russian Revolution

O. Tweedy, Russia at Random

B. Savinkov, Memoirs of a Terrorist

A. C. Noé, Golden Days of Soviet Russia

D. S. Mirsky (Suyatopolk-Mirsky), Russia, A Social History

M. G. Hindus, Red Bread

S. Taylor, Soviet and the Soul

Soviet Union Year Book

M. N. Pokrovsky, History of Russia

J. Zelitch, Soviet Administration of the Criminal Law

E. Sisson, One Hundred Red Days

K. Kautsky, Bolshevism at a Deadlock

P. Scheffer, Seven Years in Soviet Russia

J. Johnson, Russia in the Grip of Bolshevism

E. T. Cotton, X Y Z of Communism

J. de V. Loder, Bolshevism in Perspective

V. Orloff, The Underworld and the Soviet

E. G. Grady, Seeing Red
B. Hopper, Pan-Sovietism, What Russia Intends
W. H. Chamberlin, Soviet Planned Economic Order
M. Ilin (I. Y. Marshak), New Russia's Primer
R. Long, An Editor Looks at Russia
C. B. Hoover, The Economic Life of Soviet Russia
M. T. Florinsky, The End of the Russian Empire
M. Bourke-White, Eyes on Russia
E. A. Walsh, The Last Stand
C. Chesterton, My Russian Venture
S. N. Harper, Making Bolsheviks
A. Muldavin, The Red Fog Lifts
L. O'Flaherty, I Went to Russia

W. B. Lipphard, Communing with Communism
G. S. Counts, The Soviet Challenge to America
G. S. Eddy, The Challenge of Russia
A. Feiler, The Russian Experiment 1930
V. O. Kluchevsky, History of Russia
A. A. Johnson, Progress in the Soviet Union
W. C. White, These Russians
E. C. Ponafidine, Russia My Home
B. Pares, My Russian Memoirs
A. L. Strong, The Road to Gray Pamir
A. L. Strong, The Soviets Conquer Wheat
I. A. Yakovlev, Red Villages
G. I. Sokolnikov, Soviet Policy in Public Finance 1917-1928

1932

L. Fischer, Machines and Men in Russia
I. D. Levine, Red Smoke
H. Griffith, Seeing Soviet Russia
A. Hammer, The Quest of Romanoff Treasure
E. Walter, Russia's Decisive Year
J. B. Barker, Red Russia Arms
M. Buchanan, The Dissolution of Empire
M. M. Karpovich, Imperial Russia 1801-1917
T. Nurenberg, This New Red Freedom
A. Rathmanova, G. Hoyer, Flight from Terror
A. Forman, From Baltic to Black Sea
G. A. Burrell, An American Engineer Looks at Russia
G. Popoff, The Red Plague
S. Mackiewicz, Russian Minds in Fetters
C. F. A. Maitland-Makgill-Crichton, Russian Close-Up
A. de Monzie, The New Russia
W. C. White, Made in Russia (1944)
L. Lawton, Economic History of Soviet Russia
A. Livingston, Seven Years
W. A. Rukeyser, Working for the Soviets
J. W. Hird, Under Czar and Soviets
J. Stakall, Through a Communist Looking Glass
L. Trotsky, History of the Russian Revolution
W. D. Frank, Dawn in Russia

W. J. Robinson, Soviet Russia As I Saw It
J. N. Darling, Ding Goes to Russia
M. H. Dobb, Soviet Russia and the World
F. Griffin, The Soviet Scene
T. Woods, New Minds, New Men
H. T. Hodgkin, Seeing Ourselves through Russia
N. Ignatieff, The Russian Emerges
A. W. Field, Protection of Women and Children in Soviet Russia
G. E. Raiguel and W. K. Hoff, This Is Russia
W. Gurian, Bolshevism: Theory and Practice
T. Seibert, Red Russia
H. Kohn, Nationalism in the Soviet Union
J. S. Huxley, Scientists among the Soviets
G. T. Robinson, Rural Russia under the Old Régime
E. M. Friedman, Russia in Transition
T. D. Campbell, Russia Market or Menace
J. Freeman, Soviet Worker
F. W. Halle, Woman in Soviet Russia
J. Acheson, Young America Looks at Russia
R. Wright, One-Sixth of the Earth's Surface
G. Dobbert, Red Economics
G. Vernadsky, The Russian Revolution 1917-1931

427

Pocket Guide to Soviet Union (State Intourist)

Guide Book for Travelers through Trans-Caucasia (U.S.S.R.)

1933

L. and J. H. Davis, A Trip to Soviet Russia
H. F. Ward, In Place of Profit—Social Incentives in the Soviet Union
E. Winter, Red Virtue
V. M. Dean, Soviet Russia
J. S. Lockhart, Babel Visited
W. J. Durant, The Tragedy of Russia
M. G. Hindus, The Great Offensive
L. Segal, Modern Russia
J. Purves-Stewart, A Physician's Tour in U. S. S. R.
M. Patrick, The Hammer and Sickle
A. Wickstead, Ten Years in Soviet Moscow
H. Spaull, Youth in Russia Today
P. H. Box, Russia
P. Malevsky-Malevitch, Russia, U. S. S. R.—Complete Handbook
M. T. Florinsky, World Revolution and the U. S. S. R.

M. I. Cole, Twelve Studies in Soviet Russia
C. and M. Lamont, Russia Day by Day
I. Skariatina, First to Go Back
B. R. Headstrom, Story of Russia
E. T. Brown, This Russian Business
V. T. Tchernavin, Escape from the Soviets
N. N. Selivanova, Dining and Wining in Old Russia
J. F. Hecker, Moscow Dialogues
J. Davis, The New Russia
K. Mehnert, Youth in Soviet Russia
C. Wells, Kapoot
A. Newsholme and J. A. Kingsbury, Red Medicine: Socialized Health in Soviet Russia
J. Stalin et al., From First to Second Five-Year Plan
G. Stewart, White Armies of Russia
N. Buchwald and R. Bishop, From Peasant to Collective Farmer

1934

A. Wickstead, My Russian Neighbors
A. L. Tolstoy, I Worked for the Soviets
L. K. Elmhirst, A Trip to Russia
C. Hamilton, Modern Russia
B. Wooton, Plan or No Plan
P. A. Markov, The Soviet Theatre
A. Rosenberg, History of Bolshevism
J. E. Abbe, I Photograph Russia
A. F. Kerensky, Crucifixion of Liberty
R. S. Durstine, Red Thunder
M. Budberg, The Russian Seesaw
B. Holmes, Travellers' Russia
E. Lamb, The Planned Economy in Soviet Russia
B. Kamyshansky, I Am a Cossack
M. Britnieva, One Woman's Story
J. H. Rubin, I Live to Tell
J. Bunyan and H. H. Fisher, The Bolshevist Revolution

B. W. Maxwell, The Soviet State
J. Stalin, The State of the Soviet Union
W. H. Chamberlin, Russia's Iron Age
W. Duranty, Duranty Reports Russia
F. E. Williams, Russia, Youth, and the Present-Day World
A. Hirsch, Industrialized Russia
M. Muggeridge, Winter in Moscow
A. Monkhouse, Moscow 1911-1933
G. S. Eddy, Russia Today
M. E. Smith, From Broadway to Moscow
J. F. Hecker, Russian Sociology
G. Mecklenburg, Russia Changes Religion
M. Travers, Moscow Excursion
W. J. Durant, The Lesson of Russia
N. Popov, Outline History of the Communist Party of Russia

1935

A. Gordon, Russian Year
S. and B. Webb, Soviet Communism
N. A. Semashko, Health Protection in the U. S. S. R.

W. Duranty, I Write As I Please
H. Griffith, Playtime in Russia
O. P. Peterson, Embers of Old Russia
M. Ilin (I. Y. Marshak), Men and Mountains

W. H. Chamberlin, History of the Russian Revolution
G. Wreden, Unmasking of a Russian
H. A. Franck, Vagabond in Sovietland
J. H. Rubin, Moscow Mirage
E. M. Lyons, Moscow Carrousel
S. P. Turin, From Peter the Great to Lenin
J. Kunitz, Dawn over Samerkand
W. H. Waters, Russia Then and Now
L. Fischer, Soviet Journey
M. S. Calcott, Russian Justice
T. A. Tarcouzio, The Soviet Union and International Law
V. T. Tchernavin, We Soviet Women
V. T. Tchernavin, I Speak for the Silent Prisoners of the Soviet
V. A. Nadel, Supply and Trade in U. S. S. R.
A. L. Mikhelson, I Came Out Alive
A. Lobanov-Rostovsky, Grinding Mill: Reminiscences of War and Revolution 1913-1920
I. Spector, Russia

A. P. Pinkevitch, Science and Education in the U. S. S. R.
F. Stepun, The Russian Soul and Revolution
S. M. Kingsbury and M. Fairchild, Factory, Family, and Woman in Soviet Russia
B. Brutzkus, Economic Planning in Soviet Russia
G. Solomon, Among Red Autocrats
M. S. Farbman, Pialiletka, Russia's Five-year Plan (1931)
T W. Boldgriff, Russian Born
J. Oneal, Socialism vs. Bolshevism
C. Bobrovskaya, Twenty Years of Underground Russia
L. von Koerber, Soviet Russia Fights Crime
J. Seymour, In the Moscow Manner
W. E. Reddaway, The Russian Financial System
The Soviet Union (various writers)
Development of the National Economy of the U. S. S. R. (State Planning Commission)

1936

V. K. Chernov, The Great Russian Revolution
L. E. Hubbard, Soviet Money and Finance
M. Spinka, Christianity Confronts Communism
F. J. Miles, Changing Russia
M. G. Hindus, Moscow Skies
V. Fediaevky and P. S. Hill, Nursery School and Parent Education in Soviet Russia
G Vernadsky, Political and Diplomatic History of Russia
B. Magnus (B. Mohoff), Smell of Smoke
J. G. Crowther, Soviet Science (1930)
W. L. Citrine, I Search for Truth in Russia

B. Pares, Moscow Admits a Critic
A. L. Strong, This Soviet World
I. Schwezoff, The Russian Somersault
J. Bunyan, Intervention, Civil War, Communism in Russia
M. Yurluva, Russia Farewell
J. F. Hecker, Religion and Communism
W. Gurian, Future of Bolshevism
H. Iswolsky, Soviet Man Now
B. Carr, Black Bread and Cabbage Soup
G. Trease, The Comet
E. Ammende, Human Life in Russia
American-Russian Chamber of Commerce, Handbook of Soviet Union (also other years)
U. S. S. R., Handbook

1937

E. Lyons, Assignment in Utopia
V. Connolly, Soviet Tempo
E. D. Simon, Moscow in the Making
H. Lee, Twenty Years After
W. H. Chamberlin, Collectivism: False Utopia
M. Gould, I Visit the Soviets

H. S. Marchant, Scratch a Russian
C. R. L. James, World Revolution, 1917-1936
V. Serge, Destiny of Revolution (Russia after Twenty Years) (From Lenin to Stalin)
F. E. Beal, Proletarian Journey

D. Blair and C. H. Dand, Russian Hazard

V. Koureg, Once a Commissar

R. W. Dunn and G. Wallace, Life and Labor in the Soviet Union

H. G. Pratt, Russia from Tsarist Empire to Socialism

P. Stuchy, Russian Spring

A. Luzovsky, Handbook of Soviet Trade Unions

L. Feuchtwanger, Moscow—1937

T. L. Harris, Unholy Pilgrimage

E. Bigland, Laughing Odyssey

K. London, Seven Soviet Arts

N. Zornov, Moscow the Third Rome

A. Gordon, Russian Civil War

A. Z. Arnold, Banks, Credit, and Money in Soviet Russia

G. N. Serebrenikov, Woman in U. S. S. R.

N. M. Kraylov, Soviet Geography

A. P. N. Gide, The Return from Moscow (U. S. S. R.) (After Thoughts)

R. Terrell, Soviet Understanding

H. Stekall, Humanity Made to Order

E. M. Delafield (De la Pasture), I Visit the Soviets

N. Wonlar-Lavsky, The Land That I Loved

A. and M. Smith, I Was a Soviet Worker

L. A. Owen, The Russian Peasant Movement, 1906-1917

N. A. Berdyaev, The Origin of Russian Communism

B. King, Changing Man: The Education System of the U. S. S. R.

H. E. Sigerist, Socialized Medicine in the Soviet Union

P. Sloan, Soviet Democracy

W. P. and Z. K. Coates, Scenes from Soviet Life

A. L. Strong, The New Soviet Constitution

A. R. Williams, The Soviets

M. Eastman, The End of Socialism in Russia

1938

A. Shestakov, Short History of U. S. S. R.

S. and B. Webb, Soviet Communism: a New Civilization

S. N. Harper, The Government of the Soviet Union (also 1949)

W. A. H. Gantt, Russian Medicine

B. Malnick, Everyday Life in Russia

S. I. Luck, Observations in Russia

M. E. Tracy, Our Country, Our People, and Theirs

L. E. Hubbard, Soviet Trade and Distribution

P. Sloan, Russia without Illusions

I. Solonovitch, Russia in Chains (Escape from Russian Chains—Soviet Paradise Lost)

J. D. Littlepage and D. Bess, In Search of Soviet Gold

S. R. Allan, Comrades and Citizens

W. P. and Z. K. Coates, From Czardom to the Stalin Constitution

B. Silver, Russian Workers' Own Story

N. de Basily, Russia under Soviet Rule

A. Barmine, Memoirs of a Soviet Diplomat

Soviet Russia Comes of Age (by Twenty-eight of Foremost Citizens)

J. Lehmann, Prometheus and the Bolsheviks

1939

M. T. Florinsky, Toward an Understanding of the U.S.S.R.

N. Mikhailov, The Land of the Soviets (Soviet Geography)

A. Yakhontoff, Over the Divide

H. Hauser, The Battle against Time

P. Sloan, Russia Friend or Foe (Russia without Illusions)

J. N. Hazard, The Soviet Housing Law

C. S. Seely, Russia and Approach of Armageddon (Battle of Liberation—1945)

W. G. Krivitsky, In Stalin's Secret Service

L. E. Hubbard, The Economics of Soviet Agriculture

B. Pares, The Fall of the Russian Monarchy

Land of Socialism Today and Tomorrow (Congress of Communist Party)

M. Gorki, Culture and People

J. R. Campbell, Soviet Policy and Its Critics

H. Johnson, Socialist Sixth of the World

History of Communist Party of the Soviet Union

E. Varga, Two Systems: Socialist Economy and Capitalist Economy

H. and R. Timbers, We Didn't Ask Utopia: A Quaker Family in Soviet Russia

C. Clark, Critique of Russian Statistics

P. Francis, I Worked in a Soviet Factory

H. Unger, Hammer, Sickle, and Baton

D. Fedotoff-White, Survival through War and Revolution

N. Thomas and J. Seidman, Russia—Democracy or Dictatorship

Soviet Russia Today (U.S.S.R. at New York World's Fair), Facts about the Land of the Soviets

1940

F. Utley, The Dream We Lost

H. C. Wolfe, The Imperial Soviets

H. Koehler, Inside the Gestapo

M. Polanzi, Contempt of Freedom

O. N. Pritt, Light on Moscow

M. Eastman, Stalin's Russia and the Crisis in Socialism

H. Johnson, The Soviet Power

L. P. Kirby, The Russian Revolution

G. Botkin, Firebird

S. R. Tompkins, Russia through the Ages

J. S. Curtiss, Church and State in Russia

O. H. Gankin and H. H. Fisher, Bolsheviks at Work (Origin of the Third International)—(Bolsheviks and the World War)

G. Bennigson, Religion in Russia

E. Lyons, Stalin Czar of All the Russias.

1941

J. Maynard, Russia in Flux (also 1948)

V. Lansbury, An Englishman in the U.S.S.R.

M. Lovenstein, American Opinion of Soviet Russia

M. Gordon, Workers before and after Lenin

W. Duranty, The Kremlin and the People

E. Hampel, Yankee Bride in Moscow

M. H. Dobb, Soviet Economy and the War

V. Gollancz, Russia and Ourselves

P. P. Sloan, How the Soviet State Is Run

A. Efron, New Russian Empire

W. H. Chamberlin, The World's Iron Age

A. Koestler, Darkness at Noon

J. Amul, Red Hell—Twenty Years in Soviet Russia

E. M. Almedingen, Tomorrow Will Come

U.S.S.R. Speaks for Itself

H. Best, The Soviet Experiment

J. T. Murphy, Russia on the March (New Horizons)

A. L. Strong, The Soviets Expected It

M. G. Hindus, Hitler Cannot Conquer Russia

J. E. Davies, Mission to Moscow

The Truth about Religion in Russia (Moscow Patriarchate)

1942

E. Strauss, Soviet Russia—Anatomy of a Social History

M. H. Dobb, Soviet Planning and Labor in War and Peace

P. N. Miliukov, Outlines of Russian Culture

M. G. Hindus, Mother Russia

L. E. Hubbard, Soviet Labor and Industry

S. and B. Webb, The Truth about Soviet Russia

A. Ciligia, The Russian Enigma

A. Yugov, Russia's Economic Front in War and Peace

D. J. Dallin, Soviet Russia's Foreign Policy

J. Scott, Beyond the Urals

E. Caldwell, All Out on the Road to Smolensk

K. Gibberd, Soviet Russia
A. Rothstein, Workers in the Soviet Union
N. S. Timasheff, Religion in Soviet Russia
E. Bigland, The Key to the Russian Door
C. Haldane, The Russian Newsreel
M. Edelman, How Russia Prepared
V. M. Dean, Russia at War (Foreign Policy Association)
A. Werth, Moscow War Dairy (Moscow '41)
P. Binder, Russian Families
L. Zacharoff, The Voice of Fighting Russia

C. Chesterton, Salute the Soviets
M. A. Stewart, Land of the Soviets
M. Bourke-White, Shooting the Russian War
W. Carroll, We're in This with Russia
J. Maynard, The Russian Peasant and Other Studies
S. N. Kournakoff, Russia's Fighting Forces
H. Johnson, The Secret of Soviet Strength
D. Levin, Children in Soviet Russia
L. Wolfe, Short History of Russia
A. Hrdlicka, The People of the Soviet Union

1943

B. H. Sumner, A Short History of Russia (Survey)
A. R. Williams, The Russians; the Land, the People, and Why They Fight
A. Howard and E. Newman, Pictorial History of Russia
W. Graebner, Round Trip to Russia
L. Luseuer, Twelve Months That Changed the World
M. H. Dobb, U.S.S.R.—Her Life and Her People
H. C. Cassidy, Moscow Date Line
J. Cournos, A Treasury of Russian Life and Humor
M. I. Cole et al., Our Soviet Ally
W. H. Chamberlin, The Russian Enigma
H. Iswolsky, The Soul of Russia
R. Bishop, Enquire Within
B. J. Guerney, Treasury of Russian Literature

H. F. Ward, The Soviet Spirit
L. Segal, The Real Russia
L. Sava, Russia Triumphant: the Story of the Russian People
M. P. Price, Russia through the Centuries
D. J. Dallin, Russia and Post-War Europe
Science in Soviet Russia (National Council of American-Soviet Friendship)
A. Kornilov, Modern Russian History (1917)
E. H. Carter, Russian Cavalcade
S. J. Marts, The Bear That Walks Like a Man
S. G. Evans, The Church in U.S.S.R.
P. Grierson, Books on Soviet Russia
E. Yaroslavsky, Twenty-five Years of Soviet Power
B. King, Life in the U.S.S.R.

1944

L. Segal, Russia—a Concise History
American-Russian Institute, U.S.S.R. in Reconstruction
American-Russian Institute, The Soviet Union Today (also later years)
G. R. Treviranus, Revolutions in Russia
W. Duranty, U.S.S.R.—The Story of Soviet Russia
A. Bergson, The Structure of Soviet Wages
W. B. Cannon, Science in Soviet Russia
N. W. Myles, Behold Russia
J. Joesten, What Russia Wants

E. Snow, People on Our Side
X. Pruszynski, Russian Year
G. Bienstock, S. M. Schwarz, A. Yugov, A. Feiler and J. Marschak, Management in Russian Industry and Agriculture
L. M. Fischer, My Lives in Russia
N. V. and F. Hyde, Russia Then and Always
P. B. Anderson, People, Church, and State in Modern Russia
R. E. Lauterbach, These Are The Russians

B. Pares, Russia and The Peace
A. I. Nazarov, The Land of the Russian People
D. J. Dallin, The Real Soviet Russia
D. Ames *et al.*, Meet the Soviet Russians (Harvard Graduate School of Education)
A. Parry, the Russian Cavalcade
E. Winter, I Saw The Russian People

A. L. Strong, The Peoples of the U.S.S.R.
I. Ehrenburg, The Tempering of Russia
H. Dorosh, Russian Constitutionalism
J. G. Gregory and D. W. Shave, U.S.S.R., Geographical Survey
L. Street, I Married a Russian
S. P. Turin, The U.S.S.R.—an Economic and Social Survey

1945

E. Stevens, Russia Is No Riddle
A. Barmine, One Who Survived
H. Heymann, We Can Do Business with Russia
E. Snow, The Pattern of Soviet Power
S. N. Harper, The Russia I Believe In
S. Liberman, Building Lenin's Russia
P. S. Buck, Talk About Russia (with Masha Scott)
I. F. Normano, The Spirit of Russian Economics
C. Lamont, The Peoples of the Soviet Union
R. T. Dulles, The Road to Teheran
M. M. Laserson, Russia and the Western World

J. S. Martin, Picture History of Russia
G. B. Cressey, The Basis of Soviet Strength
N. Mikhailov and V. Pukshishevsky, The Russian Story (Soviet Russia: Its Land and Its People) (1948)
D. Footman, The Red Prelude
W. L. White, Report on the Russians
M. I. Bogolepov, The Soviet Financial System
R. Schlesinger, Soviet Legal Theory
A. Helpern, Conducted Tour
H. A. Freune, Russia from A to Z
S. Nearing, The Soviet Union as a World Power

1946

R. P. Casey, Religion in Russia
N. S. Timasheff, The Great Retreat
H. Salisbury, Russia on the Way
D. Erskine, Russia's Story
A. Baykov, The Development of the Soviet Economic System (Soviet Foreign Trade)
M. Sayers and A. E. Kahn, The Great Conspiracy
F. L. Schuman, Soviet Politics at Home and Abroad
V. M. Dean, Russia—Promise or Menace
W. C. Bullitt, The Great Globe Itself
B. King, Introducing the U.S.S.R.
Blue Print for World Conquest (Moscow Communist Plan-documents)
V. Kravchenko, I Chose Freedom
N. Barov, Coöperation in the Soviet Union
L. Fischer, The Great Challenge

N. K. Chadwick, Beginnings of Russian History
W. West and J. P. Mitchell, Our Good Neighbors in Soviet Russia
W. Mandel, A Guide to the Soviet Union
J. Davis, Behind Soviet Power (also 1949)
G. Moorad, Behind the Iron Curtain
J. Somerville, Soviet Philosophy
G. Soloveytchik, Russia in Perspective
R. P. Fedotov, Russian Religious Mind
W. van Narvig, East of the Iron Curtain
R. E. Lauterbach, Through Russia's Back Door
E. J. Simmons, U.S.S.R.—Concise Handbook
M. V. Condoide, Russian-American Trade
J. S. Gregory, The Land of the Soviets

1947

E. H. Carr, The Soviet Impact on the Western World

F. Lorimer, The Population of the Soviet Union

433

B. J. Stern and S. Smith, Understanding the Russians
B. Parker, How Do You Do Tovarish
E. Ashby, The Scientist in Russia
C. Ciliberti, Backstairs Mission in Moscow
A. A. Lobanov-Rostovsky, Russia and Europe
J. Fischer, Why They Behave Like Russians
E. Snow, Stalin Must Have Peace
H. D. Carter, Sin and Science
H. G. Pratt and H. L. Moore, Russia: A Short History
J. L. Strohm, Just Tell the Truth
O. Atkinson, Over at Uncle Joe's
C. Norberg, Operation Moscow
W. O. Lucas, East of the Iron Curtain
D. J. Dallin and B. I. Nicolaevsky, Forced Labor in Soviet Russia
J. Kunitz, Russia, the Giant That Came Late

H. Schwartz, Russia's Post-War Economy
B. P. Yesipov and N. K. Petrovich (Goncharov), I Want to Be Like Stalin
M. J. Shore, Soviet Education
H. Johnson, Soviet Russia Since the War
R. Schlesinger, The Spirit of Post-War Russia: Soviet Ideology 1917-1947
E. Podolsky, Red Miracle
H. E. Sigerist, Medicine and Health in the Soviet Union
V. M. Dean, United States and Russia
M. Beloff, The Foreign Policy of Soviet Russia
J. Aleksander, This Is Russia
H. Lehrman, Russia's Europe
W. B. Walsh and R. A. Price, Russia—a Handbook
W. Kirchner, Outline History of Russia
J. Lawrence, Life in Russia

1948

G. D. B. Gray, Soviet Land: The Country, Its People, and Their Work
E. Crankshaw, Russia and the Russians
J. Kucharzewski, The Origins of Russia
H. Lamb, March of Muscovy
H. Lamb, The City and the Tsar
N. Berdyaev, The Russian Idea
F. Sternberg, How to Stop the Russians without War
Ʌ. Steinbeck, Russian Journal
M. H. Dobb, Soviet Economic Development since 1917
B. King, Russia Goes to School
M. Gliksman, Tell the West
D. Shub, Lenin—a Biography
W. B. Walsh, Readings in Russian History
R. Fischer, Stalin and German Communism
M. Koriakov, I'll Never Go Back
T. Lysenko, The Science of Biology Today
G. P. Fedotov, A Treasury of Russian Spirituality
As We See Russia, by Members of the Overseas Press Club of America
S. Welles, Profile of Europe

J. Dagras, Calendar of Soviet Documents on Foreign Policy 1917-1941
S. K. Margold, Let's Do Business with Russia: Why We Should and How We Can
F. Utley, Lost Illusion
J. Towster, Political Power in the U.S.S. 1917-1947
W. H. Bruford, Chekhov and His Russia
V. Gsovski, Soviet Civil Law
M. Lovell, The Soviet Way of Life ..
D. J. Dallin, Soviet Russia and the Far East
J. Smith, People Come First
J. Kunitz, Russian Literature since the Revolution
A. Y. Vishinsky, The Law of the Soviet
P. Crowson, History of Russian People State (1938)
N. A. Voznesensky, The Economy of the U.S.S.R. during World War II
R. Bishop and E. S. Crayfield, Russia Astride the Balkans
H. Kelsen, The Political Theory of Bolshevikism

1949

R. Parker, Russia Rebuilds
R. Parker, Moscow Correspondent

Father George, God's Underground (G. Palmer)

R. H. S. Crossman, Why I Changed My Mind about Communism

R. Magidoff, In Anger and Pity

W. L. White, Land of Milk and Honey

G. Creel, Russia's Race for Asia

L. Roberts, Home from Cold Wars

W. Duranty, Stalin and Company

E. E. Cummings, Eimi, Journal of a Trip to Russia

J. Balser-White, The Soviet Spy System

P. I. Lyashchenko, History of the National Economy of Russia to 1917 (1930)

A. Rothstein, Man and Plan in Soviet Economy

O. Kasenkina, Leap to Freedom

R. G. Emmens, Guests of the Kremlin

L. Fischer, Thirteen Who Fled

S. S. Balzak, V. F. Vasyutin, and Y. G. Feigin, Economic Geography of U.S.S.R.

D. J. Dallin, Rise of Russian Asia

I. Spector, Introduction to Russian History and Culture

S. Lubin, Stalin's Russia

F. Virski, My Life in the Red Army

G. S. Counts and N. P. Lodge, The Country of the Blind

G. F. Eliot, If Russia Strikes

I. Deutscher, Stalin: A Political Biography

H. Schwartz, Soviet Economy

A. Guillaume, Soviet Arms and Soviet Power

N. Jassny, Socialized Agriculture of U.S.S.R.

B. D. Wolfe, Three Who Made a Revolution: A Biographical History

R. Fischer, German Stalin and German Communism

W. Knup, Prowling Russia's Forbidden Zone

V. Petrov, Soviet Gold

C. Zirkle, Death of a Science in Russia

1950

W. B. Smith, My Three Years in Moscow

Y. M. Sokolov, Russian Folklore

R. Schlesinger, Changing Attitudes in Soviet Russia (Documents and Designs concerning the Family, Experiments in Administrative Devolution, Foreign Policy)

C. Thompson, The Public State

P. Pirogov, Why I Escaped

A. Goodfriend, If You Were Born in Russia

C. Hill, Lenin and the Russian Revolution

E. Moos, The Educational System of the Soviet Union

H. J. Berman, Justice in Russia

W. A. Wood, Our Ally: the People of Russia

W. H. E. Johnson, Russia's Educational Heritage

J. Steinberg, Verdict of Three Decades

Kravchenko versus Moscow (T. Humphrey)

T. A. Bailey, America Faces Russia

E. Seeger, Pageant of Russian History

A. Arakelian, Industrial Management in U.S.S.R.

B. Shub, The Choice

S. Bolshakoff, Russian Non-Conformity

V. Petrov, My Retreat from Russia

G. Jorre, The Soviet Union

F. C. Barghoorn, Soviet Image of U.S., a Study in Distortion

J. Garelik, A Soviet City and Its People

G. Backer, The Deadly Parallel (Ivan the Terrible and Stalin)

V. Kravchenko, I Chose Justice

E. D. Carman, Soviet Imperialism: Russia's Drive toward World Domination

L. S. Berg, Natural Resources of U.S.S.R.

A. Inkeles, Public Opinion in Soviet Russia

O. H. Radkey, Elections to the Russian Constitutional Assembly of 1917

G. Gorer and J. Rickman, The People of Great Russia

B. Moore, Soviet Politics—Dilemma of Power

J. Wortis, Soviet Psychiatry

E. Stevens, This Is Russia Uncensored

Periodicals in English Relating to Russia

(With date of beginning of publication, some continuing only a short time—certain short-lived or mainly economic periodicals omitted)

Darkest Russia (1912)
Russian Review (1912)
Russian Review (1916)
Russia (1916)
Soviet Literature (1916)
Struggling Russia (1919)
Soviet Russia (1919)
Soviet Russia Pictorial (1919)
New Russian Magazine (1920)
Russian-American Register (1920)
Russian Life (1921
Russian Review (Soviet Union Review)
  (1921) (1923) (1934)
Slavonic and East European Review
  (1922)
Weekly News Bulletin (1925)
Soviet Union Monthly (1926)
Economic Review of the Soviet Union
  (1926)
Russia Today (1930)
Moscow News (1930)
Soviet Cultural Review (Bulletin)
  (1931)
Soviet Land (Travel) (1932)
Soviet Russia Today (1932)
Russian Review (1932)
Facts about the Soviet Union (1935)

Contemporary Russia and Her Relations
  with Her Neighbors (1936)
Research Bulletin on the Soviet Union
  (1936)
Russian News Bulletin (1937)
Bulletin on the Soviet Union (1938)
Russian Review (1938)
American (Quarterly) Review on the
  Soviet Union (1938)
Anglo-Soviet Journal (1940)
Russia at War (1941)
Russian Review (1941)
Information Bulletin of U.S.S.R.
  (1941)
American Review of Soviet Medicine
  (1943)
Russia (1944)
Russian Affairs (1944)
Russian American News (1944)
Reporter on Soviet American Relations
  (1945)
American Slavic and East European Re-
  view (1945, 1934, 1941)
Russian Review (Penguin) (1945)
Soviet Culture in War Time (1946)
Soviet Woman (1946)
Current Digest on Soviet Press (1949)
Soviet Studies (England) (1949)

Miscellaneous Publications

Books by or about certain Soviet lead-
ers, as Lenin, Trotsky, Stalin
Soviet Year Books (different years)
Publications (in English) of Soviet
Government
Publications of U.S.S.R. Society for
Cultural Relations with Foreign
Countries (including Weekly News
Bulletin, VOKS—All-Union Society
for Cultural Relations Abroad)
Publications of American-Russian Insti-
tute for Cultural Relations with the
Soviet Union
Publications of American-Russian Insti-
tute (New York and elsewhere)

Publications of National Council of
American-Soviet Friendship (Ameri-
can Council of Soviet Relations)
Publications of Russian-American
Chamber of Commerce
Publications of American Soviet Science
Society
Publications of American-Soviet Med-
ical Society
Publications of Academy of Science of
Union of Socialist Soviet Republics—
Doklady (partly in English)
Publications of Russia Today Society
(England)

436

BIBLIOGRAPHY

Publications of East and West Associations

Publications of Four Continent Book Corporation

Official publications of Communist Party of U.S.S.R. (in English)

U.S.S.R. Embassy in United States, *Information Bulletin*, and other publications

Soviet Calendar, 1944

Publications of U.S.S.R. at World's Fair in New York, 1941

Thirty Years of Soviet State-Calender, U.S.S.R., 1947 (also other Soviet documents in English)

Publications of Press Department of Soviet Embassy in London

Publications of Russian Economic Institute (London)

Publications of Russian Economic Institute (United States)

Publications of Russian Institute, Columbia University

Publications of Russian Research Center, Harvard University

Publications of Foreign Policy Association

Current Digest on Soviet Press, passim

American Review on Soviet Union, passim

Soviet Russia Today, passim

American Slavic and East European Review, passim

Russian Review, *passim*

Article "Union of Socialist Soviet Republics" in Encyclopedia Americana, 1946

American Sociological Review, ix., June, 1944

Life Magazine, March 29, 1943

Survey Graphic, February, 1944

Science and Society, Summer, 1943

Foreign Affairs, passim

Annals of American Academy of Political and Social Science
lxxxiv., July, 1919, p. 81
cxiv., July, 1924, p. 49
cxxxviii., July, 1928, pp. 82, 153
clxxiv., July, 1934, p. 153
cc., Nov., 1938, p. 254
cclxiii., May, 1949
cclxxi., Sept., 1950

Various magazines with articles on Russia or the Soviet Union

United States Department of State, Extent of Russian Expansion in Less Than One Hundred Years, 1947

United States Department of State, Documents on Nazi-Soviet Relations, 1939-1941, 1948

United States Department of State, Cultural Relations between the United States and the Soviet Union, 1949

Publications of United States Office of Education and other Governmental Agencies on Russia

Publications of American Council of Learned Societies on Russia

New Times, formerly *War and Working Class*

Soviet Union, formerly *U.S.S.R. in Construction*

Soviet Literature

Soviet Woman

(All four preceding publications published by Soviet government, in Russian, English, French, and German—two also in Chinese).

INDEX

INDEX

441

INDEX

China, 7, 11, 36

Church, 38, 45-53, 65, 73, 306-308, 378-380. *See* Religion

Circus, 76, 277

Cities, 21, 43, 73

City, movement to or from, 44, 57, 63, 65, 70, 81, 106, 115, 207, 215

City worker, 106, 151, 320. *See* Revolution

Civil rights, 44, 122, 128, 135, 328-331, 365, 412-418. *See* Communism

Civil war, 153-155. *See* White Russians

Class struggle, 98. *See* Marx; Socialism

Classless society, 99, 220, 391, 405

Clergymen, 48-51, 308, 309, 377. *See* Church; Religion

Climate, 4, 5, 8, 17, 80, 82

Clothing, 75, 238. *See* Consumer goods

Clubs, 230, 277, 278, 285, 291

Coal, 17, 69, 70

Collective bargaining, 233. *See* Trade unions

Collective farming, 169, 199, 204-215, 235. *See* Farms

Combines. *See* Trusts

Commissars, 172, 381. *See* Government

Communal land, 77, 78. *See* Farms; Mir

Communal organizations. *See* Assemblies; Mir

Communism, 101-104, 109, 110, 220, 230, 261, 268, 269, 360-366, 384-389, 412-418. *See* Constitution; International; Political structure; Socialism

Communist Manifesto, 95, 96, 100, 327, 332

Communist party, 233, 315-323. *See* Bolsheviki; Political structure; Soviets

Compulsory education, 256

Comte, 108

Concentration camps, 325. *See* Forced labor

Confessions, 297, 317. *See* Purges

Confiscation of property, 161-168, 170, 177, 181, 182

Conscription of labor, 167, 266. *See* Forced labor

Constantinople, 18, 23, 30, 33, 40, 45, 46. *See* Byzantium

Constituent assembly, 141, 145, 150-152

Constitution, 34, 90, 105, 127-132, 327-331, 415

Constitutional Democrats, 124, 125, 131, 141, 151

Consumer goods, 220, 222, 225, 238, 239, 242, 243, 411

Convict labor, 227. *See* Forced labor; Prisons

Coöperative associations, 71, 72, 167, 180, 185-190, 205, 230, 280, 302, 411. *See* Collective farming; Trade unions

Coöperative housing, 189, 286

"Correctional institutions." *See* Forced labor; Prisons

Corruption, political, 44, 89, 138, 305, 310. *See* Bribery; Illegal trading

Cossacks, 22, 88, 149

Council of Empire. *See* Council of Ministers

Council of Ministers, 41, 128

Courts, 287, 295-297, 328. *See* Crime; Law

Craft industries. *See* Home industries

Crime, 87, 88, 168, 190, 298-305, 382. *See* Punishment

Crimea, 6, 8-11, 34, 58, 68, 70

Crusades, 11, 53

Culture, 273, 274, 381-383, 392, 393, 409, 412. *See* Art

Currency. *See* Money

Cyril, 46

Czar, 13, 30, 47, 48, 51, 111-114, 129, 132, 133, 140, 141, 306. *See* Government

Czechoslovakia, 341

Dancing, 76, 273, 383

Darwin, 97

Deaf, 283, 284

Death rate, 85, 86, 112, 288, 289

Debt, 39, 54, 62, 80, 170, 204. *See* Serfs; Peasants

Decembrists, 105

Declaration of Rights of People, 162

Democracy, 315, 348, 365, 366, 372, 381, 386. *See* Communism

Dickens, 120

Diseases, 86, 111, 280-283. *See* Death rate

Disputes, settlement of, 234, 287, 295, 296

Divorce. *See* Family; Marriage

Dmitri, 31

Dnieper river, 18, 23, 24, 45 *See* Kiev

Don river, 18

442

444